RAMEAU

Also by Simon Trowbridge

NON-FICTION

Peter Hall's Royal Shakespeare Company:
The Artists of the RSC During the Era of
Peter Hall, Trevor Nunn and Terry Hands,
1960-1999

Aix: A History of the Aix-en-Provence Festival

The Music of Bruce Springsteen and the E Street Band

The Rise and Fall of the Royal Shakespeare Company:
An Illustrated History

The Comédie-Française from Molière to Éric Ruf

The Company

FICTION

Cease to Weep

Élodie Duquette

RAMEAU
A LIFE

SIMON
TROWBRIDGE

ENGLANCE *PRESS*

Rameau: A Life

New paperback edition, corrected, revised and expanded. Published in 2025 by Englance Press, Oxford

First published in hardback with colour illustrations in 2023

Originally published under the title *Rameau* in 2016

ISBN 978-1-7384215-7-2

Copyright © Simon Trowbridge 2023, 2025

All rights reserved. No part of this book may be reproduced, copied, adapted, displayed, stored, distributed or transmitted in any form.

For my father

Rameau a le malheur de savoir plus de musique que Lully.

VOLTAIRE

Rameau est d'autant plus digne d'estime, qu'il a osé tout ce qu'il a pu, et non tout ce qu'il aurait voulu oser; il a eu le mérite de voir au-delà du terme où il a conduit ses auditeurs, et le mérite peut-être aussi grand, de juger jusqu'où ils pouvaient être conduits. Il eût manqué son but en allant plus loin; ils nous a donné, non la meilleure musique dont il fût capable, mais la meilleure que nous puissions recevoir. Ce n'est pas seulement par leurs ouvrages qu'il faut mesurer les hommes, c'est en les comparant à leur siècle et à leur nation.

D'ALEMBERT

Contents

Preface 13

Introduction 15

1 Early Life 23
  i Upbringing and Education 23
  ii Travelling Musician 26
  iii Traité de l'harmonie 35

2 Beginning Again in Paris 42

3 Interlude: France During the Age of Rameau 57
  i The International Context 57
  ii Politics and Society 58
  iii Rameau's Paris 61
  iv The Organisation of Music-Making 63

4 The Opéra 67
  i Life at the Palais-Royal and the Opéra 67
  ii Hippolyte et Aricie 76
  iii The Premiere 85
  iv Rameau and Voltaire: Samson 88
  v Les Indes galantes 93

5 An Argument in the Courtyard of the Louvre 100
  i Lullists versus Ramists 100
  ii La Génération harmonique 103

  iii Castor et Pollux 111
  iv Les Fêtes d'Hébé 118
   v Dardanus 126
   vi Hiatus 133

6 La Pouplinière 137

7 Versailles 144
 i Rameau and Voltaire: La Princesse de Navarre 144
 ii Platée, Rameau's Satirical Masterpiece 150
iii Rameau and Voltaire: Le Temple de la gloire 157
  iv Rousseau Enters the Scene 162
 v Rameau's Librettist: Louis de Cahusac 166
 vi Rameau, Cahusac and Freemasonry 172
   vii Pygmalion 175
  viii The End of the War 178
 ix Zoroastre, Rameau's Opera of Ideas 182

8 Philosophers and Fools 190
 i Diderot, d'Alembert and Rameau before 1752 190
  ii Rameau's Fragile Victory 200
 iii The Philosophers Dance to an Italian Tune 206
 iv Rousseau's Lettre sur la musique française 214
  v Rameau versus d'Alembert 219
   vi Rameau's Nephew 224

9 The Part-Time Composer 232
  i In the Forest of Fontainebleau 232
 ii Castor et Pollux and the End of the Querelle 235
  iii From the Court to the Opéra 239
   iv Les Paladins 244

10 The Solitary Walker 249
  i Les Boréades 249
  ii The End 257

Epilogue 264

Appendices 269
I Chronology of Rameau's Life, Work and Times 270
II Rameau's Theoretical Writings 281
III Rameau's Compositions 286
[A] Chronology 286
[B] By Genre 289
IV Rameau's Stage Works 293
V Rameau and His Contemporaries 313

Works Cited 321

Notes 331

Index 358

This painting, attributed to Joseph Aved, is likely to be a portrait of Rameau (ca.1728). Musée des Beaux-Arts de Dijon.

Preface

It is now over fifty years since the only general study in English on Rameau's life and work, by Cuthbert Girdlestone, was first published. In France, eighty-four years separated the key texts, Paul-Marie Masson's *L'Opéra de Rameau* (1930) and Sylvie Bouissou's *Jean-Philippe Rameau: Musicien des Lumières*, published in 2014 to coincide with the two hundred and fiftieth anniversary of the composer's death.

Cuthbert Girdlestone's landmark book was essentially an in-depth study of Rameau's music with two chapters on his life. My aim in the present work is to provide a general introduction to Rameau's life, work and times that places its emphasis on his importance as a major figure in the cultural and intellectual life of Paris during the middle decades of the 18th century. His relationships with Voltaire, Jean-Jacques Rousseau, Denis Diderot and Jean le Rond d'Alembert form the core of the book. I have deliberately avoided using the label 'the Enlightenment' in the text. Rameau would not have recognised that he was a participant in a broader intellectual movement, and it seems to me that it is misleading to write emphatically about him in such terms.

The book includes chapters on all of Rameau's major stage works. I'm not a musicologist and have not attempted to provide a detailed technical analysis of Rameau's music. Since the book is aimed at the general reader and not the music scholar, I've made use of technical terms as infrequently as possible. In writing about the operas, I've interpreted the music – instrumental as well as vocal – in terms of the feelings, thoughts and situations it expresses and describes, from a character's state of mind to a phenomenon of nature. This conforms to the aesthetics of the time and Rameau's primary purpose as a composer. Rameau's contemporary Jean-Baptiste Dubos wrote in his *Réflexions critiques sur la poésie et sur la peinture* (1719) that instrumental passages (*symphonies*) in an opera should 'agitate us, calm us, move us; in short, they act upon us in the same manner as the verses of Racine and Corneille'.[1] Similarly, d'Alembert stressed the importance of music speaking to the mind and to the soul, writing, in his *De la liberté de la musique* (1759), that 'composers of instrumental music will make nothing but an empty noise as long as they do not have in their heads, like the celebrated Tartini, as they say, an action or an expression to be represented'.[2]

I recognise that, on occasion, I may have remarked on an aspect of the music, such as a detail of orchestration, that exists because of a judgement made by the editor of the modern edition of the score or by the conductor of a recording, considered scholarship rather than absolute fact. Because Rameau was always revising his scores, not only for each revival but also within runs of performances, it is impossible in a general study to do full justice to the scope and richness of his musical output.

The text includes quotations from the writings of Rameau, Voltaire, Diderot and d'Alembert, among other primary sources, translated into English. Many of these passages have not previously been translated (if a translation isn't my own, the source is given in the endnotes). The supplementary section at the end of the book contains chronological and other information on Rameau's life, work and times, along with an overview of the repertoire of the Paris Opéra during his career and a performance history of his operas from their premieres in the 18th century to today.

Introduction

Jean-Philippe Rameau was a fascinatingly paradoxical figure. Before finding success, at the late age of fifty, as a composer of operas, he was best known as the author of a learned treatise on the science of music that transformed thinking on the subject; but this progressive thinker, and church organist, also wrote musical farces for the Paris fairs. When he finally gained admittance to France's official opera theatre, the Académie Royale de Musique, he polarised opinion like no other artistic figure of his time. Rameau was an intellectual fundamentalist who believed that music was governed by a natural principle of his own discovery; and yet he excelled at entertaining the opera-going public, not least by writing the finest dance music of the 18th century.

Rameau was obsessed with his reputation as a scientist. During the last decade of his long life he devoted most of his working hours to defending his theories in books, pamphlets and letters, struggling to express his ideas clearly on the page. In contrast, his remarkable facility to compose music effortlessly never left him. The orchestral interlude 'Entrée de Polymnie', from *Les Boréades*, was among the last music he wrote. It was part of his enigmatic nature that he placed more value on the significance of his theoretical work than on the lyrical beauty of this music.

Harmonic and rhythmic inventiveness and an orchestral sound world of rich sonorities characterise Rameau's art; he was as forward-looking as any of his contemporaries. Leaving aside the syncopated rhythms and modulations that cause his dances to leap and swing, Rameau's music has a tonal ambiguity, a chromatic and harmonic daring, that makes it highly distinctive. Take, as an example, the orchestral air 'Calme des sens' from act four of *Dardanus*. A slow descending phrase, its melancholy ironically heightened by the dotted rhythm, is passed from the basses to the violins, doubled with the flutes, without achieving resolution. Rameau's supporters valued his originality and the variety of ideas contained in his compositions while believing that his mastery of French recitative made him the musical heir of the great classical dramatists Racine and Corneille. In this regard the following words by Jean-Baptiste-André Gautier-Dagoty, written in 1770, were typical: '[Rameau] was always new and yet always himself. Sublime, like Corneille; sombre, like Crébillon; and tender, like Racine.'[1] Many of Rameau's detractors, confronted by the same aspects of his art (originality, variety, complex recitative), were shocked and repelled. An anonymous writer in the *Mercure de France*, responding to the success of Rameau's first opera, *Hippolyte et Aricie*, complained about the endless use of dissonance and of two notes repeated for minutes at a time: 'As soon as [the composer] stumbled upon a good tune, he immediately changed the tone, mode and metre. There is sadness in place of tenderness, turbulence in place of gaiety. Nowhere do we find gentleness or anything that touches the heart.' The reviewer called the music 'baroque', meaning misshapen, rough, distorted.[2] This was the earliest use of the term as applied to either music or the fine arts.[3]

Perhaps most fascinating of all, although Rameau eventually worked at the heart of France's official cultural institutions, the Académie Royale de Musique and the court, and within the parameters of established forms, he remained all his life a non-conformist, a singular artist who followed his own path and whose originality shocked his first audiences; and he did all this under the radar of state censorship. Rameau's most radical work, the opera *Zoroastre*, had a political dimension, dangerously seditious, that was undetected by the guardians of the autocratic state.

Rameau's music was largely ignored for almost a hundred years after the Revolution (*Castor et Pollux*, adapted and re-orchestrated, was occasionally performed up until 1820). Rameau was remembered, particularly in his birthplace, Dijon, as an important figure of the 18th century, but his style of music was deemed to be part of the dead heritage of the past. The process of rediscovery began, tentatively, in 1876, in the climate of renewed patriotism that followed the Franco-Prussian war. The town council of Dijon organised a Rameau festival that included two concerts of extracts from his operas as well as a parade and the unveiling of a statue created by Eugène Guillaume (insufficient money had been raised to cast the statue in bronze, so a temporary plaster copy was erected instead). It was at this time that establishment figures and the press, reacting to German musical dominance and the cult of Wagner, took up the 'father of harmony' not so much as a composer of music to be played but as a symbol of past French musical greatness. (The bronze statue was finally funded and erected in 1878, only to be melted down by the Germans during the Second World War.)

The case for Rameau's music was made by Camille Saint-Saëns, Charles Bordes, Claude Debussy and others in the subsequent decades, but progress was patchy at best. A version of *Castor et Pollux* was produced at the Opéra de Paris in 1930. After the war, Rameau's most important advocate was Gabriel Dussurget, the founding artistic director of the Aix-en-Provence Festival. During the very first edition of the festival, in 1948, Dussurget mounted a chamber concert devoted to Rameau's music in the grand salon of the Musée des Tapisseries: the Quatrième and Cinquième *Concerts* and the Cantatas *Orphée* and *Aquilon et Orithie* were performed by the harpsichordist Pauline Aubert, the violinist Paolo Borciani, the cellist Franco Rossi, and the singers Ninon Alexander and Julien Giovannetti. The following year, Dussurget invited the pianist Robert Casadesus to perform pieces by Rameau (from the keyboard suites) and Debussy (the second book of Preludes), in the open-air, accompanied by the cicadas. This illuminating pairing predated Víkingur Ólafsson's album *Debussy-Rameau* by seventy years. In 1950, at the Théâtre de l'Archevêché, Nadia Boulanger conducted 'musiques oubliées' by Monteverdi, Rameau, and Graun. Then, in 1956, Aix was responsible for the first full-scale production of Rameau's *Platée* since the 18th century. This was years before the rise to prominence of period instruments and historically informed performances. However, whereas a successful production of *Les Indes galantes* at the Opéra de Paris in 1952 had used a re-orchestrated and edited score, Dussurget wanted to present *Platée* as faithfully as the current scholarship would allow. The score was reconstituted from the original manuscripts by the musicologist Renée Viollier.

Dussurget worked for weeks in Paris with his chef de chœur, Elisabeth Brasseur, and the members of the Chœur du Conservatoire. The conductor, Hans Rosbaud, directed the musicians sensitively, and Michel Sénéchal excelled in the title role. The distinguished cast also included Nicolai Gedda (Thespis), André Huc-Santana (Jupiter), David Thaw (Mercure), and Janine Micheau (La Folie). Jean-Pierre Grenier and designer Jean-Denis Malclès staged the work with style and panache. The critic of *Le Monde*, Yves Florenne, recognised that *Platée* was a unique opera that combined comedy with profoundly beautiful music.[4] The production was an important marker in France, but for most foreign music critics Rameau remained a minor figure. 'Musically speaking [*Platée*] is insignificant,' proclaimed *The Times*, 'but it has been revived with a blend of imagination and scholarship, and it deserves a good airing before being put back in the dusty cupboard with the rest of Rameau's operas.'[5]

Pierre Boulez, who, as a controversial and divisive intellectual who changed the way people thought about music, was in some ways Rameau's 20th century equivalent, admired Rameau's music and conducted a concert performance of *Hippolyte et Aricie* as part of the events marking the bicentenary of the composer's death in 1964; but the bicentenary didn't have a lasting influence. In England, the major figure was Lina Lalandi, director of the English Bach Festival, who mounted productions of Rameau's operas in the 1970s and 80s. Louis Erlo, director of the Aix Festival in the 1980s and 90s, believed that the neglect of Rameau's music was shameful. He formed partnerships with John Eliot Gardiner and William Christie and made Rameau's music, in performances by the period instruments of the English Baroque Soloists and Les Arts Florissants, central to his programmes at Aix. Gardiner's resurrection of *Les Boréades* – a concert performance at the Queen Elizabeth Hall in London in April 1975 was followed by the opera's glorious premiere at Aix in July 1982 – inspired many young musicians. Marc Minkowski would later write that the 'shock was indescribable' and that it 'changed the lives of so many musicians'.[6] Edward Greenfield was one of the critics caught off guard by *Les Boréades*: 'Our whole view of Rameau […] is at one leap altered. What can you say when an opera by Rameau, his final testament in music, never performed before, is suddenly produced from the shelves of a library, and found to be a masterpiece?'[7] Aix followed *Les Boréades* with productions of *Hippolyte et Aricie* in 1983, *Les Indes galantes* in 1990, and *Castor et Pollux* in 1991. Not since Rameau's lifetime had his music been an important part of the repertoire of a major opera house.

It was largely, then, because of Gabriel Dussurget, Louis Erlo, John Eliot Gardiner and William Christie that the operas were staged by major companies in France and recorded. Christie, more than anyone, was responsible for the emergence of a new generation of French Baroque music specialists, led by Marc Minkowski, Hervé Niquet, Christophe Rousset and Emmanuelle Haïm. In 2014, a major anniversary year, there was an outpouring of renewed interest in Rameau's life and work in France that intruded beyond academia into the realm of public opinion. In Dijon that October people of all ages assembled in the place de la Libération with whatever instrument they happened to play to perform, under Thierry Caens's direction, a version of the air 'Hymne à la nuit' from *Hippolyte et Aricie*. It was around this time that France's leading Rameau scholar, Sylvie Bouissou, published research that indicated that the composer wrote the melody of one of the world's best-known songs, the canon *Frère Jacques*, an indelible marker of childhood. The song was attributed to Rameau on one of eighteen manuscript sheets of music found in a copy of a book in the Bibliothèque Nationale written and once owned by the nephew of the composer Francœur, *Diapason général de tous les instruments à vent*.[8]

The truth, though, is that Rameau's operas are still not performed that often, especially outside of France. The pioneering work of Lina Lalandi did not lead to a rush of Rameau productions in England. In London, the Royal Opera offered its stage for one-off performances by the English Bach Festival of *Hippolyte et Aricie* in 1980 and *Castor et Pollux* in 1981 but has yet to mount its own production of a work by Rameau at Covent Garden, and the English National Opera has presented only one, *Castor et Pollux* in 2011. Barrie Kosky's staging was a qualified success, while Christian Curnyn's conducting of the score was admired both for its commitment and its sensitivity. However, the production was not a game-changer as far as the unbelievers were concerned. In his review in the *Daily Telegraph* Rupert Christiansen declared wearily: 'I really have tried hard with the operas of Rameau. [...] I am reliably informed of his genius and have given it my best shot, but I still don't get it.'[9] Glyndebourne, a house with an interest in the Baroque repertoire, waited until 2012 before turning its attention to the composer. In the years since, pioneering work has been undertaken in England by Jonathan Williams, who, as founder and director of the Rameau Project in Oxford, has mounted productions of *Anacréon* (Sheldonian Theatre, Oxford, 2012) and *Zaïs* (South Bank Centre, 2014) with the Orchestra of the Age of Enlightenment; *Les Fêtes d'Hébé*, a collaboration with the Baroque Orchestra of the Royal College of Music, soloists from the Académie de l'Opéra national de Paris and the choir of the Centre de musique baroque de Versailles (Amphithéâtre Bastille, Paris, and Britten Theatre, London, 2017); *Dardanus* with English Touring Opera (2017); and the 1737 version of *Castor et Pollux* (its UK premiere) with the Rameau Project Orchestra (Sheldonian, 2022).

The various genres of French opera, combining allegory, fantasy, classical drama, ballet and extravagant spectacle, fell out of fashion during Rameau's lifetime, and, three centuries later, they remain problematic. They lack the primary element that makes opera a popular art form – melodrama. Laurent Pelly's production of *Platée* at the Paris Opéra in 2002 revealed that Rameau's theatre can work in the 21st century if the director respects the aesthetics but has the imagination to update them (admittedly, a satire like *Platée* is easier to modernise than a tragedy). José Montalvo's production of *Les Paladins* at the Théâtre du Châtelet in 2004, involving modern styles of dance, vivid colours and astonishing video projections, was dazzlingly creative, but the staging took attention away from the music because all the senses were being bombarded at once. Jonathan Kent set the action of the prologue of Glyndebourne's *Hippolyte et Aricie* in a huge kitchen fridge, but the production went on to offer a number of insights, not least in the choreography of Anthony Page. Page interpreted the music psychologically. Too often choreographers resort to an exaggerated, over-emphatic style of movement.

While Rameau's music has been revalued, a reassessment of his character is overdue. The mocking contempt of Denis Diderot[10] and the other *philosophes* was extreme, even if one takes into account the methodical way Rameau set out to publicly demolish Jean-Jacques

Rousseau's articles on music in the *Encyclopédie*. Rameau was a progressive whose achievement, particularly as a theorist, was initially acknowledged by Diderot and d'Alembert. They later came to view him as an egotist and an enemy of their project. The arrival of Italian opera in Paris in 1752 was the catalyst. The social comedies of Italian *opera buffa*, about ordinary people, could not have been more different from the allegorical classicism of French *tragédie lyrique*, written with the tastes of the king and his courtiers in mind. The social and political significance of *opera buffa* was clear, but Rousseau's absolute conviction that the simplicity of the Italian works he saw in Paris made them superior to Rameau's complex art is perplexing until one remembers that he was motivated by personal rivalry and an acute sense of grievance.

We can agree that Rameau was a difficult man to work with and for, unprepared to suffer fools and determined to have the last word. An argument between Rameau and his fellow musician Royer, conducted on a café terrace, was jokingly said to have lasted for two days.[11] The historical record reveals that Rameau could be intimidating, prickly and obsessive. However, the view fostered by Rameau's enemies that he was a miserly misanthrope needs to be questioned. At least until old age, Rameau didn't shun company, and was active in a number of social circles, at the Opéra, at the homes of his patron La Pouplinière and at one of the most prominent dining and drinking clubs. There is very persuasive circumstantial evidence to suggest that Rameau was a Freemason. The following pages will show that Rameau could inspire loyalty and affection in people who did not have a vested interest in despising him because they were in an opposing intellectual camp. After Rameau's death, in 1764, the composer and writer Michel Paul Guy de Chabanon (1730-1792), who had studied under Rameau, wrote: 'I knew Rameau, and I loved him; I practised his art and respected his talent. I burn with desire to contribute something to his fame.'[12] For Chabanon, Rameau created 'a theatre of enchantment'.[13]

Rameau's students were unable to prevent Rousseau's dismissive view of their late teacher from becoming orthodoxy within the musical establishment. Like the English, the French can be dismissive of their native music. This was in Debussy's mind when he wrote:

I would strongly recommend a certain Rameau... For almost a century he has been waiting for a just revenge. His position is close to that of Watteau. He died, the years went by and the silence was organised by colleagues who knew what they were doing. Now the sun illuminates the glorious name of Watteau, and no era of painting can forget the greatest, most affecting genius of the 18th century. We have in Rameau the exact double of Watteau. Is it not high time to restore him to the place he has the sole right to claim, instead of obliging French music to rely on cosmopolitan traditions that prevent its natural genius from developing freely?[14]

1

Early Life

1683 to 1722

i Upbringing and Education

Jean-Philippe Rameau was born in Dijon, the capital of Burgundy, in September 1683.[1] The region was already renowned for the quality of its cuisine and wines, but Dijon's skyline, dominated by the spires of its many churches, contradicted such worldly matters. Dijon offered opportunities for clerics, cooks and musicians. Rameau's father, Jean, was an organist of humble origin who moved between the churches. His mother, Claudine Demartinécourt, came from Gemeaux, a small village encircled by vineyards[2] some thirteen miles north-east of Dijon on the road to Langres. Jean had married well, for Claudine was the daughter of a *notaire royal* and a member of the lesser nobility. She brought to the marriage five hundred *livres* and an estate in Gemeaux worth three thousand more, whereas Jean's assets amounted to around two thousand *livres*. Senior members of Dijon's *haute bourgeoisie* witnessed the marriage contract.[3]

Jean-Philippe was the seventh-born of eleven children.[4] His birthplace, in the cour Saint Vincent, rue Saint Michel (today's rue Vaillant), has survived.[5] A typical off-white four-storey Dijon building with tall chimney stacks and a central gateway into an inner courtyard, it stands across the road from the church of Saint-Etienne. Jean Rameau was organist of Saint-Etienne at the time, and his new son was christened there on 25 September. A few paces further on stands an even more imposing church, Saint-Michel; and in the opposite direction the street leads to the ducal palace. Rameau's godfather was no less a figure than Jean-Baptiste Lantin, *Conseiller du roi* at the Burgundy *parlement* and an intellectual whose interests included both mathematics and music, especially Italian music. Lantin died in 1695, when Rameau was only eleven, but it is perhaps not fanciful to believe that he had a lasting influence on his young godson.

Only five of Jean-Philippe's siblings survived alongside him into early adulthood. He was fourteen when his mother died, a devastating blow. The eldest daughter, Marguerite, aged twenty-three, abandoned her own hopes to take charge of her brothers and sisters – Élisabeth (nineteen), Marie-Claude (sixteen), Jean-Philippe, Philippe-Eugène (eleven) and Claude Bernard (eight). Further tragedy befell the family in 1706, when Philippe-Eugène, the brother closest to Rameau in age, died at only twenty. Intriguingly, in his will and testament, Philippe-Eugène asked his father to pardon his ingratitude and the worry he had given him during his 'indiscrette jeunesse'.

Dijon, rue Vaillant and the church of Saint-Etienne in 2011. Rameau was born in the house with shutters (left side of photo, second house). Photo: SAT.

The Gemeaux estate, managed by Marguerite, brought in a steady income, but Jean had to work hard as an organist to support his extended family. He decided that the best start in life he could give his children was to ensure that they could earn a living through music. He taught them well. Élisabeth, Marie-Claude and especially Claude Bernard all became keyboard players of note, but it was Jean-Philippe who possessed the special talent, mastering the organ, harpsichord and violin by the time he reached maturity.

For his general education, Rameau was sent to be taught by the Jesuits at the collège des Godrans in the city,[6] something that would not have been possible if his father had not risen in society. Rameau was the first member of his family to be given the opportunity to benefit from a rigorous and proven system of learning, and to join the elite of the educated classes. The Jesuits taught morality, civility and self-discipline alongside major subjects such as grammar, ancient languages and theology.

Students began at the college at around the age of eleven and were expected to progress from the *première classe* to the *sixième classe*. Confusingly, the six levels of the course were also named first to six, but in descending order: in other words, students progressed from the *sixième* to the *première*. One of Rameau's classmates would remember him as a vivacious boy who wrote music and sang during lessons, and who didn't pass the *quatrième*.[7] It is not clear whether this meant the fourth class (i.e. year four of the course) or the fourth level (i.e. year three of the course). This little morsel of arresting testimony, quoted by Rameau's first biographer, shouldn't be read too literally as evidence that Rameau was a disinterested and academically poor student. He did not complete the six years, but this may have been related, as Sylvie Bouissou suggests, to the death of his mother and not a consequence of academic failure.[8] Whatever the cause, Rameau certainly learned enough to be set on the path of an intellectual life. Most important of all, it was at the collège des Godrans that he discovered the theatre. The study of the theatre formed an important part of a Jesuit education, and performances of plays and operas, often of a semi-professional standard, were mounted at the end of each school year. Sylvie Bouissou is surely right when she pin-points the elderly Rameau's confession in a letter that 'I have followed the theatre since the age of twelve'[9] as a reference to his formative experience of theatre at the collège des Godrans.[10]

ii Travelling Musician

The crisis of the death of his mother and the abandonment of his schooling to join, at the age of fifteen, his father as a city organist, out of filial duty, were factors that left the young Rameau yearning for escape. The stubbornness and independent spirit that marked his life revealed itself for the first time. At the age of eighteen, in 1701, he travelled to Italy, drawn by the country's music. Italian music was fashionable in Dijon, frequently performed at the concerts arranged by the important men Jean Rameau knew through his marriage to Claudine, concerts surely attended by the young Rameau. Rameau's time in Italy remains obscure. In old age he told his student Michel Paul Guy de Chabanon that he regretted not staying longer there 'perfecting his taste'.[11] It seems that he never reached Venice, the centre of Italian music-making, travelling no further than Milan, where perhaps his money ran out. At any rate, his Italian adventure ended suddenly. Within a few months he was back in France, touring the southern cities as the violin player in a troupe of travelling players.

For this and other details of Rameau's early life, we have to rely on the uncorroborated anecdotal evidence collected by Chabanon and Hughes Maret,[12] who both published tributes to the composer shortly after his death. We know that he stayed for a time in Montpellier because during a public spat with another musician, conducted in the pages of the *Mercure de France* in 1729/30, Rameau stated that he learned the 'octave rule' from an organist called Lacroix in that city;[13] and he was in Avignon in 1702, temporarily engaged as organist at Notre-Dame des Doms. The church had offered the position to the highly-regarded Jean Gilles, but it seems that Gilles was stringing Avignon along in the hope of securing better terms from his employers at Toulouse: there is no record that he formally left Toulouse and he would die in the city in 1705. (Gilles's *Requiem* was performed at Rameau's funeral sixty years later.) While

Avignon waited for the matter to be resolved, an organist was urgently needed. Perhaps Rameau was passing through the city at the time. Rameau stayed in Avignon only for a few months; at the end of April he secured the permanent position of organist of the cathedral in Clermont-Ferrand. This ended Rameau's brief spell of travelling and working in Provence and Languedoc. Something of the heat, light and character of the South stayed with him all his life, evoked in his operas' many tambourins and rigaudons.

The Clermont contract commenced in May 1702 and was for six years. As *maître organiste*, Rameau's duties included teaching the organ to one of the choristers as well as playing at all the services. The position was reasonably well paid (some three hundred *livres* per annum) but demanding, particularly during the initial period when Rameau was finding his way: he was unable to return to Dijon, at the end of his first month of work, to attend the marriage of his sister Élisabeth. Rameau was a diligent and highly regarded employee at Clermont. During the course of his life he would spend ten years in the Auvergne, so he must have found life in the city congenial. However, as an ambitious musician, he was only ever treading water in Clermont, a city without either an academy or a theatre. When Rameau, having completed the music that would form his first published composition, a suite for harpsichord, relinquished the position, two years early, and left for Paris, he did so with the support of his masters, particularly of Jean Villenaud, one of the canons. We can find connections that explain Rameau's early career progression. He probably secured the job at Clermont cathedral on the recommendation of the composer Collet, a former organist there, who lived in Dijon during Rameau's youth. When Rameau travelled to Paris, in 1706, he surely carried with him a letter of introduction to the eminent organist Louis Marchand from Villenaud. Marchand's father, Jean, had been the organist at Clermont cathedral back in the 1680s, and also Villenaud's teacher.

By the autumn of 1706 Rameau was living in Paris. No doubt one of the first things he did was to attend a service at the church of the Cordeliers, in the rue de l'École de Médecine on the Left Bank, to listen to Marchand. On the recommendation of Marchand, Rameau secured the organ at the Jesuit collège de Louis-le-Grand in the rue Saint-Jacques in the Latin Quarter. This position, previously held by Marchand himself, was not without cachet since the college was among the most renowned in Paris.[14] Molière had studied there; Voltaire was currently a pupil; Diderot, Sade, Robespierre and many other great figures of the 18th century would soon follow. It was also an important venue of theatre and opera: at the end of each school year the students were joined by professionals from the Opéra in the performance of a new piece by one of the leading composers of the age. These pieces were principally short ballets, *intermèdes*, performed between the acts of Latin tragedies. André Campra, Marc-Antoine Charpentier, Michel-Richard Delalande and Joseph-Nicolas-Pancrace Royer all wrote works for Louis-le-Grand. It is clear that the Jesuits spared no expense. Joachim Christoph Nemeitz, visiting Paris in the 1720s, left a description of theatrical performances at the college:

> The students of the Jesuits perform a Latin Tragedy at the College [...] once a year at the beginning of August. As the Fathers wish to excel in all their actions, they omit nothing to augment the magnificence of their Spectacle. Not content merely to adorn their stage with the most beautiful Decorations and to clothe the Actors in the richest garments, they even bring in the best people of the Opéra whether for dancing or for playing in the Orchestra. They mount a ballet between each act [...]. The Stage is erected outdoors in the Court of the College... All the area of this spacious court is full of benches for the Spectators, of which there is such a great number that not only are all places occupied, but all the windows of the College that overlook the court are filled with people from top to bottom.[15]

Nemeitz recorded that the ballets were directed by a member of staff (naming one Mons. Blondi for the performances he witnessed). The role played by the college organist is uncertain, but it must be possible that Rameau played the harpsichord and was involved in the musical instruction of the students taking part.

Rameau also played the organ at the church of the Fathers of Mercy in the rue du Chaume, today's rue des Archives,[16] in the Marais. The title page of Rameau's *Premier livre de pièces de clavecin*, published in 1706, is the source of this information; it also tells us that Rameau was living in a house in the rue Vielle du Temple not far from the Fathers of Mercy.

The publication of *Premier livre de pièces de clavecin* was Rameau's first declaration of his talent. It was a collection of nine pieces in A minor that, in form and style, almost followed the practice of the time. The suite consisted of the usual dances (allemande, courante, gigue, sarabande, gavotte, minuet), but between the second sarabande and the gavotte Rameau inserted a *rondeau* with a descriptive title – 'Vénitienne'. The influence of Italy can also be heard in the prelude's gigue in 12/8. The suite, published when Rameau was twenty-three, was much more than an apprentice piece: Rameau was already experimental and individual in his prominent use of chromaticism and the diminished seventh chord. As James R. Anthony writes

> Every page [...] bears the personal stamp of its composer. [...] Most of the dances achieve a unity of texture and melodic material rare for this early date. Rameau's use of bold harmonies, both to lend colour and for structural purposes, is evident from the first piece, a prelude, that combines an opening free section with a measured, gigue-like conclusion in the tradition of Louis Couperin.[17]

Rameau's only other publication of his twenties was an air for two voices, a Burgundian peasant song, called *Lucas, pour se gausser de nous*. This duo was included in *Recueil d'Airs sérieux et a boire de différents auteurs*, published by Ballard in 1707. We know that Rameau was writing pieces for the organ at this time, but sadly they were not published. According to Jacques Joseph Marie Decroix,[18] Rameau showed Marchand some of these works at his request.[19] Marchand developed a jealousy of Rameau's talent and withdrew his support. In turn, for all his admiration of Marchand's virtuosity, Rameau was critical of his fugal writing and felt that he was not a 'bon musicien'.[20]

The breakdown of Rameau's relationship with Marchand may partly explain why his first stay in Paris ended abruptly in 1709. It is likely that the printing of the *Premier livre de pièces de clavecin* lost him money, and he was under pressure from his father to return home to succeed him as organist at Notre-Dame.[21]

The bitter rivalry between Rameau's father and another organist,

Esmilian Lorin, who wanted his son to be granted the position at Notre-Dame, along with the fact that the organ was in a fragile state of repair and required a major overhaul, couldn't have made a homecoming already imbued with a deep sense of failure any easier. Rameau was in love with a Dijonnaise, Marguerite Rondelet, who was also loved by his brother Claude Bernard. We don't know when the three met, but Marguerite (born ca. 1682) was close in age to Rameau: they could have known each other since before he first left Dijon in 1701. An autobiographical poem by Jean-François Rameau – Claude Bernard's son, Rameau's nephew – is the source of this important episode:

> He was an admirer of my father's talent, but he was his rival for the hand of my mother; the two brothers therefore decided to separate in order to be happy.[22]

In one of Rameau's greatest operas, the tragedy *Castor et Pollux*, the love of two brothers for the same woman doesn't sever the bond that connects them. The work was conceived not long after Marguerite died in 1736, poignant evidence of her significance in Rameau's life and of his love for his brother.

Rameau decided to leave Dijon. His father was no doubt furious that his son was breaking his contract and handing his family's birthright, the organ of Notre-Dame, to a rival. It is sad to think that they parted on such bad terms, and would not see each other again, but Rameau sought his independence and his own destiny. Dijon was the place he began, not the place he would end. He travelled to Lyon in the summer of 1712, taking up the position of *maître organiste* at the convent of the Jacobins in the place Comfort.[23] Lyon had its attractions. The Opéra de Lyon was highly regarded, licensed to tour to Marseilles and Dijon,[24] where Rameau may have seen Lully's *Armide* and *Isis* after his return to the city in 1709. Therefore, it was not surprising that he chose Lyon.

The installation of an organ in the convent was a new development. It was in Lyon that Rameau began in earnest his career as both a composer and a thinker on music. The newly established Académie des Sciences, Belles-Lettres et Arts de Lyon provided a focal point for intellectual and artistic endeavour in the city. We know that Rameau came into contact with the co-founder and permanent secretary of the academy, the scientist Jean-Pierre Christin, inventor of the centigrade measurement of temperature, because many years later, in a letter to Christin, he made reference to Lyon.[25] Lyon, then, was a city that facilitated the ambitions of a young man like Rameau. An equally important figure in Rameau's development was another co-founder of the academy, Nicolas-Antoine Bergiron de Briou, composer and later co-director of the Opèra de Lyon. Bergiron was five years older than Rameau, and would outlive him by five years. He would remain in Lyon all his life. If we don't know the specifics of Rameau and Bergiron's association, we know that their relationship was one of mutual esteem. Bergiron's library included ten volumes of works by Rameau.

We know that Rameau was starting to make his name as a composer. In April 1713 the signing of the Treaty of Utrecht marked the end of the War of the Spanish Succession. In celebration, the burghers of Lyon erected an equestrian statue of Louis XIV at the centre of the vast place Bellecour, and organised a public festival, paying Rameau 250 *livres* to write the music. For some reason the concert was abandoned, and sadly we don't know anything about the music. It is probable that Rameau wrote his first large-scale works, the motets *In convertendo*, *Deus noster refugium* and *Quam dilecta*, for the concert series of the Académie des Beaux-Arts de Lyon, since an inventory, begun in 1713, reveals that the orchestral parts of all three pieces were in the possession of the Bibliothèque du Concert de l'Académie.[26] The numbering in the inventory suggests that *Deus noster refugium* was written first.

Rameau's *grands motets* reveal that he had discovered his individual voice by the time he reached his early thirties, some twenty years before he composed his first major opera. In form, they followed the conventions established at the Chapelle Royale at Versailles during the previous century. A French *grand motet* was, typically, a setting of one of the psalms scored for soloists, a four or five-part chorus (divided between a *grand chœur* and a *petit chœur*) and a five-part orchestra. At Versailles, motets were written for the king's low Mass. The most prolific composer of motets at Versailles in the middle years of the 17th century was Henry Du Mont. Lully took up the form and published six of his twelve motets in 1684. Charpentier and especially Delalande, director of the Chapelle Royale from 1714, were the masters of the form during Rameau's formative years. Motets were composed by *maîtres de musique* at cathedrals throughout the country, with the cathedral of Saint-Sauveur and its choir school in Aix-en-Provence being particularly significant as a centre that produced a succession of fine musicians, André Campra and Jean Gilles among them. In the 18th century, motets were not only performed during church services but also at the Concert Spirituel, and during concert series arranged by the provincial academies. The form declined in importance as the age became increasingly sceptical and anti-clerical.

The first of Rameau's motets, *Deus noster refugium*, is a setting of Psalm 46, 'God is our refuge and strength', shot through with imagery of earthquakes and floods. Rameau divides the eleven verses into three sections, all in B flat, and shares the text between six soloists (sadly the music of verse ten is lost). Throughout, he shows his individuality by giving the orchestra a prominent role: along with the flourishes provided by the strings (for instance the rapid arpeggios of the storm music of verse three), there is some lyrical writing for a solo violin and oboe. There are two choruses (the first powerfully contrapuntal, the second repeated at the end of the work), a dramatic trio for the two sopranos and the bass (verse two) and a powerful fugal quartet for the male voices, accompanied only by the continuo (verse six). In verse four, 'The violence of the river filled the house of God with joy', the soprano is accompanied by a solo violin and bass viol. Verse five, describing the city of God, is a bravura air for the bass.

In convertendo is a greater work. Rameau's distinctive harmonic language, his haunting ambiguity and melancholy, is absent from *Deus noster refugium*, but we find it in *In convertendo*, along, in the final chorus, with one of the deepest expressions of joy in all of his work. If the two motets were composed in quick succession, as we believe, Rameau took a long stride between them. His voice was in the process of developing in *Deus noster refugium*; in *In convertendo* it is almost fully formed. Rameau revised the music in 1751 for a performance at the Concert Spirituel. The Lyon original was scored for a smaller orchestra. Since the original score is lost, we only know the piece from this second version; but it would be wrong to think that the revisions transformed the work and injected its special quality. Rameau chose to revisit this motet, rather than the others, because he knew its value.

The text is taken from Psalm 126, but Rameau inserts a verse from Psalm 68. Psalm 126 relates how God freed the Jews from captivity. Rameau's score begins, superbly, with a sombre air in G minor for *haute-contre* (high tenor) accompanied by violins and flutes. An immediate contrast is provided by a vibrant G major chorus in the form of a fugue (verse two) leading into a duo for soprano and bass, singing first in harmonic unison and then independently, with ornamentation provided by two oboes and one bassoon (verse three). In verse four, a solo for baritone, the music's fast scales and arpeggios describe the torrents of water released by God. In verse five, lifted from Psalm 68, the soprano praises the name of the Lord accompanied by the chorus and orchestra. The intricate writing for oboes and bassoons would not have been present in the original version. A compelling riff-like phrase played by unison strings begins verse six, and repeats throughout the trio for soprano, *haute-contre* and bass ('They that sow in tears shall reap in joy'). The motet concludes with the majestic chorus 'Euntes ibant et flebant'. The harmonically unsettling opening, consisting of descending scales and distinctive sonorities, is typical of Rameau at his finest. As the fugue progresses, three themes are combined in an impressive display of vocal textures, with the orchestra's unsettling commentary always present.

In December 1714 Rameau's father died and he returned home for the funeral. Jean changed his will frequently over the years; it was his way of responding whenever one or other of his sons displeased him. The final testament, though, was fair and equitable, something that may have relieved Rameau given his falling out with his father two years previously. As the head of the family, Rameau was responsible for settling his father's estate. The will provided for his sisters Marguerite and Marie-Claude, who were living in the family home in the rue de la Vannerie, and for his two nieces (their mother, Élisabeth, had died in 1712), and decisions had to be made about the family's assets and property. Rameau carried out this work diligently but in haste. It was as if he wanted to separate himself from his Dijon roots as quickly as possible, although in the decades ahead he always acted appropriately when it came to family affairs. He returned to Dijon for the wedding of Claude Bernard and Marguerite in 1715.

Rameau was already planning his next move. In his official position at the convent of the Jacobins he felt unappreciated and insufficiently rewarded. This gives a partial explanation for why he decided to move on, but surely only a personal crisis prompted by his father's death and his unrequited love for a woman who had just married his brother, explains why he left Lyon, a vibrant city that had given him the opportunity to write major compositions, and returned to Clermont-Ferrand, going back to his old job and signing a contract that stipulated a term of *twenty-nine* years.

When Rameau entered the solitary organ loft, like a monk entering his cell, it was as if he was retreating from the world. During his long second sojourn in Clermont, he immersed himself in learned reading, thinking and writing, and composed very little music beyond the short cantatas *Medée*, *L'Absence*, *L'Impatience*, *Aquilon et Orithie*, *Téthis*, *Orphée* and *Les Amants trahis*. It is not possible to establish the exact dates of these works. We can't rely on the dates written on the manuscript copies that have come down to us since we can't know whether these mirror the dates of composition. In his letter to Houdar de la Motte of 25 October 1727, Rameau writes that he composed *Aquilon et Orithie* and *Téthis* twelve years before, which gives 1715 as their date of origin. Maret indicates that *Medée*, *L'Absence* and *L'Impatience* were written before *Téthis* and *Aquilon et Orithie*, which could mean that they date from Rameau's time in Lyon.[27] However, Decroix, who collected Rameau's scores, clearly stated that *Medée* and *L'Absence* were written in Clermont.[28] Although this is a futile game – we can't verify Rameau's 'twelve years ago' let alone Maret and Decroix's indications – a chronology emerges that suggests that *Medée*, *L'Absence*, *L'Impatience*, *Aquilon et Orithie* and *Téthis* were written, in that order, in or around 1715, and that *Orphée* and *Les Amants trahis* date from a few years later. *Medée* and *L'Absence* are lost works.

It makes sense that Rameau was trying his hand at the popular genres of the day in a logical succession of scale – keyboard pieces, motets and now cantatas, with opera being the ultimate goal. André Campra was among the composers who popularised the cantata form in France during the first decade of the 18th century. It was a genre that, because of its brevity, encouraged spirited and graceful music, and Rameau's cantatas, if lacking the depth of his Lyon motets, are fine examples. The genre gave the young composer his first opportunity to write dramatic music, for these mini-operas consisted of recitatives, airs and duos, and demanded sensitivity to text and character. Listening to *Les Amants trahis*, for example, one is struck by the distinctiveness of Rameau's voice from the very first musical phrase. The only comedy among Rameau's cantatas, and the only one to feature more than one voice, it is the cantata that best reveals the composer's genius.

The betrayed lovers of the title are two shepherds, Tircis (tenor) and Damon (bass). At the conclusion of their dialogue, Damon persuades the despairing Tircis that the right response to misfortune in love is to laugh, for it is in 'forgetting the coquette that one finds revenge'. Damon's first air, 'Lorsque malgré son inconstance', starts with a descending phrase that could have been written by Fauré a century and a half later: the word-setting is exemplary; the musical phrasing exquisite in its lightness of touch. Damon's third air, 'Du dieu d'amour', is gravely expressive, with unexpected prominence given to the lyrical *obbligato* provided by the viol. Rameau reveals his singular talent by giving Damon music that momentarily darkens and undercuts the nonchalance of his bravado.

iii Traité de l'harmonie

Since his youth, Rameau had been thinking about music philosophically and mathematically, led by an instinct to discover its 'true principle'.[29] One day in the Lyon opera house he came across an elderly workman who was humming music. The old man wasn't singing the melody of a song but its hidden harmonic progression, its 'fundamental bass'. He had lived a hard and rough life, with little exposure to music, and was singing absent-mindedly. This was a revelatory moment for Rameau, for it demonstrated, in his own words, that 'harmony was natural to us'.[30] Rameau had identified the key principle of a new system of music theory.

During the following seven years, in Clermont, driven at first by the crisis of his flight from Dijon and then by a profound desire to succeed, Rameau worked to organise and express his ideas on the page. He was not a natural prose writer so the task must have been laborious. It is not difficult to imagine Rameau working late into the night, hunched over papers in candlelight. A book – *Traité de l'harmonie reduite à ses principes naturels* – was finally completed. It was published in Paris in 1722 by Jean-Baptiste Christophe Ballard, 'Seul Imprimeur du Roy pour la Musique'.

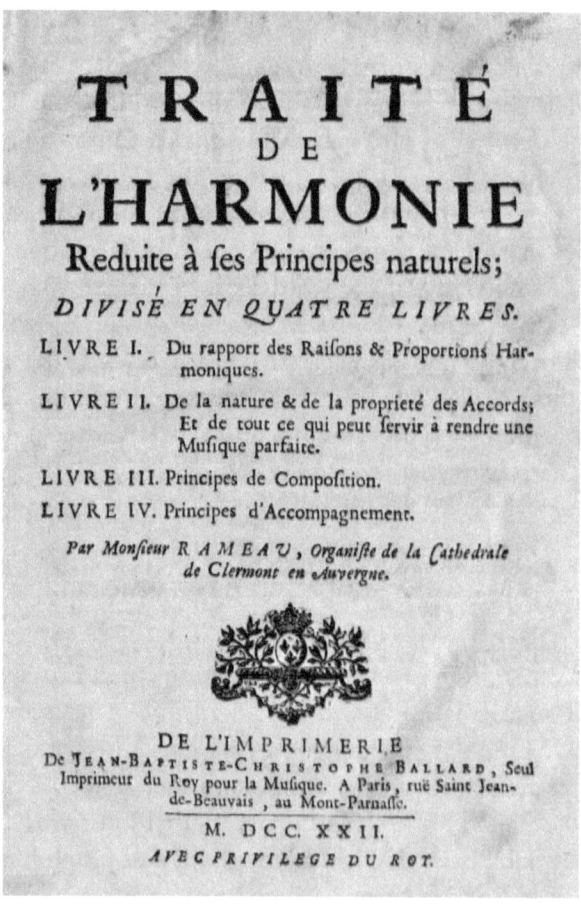

The title page of the *Traité de l'harmonie* refers to Rameau as 'Organiste de la Cathedrale de Clermont en Auvergne'. This suggests that it was only after the success of the publication that he left the position. The best-known story concerning Rameau's early life relates the circumstances. Rameau's masters at Clermont refused to release him from his career-long contract. Rameau forced the issue by sabotaging two services, the first by sitting at the organ but not playing and the second by hitting a cacophony of wrong notes. The cathedral chapter, no doubt aware of Rameau's intractable character, gave in, but reluctantly – evidence that they valued Rameau's talent and the quality of his work. The secretary of the Academy of Clermont told the story to Maret in 1764.[31] The circumstances of Rameau's departure had entered Clermont folklore, and it's reasonable to suspect that with each telling the anecdote became a little more theatrical. By 1723 Rameau was living in Paris. From now on his ambitions lay in the capital and within the secular realm.

Rameau's work as a scientist of music made him unusual among the great composers. What initially motivated his decision to devote so much time and effort to abstract thought? Was it connected to a personal crisis, as I believe? Or was Rameau always going to write the *Traité de l'harmonie*? It is part of the enigma of Rameau that his motivation eludes us. We know that, as a working musician, his prospects were limited, and would remain personally dissatisfying for many years to come. He worked mostly as an organist, a church functionary. He stopped writing motets almost as soon as he'd started (he wasn't paid to write church music in Clermont), although we can't be sure that he didn't aspire to secure the position of *maître de musique* at one of the great cathedrals.

In the preface to his book, Rameau wrote:

> Music is a science which should have definite rules; these rules should be drawn from an evident principle; and this principle cannot really be known to us without the aid of mathematics. [...] Though I did not know how to distinguish the principle from the rules, the principle soon offered itself to me in a manner convincing in its simplicity.[32]

No one had previously written about music in terms of rules drawn from a natural principle of harmony. Rameau clearly believed at this stage of his career that reason and deduction were more important than experience and perception; in this sense he was a good Cartesian – the philosophical foundation of his ideas was rather old-fashioned at a time when the empiricism of Locke was holding sway. It was René Descartes (1596-1650) who first stated that there was an analogy between the length of a vibrating string and the frequency of its vibrations. Rameau's starting point was Descartes's logical deduction 'sound is to sound as string is to string; each string contains in itself all other strings shorter than it, but not those which are longer'.[33] He refers to Descartes's *Compendium Musicae* (1618) throughout the *Traité*, and on occasion even lifts sections of text without citation.[34] Once again with Rameau, though, one is aware of a paradox, for his rationalism is not applied consistently: he constantly calls upon his own practical experiences as a musician and composer. As for other influences, Rameau didn't know Joseph Sauveur's work on acoustics at the time he wrote the *Traité*, but he was familiar with the theories of many of his other important predecessors, including the Italian Gioseffo Zarlino (1517-1590), and the Frenchmen Marin Mersenne (1588-1648), Charles Masson (d. 1700) and Sébastien de Brossard (1655-1730).

Rameau's *Traité de l'harmonie* is organised into four *livres*. The first two books examine theoretical issues; the second two provide practical instruction in the arts of composition and accompaniment. On one level, the work shows how practical music-making is built on theoretical foundations. In the first book, 'On the Relationship between Harmonic Ratios and Proportions', Rameau sets out his ideas on the special significance of harmony in the creation of music, beginning with the revolutionary statement that 'music is generally divided into harmony and melody, but we will show in the following that the latter is merely a part of the former and that a knowledge of harmony is sufficient for a complete understanding of all the properties of music'.[35] Chords, he explains, are the building blocks of music. There follows one of Rameau's philosophical leaps of thought: because all notes can be sounded in a 'fundamental source' – a single string divided by the application of bridges – it follows that a natural principle is at work. The sound produced by the undivided string is the 'fundamental sound' because all other sounds are contained within it.

> From the different distances found between this fundamental sound and those it generates by its division, different intervals are formed. The fundamental sound is consequently the source of these intervals. Finally, from the union of these different intervals, different consonances[36] are formed. The harmony of these consonances can be perfect only if the first sound is found below them, serving as their base and fundamental. Thus, the first sound remains the source of these consonances and of the harmony they form.[37]

Because the fundamental sound of a string is always the lowest sound, Rameau calls it the 'fundamental bass'. Relating this to any chord, in simple terms, the fundamental bass of a chord, its lowest note (or root), defines it, for it remains the same whatever the inversion. In the second book, 'On the Nature and Properties of Chords and on Everything which may be used to make Music Perfect', Rameau explains the progression of the fundamental bass. The harmonic basis of a piece of music can be defined as a series of chords of three or four sounds. When these chords follow each other in their fundamental state, the succession of their lowest notes forms the fundamental bass. In proclaiming the primacy of harmony over melody, Rameau demonstrates how every passage of music has a fundamental bass that reveals its shifting harmonic nature. The actual melodic bass line of a piece is not its fundamental bass because it is not the foundation of the harmony. It is not easy for the non-expert to follow the details of Rameau's exposition. As if aware of this, Rameau provides a summation in layman's terms:

> It would seem at first that harmony arises from melody, since the melodies produced by each voice come together to form the harmony. It is first necessary, however, to find a course for each voice which will permit them all to harmonise well together. No matter what melodic progression is used for each individual part, the voices will join together to form a good harmony only with great difficulty, if indeed at all, unless the progressions are dictated by the rules of harmony. [...] It is harmony then that guides us, and not melody.[38]

Philip Gossett, in the introduction to his English translation of the *Traité*, gives the best overview I know of Rameau's motivation and achievement when he writes

> Rameau himself was fully aware of the inadequacy of his theories in dealing with many aspects of music. He continually invokes taste and experience throughout the *Traité*, all his prescriptions to the contrary. When he asserts that melody is derived from harmony, he is invoking the theoretical order of precedence, not the act of composition. [...] Rameau's theoretical justifications must be accepted, in the light of 18th century philosophy, as elements in the search for universal principles. They are attempts to reduce all knowledge to central postulates, found in nature, from which all rules can be derived. In the *Traité* Rameau attempts to make music a deductive science, based on natural postulates, in much the same way that Newton approaches the physical sciences in his *Principia*. That Rameau is not wholly successful need not deter us from recognising the enormous advances in the theory of tonal music which stem from his works.[39]

The book was much talked about but little read. People understood, from Rameau, that music was a complex system and not only a succession of pleasing melodies; that it was a philosophical conundrum and not only a reason to spend a night at the opera; but little else was understood. Many years later Diderot, in *Le Neveu de Rameau*, would call Rameau this 'famous musician, who has written so many unintelligible visions and apocalyptic truths on the theory of music, not a word of which he or anyone else has ever understood.'[40] If Diderot was writing in satirist mode, there is no denying that the *Traité de l'harmonie* is a demanding work, its threads of thought difficult to unravel. Rameau's understanding of philosophy and mathematics was not especially deep, and his knowledge of the work of earlier thinkers on music was incomplete and selective. It seems remarkable, therefore, that his book is so authoritative, but not that it is so mysterious: it is the product of Rameau's own instincts and imagination and self-belief. In intellectual circles it was recognised at once that this organist from the Auvergne had written an important and original work that enriched knowledge. One of the intellectuals who endorsed Rameau's theory was the Jesuit priest and mathematician Louis-Bertrand Castel, friend of Montesquieu and co-editor of the *Journal de Trévoux*. Castel wrote a positive review of the *Traité* in the *Journal de Trévoux*[41] which, given the influence of this periodical as an arbiter of taste and thought, did much to publicise Rameau's ideas. The two became friends, at least for a time. Castel would later change his mind about Rameau.

The *Traité de l'harmonie* was only the beginning of Rameau's journey as a scientist of music: dozens of publications would follow, including two major books, the *Génération harmonique* (1737) and the *Démonstration du principe de l'harmonie* (1750). It was only in the latter years of Rameau's life, after he had made ever more eccentric claims for the broader scientific meaning of his system, that the view expressed by Diderot in *Le Neveu de Rameau* took hold and he found himself dismissed by his enemies as a crank whose ideas were obscure and unproven and, for that matter, unnecessary.[42]

2

Beginning Again in Paris

1723 to 1733

Rameau found rooms in the Palais-Royal quarter. It was a declaration of intent, since the Palais-Royal's theatre was the home of the Académie Royale de Musique, popularly known as the Opéra. Rameau would move home frequently, but he never left the fashionable neighbourhood of the Palais-Royal and the Louvre.[1] The Palais-Royal, belonging to Philippe duc d'Orléans, the nephew of Louis XIV and ruler of France as regent until his nephew, Louis XV, reached maturity in 1723, was the focal point of social and cultural life in the capital.

Paris could hardly miss Rameau. Very tall and thin, his appearance provoked particular comment. Years later, Chabanon, who would often see Rameau walking in the garden of the Palais-Royal, wrote: 'Rameau was extremely tall: thin and gaunt, he had more of the air of a ghost than of a man.'[2] The dramatist Alexis Piron was typically sharp: 'I saw him approach with the aid of a telescope: like a long organ pipe missing the blower.'[3] Many of the comments about Rameau's appearance and character date from his old age. The best portrait we have of him,[4] painted, it is believed, by Joseph Aved around 1728 when its subject was in his middle forties and still some years away from finding fame as an opera composer, shows something different. Rameau, seated, wears a plain yet handsome red coat and holds and plucks or strums a violin as if it were a guitar. His black eyes look directly out of the canvas, and his lips are parted: perhaps he is singing. The manner in which he plays the violin and the open expression on his face convey humour and conviviality.

The Louvre and rue Saint-Honoré during the 18th century. Drawing by Louis-Pierre Baltard. Bibliothèque nationale de France.

Rameau lived in the right district but his dramatic music was first heard on the other side of the river at the edge of the city. Soon after settling in Paris, he started to write music for the Saint-Germain fair. Every winter, from February to the week before Holy Week, the fair occupied a site on the left bank of the Seine between Saint-Sulpice and the abbey of Saint-Germain-des-Prés (off the rue du Four)[5] and spilt out into the streets of the quarter. The abbey owned the land; it had been allowing this annual exchange of commerce, both financial and human, since the 16th century.[6] Specially built pavilions (*loges*) and covered markets partially filled the site.

The fair presented a chaotic, boisterous and, at its dark edges, in the alleys by the river and under the bridges, illicit cavalcade of human transactions carried out in torchlight to the beat of tambourines and the shrill cries of flutes, oboes, cornets and flageolets. Thousands of people from all levels of society came together to watch the actors, dancers, tumblers, tight-rope walkers, clowns and marionettes of the fair, to seek pleasure and excitement.[7] Whores, pickpockets and beggars followed in their wake. Licentiousness and seduction, crime and hardship, sedition and the mocking of authority, were more visible than normal.

A number of troupes performed in theatres on the main site and in the neighbourhood. The organisers and performers provided entertainment of an often high quality, but without official sanction; they were adept at finding ways to circumvent the decrees of the regulator and the censor, and had to be since their existence was precarious. The state granted licences to perform plays and operas only to the official companies, and these – the Comédie-Française and the Opéra – guarded them jealously. Over the years the farces, parodies and *vaudevilles* (words sung to popular melodies) of the fair had acquired a degree of sophistication. Denied the permission to act their plays with spoken dialogue, the actors had resorted to holding up placards scrawled with the words, silent movie style; later the Opéra granted permission for the words to be sung, and from this the new *opéra comique* emerged. The theatre of the fair (théâtre de la foire) became known as the Opéra-Comique.

Contemporary accounts of Rameau's personality prompt the view that he was only writing for the fair because, to succeed as an opera composer, he had to start somewhere. There is, though, a pulse of living pleasure in much of Rameau's music. The scores of the comic operas he wrote for Alexis Piron have not survived. However, it is highly likely that some of the sections of Rameau's *Pièces de clavecin* (his second suite for the instrument), published in 1724, were lifted from Rameau and Piron's *L'Endriague*, performed at the Saint-Germain fair in February 1723. Piron's text indicates the moments of music and names them. Two of these names, Musette and Tambourin, appear in the suite side by side, the first being a stately melody marked 'tendrement', the second a short two-chord riff of percussive swagger that ends abruptly in a descending scale. One can hear the droning melancholy of the musette (an instrument of the bagpipe family, very popular at the fair and particularly associated with pastoral scenes) in the first, and the beat of drums in the second; one can imagine flickering torches and masked faces.

Rameau's contribution to *L'Endriague* would appear to have been significant. The title page of the published libretto proclaimed that the work was a 'mêlé de danses, de divertissements, et de grands airs de musique du célèbre Rameau'. One of the performers was a teenage soprano called Mlle Petitpas, later cast by Rameau in his first works for the Opéra. Piron and Rameau collaborated on three further comic operas, all created in 1726 – *L'Enrôlement d'Arlequin* for the Saint-Germain fair (in a newly opened theatre in the rue de Buci), and *La Robe de dissension, ou Le Faux-prodige* and *Le Pucelage, ou La Rose* for the summer Saint-Laurent Fair.[8] In the latter, also known as *Les Jardins de l'Hymen*, a mother attempts to prevent her daughter from giving up her virginity. Piron's sexual references displeased the censor and the work was banned.

Piron was a Dijonnais, so the coming together of these two men on the make was partly a matter of regional fellowship. Piron was a *bon vivant* who was very much at ease in the hedonistic world of the fair. He famously got around the interdiction on spoken dialogue by writing a comic hit consisting entirely of monologues – *Arlequin Deucalion*. Piron achieved success beyond the fair theatre more quickly than Rameau, moving into the official realm of the Comédie-Française with his play *Les Fils ingrats* in 1728. After Rameau's death in 1764, at the request of Maret, Piron put down on paper some thoughts about the composer. When one leaves out the comments that seem motivated by resentment or malice, the consequence, perhaps, of a rupture in their relationship that happened after their collaborations of the 1720s, Piron's account, and particularly his amusing anecdote concerning his encounters with the composer in the Tuileries, two egotists trying to have the last word, resonates strongly:

> Rameau was too singular and too out of the ordinary to make things easy for you; good luck to you! Your art will have all the more glory to jump the obstacle. [...] I was sometimes in the garden alone with him at the same time; he would see me first, would hail me from afar, and run up. [...] After he had brushed my cheeks with the impact of his own, each one of us would endeavour to lead off with the conversation; his booming voice got him in first. He would talk music and fundamental bass; I would talk Homer and Corneille. We belaboured each other's

ears with algebra, by turns; in the end he would grow impatient and send poetry where I dare not say but where I at once sent music.[9]

Rameau was unable to secure an organ for many years and turned to teaching. On 25 February 1726, at the church of Saint-Germain l'Auxerrois near the Louvre, he married a young woman called Marie-Louise Mangot (1707-1785), the daughter of a court musician who originally came from Lyon. Marie-Louise was almost certainly one of Rameau's pupils. An accomplished amateur musician, she would later sing in a number of her husband's operas at court. At the time of the marriage, Rameau was living in rue des Petits Champs and the Mangot family not far away in rue Bailleul on the other side of the Palais-Royal. Marie-Louise was only nineteen, but marriages between young girls and middle-aged men were normal. She brought Rameau no diary so it is reasonable to assume that he was deeply attracted to her. Rameau brought to the marriage two hundred *livres*.[10] Maret describes Marie-Louise thus: 'Mme Rameau is a virtuous woman, sweet and likeable, who has made her husband very happy; she has a lot of talent for music, a strong pretty voice and good taste in song.'[11] The union would produce four children, two boys, two girls.[12] In 1727 Rameau applied for the position of organist at Saint-Paul in the Marais[13] but lost out to Louis-Claude Daquin (1694-1772), a renowned virtuoso, much admired by Rameau, who had been a child prodigy. It would be some years before he finally secured a salaried position – organist at Sainte-Croix-de-la Bretonnerie, also in the Marais. It appears that playing the organ gave Rameau little pleasure. It brought a regular income but was associated in his mind with musical drudgery and low status (not that his father would have seen it that way). It certainly didn't inspire Rameau. He published no music for the instrument.

In contrast, the harpsichord was dear to him. During the late 1720s (the actual date is unknown) he published his third and final original work for the instrument, the *Nouvelles suites de pièces de clavecin*. Rameau's keyboard music doesn't represent the depth of his genius and seems small-scale when placed beside the masterpieces of his contemporary Bach, who, in the *English Suites* and the *French Suites*, the latter written around the same time as Rameau's *Nouvelles suites*, used the form in a grander and more captivating manner; but Rameau's keyboard pieces, especially when played on a modern piano,[14] explore the inner reaches of the heart and mind no less than Bach's, and by a more mysterious route. They take strange turns and are by nature enigmatic. Most of Bach's keyboard music wasn't published during his lifetime, but manuscript copies were circulated among musicians. Rameau would have met Bach's friend Georg Philipp Telemann during his sojourn in Paris in 1737/38, and was likely to have become acquainted with at least some of Bach's music by then, but the influence of Bach is not obvious in his work. In contrast, the celebrated set of variations of increasing complexity that ends the first suite of the *Nouvelles suites* – the 'Gavotte avec six doubles' – was surely Rameau's competitive response to Handel's 'Air and five doubles' from the Suite in D minor, published in 1720.

The first of the *Nouvelles suites*, in A, begins with three dances – Allemande, Courante and Sarabande – that represent Rameau at his wisest and most reflective. The rueful Allemande and stately Sarabande both feature lovely downward modulations during their reprises. 'Les Trois mains' introduces vivacity and wit, and is a technical exercise as well as a conceit, creating the illusion that three hands are playing when in fact the two hands are crossed. The second suite, in G, contains two of Rameau's best-known pieces. 'La Poule' depicts the bird through stabbing repeated notes. Designed to make its listeners chuckle along with the hen, it is the only expression of humour in the *Nouvelles suites*. 'Les Sauvages' depicts a performance given by two native Americans witnessed by Rameau at the Saint-Laurent Fair in 1725. The power of this dance would become apparent a few years later when Rameau orchestrated it for his opera *Les Indes galantes*. The contrasting minuets, light and dark, make one think of the young Beethoven. In 'L'Enharmonique', the book's masterpiece, Rameau creates a faint feeling of unease that is never resolved: this ambiguity runs through much of his finest music. The piece is much more than just a demonstration of enharmonics, although this was certainly important to Rameau: he wanted people to learn to appreciate an aspect of his art that was little grasped even by some of his fellow musicians. In his preface to the score, he wrote at length about the 'enharmonic style':

The harmony that creates this effect is not thrown in haphazardly; it is founded on reason and is authorised by Nature itself. The performer must support the intention of the author by softening his touch and by suspending the appoggiaturas more and more as he approaches the striking moment. [...] This effect is born of the difference of one *quartertone* between the *C sharp* and the *D flat*. And although this *quartertone* has effectively no place there, since *C sharp* and *D flat* are one and the same note, sound and key on the keyboard, the effect is none the less perceptible because of the unexpected succession of the different modulations that, in their passage, necessarily require the *quartertone*.[15]

This would not be the last time that Rameau wrote about the value of enharmonics.

In October 1727, Rameau wrote a long and detailed letter to the distinguished writer Antoine Houdar de la Motte (1672-1731). Houdar de la Motte was the most celebrated opera librettist of the age. His successes included works by Campra (the opéra-ballet *L'Europe galante*, 1697, frequently revived), Destouches (*Omphale*, 1701; *Le Carnaval de la folie*, 1704) and Marais (*Alcyone*, 1706; *Sémélé*, 1709). His plays included the tragedy *Inès de Castro*, first performed at the Comédie-Française in 1723. In the letter,[16] Rameau puts himself forward as a potential collaborator. Fearing that his reputation as a theoretician is having a negative impact on his chances of entering the world of the Opéra, he expends too many words on explaining the difference between his learnedness and that of a 'school musician', who has been taught the notes but nothing more. Other composers, he suggests, are governed by their temperaments and the limit of their imaginations. As for himself, he explains how learning gives a deep understanding of nature while precluding neither imagination nor the ability to give the public (who are not learned) what they require. He writes: 'I try to disguise art by art itself.'[17] Rameau goes on to cite two of his Clermont cantatas, *Aquilon et Orithie* and *Téthis*, as examples of his dramatic skill. He does not mention his music for the Paris fairs.

The letter, in essence an application, was perhaps, ironically, a little too densely learned, as well as defensively arrogant, to prompt Houdar de la Motte, who was blind and near the end of his life and reliant on others in his household, to take up a composer yet to prove himself. The letter was kept, though, and printed in the *Mercure de France* after Rameau's death in March 1765.

Rameau clearly believed that his cantatas represented his best hope of attracting a librettist, for he now wrote a new cantata, *Le Berger fidèle*, performed by the young soprano Catherine-Nicole Le Maure at the Concert Spirituel on 22 November 1728,[18] and subsequently arranged for its publication. *Le Berger fidèle*, on a text inspired by Guarini's *Il pastor fido*, was scored for voice, two violins and bass. Amarillis, the beloved of the shepherd Mirtil, is about to be sacrificed on the altar of Diana. Mirtil offers to take her place. This demonstration of true love persuades Diana to relent. Rameau composed three short recitatives, each followed by an air. The highlight of this minor work is the third air, 'L'amour qui règne dans votre âme': Rameau would re-use the music at the end of *Les Fêtes d'Hébé*, ten years later. Rameau published *Le Berger fidèle* along with *Aquilon et Orithie* in *Cantates françoises à voix seule avec symphonie, livre premier*. If Rameau planned further volumes, as the designation suggests, they never materialised.

Rameau was still best known as a music theorist. The *Traité de l'harmonie* had been received positively in 1721, but by the end of the decade a number of gossips, in defence of the thinkers Rameau had superseded, were challenging and disparaging his theories behind his back. It was the anonymity of these attacks that Rameau found hard to bear, writing in his *Nouveau système de musique théorique*, published in 1726: 'If those who are jealous for the early masters' fame wish to undertake their defence, I beg them to speak their mind openly and not rest content with giving their reasons to persons incapable of countering them.'[19] In the summer of 1729 Rameau became embroiled in an argument with another musician, the first public polemical dispute of his career. The *Mercure de France* reported that two well-known figures, named only as the 'first musician' and the 'second musician', had met on Sunday 8 May at the home of a certain individual whose daughter was a talented harpsichordist to try and resolve a difference of opinion over several aspects of harmony. The first musician can easily be identified as Rameau – he gives himself away as the originator of the fundamental bass. The second remains unknown. The report, entitled 'Conference sur la musique', was hostile to Rameau – we learn, for instance, that he arrived for the meeting with seven or eight friends, while his rival came alone.[20] It was probably written by the second musician. Rameau certainly thought so, and responded by publishing *Examen de la conférence sur la musique* in the October edition of the *Mercure*.[21] Further open letters followed.

Rameau and his opponent clashed over the art of accompaniment, that is the art of knowing how to play upper lines when only the bass line has been notated. The second musician accused Rameau of arrogance. Rameau replied that his discovery of the fundamental bass was the key that unlocked the art of accompaniment, and that it was gaining recognition throughout Europe. His opponent, who advocated the octave rule, denied the originality of Rameau's method, saying that he had learned it from another. Rameau fired back that he had always made it known that M. Lacroix of Montpellier had taught him the octave rule when he was a young man, but that the octave rule was a far cry from the fundamental bass.[22] When Rameau's integrity was impugned he responded by becoming ever more arrogant and condescending. He silenced the second musician by writing: 'Do you not know that music is a physico-mathematical science, that sound is its physical object and that the relations between different sounds are its mathematical or geometrical object?'[23]

Cuthbert Girdlestone suggested Michel Pignolet de Montéclair (1667-1737) as the second musician, on the basis of an annotation in the margin of the copy of the *Mercure* held in the Bibliothèque Nationale.[24] Montéclair was in his sixties, a highly respected music teacher, composer and double bass player in the orchestra of the Opéra. He was not a polemicist. It's hard to believe that Rameau didn't respect Montéclair. Two years later, in 1732, Montéclair's *Jephté* would inspire Rameau to create his first work for the Opéra.[25] Thomas Christensen put forward François Campion (1686-1748), the theorist who first formulated, and named, the 'règle de l'octave' in his *Traité d'accompagnement et de composition selon la règle des octaves de musique* (1716), as an alternative candidate.[26] This opinionated guitar virtuoso seems a better fit for the second musician than an elderly double bassist like Montéclair. However, in the book he published that very year, *Lettre du sieur Campion à un philosophe disciple de la règle de l'octave*, he was respectful of Rameau's theory. Rameau transformed his arguments into a new book, *Dissertation sur les différentes méthodes d'accompagnement pour le clavecin ou pour l'orgue*, published by Boivin in 1732.

Le poète Piron à table avec ses amis Vadé et Collé, ou, Les Buveurs de vin by Jacques Autreau (1747). Musée du Louvre, Paris. Piron centre; Collé right.

Rameau's association with Piron and the other artists of the fair theatre would continue into the next decade. Around 1729, Piron along with his fellow writers Crébillon fils and Charles Collé established an exclusive dining club dedicated to food, wine, poetry and satirical song, a *goguette* called the société des dîners du Caveau. The club took its name from the establishment where the twice-monthly meetings took place, the lower salle of the cabaret run by the *traiteur*

Nicolas-Alexis Landelle, on the site of no. 4, rue de Buci, near the junction where the rue de Buci meets the rue Dauphine and the rue de l'Ancienne-Comédie and not far from the Comédie-Française and the Café Procope. Rameau became a member. When, in the years ahead, he came under attack from the *lullistes*, the club provided partisan support and encouragement; it also provided three of his future librettists. To counter the unflattering comments made about Rameau in later life, we will continue to come across pieces of evidence that suggest that he could be good company, pleasure-loving and satirical. His participation in the Caveau suggests something positive about his character at the beginning of the 1730s, or why else was he invited to join? Collé's future resentment of Rameau was caused by their unhappy collaboration in 1751.

In the poet Pierre Laujon's account of the club (admittedly not first-hand – Laujon was a member of the reconstituted société du Caveau later in the century), we learn something of the nature of the meetings in the rue de Buci:

> These joyous companions gathered throughout the year (but especially in the winter and autumn) on the first and sixteenth of each month, for dinner, at their common expense, at the Caveau, where each guest was, in turn, the subject of an epigram (too risqué to admit women). If the epigram was deemed to be just and piquant, its target drank a glass of water to toast his critic; if unfair or inane (it was their word), as punishment the critic downed the glass of water. The other guests drank merrily to the health of the winner. Drama, above all, was the perpetual object of their epigrams.[27]

These gatherings would become more indulgent than Laujon's account suggests. Crébillon fils, Charles Collé and Piron moved between the fairs and the official theatres, but also wrote erotic farces and pornographic dialogues for influential figures such as La Pouplinière (a man we are about to meet), performed in private theatres. Rameau, then, was participating in the literary and theatrical life of the capital as a member of the alternative, and fashionable, Saint-Germain scene of young artists, while seeking a breakthrough in his own career. When his luck changed, at the beginning of the 1730s, it did so suddenly and irrevocably. The established poet Simon-

Joseph Pellegrin,[28] librettist of Montéclair's *Jephté*, agreed to collaborate with him in the creation of an opera and delivered a text of acceptable quality – *Hippolyte et Aricie*. Rameau had come to the attention of La Pouplinière,[29] wealthy *fermier général* (tax collector) and influential patron of music and literature, who at some point made him director of his private orchestra at his home in the rue Neuve-des-Petits-Champs.[30] The orchestra consisted of players of the highest calibre, helping to make La Pouplinière's house one of the most fashionable addresses in the capital. Modern scholarship suggests that *Hippolyte et Aricie* came first but as is so often the case we can't be sure of the exact timing or order of events. It is possible that Piron, who knew an associate of La Pouplinière called Durey d'Harnoncourt,[31] first introduced Rameau to the tax collector's circle back in the 1720s; and it feels right to assume that Rameau met Pellegrin there after La Pouplinière's return from a long stay in Marseille in the early 1730s. If there is a certain logic to believing that Rameau became La Pouplinière's director of music before the premiere of *Hippolyte et Aricie*, not least because two near contemporary sources – Maret's *Éloge historique de Mr. Rameau*[32] and the *Almanach des spectacles pour l'année 1763* – mention that the opera was tried out in his private theatre in the spring of 1733, Graham Sadler has convincingly argued that references to Rameau in Voltaire's letters suggest that he did not take on this role before 1735 at the earliest.[33]

One of Rameau's pupils was a young woman called Thérèse Boutinon des Hayes.[34] Thérèse was born into a theatrical family: her mother, Mimi Dancourt, and aunt, Manon Dancourt, were both members of the Comédie-Française. Rameau and Thérèse formed a close relationship, further evidence, following his marriage to Marie-Louise, that Rameau could have a powerful effect on the young women he taught. Thérèse was the young mistress, and future wife, of La Pouplinière. It is likely that Rameau owed his appointment to her advocacy and that it came about after she became the financier's mistress in 1734.

Portrait said to be of Thérèse Boutinon des Hayes. Artist unknown (ca. 1735). Musée Carnavalet, Paris.

Rameau's relationship with another key figure, the prince de Carignan,[35] also needs to be considered. The prince de Carignan outranked La Pouplinière. He was a senior court official (Intendant of the Menus-Plaisirs) and the Inspector-General of the Opéra. He must have been at the top of Rameau's wish list of potential patrons.

In 1727 Carignan discovered that La Pouplinière was having an affair with his mistress, the singer and actress Marie Antier.[36] Marie Antier was both *première actrice* at the Opéra and a *musicienne de la chambre du roi*. She would later create the role of Phèdre in Rameau's *Hippolyte et Aricie*. Carignan's influence at court was such that he was able to arrange La Pouplinière's removal from Paris – the aforementioned long stay in Marseille that lasted until the early 1730s.

There is no definitive evidence that Rameau worked directly for Carignan. He may have been wary of aligning himself too closely with this notorious libertine and gambler. But we know, again from Voltaire's letters, that Rameau frequented the prince's palatial home, the hôtel de Soissons in Les Halles (not far from the Palais-Royal),[37] and was enjoying some degree of patronage from him at the time of *Hippolyte et Aricie*. Given the prince's position at the Opéra, Rameau's opera would not have been accepted for performance without his consent. We know that new operas were tried out at the hôtel de Soissons, and it is tempting to agree with Graham Sadler[38] that the author of the anecdote in the *Almanach des spectacles* simply got the location of the trial performance mixed up (we know that the performance happened somewhere because Rameau refers to it himself in his *Démonstration du principe de l'harmonie*, 1750). Given the personal grievance and rivalry that existed between La Pouplinière and Carignan, it seems unlikely that Rameau was working for the former at a time when he needed the goodwill of the latter at the Opéra. In the subsequent years, after Rameau had gained his first success and was bringing prestige and money to the Opéra, Carignan would have tolerated his association with La Pouplinière. There is a reason why Maret and others, later on, may have consciously or subconsciously erased Carignan from the record. Carignan fell from grace, his life ending ruinously and prematurely in 1741.

Whatever the truth, the important factor was the meeting with Pellegrin and the creation of *Hippolyte et Aricie*. Rameau, at fifty, was finally able to release the creativity that for years had been kept in check. One can imagine the intensity of the relief that Rameau must have felt at this moment. By the end of 1733 this intensely beautiful tragédie lyrique had been staged to great acclaim and no little controversy at the Opéra.

3

Interlude: France During the Age of Rameau

i The International Context

Rameau was a child of the 17th century, of a France at the height of its political and cultural influence under Louis XIV. Relative decline started during the Sun King's last years, and by the middle years of the 18th century, during the reign of Louis XV, France was facing the challenge of an increasingly assertive England. In Europe, conflict between the two great powers resulted in periods of warfare, but the overriding policy of both England and France was to maintain the *status quo*. The War of the Austrian Succession of the 1740s (Prussia, France and Spain against Austria, England and the Dutch Republic) ended in a conciliatory peace deal (the Treaty of Aix-la-Chapelle) that saw France abandon its most significant gain, the Austrian Netherlands. In return, England handed back Louisbourg (Nova Scotia) to France. Rameau, recently appointed *Compositeur du Cabinet du Roi*, composed an opéra-ballet to mark the highpoint of France's campaign during the war, the defeat of English and allied forces at Fontenoy – *Les Fêtes de Polymnie*, premiered at the Opéra on 12 October 1745; and was commissioned by the king's mistress Mme de Pompadour to write a work to celebrate the Treaty of Aix-la-Chapelle – *Les Surprises de l'Amour*, performed at Versailles on 27 November 1748.

Retaining Louisbourg and its other colonies in the New World was more important to France than permanently removing Austria from the Low Countries, for, beyond Europe, in the Americas, India and Africa, the rich-pickings of trade and commerce demanded a fight with England for global supremacy. The next major conflict, the Seven Years' War (1756-63), coincided with Rameau's last years. The war started well for France with victories against the English in America (infamous because of atrocities committed by native auxiliaries,[1] a challenge to the idealised European view of native Americans expressed in the last act of Rameau's *Les Indes galantes*, revived in Paris during the war), the Mediterranean and Hanover. The extent to which London was rattled by such humiliations was revealed when Admiral Byng, blamed for the fall of Minorca, was court marshalled and shot, provoking Voltaire, who despised both nations for engaging in a ridiculous and futile fight over 'a few acres of snow on the Canadian border', to write the chapter of *Candide* (1759) in which the hero witnesses the execution of an admiral in Portsmouth and is told 'in this country we find it pays to shoot an admiral from time to time to encourage the others'.[2] The tide quickly turned, however, when England's ally Prussia surprisingly defeated the French at Rossbach. The long and bitter struggle that followed saw the England of William Pitt ruthlessly assert its global power through naval superiority and precipitated a profound crisis of confidence within the splendour of Versailles: Mme de Pompadour's famous remark 'Après nous, le déluge' is alleged to have been spoken during the war in an attempt to lift the spirits of the king, who was diminished by the setbacks of the war and depressed following an assassination attempt. The war ended with France's eviction from North America. The mood of the French public was as despondent and angry as it was rabidly anti-English. The monarchy suddenly appeared weak and fallible. This was the state of things as Rameau wrote his last operas, *Les Paladins* and *Les Boréades*.

ii Politics and Society

Despite the cost and suffering of war, France remained, on the continent, the *grande nation*, and, domestically, up until the Seven Years' War, the period was one of relative calm.

Louis XIV died in 1715, the year Rameau returned to Clermont. France then entered the potentially difficult period of the Regency of

Philippe d'Orléans. The predicted political strife, as powerful factions jostled for position in the hope that the young king in waiting, Louis XV, would die before reaching the age of majority, never happened. The country had feared that the famously hedonistic Orléans would not be equal to the task. On the contrary, he governed with firmness and skill, manoeuvring his enemies into positions of weakness, negotiating his way through domestic and international crises, and taking his responsibility as the protector and educator of the future king with the utmost moral seriousness. (As we have noted, Orléans's Paris home, the Palais-Royal, housed the Opéra.)

Louis reached maturity, as tradition dictated, at the age of thirteen in 1723, the year Rameau settled in Paris. Orléans still governed behind the scenes, supported by his first minister, the abbé Dubois. At only thirteen Louis was not ready to take on an active role. Then, in quick succession, Orléans and Dubois died. The senior Prince of Blood, Louis Henri, duc de Bourbon, became first minister but was error-prone in both domestic and international affairs as well as unsubtle in his attempt to overload the court with his own nominees, including his unpopular mistress. With Louis's support, André-Hercule de Fleury moved against Bourbon and the latter was forced into exile (1726). Louis declared that from now on he would rule without a first minister but in reality he turned to Fleury, his old tutor and confessor. Louis was in need of both emotional support and political guidance, and Fleury had been managing his life since his early childhood. With Orléans gone, this seventy-six-year-old churchman occupied the centre stage and would do so for the next seventeen years. He was a master of political manoeuvring. As Colin Jones explains in his study of 18th century France, *The Great Nation*,[3] Fleury even took advantage of his old age. He was adept at giving the impression that he was too old to know what was going on, and blameless, when, in truth, he was behind everything the state did. He made sure that none of the factions had reason to feel excluded, while consolidating his own power at the heart of government – the secretaries and officials of state were his people. It was Fleury who, in 1727, arranged for La Pouplinière to be posted to Marseille.

Fleury presided over a France that, like a son breaking free from a dominant father, was finally emerging from the long shadow of Louis XIV. For the top and middle ranks of society, this was an age of stability and prosperity. However, if no one was predicting the catastrophe of the Revolution, just half a century ahead, there was a constant noise of dissatisfaction and criticism, a new constituency of dissent that united salon intellectuals and backstreet pamphleteers and which threatened to break unchecked into the mainstream. The state was wary of independent thought. It remained ever watchful, but, given the spread of printing, struggled to keep up. Also, some officials were reluctant to banish intellectual thought from the borders of a country they considered to be the most civilised in the world. As the century wore on the state would find it increasingly difficult to control public opinion. Nevertheless, France's leading thinkers, scientists and writers had to work and publish, if they dared, under the most trying conditions.

Voltaire, by issuing work abroad or in clandestine editions, was one who dared, albeit with understandable trepidation and in the hope that he could escape the consequences by denying responsibility or by talking himself out of trouble with the help of his connections: Voltaire was no anti-establishment rebel, but his profound belief in the principles of free speech and religious tolerance, pushed him into risk-taking. In 1733, the year of *Hippolyte et Aricie*, he published in London his *Letters Concerning the English Nation*; the work appeared in France the following year as *Lettres philosophiques*. Here Voltaire analysed and extolled (and exaggerated) the virtues of the English model of politics and society as a means of throwing a critical light on France, comparing England's constitutional monarchy and parliamentary politics to France's despotism, England's relative freedoms and religious tolerance to France's censorship and intolerance. Relative to their French counterparts, English thinkers and scientists were granted some leeway by the state when it came to freedom of expression, and were honoured as great men: Voltaire attended Newton's state funeral in Westminster Abbey in 1727. On the publication of the *Lettres philosophiques* the French authorities proved Voltaire's point by banning the work and forcing its author to flee from Paris.

Voltaire had first found himself in trouble with the authorities when, at the age of twenty-two, just before the success of his first play, *Œdipe*, he wrote some satirical verses accusing Philippe d'Orléans of committing incest with his daughter. Although the verses were circulated anonymously the gossips rightly declared Voltaire to be the author. Orléans dispatched him to the Bastille. Voltaire sent contrite and sycophantic letters and was eventually released almost a year later. Most writers were more exposed than Voltaire because they lacked his aristocratic friends. They dreaded informers and police spies; they knew that if a minister signed a *lettre de cachet* against them they would be arrested and imprisoned without trial. This fate befell Denis Diderot in 1749 after the publication of his *Lettre sur les aveugles*.

There is no direct evidence that Rameau held radical views on social, religious or political issues. He comes across as a man absorbed in his own art to the exclusion of all other concerns, and when he got to know Voltaire, at the time of the *Lettres philosophiques*, it was in professional circumstances that proved difficult and which prevented a meeting of minds. However, at least three of his major operas, *Platée*, *Zoroastre* and *Les Boréades*, contained material that indirectly mocked or challenged the authority of the royal state, and with very little subterfuge involved. If the messages contained in these works had not been dressed up in the fancy paraphernalia of opera they surely would have been read not as humour and spectacle but as dangerously subversive acts of disobedience.

iii Rameau's Paris

Despite over two centuries of change, Paris has retained many of the buildings that were standing during Rameau's lifetime. This is particularly true of the Left Bank quarter of Saint-Germain between the river and the boulevard Saint-Germain, and of the Right Bank quarter of the Marais. The buildings are tall, off-white and stuck together in a largely uniform fashion; the streets are relatively narrow (they were wider, though, in the 18th century because there were no pavements). To sense Rameau's Paris, leave those streets in Saint-Germain that are cluttered with market stalls, café terraces and shops and turn into the quieter and more secretive roads that run parallel to the river.

On the Right Bank, the major redevelopment schemes of the 19th century tore away large areas, clearing medieval streets and buildings to create wide boulevards and 'modern' housing. If the district most associated with Rameau, that of the Louvre and the Palais-Royal, was radically altered by the creation of the rue de Rivoli, the rue du Louvre, the rue du Colonel Driant and the avenue de l'Opéra, many streets and buildings were left intact. The same can't be said of Les Halles: here the church of Saint-Eustache, where Rameau is buried, rises like a stone ship over one of Paris's few 20th century lapses in taste.

If Paris retains the contours of its past, we need to fill in the particularities of 18th century life. 18th century Paris had great monuments and fashionable quarters where the rich built beautiful townhouses with enclosed formal gardens, but, other than the gardens of the Tuileries and the Palais-Royal, there were no green public places in the centre and the river was an open sewer. A city renowned for its elegance was notorious for its squalor. In *The Embellishments of Paris*, written in 1739, Voltaire described the dual nature of the capital:

> Whilst the triumphal arch of the Porte Saint-Denis and the equestrian statue of Henri IV, the two bridges, the Louvre, the Tuileries and the Champs-Elysees all equal or surpass the beauties of ancient Rome, the city centre – dark, enclosed and hideous – stands for an age of most shameful barbarism.[4]

Contemporary guidebooks warned travellers of filthy lodging houses and the impossibility of keeping clothes clean because of the muddy streets. The Seine was the main source of drinking water. Parisians were immune to the germs, but visitors often became ill. In Paris, more so than in London, which had pavements, horse-drawn carriages posed a constant threat to life and limb. Most inhabitants lived cheek-by-jowl in cramped medieval tenements. Daily existence was hard and unrelenting, and life expectancy low. Ordinary Parisians, of course, took all this for granted and didn't find their city extraordinary at all. The rich and middle classes were removed from the worst but shared the air, the water and the diseases. Although they were inconvenienced by the slums, and fearful of the social consequences of Paris's seemingly uncontrollable rate of expansion

(Rétif de la Bretonne: 'I marvelled at the way in which Paris devours its surroundings, converting nourishing gardens into sterile streets'[5]), they mostly saw their city as the paragon of culture, taste and modernity (Marivaux: 'Paris is the world; the rest of the earth is nothing but its suburbs'[6]). Paris as a whole had an unruly swagger, a dynamism, which drew many thousands of foreign visitors but which kept the lieutenant of police's army of spies continually on manoeuvre and caused France's people-wary king to order the building of a new road so that he could travel from Saint-Denis to Versailles without entering its gates.

iv The Organisation of Music-Making

To understand the music of Rameau's time we need to go back to the reign of Louis XIV and to Jean-Baptiste Lully (1632-87), the Italian who was France's greatest composer in the second half of the 17th century. Lully was not only the leading creator of French stage music; he was also, thanks to the patronage of the king, its controlling master. If a composer wanted to write for the Paris stage he had a problem if Lully considered him to be a rival; if a theatre owner in Marseille wanted to present operas he had to pay Lully to obtain a licence.

The young Lully had come to the attention of Louis XIV as a dancer and a composer of ballet music at court. The king was a keen performer himself and well able to recognise Lully's particular genius. As well as fulfilling his duties as the king's *Surintendant de Musique*, Lully formed an association with Molière, composing music for the great playwright's comedies and creating the new theatrical form of the comédie-ballet.

After 1670 Lully turned his attention to opera. This may have been partly because the king, now beyond his performing years, had lost some of his passion for the dance; it was certainly about building an empire and making money. Louis XIV had granted the sole *privilège* of establishing academies for the performance of operas in French to the writer Pierre Perrin in 1669. The crown wanted to encourage artistic creation while at the same time regulating it. Perrin endeavoured to establish a national opera by taking elements from the *ballet de cour* and combining them with recitative and airs: with the composer Robert Cambert he wrote the first true opera in French – *Pomone*, a *pastorale* in five acts and a prologue (1671). When Perrin fell into debt, Lully bought the privilege with the king's blessing (1672). The Académie d'Opéra became the Académie Royale de Musique.

The Académie Royale de Musique (referred to henceforth in these pages as the Opéra) was at the apex of a complex network of cultural bodies – academies, orchestras, choirs – established and monitored by the crown.[7] This meant that support of the arts was inseparable from censorship of the arts. Louis XIV was a master of this kind of control politics. The Opéra was originally based at a theatre in the rue de Vaugirard. On Molière's death in 1673 Lully was understandably quick to move his organisation into the prestigious theatre in the Palais-Royal.[8]

As well as taking control of the Opéra, Lully was its primary composer (Cambert, excluded by Lully, left for London). Lully and his librettist Philippe Quinault (1635-1688) created a form of national opera – called *tragédie en musique* or *tragédie lyrique* – that, in its grandeur of scale, was carefully designed to appeal to the king. Lully understood the king's artistic likes and dislikes better than anyone else in the kingdom.

Lully and Quinault took their subject matter from either classical mythology or the tales of chivalry, and gave their tragic dramas happy endings. The structure of a tragédie lyrique consisted of an allegorical prologue and five acts. Each act consisted of long *airs* (arias), in which a character expressed his or her innermost feelings; *recitatives* (dialogues between characters) punctuated by *petits airs* (short arias); and a concluding *divertissement*. The overriding characteristic of French opera, in contrast to Italian, was the integration of these elements to give the music and drama a continuous forward movement.

A special feature of French opera was the splendour of the design. French opera became synonymous with visual spectacle on the grandest of scales. Elaborate stage machinery created stylised depictions of clouds, waves, temples and forests, each picture replacing the previous without interruption. Another feature was the importance given to dance. The poetry of the text was viewed in the abstract as having primacy over all the other elements, including the music. For Antoine Louis Le Brun, writing in 1712, opera was a 'monstre en fait de poésie'.⁹ In practice, though, the words served the music. Le Cerf de La Viéville's contemporary account of Lully's working methods reveals that his controlling intellect made him Quinault's master:

> Quinault wrote out a plan for the action of the Piece. He gave a copy of this plot to Lully, and Lully, seeing the subject of each Act, prepared some divertissements from his imagination. [...] Quinault composed his Scenes. [...] He brought the scenes to Lully [who] examined [this] poetry word by word, which he corrected or from which he cut out half when he judged it appropriate.¹⁰

These sentences could have been written about Rameau half a century later. Lully and Quinault established their new national opera at the first attempt, *Cadmus et Hermione*, staged at the Opéra before the king in 1673. The king and his courtiers adored a work that found a place for ballet and scenic spectacle within the parameters of a play about mortals and gods that took its inspiration from the verse tragedies of the spoken theatre. In the recitatives, Quinault adopted the alexandrine couplets of Racine, but rarely rigidly. To avoid monotony in the music, Lully demanded variations in the number of syllables per line. Whereas Italian recitative used a uniform rhythm, Lully's French style was characterised by changes in metre.

During the next fifteen years, Lully produced a new *tragédie lyrique* every year, such was the popularity of the form. His final completed work, *Armide* (1686), performed at the Opéra but not at Versailles, for Lully, embroiled in a homosexual scandal, had fallen out of favour with the king, was widely considered to be his masterpiece. The following year, while directing a performance of his *Te Deum*, Lully accidentally struck his foot with his conducting staff. He refused to have his leg amputated and died from gangrene. The composers who took up the form included Marc-Antoine Charpentier (*Médée*, 1693), Marin Marais (*Alcyone*, 1706) and André Campra (*Idoménée*, 1712).

Rameau adopted Lully's model but made it his own in a number of important respects. He gave a more prominent role to the orchestra, with overtures that were varied in character and ballet music that dazzled in its profusion of different dance forms. Likewise, his choral writing was far more elaborate than Lully's. Eventually, Rameau abandoned the prologue, an innovation.

4

The Opéra

1733 to 1735

i Life at the Palais-Royal and the Opéra

In September 1733 Rameau walked across the garden of the Palais-Royal and entered the Opéra for the first time as the composer of a tragedy, *Hippolyte et Aricie*. Because he had waited so long for the opportunity he would not have taken it for granted. Ten years later, in a fascinating letter to a young composer called Mongeot, Rameau wrote that even at fifty he had feared that he was not ready:

> I have followed the theatre since the age of twelve. I didn't work for the Opéra until I was fifty, and even then believed myself to be incapable of it. I took a chance, I had good fortune, I continued.[1]

Mongeot had asked for advice, and Rameau wrote a warm, considered and honest reply. In the letter he reveals his thoughts on the essential requirements of becoming an opera composer: a detailed and sensitive knowledge of the stage, of actors, choreography and the voice; but also, crucially, an understanding of human nature, so as to be as true as possible. Rameau advises Mongeot that it is better to write small pieces, such as cantatas, or a 'thousand bagatelles' that nourish the mind, before tackling a grand work. Make your opera debut with a ballet, he writes, and not a tragedy.[2] The letter reveals the private Rameau, confessional and self-doubting. He would not have publicly expressed these doubts as he entered the world of the Palais-Royal and the Opéra.

At the Palais-Royal the Orléans family was served by a household that was second only to the royal court at Versailles. Later in the century, the Palais-Royal would be transformed, with the building of new arcades and rooms, into a highly profitable commercial centre, a top end red-light district frequented by both aristocrats and the young men of the professions; but in Rameau's time it was a more exclusive, more enigmatic, purveyor of pleasure. The artists of the Opéra worked in a continually shifting world of rumour, ridicule and gossip. The female singers and dancers were viewed by many as prostitutes, for the Opéra's stage was a shop window. A star singer or dancer was usually the mistress of a rich aristocrat; the others had a rougher and more precarious time of it.

Montesquieu, in his philosophical epistolary novel *Persian Letters* (1721), imagines the experience of one of his Persian travellers on his first visit to the Opéra:

> A few days ago a friend of mine took me into the box where one of the principal actresses was changing out of her costume; we became so well acquainted that the next day I received this letter from her: 'Monsieur, I am the most unfortunate girl in the world; I have always been the most virtuous actress of the Opéra. About seven or eight months ago I was in the box where you saw me yesterday; as I was costuming as a priestess of Diana, a young abbé visited me, and without the least respect for my white robes, my veil, and my virginal headband, violated my innocence: no matter how fiercely I complained to him of the sacrifice I made him, he laughed at me, assuring me he found me very profane; however, I am so big with child that I no longer dare show myself on the stage, for when it's a matter of honour I am fastidious to a fault; I believe that it's easier to persuade a well-born young woman to lose her virtue than her modesty: consequently, in view of my fastidiousness you will readily believe that the young abbé would never have succeeded, had he not promised to marry me. [...] Since I have been dishonoured by his bad faith, I no longer want to stay at the Opéra where, between you and me, they barely give us enough to live on.'[3]

From Lully's time onwards there was a constant chorus of complaint, genuine or hypocritical, from clerics and other moralists outraged by the culture of decadence at the Opéra, and concerned that the presumed promiscuity of its young women would influence the behaviour of respectable women in the audience.[4] Opera became synonymous with sensuality – in the works presented, in the manner of their presentation and in the physical interactions of performers and spectators. The female performers were chosen by the management more for their attractiveness than their dancing or singing ability. There was a deeply established, if officially unacknowledged, culture of prostitution that the creators of operas had no choice but to tolerate, building their productions in spite of the distractions and the artistic weaknesses of the dancers and singers.

Casanova, in the chapter of his memoirs that concern his sojourn in Paris in 1750, writes of how he rushed to see the renowned Palais-Royal soon after his arrival in the city, describing a magnificent garden of tree-lined pathways and fountains surrounded by tall buildings. Rameau lived in houses[5] overlooking the garden from 1735 to 1744, and from 1753 to his death. The view was one of the finest in Paris. Today's garden, although narrower, retains the rows of lime trees and pathways of hard sand. To visit it on a breezy summer's day, when the leaves rattle and the pathways release swirls of white dust (Rameau wrote a harpsichord piece inspired by this sight – *Les Tourbillons*), is to share an experience with the composer across the centuries. Different activities took place in different parts of the garden. The avenue of trees on the east side, the allée d'Argenson, was a place for solitary walks and quiet contemplation. Prostitutes worked in the allée de Foy, opposite.[6] Casanova writes of stalls selling news sheets, bottles of perfume, snuff and toothpicks, and of the many young men and women strolling under the trees or sitting alone at the café tables. At the house of the ballet master, Lany,[7] he meets some of the *filles de l'Opéra*, aged only thirteen or fourteen, and finds their conversation provocative and shameless. The libertine is similarly taken aback when the celebrated actress of the Opéra, Marie Fel,[8] tells him that her three children have different fathers. Within pages he is coldly relating the story of his seduction and abandonment of his landlady's fifteen-year-old daughter. The girl runs away from home and he next sees her singing on the stage of the fair theatre. When he tells her that he didn't know that she was a musician, she replies: 'I'm no different from the others. The girls at the Paris Opéra can't read a note but they sing all the same.' Casanova concludes by writing: 'Later she was taken for all she had by a violinist called Bérard and she disappeared.'⁹

Portrait de Louise Jacquet by Jean-Étienne Liotard (ca. 1748).

There was a parallel culture of hypocrisy, for a young actress (as the singers were called) or dancer could be disciplined or even sacked for immoral behaviour. Because of the intense rivalry that existed in the ranks of the Opéra, back-stabbing and snitching were common. In 1740, the attractive young leading soprano Louise Jacquet, then at the beginning of her career, accused the young dancer Marie-

Antoinette Petit of having sex with the marquis de Bonnac in a dressing room. Mlle Petit was dismissed from the company. She asked her friend La Mare (librettist of Royer's *Zaide*) to help her write a public essay in which she accused Mlle Jacquet of malice: 'The supposed witness of my infamy bears a resemblance by the blackness of her nature to the chief of the Cyclopes. Her soul is worthy of the body she occupies; she has all the vices of her profession but none of the virtues.' Mlle Petit wrote that she had only been flirting with the marquis. 'He told me crazy things to which I replied wisely. Finally, he choked me up with conversation and we gave each other a few knocks, playfully. I ran after him with the intention of avenging myself. He asked for mercy and kissed my hand; I calmed down. Mlle J, who passed at that moment, pretended to take the preliminaries for the very thing.'[10]

The result was a minor scandal. Mlle Jacquet was condemned as a 'bad colleague'. Mlle Petit was reinstated by the Opéra, but not until 1742. She only lasted a few more years. In 1745 she made an official complaint against the *sous-fermier général* Bouret de Valroche, who was subjecting her to systematic abuse and violence.[11] The documentary evidence, then, confirms that the literary writings of Montesquieu, Casanova and others on this subject were not exaggerated. The national archives hold plentiful examples of young actresses and dancers seeking help and redress because of exploitative and abusive relationships.

Mlle Jacquet went on to peform many named roles, particularly in works by Lully. For Rameau, she sang Isbé in *Les Fêtes de Ramire* and Arsine in *Le Temple de la Gloire* in 1745; Junon in *Platée* in 1749; Zélize in *Zoroastre* in 1749; Mnémosyne and Oriade in *Les Fêtes de Polymnie* in 1753; and Diane in *Les Surprises de l'Amour* in 1757. She inspired the verses:

> Jacquet par son air de gaîté
> Animerait le plus farouche;
> Le plaisir et la volupté
> Brillent en ses yeux et sur sa bouche.

> Jacquet by her jollity would rouse the most timid; pleasure and voluptuousness linger in her eyes and on her mouth.

Despite the circumstances of their selection for the Opéra, the female performers were still expected to master difficult music and choreography. Performances, not surprisingly, were often accident-prone and chaotic. How did Rameau fit into this milieu? Some of the young women in the company would have been ambitious in their stage careers and eager to catch his eye. We cannot know whether he exploited this power. We do know that it was opera that inspired him as a composer, for he had little or no interest in other forms or outlets. He was attracted to this world of intimate collaborations, of youth, beauty and sensuality, of pleasure and fantasy (his writing, particularly for the female voice, is the musical representation of all of the above); attracted by the nature of the thing itself, by the importance of its role within fashionable Parisian society and by the rewards of fame and adulation that it alone could bring.

The actual process of bringing a work to life in the theatre was, then as now, a stressful business, relying on the skill, commitment and ability to collaborate of a large and disparate group of people, from temperamental star singers to overworked costume makers, from bullied young dancers to struggling musicians, from money-obsessed theatre managers to ambitious composers and librettists. It comes as a surprise to learn that the theatre of the Opéra was ill-suited to the presentation of a piece like *Hippolyte et Aricie*. The stage was small. The auditorium was a thin rectangular box into which a gallery, three rows of boxes and a balcony had been squashed. The theatre had been recently renovated (in 1732) and it was handsomely decorated. Nevertheless, a traveller from Italy, familiar with the grand houses of Milan and Venice, would have felt contentedly superior. We can easily imagine the cramped and chaotic conditions backstage. Because the Opéra had a studio and storage facility in the rue Saint-Nicaise,[12] the Magasin de l'Opéra, the preparation work was better served. It was here, just across the road from the Palais-Royal, close to the place de Carrousel, that costumes and sets were created, décor stored, singers and dancers trained and productions rehearsed.[13]

From his conversations with some of Rameau's friends and colleagues, Hugues Maret was able to write convincingly about the composer's working methods and temperament. His portrait of Rameau at work includes small but telling details that testify to its authenticity. On receiving a libretto, Rameau would study the text carefully, and often demand changes that would try the author's patience. When composing his music he would have a violin to hand, although sometimes he would sit at the harpsichord. He did not suffer to be interrupted. If the process went well he would be in high spirits; if badly, he would fall into a state of sorrow and anger. He was frustrated by the inability of the orchestra at the Opéra to master his music. During rehearsals, to get things right, he was forced to talk so much that his mouth became dry; only by eating a piece of fruit was he able to re-find his voice. Often he would sit alone in the *parterre* and brush people away with a gesture of his hand. During performances he would attempt to stay hidden in one of the small boxes. If the public saw him, though, he would acknowledge their applause with a dignified modesty.[14]

How was a work chosen, rehearsed and directed? In 1733, the Opéra was managed by the prince de Carignan (as Inspector-General) and Louis-Armand Eugène de Thuret (as Director).[15] The two men had joint responsibility for programming, but all works selected for production had to be approved by the relevant minister of state. Thuret held the *privilège* and was in charge of financial matters. The Opéra employed a conductor (*batteur de mesure*) who directed rehearsals and performances, and a music master (*maître de musique*) responsible for instructing the performers. At this time, the orchestra of the Opéra consisted, typically, of thirty-four string players and nine woodwind players,[16] an appropriate line-up for the size of the theatre. Contemporary sources, though, reveal that the Opéra's staff faced a constant struggle to get the balance and tone of sound right. The role of the conductor was crucial in this respect.

The articles of the Opéra reveal that the composer had the right to direct proceedings if he so wished. We know that Rameau was in charge of his opera *Dardanus*, six years later, because an eye-witness account of the dress rehearsal has survived. This account, by Mme de Graffigny[17] in a letter, brings a Rameau rehearsal at the Opéra to life. We learn that the dancers were comically incompetent, that the mistakes provoked constant interruptions and scoldings, and that Rameau was mocked by wits in the audience:

> I've been to the rehearsal of *Dardanus*. I was enchanted by it

and all of a sudden converted into a *ramoneuse*. As for the lyrics, I cannot say anything yet, I did not hear more than four words. We were too close to the orchestra to hear. Oh, rehearsals are funny and ridiculous things! While someone sang mournfully, a dozen people were dancing at the rear of the stage, neither together nor in time to the music, but each one by himself and against the count of the vocal accompaniment. How can I express the ridiculousness of it? The interruptions, the scoldings. Rameau, with the air and the figure of a great devil, sang to indicate the note; the *parterre*, where there were more than one hundred and fifty people, mocked him by clapping hands, for he sings a little like you, and he clapped back at them. All this made for a singular experience, and because of all the buffoonery, the beauty of music, the charm of Jélyotte's voice,[18] I cried behind my fan for much of the time.[19]

Given what we know of Rameau's character, it seems unlikely that he did not supervise most of his major works, including *Hippolyte et Aricie*. He would have been worried that *Hippolyte et Aricie* was in places too difficult and in others too new to be left to the Opéra staff. However, as a relatively inexperienced theatre man, he must have relied upon the conductor and the music master up to a point. In the event, the performers struggled to master their parts. Rameau was intimidating and intolerant of errors. We know that he cut or altered some of the most difficult sections. The enforced alteration of one particular section – the trio of Fates at the end of act two, a bravura passage of diatonic enharmony – clearly rankled with him, for he mentioned it in print on two separate occasions: in 1737, when he stated that some of the singers and musicians at the Opéra had been incapable of mastering the style;[20] and in 1750, when he praised the musicians of the private orchestra who had played the work at the trial concert.[21]

Casanova wrote an account of his first visit to the Paris Opéra in 1750. The piece was not by Rameau,[22] but by Campra – *Les Fêtes vénitiennes*. Casanova watched from the *parterre* at a cost of forty sous. He praised the orchestra, but found the music's style to be outmoded, its recitatives monotonous (Campra's opéra-ballet dated from 1710). Casanova admired the representation of St Mark's Square in Venice, despite the comical inaccuracies, and was delighted by the speed of the scenic changes, which were signalled by the blowing of a whistle. Casanova wrote one of the first descriptions of the egotistical conductor in the history of music: 'The leader of the music violently waved his baton from right to left as if his actions were responsible for bringing the instruments to life.' Casanova's compatriot Carlo Goldoni, who settled in Paris in the early 1760s, was similarly dismayed by a style of opera that was not, to his ears, neatly divided into clearly defined segments, writing:

> I patiently waited for the airs, in expectation that I should at least be amused by the music. The dancers made their appearance, and I imagined the act finished, but heard not a single air. I spoke of this to my neighbour, who laughed at me, and assured me that we had had six in the different scenes which I had heard. 'What!' said I, 'I am not deaf; the instruments never ceased accompanying the voices, sometimes more loudly and sometimes more slowly than usual, but I took the whole for recitative'.[23]

Goldoni was at least impressed by the visual opulence of French opera, the decorations, machines and costumes: 'Everything was beautiful, grand and magnificent, except the music.'

Casanova described how the audience applauded the entrance of the tall figure of the dancer Louis Dupré,[24] sixty years old but still physically strong. Wearing a mask and a large black wig that stretched half-way down his back, the *grand Dupré* made a stately journey to the footlights, where he gestured gracefully with his arms, moved his feet with delicate precision, and pirouetted. Casanova's French companion told him: 'It is always the same, but every time it seems new to us, such is the power of beauty and truth penetrating the soul: this is the true dance, of which you have no idea in Italy.' There followed a female dancer, also of mature years. 'This is the famous Camargo,'[25] the Frenchman told Casanova. 'She is the first dancer who has dared to leap, before her no one did so; and the admirable thing is that she doesn't wear *culottes*.'[26]

Whether the overall effect of these dances was, to our modern eyes, more comical than sublime is hard to know, but Casanova's account helps us to imagine the dancing in a Rameau opera. Casanova saw Dupré and Marie Camargo at the end of their careers.

Rameau met them now, in 1733, as he entered the Opéra to stage *Hippolyte et Aricie*. We know that Camargo, aged twenty-two, was in the *Hippolyte et Aricie* company and if Dupré wasn't involved he certainly worked (as dancer and choreographer) on Rameau's second opera, *Les Indes galantes*, two years later.

Marie Camargo would become a follower of Rameau. His vivacious, fast, rhythmical music for dance influenced her style of quick, intricate footwork and entrechats and other steps performed in the air. To allow and display these movements, she abandoned her high heels for slippers and wore calf-length dresses, both innovations. As for Dupre's mannered and graceful style, appropriate for slow, formal dances, this was also a feature of all of Rameau's operas.

The composers of works staged at the Opéra wrote for a permanent company and needed to match their music to the abilities and personalities of the company's leading players. 'Most composers,' wrote the renowned choreographer Jean-Georges Noverre, 'followed [...] the old decrees of the Opéra: they composed *passepieds* and *musettes* because Mlle Prévost danced the former with such elegance and Mlle Sallé and M. Dumoulin the latter with as much grace as voluptuousness; *tambourins*, because it was a form at which Mlle Camargo excelled; and *chaconnes* and *passacailles* because these fitted the noble gestures of the celebrated Dupré so well.'[27]

The acting ability of the leading singers was an issue of much concern and debate, perhaps more so in the 18th century than in the centuries since. A female singer was, officially, an *actrice*, required to be able to act as well as she could sing, and composers had a responsibility to try to aid the singers by writing music that helped them to pitch the emotional level of their acting of a scene; but, in reality, singers who could act were few in number. Rameau wanted his singers to be able to inhabit the characters in his operas, as his letter to Mongeot implied, and he wrote repeatedly for those few who could meet his demands.

ii Hippolyte et Aricie

The originality of Rameau's first tragédie lyrique wasn't in the form, structure, themes or words, which largely conformed to Lully and

Quinault's model, but in Rameau's treatment of them. As was usual, the characters and story were drawn from Greek mythology. Pellegrin based his libretto on Racine's play *Phèdre*, a masterpiece written fifty-six years earlier in 1677, but also drew on Racine's ancient Greek sources, Euripides's *Hippolytus* and Seneca's *Phaedra*, and added opera-friendly elements of his own invention.

Pellegrin was seventy in 1733. Born in Marseille, he was ordained in the order of Servites but was too ambitious to settle. According to an 18th century biographical dictionary, he took to the seas as a ship's chaplain, finally washing up in Paris in 1703.[28] He made his name thanks to a calculated act of sycophancy, an ode to the king called *Epître à Louis XIV* that brought him to the attention of the king's mistress Mme de Maintenon. His tragedy *La Mort d'Ulysse* was performed by the Comédie-Française in 1706, while at the Opéra, the focal point of his ambitions, he collaborated with Destouches on the creation of *Télémaque* in 1714. Pellegrin didn't restrict his activities to the official theatres. For a period, under the name of his brother, he ran one of the theatres of the Saint-Laurent fair. He wrote farces such as *Arlequin à la guinguette* (1711) while fulfilling his duty to the church by producing thousands of *cantiques spirituelles*, adapting verses from the Bible and setting them to popular tunes. Pellegrin was both a devout clergyman and a *bon vivant* and this double life inspired an epigram – 'Le matin catholique et le soir idolâtre, il soupait à la messe et dînait au théâtre'[29] – as well as the constant contempt of Voltaire, who smelt hypocrisy along with incense, mediocrity and old age. His church masters, meanwhile, banned him from saying mass. Most accounts of Pellegrin suggest that he was a good-natured and modest man who once referred to himself as 'poet [et] pauvre prêtre Provençal'.[30]

Pellegrin, then, was a senior member of the theatrical scene, successful and no doubt set in his ways. Rameau was fortunate to secure Pellegrin, for his libretto was arguably the most dramatically satisfying he was ever to set. He would not have felt the need to try the older man's patience. An anecdote concerning the contract between Rameau and Pellegrin would soon circulate. Pellegrin, it was said, was so unsure of the novice opera composer that he demanded a fee of five hundred *livres* for writing the libretto; but when he attended a rehearsal he was so delighted by the music that he tore up the contract.³¹

Following a prologue set in the forest domain of Diana, in which the goddess attempts to defend her subjects from the predatory intrusion of Cupid (chastity versus desire), a conflict which ends with Jupiter allowing love to reign for one day a year as long as marriage is the outcome, the opera tells the story of Thésée, his wife Phèdre, his son (from a previous marriage) Hippolyte, and Aricie, the young daughter of Thésée's defeated enemy Pallas, held captive. Thésée has gone down into the underworld to try and rescue a friend only to be trapped there too. At home, Phèdre is tortured by a secret passion for her stepson and enraged when she learns that Hippolyte and Aricie are in love. This union is impossible because Aricie has been ordered to live a chaste life. Believing that Thésée won't return, Phèdre finally declares her love to Hippolyte. He rejects her. She takes his sword and tries to kill herself. As they struggle Thésée, who has been released from the underworld, enters the scene and mistakenly believes that Hippolyte is attempting to rape Phèdre. Hippolyte goes into exile and is seemingly killed by a sea monster summoned by Neptune, at Thésée's request. Phèdre takes poison but confesses to Thésée before dying.

Whereas Racine's play closes with the deaths of Hippolyte and Phèdre and Thésée's act of atonement (he pardons Aricie and adopts her as his daughter), Pellegrin substituted his own ending. Hippolyte is saved by Destiny, and taken to an idyllic place in Diana's forest where he is reunited with Aricie. Racine's ending was too austere for the contemporary operatic stage, which expected the innocent to triumph.

Despite the compromise of Pellegrin's ending, Rameau's approach was essentially tragic, giving depth to the emotional dilemmas faced by the four main characters in music that is dark-hued and melancholy. Even the celebratory music of the final scene is weighed down by a gravity of expression. The work is full of ideas. I suspect that some of the music had been created during the previous years, to be released all at once in an outpouring of creativity. Rameau had waited so long; it was as if he feared this would be his only opportunity. For Rameau's contemporaries, *Hippolyte et Aricie* was shockingly new. Maret, writing in the 1760s, left an illuminating summation of this aspect of the work:

One heard, for the first time, airs in which the accompaniment augmented the expression, unexpected chords, intonations previously thought to be unworkable, choruses, and symphonies with numerous parts that nevertheless merged to form a cohesive whole. The movements were combined with a previously unknown artistry; and this artistry, applied to different emotions with precision, produced the most wonderful effects. It was not only to the heart that the music spoke; all the senses were touched and the harmonies lifted the spectators out of themselves, without giving them time to reflect on the nature of the marvels that were being created.[32]

James R. Anthony, writing over two hundred years later, also stressed Rameau's originality. Rameau's revolution was built on his mastery of the style created by Lully and enriched by Campra, Charpentier, Destouches and others:

[Rameau] parallels Bach in that he culminates a style, in his case, that of the *grand siècle*; but more than Bach, he portends and in places even creates the sound of the future. [...] New to French music were his use of independent second violin and viola parts and his use of sustained winds in pairs to support the strings. In accompanied recitatives such as Phèdre's 'Quelle plainte en ces lieux m'appelle' that closes act four, we may observe Rameau's progressive features to best advantage. In this scene, we are on the threshold of high classical opera. Rameau's Phèdre and Gluck's Iphigénie and Clytemnestra speak the same language, and it is no longer the language of Lully's Armide.[33]

In composing the overture of *Hippolyte et Aricie* Rameau followed the Lullian model of a slow introduction giving way to a fast *fugato*, but his scoring and harmonic language opened up a previously undiscovered world. The bleak opening motif in D minor, played by the strings, gives a forewarning of the tragic drama that will begin once the prologue has ended.

In scoring the long prologue Rameau was clearly on Cupid's side. Even before Apollo decrees in favour of love, Diana's music, ironically sensuous, is at odds with the severity of her rule. Cupid easily seduces Diana's subjects. As they dance, though, and a Follower of Cupid sings the air 'Plaisirs, doux vainqueurs', accompanied only by the continuo, the spare beauty of the melody has a quality that conveys yearning rather than fulfilment: it defies expectations. The tone of the prologue is in keeping with the tragedy that follows, and the figure of Diana will reappear as a character in the main action.

The opera proper begins with Aricie (soprano) alone in the temple of Diana. The contrast with the teeming stage of the prologue could not be starker. Aricie, obeying the order of Thésée, has come to the temple to take her vows of chastity; but she is in love with Hippolyte and sings of her agitated heart. In the scene that follows, Hippolyte (*haute-contre*) pleads with Aricie not to ruin her life. This tentative love scene, relatively short, and scored only for strings and flutes, is a fine example of the economy of expression in Rameau's music. With the entry of Phèdre (mezzo-soprano) the music switches dramatically from G to D minor, the key of the overture. In love with Hippolyte, and suspecting his passion for Aricie, Phèdre treats the girl with disdain. Aricie refuses to go ahead with the ceremony, emphatically in Rameau's scoring; she tells Phèdre that in her heart she is unworthy to enter this sacred place, and the priestesses agree that the gods will not accept vows that are given unwillingly. Outraged, Phèdre turns to Hippolyte; but Hippolyte refuses to coerce Aricie. Phèdre tells him, 'La vertu quelquefois sert de prétexte au crime'. She calls on the gods to punish Aricie, an invocation that unleashes a tempest. Phèdre is the target of the gods' anger, for Diana values Aricie's chastity, and is just as content to be served outside the temple as within it.

Once Phèdre is left alone with her confidante Oenone (mezzo-soprano) she admits to a venomous jealousy. The news reaches them that Thésée has gone down into the underworld. Oenone, a malign influence, tells Phèdre that she can now marry Hippolyte. Phèdre already senses her fate, disclosing that if Hippolyte rejects her she will kill herself – 'La mort est mon dernier recours'. This single phrase, the last of the act, reveals Rameau's sensitivity to text, for the nakedness of the music, just harpsichord and cello, and the way Rameau sets the words 'La mort' as a descending phrase, aware of the double association ('La mort' sounding the same as 'L'amour'), are powerful responses to the dramatic moment and the character's predicament.

Following a stormy orchestral prologue in B flat, a key frequently used by Rameau and other composers of the French Baroque to denote fury and disquiet, the second act begins at the gates of Hell, where Thésée (bass) is confronted by a Fury, Tisiphone (tenor). Thésée wants to take his friend Peirithous's place, but Tisiphone tells him that the underworld will keep them both. They sing their contrasting lines simultaneously, in a duo that establishes Thésée as a figure of courage and dignity. The setting changes to reveal Pluto (bass), king of the underworld, surrounded by his court. At the beginning of scene three, Pluto sings a demonic air, and the chorus responds in a sudden and magnificent unleashing of all of the resources at Rameau's disposal, momentarily breaking the austerity that characterises the work as a whole, the orchestra producing waves of sound upon which the vocal line balances precariously – the effect was too startling to be appreciated by many of the opera's first listeners. The dance music that follows has the infectious physicality so characteristic of Rameau, and the overall grandeur of expression is completed by Thésée, who having failed in his mission, appeals to his father, Neptune, in an air – 'Grand dieu, daigne me render au jour' – that might be considered Lullian if it wasn't for the striking oscillating *arpeggiando* figure in the strings, Rameau using the orchestra as an equal partner. On the subject of Rameau's innovative use of the orchestra in *Hippolyte et Aricie*, the work's most important modern interpreter, William Christie, has written of how 'Rameau the theorist applies his ideas to the expressive force of melodic intervals and harmonic progressions in order to give his orchestra a new harmonic language, more dissonant, richer and more powerful than that of his contemporaries':

> By means of orchestration, harmony and rhythm, Rameau drew his new orchestra together into one new 'lyric partner' to the vocal line in a manner that was unusually active for the time. As was to be the case later for Berlioz and Wagner, the 'lyric' function of the orchestra is here as important as the voice itself. The orchestra initiates or anticipates vocal melody and dialogue, interpolating phrases rather than constantly supporting the voice.[34]

In scene five, Neptune sends Mercury to appeal for mercy; Pluto agrees but takes pleasure in ordering the three Fates to reveal to Thésée his tragic destiny: 'You are leaving Hell only to find another hell at home.' This is the trio that had to be cut because the singers and musicians could not master the enharmonic passage at its heart. Enharmonics – a downward modulation of semitones from G minor to D minor in this instance – are employed by Rameau to achieve a sense of fear and foreboding.

Following the trio of Fates, act three sees a return to the opera's default mode of classicism. The act opens with Phèdre alone in Thésée's palace beside the sea, praying to the goddess of love. She sings one of Rameau's finest airs, 'Cruelle mère des amours'. Pellegrin's words are dull; it is left to Rameau to create the forlorn Phèdre of Racine's play. The melody is grave and beautiful, but Rameau is not content with this alone. The vocal line progresses in a mostly downward flow, in concert with the flutes; the intervals are in places unexpected and the orchestra provides a harmonic underpinning that must have sounded strange and decadent in 1733 (indeed, the air was quickly replaced by a more conventional offering). It is through the intervals and the harmonic language that Rameau conveys the character's emotional state.

Hippolyte has no idea that Phèdre is in love with him. As naive as he is good, he hopes that she will release Aricie from Thésée's decree so that he can marry her. Phèdre, misunderstanding, offers him her throne. He says that he only wants Aricie. In her despair, Phèdre finally reveals the truth. Rameau's mastery of dramatic recitative keeps the tension high throughout these tense exchanges. Phèdre asks Hippolyte to kill her, and when he refuses she takes up his sword to do the deed herself. The Fates' prophesy is fulfilled, for it is at this moment that Thésée returns. Hippolyte cannot bear to tell his father the truth about Phèdre, and departs, while Phèdre, ashamed, remains silent. Thésée turns to Oenone, who implies that Hippolyte was about to rape Phèdre. Thésée's subjects arrive to celebrate his return from the underworld, and the king is obliged to suffer in silence through the divertissement that follows. By placing the divertissement here, interrupting the unfolding domestic drama, Rameau seems to be making a political point about kingship and public duty. The divertissement contains the most joyous music of the opera and is therefore an exercise in dramatic irony. Once the revellers have departed, Thésée steps forward, torn between his love for his son and the obligation to punish his supposed crime. Sombre music in the strings is quickly snuffed out but returns as Thésée addresses Neptune ('Puissant maître des flots') in the same key, B minor, as Phèdre's lament at the beginning of the act. After the bright orchestral colours of the divertissement, the music is denied rhetorical flourishes. Thésée's sombre voice is enveloped in the silky embrace of the strings alone. Rameau refuses, though, to let sentimentality weaken his portrait of a king whose judgement has been flawed throughout, from his cruel treatment of the innocent Aricie to his willingness to sacrifice everything for his male friend. The final section of his invocation ('Mais, de courroux l'onde s'agite'), closing the act, is a clarion call to Neptune to drown Hippolyte without delay, the strings playing rapid arpeggios in 6/8.

Act four is set in a grove sacred to Diana beside the sea. Hippolyte, facing exile, is given tender music, notably different from the anguished airs sung by Phèdre and Thésée in the previous act. The innocent Hippolyte has the greater cause for anger and bitterness, but can only manage sorrow and regret – 'Ah! Faut-il, en un jour, perdre tout ce que j'aime'. The music, in A minor, reflects his stoicism. Respect for his father prevents Hippolyte from telling Aricie the truth about Phèdre. Aricie accuses Hippolyte of abandoning her. He asks her to go with him as his wife, but Aricie knows that this is impossible without Diana's blessing. They address Diana, and the goddess sends her followers – hunters and huntresses – to witness their vows of fidelity. A fanfare in D, played by the horns, announces the divertissement. In the second *air en rondeau*, a stately but infectious six-note phrase underpins repeated staccato notes played by the horns and woodwinds. It begins as a dance before being taken up by a huntress singing 'À la chasse, à la chasse; armez-vous'. Suddenly the sea rises and a monster drags Hippolyte beneath the waves. Aricie, desolate, faints. In the space of only a few minutes Rameau's music has taken us from joy to terror and finally to desolation, and yet these changes of mood, powerfully juxtaposed, seem neither artificial nor cursory. Rameau's ability to express a profound emotion in just a few bars of music is at its most striking in the swooning Aricie's 'Tout se dissipe… Hélas! Hippolyte ne paroît pas… Je meurs', her voice emerging from the terror of the storm, the storm music ending, so that she sings alone, answered by descending notes in the orchestra. This sudden stripping away of the full forces to leave Aricie alone and vulnerable is a great dramatic moment, capped almost immediately by the chorus's devastating response – 'Ô disgrâce cruelle! Hippolyte n'est plus'. Phèdre, arriving at this moment, demands to be told the cause of such grief. The chorus repeats 'Hippolyte is no more'. Wracked by remorse, Phèdre blames herself. At the end of her monologue, a sustained note, as portentous as an organ chord, announces the air 'Dieux cruels, venguers implacables'. Long drawn-out chords, building tension, continue to underscore Phèdre's poignant confession. After she sings 'Laissez-moi révéler á l'auteur de ses jours, et son innocence et mon crime' the chorus repeats its lamentation for a third and final time. In this remarkable passage Rameau's Phèdre has the depth and intensity of Racine's. William Christie's love of Rameau's music was initiated when, as a student at Harvard, he heard a recording of Janet Baker in the role and was astounded by the act four monologue: 'Nothing that I had heard previously of French music had seemed so intense to me.'[35]

Act five continues the action at the same place. Thésée has just seen Phèdre die. Before committing suicide she told him the truth about Hippolyte. He sings of his grief and his guilt, and asks Neptune to take him too. But as Thésée is about to commit suicide by jumping into the sea Neptune intervenes, telling him that Destiny decreed that Hippolyte should live. For a moment Thésée is overjoyed at the thought of seeing Hippolyte again, but Neptune tells him that he will never see his son again. As Thésée accepts this 'just punishment' a flute enters the scoring, linking Thésée's resigned grief to that expressed by Hippolyte at the beginning of act four. Given the difficult nature of Rameau's relationship with his father, and the way they parted on bad terms, it is legitimate to believe that Rameau poured his private feelings into the opera, his perception of the regret his father must have felt along with his own.

At the beginning of scene three the setting changes to the woods where Aricie, rescued by Diana, is living. (This breaking of the rule of unity of place within an act would be heavily criticised after the premiere, leading Rameau to make significant changes when the work was next revived.) A sweet melancholy lingers from the previous scene. Aricie mourns the loss of Hippolyte. Shepherds and shepherdesses sing a chorus to Diana. The goddess tells Aricie not to mourn and brings Hippolyte before her. The lovers sing of their joy, but Rameau resists gaiety, preferring to give expression to their longing in dances dominated by subtle scoring for a musette. As the girls dance, a shepherdess sings of 'amorous nightingales', and the flutes, so closely aligned to Aricie at key points of the work, are given a predictably prominent role. In his 2012 Glyndebourne production Jonathan Kent set the scene in a morgue, and the dancing shepherdesses wore veils and black dresses. The staging reflected the character of the music and the drama, from the disorientation that Aricie must feel on waking in a strange place to the enigmatic sadness of the wedding music.

iii The Premiere

Hippolyte et Aricie opened the Opéra's winter season. The glitterati came out in force to watch Claude Chassé,[36] Marie Antier, Denis-François Tribou and Marie Pélissier[37] sing the leading roles of Thésée, Phèdre, Hippolyte and Aricie. Carriages clogged the rue Saint-Honoré and the narrow streets to either side in the rapidly fading light (performances started at five in the evening).

The Opéra's auditorium was class-conscious, reflecting the social hierarchy of the age. Where an individual was meant to sit in the theatre was dictated by his or her social status, although practical factors, such as availability of seats and personal preference, could lead to a small dilution of the social order. For instance, people of rank sometimes chose to watch from the *parterre*, partly to enjoy the thrill of interacting (usually critically) with the performers, and partly because from the ground it was possible to go in and out of the auditorium without disturbing other people. In general, audiences at the Opéra were more exclusive than those at the Comédie-Française, where the price of entry was cheaper, but the range of people was nevertheless impressive, with the *parterre* largely the domain of the middle classes and the *paradis* (top level) of 'all sorts of riffraff'. The phrase was used by Nemeitz to convey the social character of the amphitheatre of the Comédie, but he could have been writing about the top level of the Opéra. Nemeitz's descriptions of the Comédie-Française, the Comédie-Italienne and the Opéra formed part of his account of the Parisian scene of the 1720s:

> At the Comédies a man of quality takes his place on the Stage and in one of the first Loges or in the Parterre, if there are not too many people. But rarely in the second Loge which is for the bourgeois, and never in the Amphitheatre where all sorts of riff-raff are assembled. But the Amphitheatre of the Opéra is honourable and has the rank of the first Loge. The second Loge is still passable. But no one would willingly seat himself in the alleged *Paradis*, excepting the Balcony which is on the side. The Balcony, below, to the side of the stage, is for gentlemen of distinction and costs ten livres per person. But the Parterre is sometimes visited by people even of the first quality [...]. When one is in the Parterre of the Comédie or the Opéra, one takes care to whistle at some Actor or to clap [...] hands in order to mock him.[38]

The grandeur of a performance at the Opéra as a society occasion, the prelude to a *fête* in the gardens of the Palais-Royal or the Tuileries, was conveyed by the English visitor Charles Burney: 'One of the finest sights at Paris used to be the Tuileries in summer, after the opera; which being over between seven and eight in the evening, all the company, in full dress, consisting of the flower of this capital, poured into the grand avenue and formed an assembly not to be met with in any other part of the world.'[39]

Curiosity surrounded Rameau, still best known as the author of the ten years old *Traité de l'harmonie reduite à ses principes naturels*. Would this middle-aged scientist of music and occasional composer of harpsichord pieces be able to validate his theory by creating an opera of merit? The performance went well despite the demands made on the players. The *Mercure de France* commented: 'The music of this opera was a little difficult to execute, but by the skill of the symphonists and other musicians the difficulty was overcome.'[40]

Voltaire attended the premiere and the day after wrote in a letter:

> I witnessed yesterday the premiere of the opera *Aricie et Hippol-*

yte. The words are by the abbé Pellegrin and worthy of the abbé Pellegrin. The music is by a certain Rameau, a man who has the misfortune of knowing more about music than Lully. He is a pedant in music. He is exact, and tedious.[41]

The inclusion of a cleverly phrased put-down or backhanded compliment was a feature of letter writing in 18th century France, and Voltaire was a very subtle exponent of the art. In declaring that 'Rameau has the misfortune of knowing more about music than Lully' Voltaire was converting the consensus view of the first night crowd into a perceptive witticism. People were struck by the abundance and richness of musical invention and the originality of the harmonic language, and by how the score dominated Pellegrin's libretto. For supporters of the work, this was a great moment of change in French music. André Campra, when asked his view of *Hippolyte et Aricie* by the prince de Conti, said 'There is enough music in this opera to make ten, this man will eclipse us all',[42] and the anonymous reviewer in the *Mercure de France* wrote '[Rameau] has forced the harshest critics to agree that, in his first operatic work, he has created virile and harmonious music, of a new character'.[43] But for others the work's very complexity and 'virile' character were problematic: it lacked, they thought, the elegant proportions, the balance between words and music, of the Lullian heritage. It was, they complained, too fussy, too Italianate. Rameau, who in some respects was a follower of Lully, found himself being portrayed as the anti-Lully.

Strong opinions on either side ensured that the opera was a *cause célèbre*. Parisian society enjoyed nothing better than a public quarrel, and the success of *Hippolyte et Aricie* was intensified by the controversy it provoked. It was a quarrel between tradition and innovation, paternalism and rebellion; between the comforting certainties of the age of Louis XIV and the exciting uncertainties of the modern age. Years later, looking back at the impact of Rameau's breakthrough, d'Alembert would write:

> Finally in 1733 Rameau arrives with his opera *Hippolyte et Aricie*. This is when the clamour redoubled; the abusive and mocking pamphlets, the dark secrets, all the little devices that the ignorant and envious have at their disposal, were directed

against this dangerous innovator; the public was influenced at first, but in the end came to appreciate the genius of this persecuted talent.[44]

iv Rameau and Voltaire: Samson

Voltaire quickly changed his opinion of Rameau's music. He realised that the composer was an innovator walking alone ahead of the crowd and that the crowd would need time to catch up.

Voltaire was thirty-nine, eleven years younger than Rameau. He had only recently returned to France after his years of exile in England and was working prolifically. After the success of his verse play *Zaïre* at the Comédie-Française in 1732 he worked to complete the *Lettres philosophiques*. He had yet to publish a libretto: if this form of theatre didn't especially attract him, the idea of creating a great opera with Rameau certainly did.

Within a couple of months of the premiere of *Hippolyte et Aricie* Rameau and Voltaire started a collaboration that would drag on for years without reaching fruition and which would leave Voltaire contemptuous of a man who was as uncompromising in his relationships with people as he was in his relationship with his own art. Voltaire had been a student at the collège de Louis-le-Grand during Rameau's tenure as organist, and it is fascinating to wonder whether they made the connection. Physically the two men were remarkably similar, a coincidence that would link them in the public imagination for the rest of their lives, but temperamentally they proved to be incompatible

The chosen subject of the opera was the biblical story of Samson and Delilah. This was provocative because the enactment of an episode from the Bible on the stage was considered inappropriate and even blasphemous. The most recent tragédie lyrique on a religious theme, Montéclair's *Jephté*, presented at the Opéra the previous year, had been banned after a few performances. It is perhaps too easy to assume that the story of Samson was Voltaire's idea. Maret records that Rameau was inspired to write his first opera by *Jephté*,[45] a claim backed up by the fact that he sought out the work's librettist, Pellegrin. Rameau must have known that the choice of subject matter was likely to provoke the church and worry the censor, but he began work. The project's artistic strengths would have, I suspect, pushed any concerns over the reaction of the authorities from his mind.

Portrait de Voltaire by Maurice Quentin de La Tour (1735). Musée Antoine-Lécuyer, Saint-Quentin.

We know Voltaire's flow of thought during this process because his letters have survived. We don't know Rameau's. It would seem that Rameau, flushed with the success of *Hippolyte et Aricie* and eager to begin work on a follow-up, initiated the collaboration. In a letter to Rameau, dated December 1733, Voltaire writes '…your repeated letters press me so forcefully, and you're so convinced that it is in your best interest to give your opera this winter, it is necessary that I overcome my reticence'. Voltaire flatters the composer and condemns his enemies: 'Your music is magnificent, but even that makes you enemies and cruel enemies. I'd have less than you if we were to compare our talents.'⁴⁶ Of greater meaning, Voltaire takes pains to explain that he doubts his aptitude to write the libretto of a conventional tragédie lyrique:

> I will have to work hard to change the prejudices of the public. They will not accept willingly an opera heroine who is not in love, and while my detractors will say that my work is impious, the *parterre* will find, perhaps, that it is too virtuous and too austere. They will be repelled by seeing love treated only as seduction on a stage where it has always been consecrated as a virtue. My poem for *Samson* is more a feeble sketch of a tragedy in the manner of the ancients with choruses than an opera with divertissements. I don't believe I have the talent to write lyrics, and fear I will never master this particular harmony. Above all, I'm incapable of writing an acceptable prologue; I would sooner fashion lyrics from an epic poem. These, Monsieur, are the reasons why I hesitate.⁴⁷

In the first months of their collaboration Voltaire worked slowly and was chased by Rameau. Rameau needed to receive the finished libretto in time to allow the work to be staged during the 1734/35 winter season. Writing to Rameau in April 1734, Voltaire blamed the marriage of his friend the duc de Richelieu⁴⁸ for his tardiness (during the next decade Richelieu would become one of the most powerful figures in France, and we will meet him at some significant moments in Rameau's story). In a style that combined flattery, familiarity and elaborate wit, Voltaire promised to 'marry' Rameau and to 'bear his children'.⁴⁹ He soon discovered that this kind of language didn't work with Rameau. Rameau's harrying was effective, though, for by June 1734 Voltaire had completed most of the libretto.

Rameau kept his hand in by writing instrumental music (sadly mostly lost) for Alexis Piron's one-act play *Les Courses de Tempé*, a *pastorale* staged at the Comédie-Française that August. It seems that their fragile friendship was still intact and that Rameau's contribution was significant. In the preface to the published text, Piron wrote: 'I like to think that I enjoyed some success because of the illustrious Rameau, my dear compatriot, who agreed to embellish the divertissement with the sparkling sounds of his music.'[50]

In May 1734 Voltaire's life was turned upside down by the publication of the *Lettres philosophiques*. He had arranged clandestine editions with two booksellers but hadn't actually authorised publication at the time the book appeared. He wrote a letter to Fleury in which he denied all responsibility and blamed the booksellers. It did no good. Voltaire, tipped off by his close friend the comte d'Argental[51] that an arrest warrant had been issued, left Paris just in time, fleeing in secret to a remote estate in Champagne owned by the husband of his friend Mme du Châtelet. Here, at Cirey-sur-Blaise, he evaded the authorities and waited to be forgiven. It wasn't until the late summer that he re-engaged with *Samson*, provoked into action by Rameau's indignant and bitter recriminations. Voltaire wrote to d'Argental that 'I had completely abandoned [*Samson*], but Rameau rants, Rameau says that I've cut his throat, that I treat him like a Philistine'.[52] It seems that Rameau, ignoring Voltaire's comments about his deficiencies as a librettist, was demanding additional material, including a prologue. Voltaire returned to work, and at speed. Voltaire's letters to his friend and business agent, Nicolas-Claude Thieriot, who acted as his intermediary in Paris, show that he had strong ideas about structure and style, advocating fewer uniform recitatives and more airs in the Italian style.[53] Voltaire was at least partly motivated by a personal desire to modernise the tragédie lyrique genre: in November 1733, his friend Formont wrote to Cideville that '[Voltaire] will include in his libretto very little recitative and will try to give the musician the best opportunity to exercise his talent'.[54] However, Rameau, at this delicate point in his career, was not ready to take risks with the form and wanted his librettist to stick to his brief; it seems that he dismissed Voltaire's ideas as interference. Their differences didn't prevent the work from reaching enough of a finished form to be submitted to the censor and to be previewed before a private audience at the home of Louis Fagon, Intendant des Finances, in the rue Neuve-des-Petits-Champs, that October.

The opera's prospects were uncertain. According to Mme de Châtelet, the theologians of the Sorbonne would not accept even the slightest contradiction of scripture: if the libretto stated that one column of the temple fell rather than two it would be a great heresy.[55]

Aware of the tension that existed between Rameau and Voltaire, Mme de Châtelet was delighted when the composer invited her to attend the private performance (Voltaire couldn't risk returning to Paris). 'Rameau had the gallantry to invite me to the rehearsal at M. Fallon's,' she wrote in a letter. 'The music includes an overture, a chaconne, some airs for violin and a third and fifth act that are admirable.'[56] It was all in vain, for the official tasked with examining the text, the abbé Hardion,[57] refused to authorise for performance an opera that took liberties with the Bible co-written by a fugitive from justice.

The deadline for the winter season passed and early in 1735 Rameau put *Samson* to one side and never really returned to it. By the spring he had a new piece, the opéra-ballet *Les Indes galantes*, ready for production. Voltaire was not disheartened. He believed that *Les Indes galantes* confirmed Rameau's genius. He wanted to align himself to Rameau's new music despite his scepticism as to whether the public would ever understand it. From now on it was Voltaire who did the chasing. Rameau ignored him. He was by now a member of La Pouplinière's circle. Thieriot, who knew La Pouplinière well, represented Voltaire somewhat imperfectly. Voltaire would come to believe that La Pouplinière had turned Rameau against him, but his letters to Thieriot reveal that he endeavoured to keep La Pouplinière, and Thérèse, whom he called 'Polimnie', on side. Voltaire flattered them in his letters to Thieriot, in the expectation that Thieriot would let them know. In one letter he asked after La Pouplinière's health, continuing: 'I would commit a massacre of fools to save a kind man from rheumatism.' In another he wrote of Thérèse discussing philosophy while playing a sonata. Initially, Voltaire was happy for La Pouplinière and Thérèse to know confidences, such as the secret that he was the author of the play *L'Enfant prodigue*, staged at the Comédie-Française in October 1736.

Rameau was well able to make up his own mind about Voltaire. Whatever his views on Voltaire's personality, there can be little doubt that he had come to dislike him as a collaborator. If Rameau had entered into a partnership with Voltaire on *Samson* because he wanted to work with a great writer, by the end of the process he was wishing for a pliable and reliable professional librettist. Voltaire was surprisingly slow to realise this. He had, after all, in his letter of December 1733, generously volunteered to waive his part of any royalties achieved by the work in favour of Rameau, who he knew to be hard up,[58] and therefore would have been justified in expecting a modicum of courtesy in return. It wasn't until Rameau began work on a new tragédie lyrique, *Castor et Pollux*, in March 1736 that Voltaire accepted the inevitable. Around this time the censor decreed against *Samson* for the second time.

v Les Indes galantes

Whereas Voltaire always regretted the stillbirth of *Samson*, referring to the subject in a letter of thirty years later as 'ce paillard de Samson, et à cette putain de Dalila' (a startlingly unusual use of language in this context), before going on to tell the recipient, Chabanon, that 'Rameau created delightful music for *Samson*',[59] Rameau ruthlessly erased it by diverting the music into other works, notably *Les Indes galantes* and *Castor et Pollux*.

Rameau first met the writer Louis Fuzelier (1672-1752) at the Saint-Germain fair during the 1720s. They were fellow members of the Caveau. A prolific author of plays, parodies and comic operas, mostly for the fair theatres, Fuzelier had produced, alone or in collaboration, more than two hundred pieces by the time of his death. It is tempting, but wrong, to think of him as simply a jobbing writer. He presented work at the Comédie-Française and the Opéra and he was a co-editor of the *Mercure de France*.

Fuzelier was a veteran of the opéra-ballet genre, the author of libretti for Bourgeois (*Les Amours déguisés*, 1713), Campra (*Les Ages*, 1718), Colin de Blamont (*Les Fêtes grecques et romaines*, 1723), and Mouret (*Les Amours des Dieux*, 1727). Having wasted many months on *Samson* and needing to offer the public a new work without further delay, Rameau turned to this highly popular form of opera, lighter and less portentous than tragédie lyrique, and to one of its most experienced librettists. Fuzelier, unlike Voltaire, was used to writing to order and he delivered work at speed.

The genre of opéra-ballet was created at the end of the previous century at a time when, following the death of Lully and the withdrawal of Louis XIV to Versailles, the knot of official control had loosened a little and people were seeking an escapist theatre that reflected contemporary life. Campra and Houdar de la Motte's *L'Europe galante* of 1697 was the defining work. This pursuit of pleasure based on style intensified during the Regency of Philippe d'Orléans. There were two main elements that defined the genre in contrast to Lully's tragédie lyrique. First, although there was often a unifying theme, each act (*entrée*) was written to stand alone, thereby allowing frequent revivals of a work either in part or whole. This made compelling commercial sense. It satisfied the desires of those operagoers, the majority, who quickly became bored during the long single narrative of a tragédie lyrique and allowed every last drop of revenue to be squeezed from the most successful entrées. Second, each entrée was dominated by the songs and particularly the dances of its divertissement.

A third important factor distinguished opéra-ballet in the period up until the end of the Regency: its characters were drawn from the contemporary world, and its stories were comedic rather than tragic. A typical opéra-ballet of this period consisted of a number of separate human comedies about the game of love that were designed to do little more than charm and divert. People saw very clearly the thread that linked opéra-ballet to the plays of Marivaux at the Théâtre Italien to the paintings of Watteau to the real interactions of men and women in the gardens of the Palais-Royal or the Tuileries at dusk in summer. It was a movement that saw high society and the arts circumvent the strictures of the court and the church as Parisian townhouses and salons became more fashionable than Versailles and as the depiction of personal pursuits in paintings and plays challenged the authority of the academies.

After Louis XV reached maturity, in 1723, the genre of opéra-ballet changed. Works derived from history or mythology had never lost their greater status. *L'Europe galante*, an opera that took and gave pleasure in contrasting national styles of courtship, was much loved, as was Campra and Danchet's *Les Fêtes vénitiennes* (1710), but even admirers of these works believed that their lack of grandeur limited their artistic worth. La Motte appeared to agree, for he didn't attempt to repeat the success of *L'Europe galante*. Louis de Cahusac regretted La Motte's abandonment of the genre he had created: 'The spectacle created by La Motte is composed of several acts, each representing a single action. These are pretty Watteaus, piquant miniatures that demand precision of design, grace of brushstroke, and brilliance of colour.'[60] Cahusac, though, wanted opéra-ballet to embrace the *merveilleux* and to address deeper themes. By the time Rameau came to write *Les Indes galantes* elements from tragédie lyrique had seeped into opéra-ballet to the extent that the latter genre had become known as *ballet héroïque*.[61]

One of the fascinating things about Rameau's first opéra-ballet, though, is that it belongs to the first phase of the genre, to the opera of real people created by La Motte and Campra, and not to the second. This makes it unique, for all of Rameau's subsequent opéra-ballets belong firmly in the world of myth and fantasy of the genre's second phase. In creating *Les Indes galantes*, Rameau was in a sense looking back to look forward: it was as if he wanted to revive the inclusive, non-monarchical opéra-ballet of his youth. Professionally, it made sense for Rameau to temporarily abandon the prestige of tragedy for the lighter pleasures of Campra's opéra-ballet. It was a way of showing that he was a composer of range and versatility. Not that he compromised in the music.

The first version of the opera, premiered on 23 August 1735, consisted of a prologue and three entrées, *Le Turc généreux*, *Les Incas du Pérou* and *Les Fleurs*. *Les Fleurs* was quickly revised. Then, in March 1736, Fuzelier and Rameau added a fourth entrée, *Les Sauvages*. By inventing stories set in the Orient and the Americas, Fuzelier was responding to the public's fascination for these remote and seemingly exotic worlds. The stories set in the Americas are concerned with the conquest by Europeans of ancient civilisations, and, in the case of *Les Sauvages*, with the concept of the 'noble savage', but Fuzelier does not labour the point. It would appear, though, that the simple message of the libretto – true love is both universal and triumphant – was informed by serious ideas on aesthetics. In the foreword to the published libretto, Fuzelier concluded that 'judicious taste must be the product of an enlightened century, a century witnessing the progress of [artistic] talent, driven by sure principles, acquiring understanding without forsaking grace'.[62]

The overture's stately opening theme and quick *fugato* don't surprise, but the conception is grander than anything attempted by Lully. The prologue, in the gardens of Hébé's palace, sets up the rest of the work. Hébé (soprano) calls upon the youth of four nations, France, Italy, Spain and Poland, to celebrate love. Rameau composes a languid theme, dressed in melancholy, to accompany their entrance, but Hébé's air 'Amants sûrs de plaire', with its repeated trills and lilting melody, lifts the spirits, and musettes and piccolos establish a mood of pastoral calm. Drums announce the intrusion of Bellone (baritone), the goddess of war. Bellone exhorts the people to take up arms, and the people are enticed by this promise of glory. Hébé appeals to Cupid to save the day. Cupid (soprano) descends with his retinue, all armed with firebrands. Cupid commands his followers to scatter to every corner of the earth to replace the hearts lost to Bellone.

The story of *Le Turc généreux* follows a favourite scenario of contemporary erotic literature. In his gardens by the sea, the Turk Osman Pasha (bass) is pursuing a French girl he holds captive, Émilie (soprano). In a compelling monologue, 'Dans le séjour témoin de ma naissance', she tells the woeful story of how on her wedding day in her homeland she was abducted by a gang of pirates. Their ship went down off the coast of Turkey. Osman tells Émilie to forget the past, for the only law that matters is the law of pleasure. Finding herself alone (scene three) Émilie calls Osman a barbarian. Although she believes that her husband is dead, she will not forsake him. Out to sea the waves rise ominously and a ship founders. The storm music is impressive but the techniques involved were not new: wind machine, whistling flutes and the key of B flat. The sailors survive the storm only to be enslaved by Osman. In scene three, Émilie greets one of the sailors and discovers that he is Valère (*haute-contre*), her husband. In scene five, Osman defies expectations by handing Émilie to Valère and granting the pair their freedom. He knew Valère in a former life. As Valère and Émilie prepare to embark on ships that Osman has stocked with precious goods they sing a lovely duo, 'Volez, Zéphyrs'. The refrain is passed to the chorus and then returned. Rameau's choral writing here is close to Bach's, in form as well as in spirit. The chorus is followed by a lyrical air for Émilie, 'Fuyer, vents orageux', in which the voice combines deliciously with the woodwind. Provençal youths and maidens lead the short ballet. The dances – two rigaudons followed by two tambourins – are measured and elegant: Rameau composed more rhythmically striking equivalents elsewhere.

Les Incas du Pérou begins with a five-part fugue that develops from a four-note phrase that is similar to the subject of the first fugue in the finale of Beethoven's Piano Sonata Opus 110. The setting of an arid landscape beneath a volcano promises a concluding *coup de théâtre*, and Fuzelier and Rameau don't disappoint. They also create a compelling character, the High Priest Huascar. The Inca princess Phani (soprano) is in love with one of her people's conquerors, a Spanish nobleman called Don Carlos (*haute-contre*). Phani defies Huascar (bass), who, in love with the princess himself, plans to use the festival of the sun to entrap her. The sombre A minor 'prelude for the adoration of the sun' has masterly polyphonic writing for the strings; it initiates the long continuous sequence of the sun festival and the eruption of the volcano, a *tour de force* of musical organisation, in which Huascar leads the chorus and the dances never seem episodic. Huascar tells Phani that the eruption is a sign that the gods are angry, and that they will only be appeased if she returns his love. Carlos arrives in time to expose Huascar's treachery. The priest is responsible for the natural disorder. The volcano erupts again and Huascar is buried beneath burning rocks.

The third entrée, *Les Fleurs*, is the weakest dramatically. The action takes place in Persia, in the gardens of the palace of Ali, on the day of the festival of flowers. In this pantomime of the fair, the Persian prince Tacmas (*haute-contre*) disguises himself as a merchant-woman of the seraglio so that he can gain access to one of Ali's slaves, Zaïre (soprano). He reveals his plan to Ali (baritone), who gives him his blessing. Ali is now free to pursue Fatime (soprano), the beautiful girl Tacmas has scorned. Fatime, already in love with Ali, disguises herself as a Polish man to get close to him. Thankfully, the plot is quickly brought to its happy conclusion. The lovers' quartet, 'Tendre amour', is the finest number of the entrée and of the opera as a whole. The four vocal lines entwine sensually above the continuo. The sublime melody, darkened by one harmonic oddity, is reminiscent of Purcell's *An Evening Hymn*, a song underpinned by the ground bass of a chaconne. *An Evening Hymn* was published in *Harmonia Sacra* (1693) so it's possible that Rameau knew of it. The solos and choruses of the festival are charming but unremarkable. The closing dances feature intricate writing for the violins and flutes.

They are good examples of Rameau's melancholy lyricism, if not of his harmonic originality.

The origins of *Les Sauvages* can be traced back to 1725. That autumn, at the Théâtre Italien, Rameau witnessed a performance of tribal dances by two Native Americans from France's Louisiana colony[63] and responded by writing a piece of music. He mentioned the 'Danse des sauvages' in his letter to Houdar de la Motte, citing it as an example of his ability to write descriptive music, and included it in the *Nouvelles suites de pièces de clavecin* (1728). Now Rameau created an operatic act inspired by the exoticism and dignity of those Indian dancers.

The setting is a clearing in a forest, close to where the French and Spanish colonies meet. In this fantasy world, the French and Spanish are living in harmony with each other and with the people they have conquered. A native warrior called Adario (baritone) is in love with the chief's daughter, Zima (soprano), but Zima is also being courted by a roguish Frenchman, Damon (*haute-contre*), who offers pleasure, and a serious Spaniard, Alvar (bass), who offers fidelity. Fuzelier pays homage to *L'Europe galante* by having some fun with national stereotypes – French husbands are fickle; Spanish husbands are tyrannical. Zima rejects the Spaniard for loving too much, and the Frenchman for not loving enough. She chooses honest, tender Adario – in other words, the simple and noble ways of her own people over the cynicism and possessiveness of the Europeans. Damon shrugs his shoulders, but Alvar has to be prevented from drawing his sword. The rest of the entrée is taken up by the 'Ceremony of the Great Pipe of Peace'.

Fuzelier's libretto tells this simple story reasonably well. Rameau, though, finds little inspiration until the final section of the work. From the first note of the 'Danse des sauvages' to the last note of the opera the music beguiles and delights. The theme of the dance is nobler and less rhythmically driven than in its original version for harpsichord, but no less hypnotic or choreographically enticing. With each repeat its appeal deepens. The opera concludes with a glorious chaconne, lasting two hundred bars, which may have been originally intended for *Samson*.[64] The contrasting episodes are seamlessly integrated. Some passages sound uncannily like orchestrated Lennon and McCartney. Rameau combines oboes and bassoons;

beneath, the strings play a slowly descending phrase, perhaps the most magical passage of all.

The leading roles were created by Jélyotte (Valère, Don Carlos and Damon), Chassé (Huascar), Tribou (Tacmas), Dun (Osman and Alvar), Person (Ali), Cuvillier (Adario), Marie Pélissier (Émilie and Zima), Mlle Petitpas (Fatima and Amour), Marie Antier (Phani) and Mlle Eeremans (Zaïre and Hébé). The choreography was by Louis Dupré. It was said that the renowned dancer was so confounded by the demands of the music, particularly the passages that required quick and expressive movements, that Rameau had to guide him.[65] Dupre and Chasse were still performing in *Les Indes galantes* when David Garrick went to the Opéra in the summer of 1751. 'Ye show is great but ye singing execrable,' he wrote in his diary. 'There was spirit of expression in ye music & ye dancing very well. Ye best actor I have seen hitherto is Chassee, ye bass singer. I was disappointed in Dupre.'[66]

Rameau's contribution to the development of dance is a topic that warrants some investigation by scholars. His music certainly provided an impetus for change, and in his later opéra-ballets, created with Louis de Cahusac, he integrated an expressive, narrative-based style of choreography – *ballet figuré* – more successfully than most of his contemporaries. Of his general influence, Jean-Georges Noverre would write in his *Lettres sur la danse* (1760):

> It is through the diverse and harmonious compositions of M. Rameau, through the style and the spiritual conversations that reign in his airs, that dance must make its progress. Dance awoke from the lethargy into which it had been plunged as soon as this creator of a learned but always appealing and always voluptuous music appeared on the scene.[67]

5

An Argument in the Courtyard of the Louvre

and Other Matters Concerning Rameau's Reputation
1736 to 1744

i Lullists versus Ramists

The controversy that surrounded Rameau's work had intensified. One aspect of Rameau's style, greatly admired by his supporters, was the use of short notes, semiquavers, repeated rapidly or cascading to form elaborate scales. For many, this music, agitated and harmonically unpredictable, broke the rules that made them feel comfortable. It sounded to their ears that Rameau was packing more notes into a few bars of music than Lully had needed for a whole page, and this was surely unnecessary and inelegant and nothing more than a means of showing off (Rameau wouldn't be the last great composer to be accused of inserting too many notes). We find this view of Rameau's style expressed in the abbé Desfontaines's journal *Observations sur les écrits modernes*, following the premiere of *Les Indes galantes*: 'The music is endlessly fantastical; nature has no part in it. Nothing is as scabrous or as bumpy. It is a road that jolts one without cease.'[1] Voltaire, stuck in Champagne and unable to attend the premiere, gave the opposite view in a letter to Thieriot: 'I believe that the profusion of semiquavers may shock the *lullistes*, but, in the long term, Rameau's style will become the prevailing style of the nation as people become wiser.'[2]

The *lullistes*, though, would not be persuaded. Alongside the 'profusion of semiquavers' in Rameau's music, the *lullistes* objected to the complex harmonies – '[they] have a geometrical tone that frightens the heart,' wrote Cartaud de La Vilate in 1736[3] – and the ever-present orchestra. Toussaint Rémond de Saint-Mard criticised modern music in his *Réflexions sur l'opéra* (1749), writing how 'fugues, held notes, counterpoints and a prodigious crowd of chords stifled the sung part by an excess of harmony'.[4]

The debate would continue for many years. In 1748, before he had turned against the composer, Diderot eloquently summarised the issues by comparing the contrasting merits of the two masters in his fictional work *Les Bijoux indiscrets*:

> Both of these original creators had their supporters: the ignorant and the old hands were for [Lully], the young and the advanced for [Rameau]; while people of taste, young and old, could see the merits of both. The old [Lully] is simple, natural, plain, too plain sometimes, and this is a fault. The young [Rameau] is singular, brilliant, complex, learned, sometimes too clever; but perhaps this is the fault of his listeners. The former has only one overture, beautiful indeed, but repeated at the start of all of his operas; the latter has as many overtures as operas, and all are masterpieces. Nature has led [Lully] in the ways of melody; study and experience have helped [Rameau] to discover the sources of harmony. Who has ever declaimed and recited as the elder has? Who will give us light airs, voluptuous airs and character symphonies to compare with the younger's? [Lully] is a master of dialogue. Before [Rameau] no one had discerned the delicate nuances that separate the tender from the voluptuous, the voluptuous from the passionate, the passionate from the lascivious.[5]

Diderot was being fair and measured when he wrote that 'the ignorant and the old hands were for Lully, the young and the advanced for Rameau, while people of taste, young and old, could see the merits of both'. People of taste, though, were mostly silent. French society had a need to place great figures in opposition, and to take sides.

Rameau represented modernity, and some of his more vocal followers were not only scornful of his enemies, believing them to be stuck in the past, they also disparaged Lully's music as outdated, predictable and bourgeois (by which they meant popular with non-connoisseurs). Rameau did not endorse these attacks on Lully. In fact, he deliberately made publicly known his admiration for Lully's music in the preface to the printed edition of *Les Indes galantes*. 'In striving to achieve the beauty that reigns in the recitative of the great Lully,' he wrote, 'I imitate him, not as a servile copyist but as [a composer] who takes the beauty of nature as his model.'[6]

The constant criticism and jibes of the *lullistes* took away Rameau's peace of mind. We know that Rameau's rage over slights was barely controllable because of his public argument with the poet Pierre-Charles Roy. In August 1737, a satirical poem on Rameau called *Marsias allegori, ou le nouveau Carizelly* did the rounds.[7] In an age of ridicule an attack of this kind was not unusual; however, when this poem was read aloud in the Café Procope in the rue de l'Ancienne Comédie, the people present were shocked by its tone. The author was too spiteful to be witty. Rameau wasn't named, but, as the author intended, he was immediately identified as the poem's subject. His physical appearance and character were viciously caricatured.

In an introduction to the poem, the author referred to Rameau as 'the new Cariselli'. The story of how Lully sent packing a rival composer named Cariselli, newly arrived at the French court from Italy, by mocking his vocal stammer in a piece of music, was well-known thanks to the popularity of the one-act opera *Cariselli*, a comedy first performed in the compilation *Fragments de M. de Lully*. The poem that followed was more venomous. The author based his verses on the mythological figure of Marsyas, a satyr who dared to believe that his discordant music was superior to the harmonious sounds produced by Apollo. In the ancient story, Marsyas challenges Apollo to a contest of music and, having lost, is flayed alive. In *Marsias allegori*, before his execution the satyr copulates with Envy and sires a 'modern Marsyas'. For Apollo read Lully; for Marsyas's offspring, read Rameau. In describing the modern Marsyas, the poet writes:

> For in addition to his raucous music, he will have a mania for the written word. I hear the cannibal. I see him: ostrich's neck, puckered eyebrows, yellow skin and bristling hair, hollow nose, the very features of a satyr, a mouth for biting but not for

laughter, a pointed head and narrow forehead, legs dried up like Erichthonius.[8]

'A mania for the written word' ('D'écrire il lui prendra la rage'), a reference to Rameau's theoretical writings, was especially good. Roy was quickly identified as the author. A successful librettist[9] and a prominent member of the pro-Lully camp, Roy was one of Rameau's most active opponents and, besides, he made a habit of issuing poems of this kind. Despite his successes, it would seem that he had long been a divisive figure. Voltaire, in a letter written when he was twenty-four, claimed that he had changed his surname, from Arouet, because he no longer wanted to be confused with Roy (pronounced Roué).[10] The two writers would later exchange insults in print.

Marsias allegori, ou le nouveau Carizelly's circulation and the minor scandal it provoked were mentioned in some of the cheap news sheets – *Gazettes à la main* – that peddled the latest scurrilous gossip. The *gazette* gave a report of a tense encounter between Rameau and Roy.

Rameau was crossing the 'cour du vieux Louvre' (the Cour Carrée) when he saw Roy. Isolated in the open space of the courtyard, the poet had no means of avoiding the tall, stick-thin, immediately recognisable figure coming towards him. A quarrel ensued over the poem. Rameau accused Roy of being the author; Roy denied it. Rameau then threatened to beat the poet with his cane. The reporter tells us that Roy drew his sword. Fortunately, Rameau had stopped wearing a sword a year before on the advice of friends who feared that his temper would result in a fatal incident. Roy was brandishing his rapier without conviction and had good reason to fear Rameau's cane. Rameau was held back and persuaded to leave the square.

ii La Génération harmonique

Rameau was writing a new opera, *Castor et Pollux*, for presentation at the Opéra that autumn, and had recently published a new theoretical work, *La Génération harmonique, ou Traité de musique théorique et pratique* (1737). This was his third major book, following the

Traité de l'harmonie (1722) and the *Nouveau système de musique théorique* (1726). In *La Génération harmonique*, Rameau reaffirmed his theories in the context of the new experimental science of acoustics. He was influenced by the empirical science of Isaac Newton's *Opticks* (translated into French in 1721) and more directly by the ideas of Joseph Sauveur (1653-1716) and Jean-Jacques Dortous de Mairan (1678-1771). Following Sauveur and Mairan, Rameau addressed the natural phenomenon by which a vibrating string produces more than one sound (a number of faint pitches being detectable above the dominant note), the effect that became known as the harmonic overtone. This phenomenon of harmony in a vibrating body (*corps sonore*) existed, Rameau declared, inside us – 'harmonie qui est en nous' – and in all things. Mairan developed an explanation for the seeming mystery of the harmonic overtone by applying aspects of Newton's ideas on the physics of light travelling through the air to sound transmission. As Thomas Christensen writes: 'Mairan concluded that this phenomenon must originate in the sympathetic resonance of commensurate air particles. In other words, the vibrations of the string will also agitate those particles whose frequencies are integrally related in harmonic proportion to that of the original sounding frequency.'[11] Rameau had met Mairan soon after his arrival in Paris in the early 1720s, and they had discussed these ideas frequently over the years. Rameau needed time to absorb the overtone and Mairan's explanation within his musical theory. At the beginning of *La Génération harmonique* he acknowledged his debt to Mairan. Mairan's admiration for Rameau's work was sincere, but he wrote to a colleague that 'one could wish that this author, whom one cannot refuse the distinction of being a great musician, had a bit more geometry and physics, or even a certain amount of metaphysics, along with the talent of expressing himself more clearly'.[12] Rameau was not deaf to such criticism and would eventually seek the help of Diderot and d'Alembert.

The fact that Rameau continued with his theoretical work after making his name as a composer shows that his position as a scientist of music was central to his working life and, crucially, to his view of himself. He didn't separate his theoretical investigations from his work as a creator and believed that this duality made him unique among the great creative masters of his art. He was dismissive of composers who only concerned themselves with the practical rules of composition and were indifferent to the underpinning mathematical and philosophical principles of music, writing, in *La Génération harmonique*, of the 'simple practising musician who always despises the source of the science he builds upon, and who asks, What is the point of all these calculations etc. when I compose good music without them?'[13]

The question of whether Rameau would have been a different composer if he had been the kind of instinctive practitioner he gently mocks in the above passage is a fascinating one. It is logical to think that he would have been both different and lesser, but the act of creation and the mechanics of genius are matters too mysterious for logic to carry the argument. It is clear, though, that Rameau believed that the roles of thinker and artist were connected and that his learning enriched his art. Many years later, at the end of his *Démonstration du principe de l'harmonie*, he made the point himself:

> I will only say, gentlemen, with regard to practice, that when I devoted my energies to working for the theatre I was driven by the pleasure of realising there, as an artist, many pictures conceived from my own ideas, immeasurably flattering taste and imagination, but, even more than this, by the pleasure of seeing, as a philosopher, the interplay of all these phenomena, from a principle known to me, giving rise to an infinite number of effects whose causes I was in a position to know.[14]

In his writings, Rameau occasionally made reference to one of his own compositions to demonstrate how expressiveness in music was linked to the deliberate use of certain techniques, such as chromaticism or the subdominant, and those occasions are instructive. For example, he cited Télaïre's air 'Tristes apprêts, pâles flambeaux', from *Castor et Pollux*, on two occasions in the last decade of his life as an example of the expressive power of the fundamental bass.

The point shouldn't be taken too far. Rameau didn't use theory as a substitute for creativity, and his learned exploration of music didn't make him an innovator of new musical forms or modes of expression. The science of music was an important intellectual discipline in its own right; it was not a set of instructions that enabled a mediocre musician to compose great music. As early as 1726 we find him writing: 'When we compose music, this is not the time to remember the rules that could enslave our genius.'[15] Rameau the scientist could believe, without contradiction, that 'true music is the language of the heart'.[16]

Rameau sent a copy of *La Génération harmonique* to Hans Sloane, president of the Royal Society of London, in the hope that the Society would endorse his ideas. He had first attempted to engage with the Royal Society after the publication of his *Nouveau système de musique théorique* in 1726. One of the Society's secretaries wrote to an acquaintance in Paris: 'I beg the favour of you to return the Society's thanks to Mons. Rameau for communicating his Tract, entitl'd Nouveau Systeme de Musique Theorique.'[17] The mathematician Brook Taylor wrote a favourable review that was read out during a meeting in January 1728. 'After having shown how all musical relations are derived from the properties of numbers,' Brook writes, 'our author observes that the perfect and most natural harmony of any given note is that of its third fifth and octave, especially when the third is major.' The review ends:

> The principal parts of [Rameau's] system appear to be reasonable and natural, and it deserves to be esteem'd a valuable improvement to have been able so far as this author has done to reduce the confused variety of intricate and difficult rules in this art to so few and so simple principles.[18]

D'Alembert would come to exactly the same conclusion twenty-five years later. Taylor's essay is of interest as the first significant English response to Rameau's ideas, and it is still of use as a concise explanation of the key principles of his theory as they existed in 1726. Rameau didn't achieve the public recognition he was seeking, for the Royal Society made no mention of the work in its published transactions. Rameau's letter of 1737 to Sloane was read out at a meeting on 3 November of that year. The fellows recorded their thanks to Rameau in the minutes and the Earl of Abercorn was asked to submit a review of *La Génération harmonique*. It appears, though, that the review was not written. Rameau tried again thirteen years later in 1750, submitting *La Génération harmonique* and *Démonstration du principe de l'harmonie* and writing two letters, the second of them very long and detailed. These fascinating documents, identified among the Society's papers by Leta E. Miller, contain valuable summations of his ideas. More significantly, they reveal the extent to which Rameau craved recognition for his theoretical discoveries from Europe's most prestigious scientific body: 'It is on your approval that the Arts should base their glory, and it is for you to pronounce on the merit of the studies and discoveries that contribute to their progress. You have taught Europe to follow the truth in the footsteps of experience, and the rigorous attention with which you examine the workings of nature makes you the first judge of all that pertains to physics.'[19] One senses vulnerability and pain when, at the beginning of the second letter's twelve pages, he writes:

> Although the people who delivered my *Démonstration du principe de l'harmonie* together with my *Génération harmonique* to you, about nine months ago, told me that you had received them, I will only be convinced of that when you have done me the honour of assuring me so, either by your approbation or your criticism. I am too anxious for the approval of your illustrious Society to neglect the means of obtaining it.[20]

Once again, the Society commissioned a review, but there is no record in the Society's papers that it ever materialised.

The critical reaction to the book in Paris was predictably divided. Younger, progressive thinkers mostly embraced Rameau's ideas (I will turn to his relationship with the *philosophes* in a later chapter). Traditionalists mostly recoiled from them. Desfontaines hadn't changed his view of Rameau and wrote a new attack in his *Observations sur les écrits modernes*. Desfontaines had been imprisoned for sodomy in 1724. Voltaire had helped to clear his name and Desfontaines, paradoxically, never forgave him. He presumably couldn't bear to be indebted over such an issue. As a man of letters he was well-regarded (he was the translator of Swift's *Gulliver's Travels* and the author of a history of France), but literature had uses beyond itself: he used his journal to settle scores.

His case against Rameau's *La Génération harmonique* centred on what he claimed to be the sterility of its intellectualism. In Desfontaines's view, innovation in music, as in all artistic creation, depended on genius and taste and not on elaborate rules and methods.²¹ Desfontaines was perhaps deliberately missing the point, for the role played by genius wasn't in dispute, and didn't negate Rameau's conviction that the theory of music was worth studying as an intellectual discipline so as to gain an understanding of what music *is*.

Rameau didn't respond directly to Desfontaines. Instead, Thérèse Boutinon des Hayes rebutted Desfontaines's critique in the abbé Prévost's weekly gazette *Le pour et contre* (1737). Perhaps Rameau chose this clever tactic and directed Thérèse in its execution. Desfontaines was being intellectually challenged by a girl who, as La Pouplinière's young mistress, was considered by many to be a *soubrette* (La Pouplinière married her around this time, on the orders, it was said, of Fleury).

However, the lucidity of her analysis would seem to have been all her own. Her essay was praised by people sympathetic to Rameau. His enemies were unlikely to be convinced given that she was the composer's pupil and patroness; and neutral readers were unlikely to take the time needed to understand the logic of Rameau's theories. The young Rousseau made the effort and found it extremely taxing: 'I did not leave off studying my Rameau, and, by great effort, was finally able to understand it, and to make some small attempts at composition.'²²

Rameau did respond himself to one reviewer of *La Génération harmonique*, and in a manner that exposed his acute vulnerability to personal betrayal. Louis-Bertrand Castel wrote a critical appraisal of the book in the *Journal de Trévoux*.²³ The attacks of a fellow scientist and former supporter (Castel had been an enthusiastic advocate of Rameau's ideas back in the early 1720s) did more damage, and hurt more, than those of a professional point-scorer like Desfontaines, and it made no difference that Castel – a supporter of English mathematics who nevertheless challenged Newton's principles and who was most famous for building an ocular harpsichord, a contraption that replaced sounds with coloured lights – was considered by many to be eccentric. Through his English connections, Castel was elected to the Royal Society in 1730. Rameau and Castel had still been on excellent terms in 1733, for, following the success of *Hippolyte et Aricie*, Rameau, briefly fearing that he would need to abandon his theoretical investigations, offered Castel all of his papers (Castel made this known; if he had misunderstood, Rameau didn't contradict him); but, in 1735/36, they clashed in the pages of the *Trévoux*, with Rameau accused by Castel of unacknowledged borrowings of other scientists' ideas, including his own – Castel claimed to have pointed Rameau in the direction of Sauveur. Castel went further in his review of *La Génération harmonique*, writing that his earlier support of Rameau's ideas had been a consequence of his inexperience at the time. He identified an inconsistency in Rameau's theory;[24] but what Rameau couldn't bear was the attack on his integrity, leading him to publish a dismissal of Castel in *Le pour et contre* that, in its tortured sarcasm, revealed more about Rameau than it did about Castel:

> Why has this celebrated mathematician, all together geometer, physicist, metaphysician, physico-mathematician, not used his learning otherwise than to fall into errors of which he would never have been supposed, did not the proof follow closely upon them? Should not this rare talent which he says he has, p. 2143, for 'clarified exposition', for 'methodical arrangement', for 'systematic reconciling', for 'full, correct and physico-mathematical demonstration' suffice him? Why forsake it in order to give himself up to 'personal details, in which,' as he says very truly, p. 1999, 'the public takes no interest and whose only use is to feed the proper pride of those interested'? This lesson, which he gives me, concerns only him… He dares claim that he gave me lessons of very geometry, that he has even communicated to me harmonic generations… What! is it the author of *Universal Mathematics* who contests with me for the glory of my own poor discoveries – me, a mere musician! I must have succeeded; that is the proof of it… 'I agree readily,' he says elsewhere, 'that fifteen years ago I was younger by as much.' The calculation is geometrical; so let us not hurry. Fifteen years hence he will perhaps have the same excuse.[25]

At least Rameau's final point in the above passage hit its mark.

Voltaire followed these exchanges with some relish and couldn't resist writing a polemical essay in the form of a letter to Rameau in which he ridiculed the Jesuit as someone who got everything the wrong way round and advised Rameau to do as the rest of the world did and ignore him.²⁶ Voltaire adopted a humorous tone to dismiss Castel. In his letters to Thieriot he was more direct, referring to Castel as 'Zoïle²⁷ Castel' and writing, 'Castel is a mad dog, an idiot of mathematics and a troublemaker in society'.²⁸ Voltaire sent the essay to Thieriot at La Poupliniére's, where Rameau would have seen it. If Voltaire was hoping to get Rameau back on side it didn't work, for the composer ignored his offer of the libretto *Pandore* in 1740.

It wasn't only Rameau's enemies who were sceptical of the originality, philosophical basis or practical worth of his ideas. Here's the scholar and musician Charles Burney writing in 1789:

> After frequent perusals and consultations of Rameau's theoretical works, and a long acquaintance with the writings of his learned commentator D'Alembert, if any one were to ask me to point out what was the *discovery* or *invention* upon which his system was founded, I should find it a difficult task. The base to a common chord has been known ever since the first attempts at counterpoint; and it only seems as if Rameau had given new names to old and well-known combinations, when he calls the key-note *basse-fondamentale*. But the Italians, ever since the time of Zarlino, have distinguished this lowest sound by calling it the *first base*. [...] But Brossard in his Musical Dictionary, published in 1702, in defining *Trias harmonica*, or the three sounds of the common chord in its first state, calls the under-note *basse*, or *son fondamental*. [...] And what has Rameau told us more, except that the *harmoniques* produced by a string or pipe, which he does not pretend to have first discovered, are precisely the third and fifth in question. This is the practical principle of the fundamental base; the theoretic was surely known, of harmonical, arithmetical, and geometrical proportion and ratios of sound. [...] Rameau's system, as compressed by D'Alembert, is perhaps the shortest, clearest, and best digested, that is extant; and yet, from the geometric precision with which it has been drawn up by that able mathematician, many explanatory notes and examples are wanting to render Rameau's doctrine intelligible to musical students.²⁹

In the end, Rameau the theoretician was most vulnerable not to the criticisms of his enemies in Paris, but to the scepticism and broader historical knowledge of an influential figure like Burney who, although finding aspects to admire in Rameau's theories, did not believe them to be as revolutionary or as pertinent as he did.

iii Castor et Pollux

Castor et Pollux opened at the Opéra in October 1737. The usual accusations of complexity negating beauty were launched by the *lullistes*. The theme had enough resonance to become the subject of the lyrics of a satirical street song that did the rounds following the premiere:

> Against modern music
> Here is my final reply:
> If complexity is beautiful
> Then Rameau is a great man;
> But if beauty, by chance,
> Is that which is simply natural,
> And best depicted as such,
> Then Rameau is a foolish man.[30]

This kind of popular satire, targeting public figures, was rampant in Paris, and Rameau, used to raucous heckling from audience members at the Opéra and to the Comédie-Italienne's clever parodies of his operas, would have been wise to view it as an acknowledgement of his standing and influence.

We have already noted that Rameau used at least some of the *Samson* music in *Castor et Pollux*. It appears that he also retained some of Voltaire's ideas on modernising the tragédie lyrique genre by reducing action and concentrating, dramatically and musically, on the moral dilemmas faced by the characters, in the manner of classical drama. This is particularly evident in the striking beginning to act one, arguably the most sustained dramatic writing in all of his works.

Rameau's librettist was the poet Pierre-Joseph-Justin Bernard (1708-75). Bernard, from Grenoble, was in the process of becoming a star of the Paris scene thanks to his charismatic performances of his own mildly risqué verses, after Ovid, in the salons. Sociable and personable, he was, as far as we can gather from the sources left to us, that rare thing, a public figure of the time without notable enemies or bitter rivals. He soon came to the attention of Voltaire who wrote some lines in which he, enigmatically, called the poet 'Gentil-Bernard'; and to Jeanne-Antoinette Poisson, the future Mme de Pompadour, who would arrange his appointment as librarian at the royal Château de Choisy.

Once again, the connection between Rameau and his new librettist was the Caveau, although they would have also met at La Pouplinière's house. Bernard's libretto was generally admired, and Rameau would work with him on two future occasions, in 1748 on *La Surprises de l'Amour*, and in 1757 on *Anacréon*.

Following an allegorical prologue, celebrating the end of the War of the Polish Succession, Bernard's libretto tells the story of the Spartan warriors, and brothers, Castor and Pollux. The brothers are twins despite having different fathers. Pollux is the son of Jupiter and therefore immortal.

Despite the grandeur of its mythological setting, Rameau's opera is an intimate drama about the intense feelings that connect and disconnect four young people. Castor and Pollux love the same young woman, Télaïre, who loves only Castor. This is a love triangle plus one, for Télaïre's friend Phébé is in love with Pollux, but it is also a drama in which fraternal love, honour and duty win out over sexual desire.

Rameau used the substantial overture, in D minor, to establish the mood of the drama and to proclaim his individuality: the profusion of dotted semiquavers, the rise and fall, the shades of colour provided by the bassoons and flutes, and the way the surface flair is contradicted by an inner melancholy, *joie de vivre* in a minor key, are the key elements of his style that separate him from the other composers of his time. The prologue disappoints as drama – Venus seduces Mars into ending his campaign of terror against the inhabitants of the earth and the people celebrate. The divertissement contains the prologue's best music. The delicate formality of the gavottes and minuets is dismissed by a boisterous tambourin, propelled by the beat of a drum and harmonised by the woodwind. Rameau lifted the first minuet from his third book of harpsichord pieces.

Act one begins with the funeral rites of Castor, slain in battle against his enemy Lyncée, and the grief of Télaïre as expressed to Phébé. An ominous drum roll is followed by a slowly descending chromatic scale on the strings; and then the chorus begins a grave lament, 'Que tout gémisse'. Phébé (soprano) tries to comfort Télaïre (soprano) by saying that Pollux will avenge Castor's death, but Télaïre is inconsolable and tells Phébé that she is fortunate to love the immortal brother. There is an undercurrent of tension between the two women. Télaïre, left alone on the stage, sings the air 'Tristes apprêts, pâles flambeaux'. Télaïre, the daughter of the sun, yearns for perpetual darkness. The forlorn melody is carried on haunting three-crotchet phrases played by the bassoons. Rameau's mastery of expression does not require a minor key – the air is in E flat, and its mystery and beauty are partly achieved by the choice of mode. Rameau was very satisfied with his achievement here. Referring to 'Tristes apprêts, pâles flambeaux' in his theoretical writings, he explained how a 'feeling of dull pain, of prevailing melancholy, is achieved by the chromatics of the fundamental succession, during which there is not a single chromatic interval in any of the parts',[31] and went on to write:

> Is one not naturally struck by sadness along with the actress when she sings 'tristes apprêts' etc. in the opera *Castor et Pollux*, at the moment when the lower fifth, namely the subdominant, succeeds the tonic on the last syllable? And is one not a little relieved when the tonic immediately returns on the last syllable of 'pâles flambeaux'?[32]

It is fascinating, if not surprising, to learn that Rameau's intellectual approach to composition was a means of expressing heightened feeling, both to give depth to the character and to expose the character's inner life to the audience. The music of this sequence, from the opening lament to the end of Télaïre's air, pointed forward to Gluck, the Mozart of *Idomeneo*, Berlioz – who declared, in 1842, when Rameau's music was largely unknown, that 'Tristes apprêts' was 'one of the most sublime conceptions of dramatic music'[33] – and the Verdi of *Don Carlo* and *Simon Boccanegra*.

A 'Martial Symphony' announces the arrival of Pollux (bass baritone) and the Spartan army. He has killed Lyncée in combat, and lays his body before Télaïre and the people. A superb chorus – 'Que l'Enfer applaudisse... Le cri de la vengeance est le chant des Enfers' – first shatters and then subsumes the grief of Télaïre, for the swinging refrain, in C, expressing the ecstasy of victory, is punctuated by moments of desolate reflection. The 'Airs of the Athletes' have the uncomplicated charm of folk music, with subtle scoring for trumpets. When Pollux is finally left alone with Télaïre he tells her that he loves her; instead of replying she asks him to petition Jupiter to restore Castor to life. Their recitative is more subtly shaded than dramatic: the *petits airs*, unaccompanied, and lasting for only a phrase, are exquisite, but easily missed on a first listen.

Act two opens in the Temple of Jupiter. Pollux faces a classic moral dilemma, torn between his duty to his brother and his passion for Télaïre. The opening air – 'Nature, Amour, qui partagez mon cœur' – is a fine example of the importance of the orchestra in Rameau, for the voice's place in the ensemble is equivalent to that of an obbligato instrument. A long, continuous phrase of quavers, reminiscent of Bach, winds a poetic course beneath the voice. Even the presence of a middle section (the home key of D minor gives way to F major and A minor) can't interrupt the sense of forward movement. Four years after *Hippolyte et Aricie*, many of Rameau's contemporaries still found his orchestra intrusive and didn't understand its dramatic function. It was only when Rameau was rediscovered, post-Wagner, that this aspect of his style was fully appreciated. In 1903 Claude Debussy, having attended a performance of *Castor et Pollux*, wrote of the air 'Nature, Amour, qui partagez mon cœur' that 'it is so personal of accent, so new of construction, that time stands still and Rameau appears as a contemporary one could go up to and congratulate at the end of the performance'.[34] The composer of the recently premiered *Pélleas et Mélisande* had discovered a kindred spirit.

In a lengthy passage of recitative and airs, Pollux tells Télaïre that he will plead for his brother's life while expressing his frustration that he must abandon his love for her. Télaïre gives him no hope, for her response is stern and unyielding – 'You are a god, leave love to feeble humans'. The descent of Jupiter (bass) is accompanied by baleful music that recalls the opening phrase of the overture. Pollux's cry of 'O! Mon père' has a bare intensity, as if Rameau was remembering his own father. Jupiter announces that Castor can only be brought back to the living if Pollux takes his place in the underworld. Pollux passes this moral test. To show Pollux the life he is about to give up, Jupiter summons Hébé, the goddess of youth. Hébé leads a dance of Heavenly Pleasures, promising Pollux eternal youth. As the beautiful young women dance for Pollux, and sing to him, their heady music floats in the air, like a scent, dangerously feminine (we are mostly in E minor, and the mode of expression conveys the intense longing that precedes pleasure); but the young man finds the resolve to resist. A second air, a sarabande, with a solo flute prominent for the first time in the opera, ends with a girl asking, incredulously: 'Are you not beguiled?' Pollux replies: 'I will journey to Hell to forget my woes; Castor will be reborn to savour your charms.' The 'Entrée d'Hébé', reprised, concludes the divertissement.[35]

Act three, centred on the work's theme of misdirected passion, begins at the entrance to the underworld, where Phébé leads a stirring chorus, calling on the people to block Pollux's way. Pollux's indifference to Phébé is powerfully rendered in Bernard's terse writing. In reply to her poignant entreaty 'See my tears', he dismisses her with 'Castor is all that I see'. Pollux chooses this moment to reveal to Phébé that he has never loved her but only Télaïre. A sublime trio, in which Pollux and Phébé sing of their pain and Télaïre of her joy, accompanied only by the continuo, is followed by a thrilling passage of ensemble writing for the three principals and the chorus, the strings climbing two octaves in four quaver leaps. The hysteria of the two women comes to the fore. While Télaïre urges Pollux forward, Phébé tries to block his path by summoning the demons of Hell. With the help of Mercury Pollux escapes the demons and descends into the abyss. Phébé is left behind: in despair, she sings 'Hell has already entered my heart'.

Act four, in the Elysian fields, the resting place of heroes, opens with an air for Castor (*haute-contre*) – 'Séjour de l'éternelle paix' – of exquisite lyricism. Even in this place of enchantment, Castor can think only of Télaïre, and there is something slightly out of kilter about this music that suggests lovesickness: the dotted rhythm is like a fast heartbeat, and the repeated sixths convey Castor's longing. Castor's mood infects the divertissement: the Air of the Spirits has a somnolent melancholy, and the fast dances – a gavotte and two passepieds – cannot fully lift the mood. In the final scene of the act the brothers are united. Following a tender greeting, Castor refuses to accept his brother's sacrifice: he resolves to return to earth just long enough to say goodbye to Télaïre. The recitative is long and continuous, without *petits airs* and with only one short duo.

Castor's return to Sparta, in the final act, leads Phébé to think that Pollux has given up his life. She sings the work's only dramatic monologue, 'Castor revoit le jour', and her anguish interrupts the prevailing calmness of expression. The air is only as long as it needs to be, for Rameau is not interested in over-indulging the audience, or for that matter the singer. She resolves to kill herself so that she can join Pollux in the underworld. In scene two, Castor's return grants Télaïre a moment of happiness. When he tells her that he must return to the underworld she accuses him of a false love: 'I have barely seen you, I have but barely breathed again, and you forsake me?' Their conversation is interrupted when the people arrive to celebrate Castor's homecoming and his marriage to Télaïre. They join Télaïre in appealing to Castor in a heartfelt chorus – 'Why steal away from such pleasures?' – but Castor sends them away, and the recitative resumes. Castor tries to make Télaïre understand that, for him, duty comes before love: 'Do you wish me to abandon my brother in Hell? Live, and let me die'. Télaïre reveals to Castor that Pollux also loves her and is his rival. When this fails to provoke him she says: 'You never loved me; if you loved me you would be more jealous.' Castor commands her to stop: 'If I don't return to Hell Jupiter will punish me and perhaps you.' Here, as in all the highly developed passages of recitative in his operas, Rameau makes the exchanges powerfully dramatic through the elegance of his style. Edward Nye gives a succinct summary of the techniques adopted by the composer when he writes: 'Exchanges proceed with minimal musical time between the interlocutors, perhaps a single beat. Replies are marked musically with syncopation, interruptions by unresolved harmony, questions and exclamations by harmony with the dominant, caveats with a fourth interval drop.'[36]

Suddenly, a terrifying storm erupts over Castor and Télaïre and the earth begins to fracture. Télaïre faints into Castor's arms. He thinks she is dying and appeals to Jupiter.

The storm abates and a 'Melodious Symphony' accompanies the descent of Jupiter. Jupiter reveals that the Fates are satisfied. Castor has been granted immortality and the brothers will live together in the skies as the constellation of Gemini. Pollux, released from the underworld, tells Castor that he saw Phébé descending into the abyss. At Jupiter's command the skies open and reveal the Zodiac, the Sun in his chariot, and, in the distance, the Palace of Olympus. Stars, planets and Gods join Castor and Pollux in a festival of the universe. Bernard and Rameau's dramatically weak conclusion had more to do with special effects than anything else. The festival only tricks us into thinking that the ending is happy. Castor and Pollux lose the pleasures of an earthly life; and Phébé, alone in the underworld, suffers for eternity. This is only a happy ending from the point of view of the Gods.

Castor et Pollux is a less clamorous and more contained work than *Hippolyte et Aricie*. Its tone is essentially elegiac, and in this sense it is perhaps Rameau's most personal opera. The story of two brothers who love the same woman too closely mirrors Rameau's own experience for its choice to have been coincidental. The death in 1736 of Marguerite, the woman who, years before, rejected Rameau to marry his brother Claude Bernard, must have brought back feelings of regret. Rameau found in *Castor et Pollux* a drama that validated his own actions. Like Pollux, Rameau acted honourably, accepting his brother's marriage to Marguerite and leaving the stage. Writing *Castor et Pollux* was a way of expressing his feelings for Marguerite and Claude Bernard, of working out complicated emotional issues. Is the relentlessly self-obsessed Télaïre a portrait of Marguerite? If so, there is no doubting the complexity of Rameau's feelings.

Castor et Pollux, first performed on 24 October, with Denis-François Tribou as Castor, Claude Chassé as Pollux, Marie Pélissier as Télaïre and Marie Antier as Phébé, was not an extravagant popular success. It was, as often with Rameau, a *cause célèbre*, polarising opinion, and this was more beneficial to the composer's fame than generalised praise. The opera provoked extreme reactions in people who disliked Rameau and his music, as well as in some of his professional rivals. The composer Jean-Joseph Mouret was said, anecdotally, to be so jealous of Rameau's talent that he lost his reason and had to be placed in the Charenton asylum, where, deranged, he sang over and over again the demonic chorus 'Qu'au feu du tonnerre' (act four).[37] Mouret died in the asylum in December 1738.

'The opera has not succeeded,' wrote the duc de Luynes in his journal, by which he meant that there were many critical voices.[38] The reviewer in the *Mercure de France* hedged his bets, commenting on the high level of interest generated by Rameau's follow-up to *Hippolyte et Aricie* but refusing to pass judgement on its overall quality, writing only that 'the audience has yet to make up its mind'. He did, however, praise the 'gracious' and 'tender' music of Hébé in act two, and the trio in act three.[39]

Rameau's admirers were enthusiastic, and even Voltaire saw merit in Bernard's poetry (still living in exile far from Paris, he had to make do with reading the libretto, writing sadly to Thieriot, 'I wish I could watch the opera with you and afterwards take supper with the actors'[40]); but many of the neutrals were bored by the theme of fraternal love and wanted to see more of the actresses. The opera is centred on Pollux and the way his moral character is tested, dramatically compelling to Bernard and Rameau, and to fellow artists, but of little interest to many of the most vocal members of the audience. This aspect of the opera, along with the general theme of *amitié* and references to the sun, is consistent with the philosophy of the Freemasons. A number of his later works, created with the dramatist Louis de Cahusac, a known Freemason, were underpinned by Masonic ideas, but in *Castor et Pollux* the connection is uncertain (I will return to this theme in a later chapter). Rameau accepted some of the criticisms, or at least, as a practical man of the theatre, was willing to address them. When he came to revise the work, twenty years later, he radically re-thought much of the material and added new music.

iv Les Fêtes d'Hébé

Rameau wasn't making enough money from his operas to be able to give up other sources of income. His contract with La Pouplinière was therefore essential. It meant that he could finally bring to an end his career as an organist (he stepped down from his position at the church of Sainte-Croix-de-la-Bretonnerie during the course of 1738), but not that he stopped seeking further streams of revenue. In December 1737, a few weeks after the premiere of *Castor et Pollux*, Rameau opened to the public his own school of composition, taking out advertisements in both the *Mercure de France*[41] and *Pour et Contre*. There were places for twelve students, and lessons took place at Rameau's home in the rue des Bons Enfants three afternoons a week, from three to five, at a monthly fee of one *louis d'or* (a value of twenty *livres* before 1740; twenty-four thereafter). The school had the potential to earn Rameau nearly three thousand *livres* a year, a not inconsiderable sum to add to his total income at a time when people whose yearly income amounted to fifteen thousand *livres* were considered to be rich.[42]

Composing operas had to fit into a cramped working week, but it seems that Rameau had an inexhaustible capacity for work. In 1739 he delivered two major pieces: in the spring, the effervescent ballet *Les Fêtes d'Hébé*; in the autumn, the stately tragedy *Dardanus*.

It seems that the music that Rameau created for Hébé lingered in his mind during the months that followed the première of *Castor et Pollux*. The idea of creating a whole opera permeated by the beguiling spirit of the goddess may have been born over supper at La Pouplinière's. The author of the text of the resulting work – initially entitled *Les Talents lyriques* – was not revealed at the time of the premiere. The libretto was universally derided. 'Rameau said that he could put into music the *Gazette de France*,' wrote the abbé Raynal in his newsletter; 'I was not inclined to believe him until he set the words of *Les Talents lyriques*.'[43] Identifying the culprit became a matter of public curiosity, and within months numerous sources, among them Simon Henri Dubuisson in a letter dated 8 June, were claiming that a group of writers had been involved, all members of La Pouplinière's inner circle: the financier and man of letters Antoine Gautier de Montdorge,[44] Gentil-Bernard, Pellegrin and La Pouplinière himself. Montdorge, La Pouplinière's close friend and neighbour in the rue de Richelieu, was the primary author; Pellegrin was brought in after the opening to improve the second act.[45] The circumstances of the libretto's creation give one explanation as to why the authors remained undeclared; its lack of literary merit gives another. As a librettist, Montdorge was at best an enthusiastic amateur, someone the art critic Bachaumont would later dismiss as a 'financier who fancied himself a wit'.[46] A cryptic disclaimer in the form of an 'Extract from a letter written to M. Rameau', in which the librettist, presumably Montdorge, proclaimed that his words were merely pegs for music and spectacle, and were only being published because that was the convention, was inserted at the beginning of the printed libretto, published, as was customary, to coincide with the first performances. 'I console myself,' he tells Rameau, 'that when critics accuse you of setting a text that is quite different from those that succeed today, I can reply – Let the music be savoured as it deserves, and don't ask for more.'[47]

Critics of the libretto blamed Rameau. Mme de Graffigny, who later that year would become a temporary admirer of Rameau's music after attending a rehearsal of *Dardanus*, was, at the time of *Les Fêtes d'Hébé*, contemptuous of his supposed disregard for poetry. 'Playing currently at the Opéra,' she wrote to her friend Devaux,

> is a ballet by Rameau that was detested at its opening. I really can't remember the name. The words [...] are pitiful. They are the work of a man who has never before written verse. Rameau wants it so, for he has declared that it is impossible to make good music from good words. He has been given his wish, but still hasn't succeeded that well.[48]

The belief expressed by Mme de Graffigny was widely shared, and became poisonous when a rumour started to circulate accusing Rameau of collaborating with mediocre poets out of greed, for men like Montdorge, it was believed, did not demand payment.[49] This view of Rameau's character was unsubstantiated at the time, and it is not possible to either confirm or deny it. Those who expressed it were not only possibly slandering Rameau; they were also dismissing Pellegrin and Gentil-Bernard as second-rate. Voltaire offered to give up his rights, but from a position of strength, not weakness.

Intriguingly, Rameau chose a dedicatee for *Les Fêtes d'Hébé*, making it unique among his operas. At the head of the published score, Rameau dedicated the work to Mme La Duchesse Douairiere and thanked her for 'protecting' his first works.[50] Who was this royal duchess who provided Rameau with protection? There are a few possibilities, but Louise Françoise de Bourbon (1673-1743), the daughter of Louis XIV and his mistress Mme de Montespan, and the widow of Louis III de Bourbon-Condé, is the best fit. She was known to be a passionate supporter of music and opera. It is intriguing to think that this formidable woman knew and admired Rameau. She was in her sixties in the 1730s, but had been both a black-eyed beauty, infamous for the many scandalous affairs of her youth (a portrait by de Troy of the bewitching teenage Louise Françoise hangs in the Museu Nacional d'Art de Catalunya in Barcelona), and a figure of political influence (her son, Bourbon, had been a scheming first minister during the early years of Louis XV's maturity, until the young king instructed Fleury to remove him). Sadly, beyond Rameau's words of tribute, nothing is known about his relationship with his dedicatee.

Les Fêtes d'Hébé is a typical ballet héroïque, consisting of a prologue and three acts linked by a theme. The theme is the lyric arts themselves (*les talents lyriques*), with the entrées representing, in turn, poetry, music and dance. One can well understand why Rameau, an artist inspired by the aesthetics of the theatre, liked the idea of creating an opera about opera.

In the lively overture Rameau uses repeated notes and a galloping beat to set a comedic tone. The expression of humour is a facet of his genius that can surprise given the melancholia that best defines it. The prologue is set in a landscape below Mount Olympus. Hébé (soprano) has left the home of the gods, pursued by Momus (*haute-contre*), the personification of satire and censure. As the prologue begins, the two characters are in the middle of an argument. *Les Fêtes d'Hébé* was the first opera to begin in this way, with a duo.

'The fickle gods forced me out,' Hébé sings.

'You flee in vain,' Momus responds. 'They do you a favour – happiness can be found here on earth among mortals.'

Confronted by the banality of Montdorge's verses, Rameau relied on his imagination, for, as Cuthbert Girdlestone writes, 'one feels throughout this prologue, as so often in his music, that it was Rameau, not his librettists, who decided what mood to evoke'.[51] An oboe leads the orchestra as Hébé, Cupid and Momus sing 'Chérissez le jour qui vous rassemble'. Cupid tells the people to pay homage to

Hébé and, in the divertissement, a gracious air is followed by a glittering bourrée. Cupid suggests to Hébé that they leave for the banks of the Seine to witness a celebration of poetry, music and dance. Cupid and Hébé sing separately and together ('Let us fly to the banks of the Seine' etc.) in a sequence that flows effortlessly despite being tightly organised.

The first entrée, *La Poésie*, is set in a wooded grove on the island of Lesbos. Thélème (*haute-contre*) is jealous of the love of the poets Sapho (mezzo-soprano) and Alcée (baritone), and has persuaded King Hymas (baritone) to banish Alcée. Sapho uses poetry to beguile the king into revoking Alcée's banishment.

The entrée begins with a short orchestral prologue leading into Sapho's air 'Bois chéri des amours'. She remembers her secret trysts with Alcée in the woods, and mourns his banishment. Sapho knows that Thélème is to blame for Alcée's banishment. In the next scene, when Thélème declares his love, in one of those *petits airs* that Rameau challenges the listener to notice, Sapho indicates that she will submit if he brings the king to this solitary place to watch an entertainment that she has devised. Scene three is devoted to Sapho and Alcée. Only now does Alcée learn of Thélème's villainy, and, in the first dramatic air of the opera, 'Par les horreurs du noir Tartare', his anger is propelled by vivacious fugal writing for the strings in C minor. He appeals to the gods for vengeance, but Sapho stops him – 'Through my art, my poetry, infused with the pain of unhappy lovers, love will triumph' – and together they invoke the god of poetry.

Horn fanfares announce the arrival of the hunt. As Alcée hides behind the trees, Sappho greets King Hymas. The back of the stage is transformed to show a landscape with a river, and a water nymph leaning against an urn. The nymph is in love with a stream, but the stream has disappeared, leaving her grief-stricken. Suddenly the waters swell and the river takes on human form to tell the nymph that the stream will return. Hymas is moved by the story of the stream. When Sapho compares herself to the nymph, and tells Hymas that she loves the banished Alcée, he revokes Alcée's banishment. Alcée steps forward while Thélème sneaks away. 'I see now,' the king tells Alcée, 'that your only crime was to hide your love from me.' In the celebrations that follow, Rameau's dances – a pair of tambourins and a pair of rigaudons – are melodically and rhythmically exuberant.

Between the fast dances there is a gavotte and an air for the nymph that Rameau cannot resist infusing with disquietude.

In the second entrée, *La Musique*, the action takes place outside a temple. Iphise, daughter of Lycurge, King of Sparta, has been seduced by the beautiful singing of the warrior Tirtée and is about to marry him. Inside the temple her father is seeking the gods' approval by offering a sacrifice. Iphise (mezzo-soprano) sings of how Tirtée won her heart in languorous phrases shared by the strings and flutes, Rameau opting to portray her as a sensual young woman rather than as an excited ingénue. Lycurge (*haute-contre*) and Tirtée (baritone) emerge from the temple with bad news: the Oracle has decreed that Iphise can only marry the conqueror of the Messenians. Tirtée departs to lead the army into battle against them. The Oracle allows Iphise to witness the battle in the form of a ballet. In these central scenes (four and five) Rameau's creativity is at its most profound. Iphise's fear of death – 'O mort, n'exerce pas ta rigueur inhumaine' – is expressed in music that is unflinchingly bare and desolate, more so, perhaps, than any other comparable music in Rameau's work. It is followed by a beautiful orchestral passage, fragile and poignant, scored for the violins and flutes, that Rameau based on the first part of *Entretien des Muses* from his second suite of harpsichord pieces (1724). Rameau's self-borrowings were quickly spotted and commented upon. Mme de Graffigny, in her letter on *Les Fêtes d'Hébé*, took a very low opinion of the practice, writing: 'Je ne trouve pas cela bon pour un grand musicien.'[52] The quality of *Entretien des Muses* merited its re-use. The mood changes abruptly to reflect Tirtée's victory over the Messenians. With drums, horns and piccolos providing a martial flavour, the most uplifting of the dances have something of the foursquare optimism employed by Handel when composing celebratory music. At times, though, the music slips back into ambiguity, notably in the fine chaconne that ends the sequence. The divertissement celebrates music, and is perhaps the most extravagant example of ceremonial music in Rameau's output. Trumpet fanfares decorate a chorus in which the people praise Iphise's beauty. During the ensemble the librettist addresses the composer: 'Apollo, too, wants to take part; everything confirms the oath of the god of harmony.'

The final entrée, *La Danse*, is set in a rural paradise. Encouraged by Cupid, Mercury (*haute-contre*) disguises himself as a shepherd so that he can seduce the shepherdess Eglé, renowned for her beauty and her dancing. The shepherd Eurilas (baritone) tells him that Terpsichore, the muse of dance, has promised on this day to find Eglé a husband worthy of her. Mercury mocks the shepherd for believing that he will be chosen. Eglé, garlanded, dances to the sound of an oboe played by another of her suitors, but when Mercury begins to sing, in concert with the oboe and accompanied only by the continuo, the quality of his voice seduces her away from the oboist, who breaks his instrument in a jealous rage. Rameau writes a love duet for Mercury and Eglé in vocal phrases that exploit the sensuality of the human voice without resorting to ornament, repetition or the backing of strings, during which the god reveals his true identity. Eglé doubts Mercury's constancy, but Mercury reassures her. Their dialogue ends when they sing in harmony for the first time ('Non, non, je n'aimerai que vous'): the whole sequence builds up to this moment of resolution. All is now set for a divertissement that contains Rameau's fullest expression of pastoral music. Throughout, Rameau's genius ensures that Mercury's corrupting presence can be detected beneath the Arcadian surface. Watched by her suitors, Eglé dances with the other shepherdesses and at the appropriate moment places a nosegay over Mercury's head. The setting changes to reveal an ornate garden where Terpsichore reigns over the nymphs. A piccolo leads the first gavotte, and oboes and bassoons interrupt gliding strings in the second. A short but sharp rigaudon precedes Eurilas's expression of disappointment and Mercury's rebuke. A loure marked 'grave' is followed by two minuets. Mercury sings to the 'jeunes beautés' and a mysterious dance, a *musette*, richly orchestrated, evokes a feeling of elusive happiness. A vivacious *tambourin en rondeau* is propelled by a mesmeric beat, but the melody of the *musette* returns as a chorus. Rameau lifted these two celebrated dances from his second book of harpsichord pieces, but they were probably first composed, and orchestrated, for his comic opera *L'Endriague*, presented at the fair theatre in 1723. Terpsichore takes hold of Eglé and together they dance for Mercury's pleasure. Accompanied by cascading violin runs, Mercury sings a virtuosic *ariette* – 'L'objet qui règne dans mon âme' – lifted by Rameau from his early cantata *Le Berger fidèle*. The final pages of the opera contain the sweetest music. A hauntingly lovely lilting phrase, in 6/8, is passed between the oboes, violins and basses before being taken up by Mercury – 'Je fais mon bien suprême' – and finally by the chorus. As this beauty lingers, a short, wittily casual *contredanse* closes the opera with a nonchalant flourish.

Les Fêtes d'Hébé opened on 21 May. Critical comments about the libretto and the tone of the second entrée – it was felt to be too dark for a ballet, prompting Rameau to cut Iphise's air 'O mort, n'exerce pas ta rigueur inhumaine' from scene four – were of little concern given the public's extravagant enthusiasm for the music and the dances. Over seventy performances were given in the first year alone, and the clamour for places led to confusion and disappointment at the Opéra on a nightly basis. People would arrive thinking they had reserved a box only to find another party occupying their seats (the trick was to send a servant to occupy a box early in the morning). This indignity befell Mme de Graffigny three months into the run.[53] Part of the appeal of *Les Fêtes d'Hébé* lay in the way it showcased the charms of the Opéra's star actresses and placed them in direct competition. The allure of Marie Pélissier – Iphise in *La Musique* – and especially of Mlle Mariette and Mlle Sallé[54] – Eglé and Terpsichore in *La Danse* – was considerable ('Sallé, grands dieux, est ravissante!'[55] wrote Voltaire a few years earlier); but there was the added piquancy of knowing that an intense rivalry existed between these women, and between them and the nubile youngsters who challenged their prominence. On this topic, Mme de Graffigny remarked, 'La Pélissier and La Sallé are piqued because La Mariette has the most beautiful entrance […] and for eight days now a new Italian dancer has appeared who leaps higher than Camargo but without her gracefulness, and who has legs like a man'.[56] The Italian girl – eighteen-year-old Barbara Campanini – inspired Rameau to the extent that he inserted some new music into the third entrée especially for her. She caused a sensation despite disapproving shakes of the head of older women like Mme de Graffigny who were admirers of either La Mariette or La Sallé.

v Dardanus

Less than six months after the opening of *Les Fêtes d'Hébé*, in November 1739, Rameau presented a new tragedy at the Opéra, *Dardanus*. Rameau was breaking his established pattern of producing a new work every other year in what was perhaps a deliberate move to proclaim his dominance. Like many great artists, Rameau was unapologetically egotistical and competitive.

The writer of the libretto was Charles-Antoine Leclerc de La Bruère (1714-1754). Leclerc de La Bruère threatened to become a phenomenon when, five years before, at the age of nineteen, he wrote a one-act comedy for the Comédie-Française called *Les Mécontents* (1734). Two years later, his ballet *Les Voyages de l'amour*, with music by Boismortier, was staged at the Opéra: Voltaire read the libretto in Cirey and found it to be 'full of grace and spirit'.[57] Although Leclerc de La Bruère was still only twenty-five, his literary career was in danger of fizzling out. It seems that he wrote *Dardanus* independently of any composer and then spent months trying to place it. Early in 1738 he contacted Voltaire in the hope that the great man would become his mentor. Voltaire agreed to take a look at Leclerc de La Bruère's manuscript, and even before he'd received it he wrote to François Berger[58] (secretary to the inspector-general of the Opéra, Carignan) that 'a certain student of Apollo and Minerva, named La Bruyère [sic], is one of the young men of Paris of whom I have the best opinion'.[59] Voltaire's appraisal of *Dardanus*, sent via Thieriot to Leclerc de La Bruère that November, has not survived, but it's clear that he made some positive comments because Thieriot took him to task for over-rating the libretto in a subsequent letter. 'I am less severe than you,' Voltaire wrote back.[60]

Voltaire still hoped to write a tragedy with Rameau, so it feels wrong to think that he recommended *Dardanus* to him. Rameau knew Leclerc de La Bruère. They mixed in the same circles, and Rameau may have been present when the poet read extracts from *Dardanus* at the Caveau. Rameau didn't rush to work with Leclerc de La Bruère, and his acceptance of *Dardanus* was driven more by pragmatism than anything else. If his intention was to deliver a new opera in time for a November opening, he couldn't wait for a libretto to be written. *Dardanus* was ready, and serviceable. It had the grandeur of scale required of a tragédie lyrique. Its deficiencies as drama would become clearer when it was performed on the stage.

There are various and conflicting accounts of Dardanus in classical literature. In the *Aeneid*, Dardanus is the son of Jupiter and Electra. He establishes Troy and marries the daughter of his ally Teucer, king of Phrygia. Leclerc de La Bruère took inspiration from the *Aeneid*, but invented his own pre-story.

The overture begins in the Lullian manner, but Rameau breaks the mould by introducing a second subject that is briefly developed. For Girdlestone, the overture 'points to the early symphony'.[61] Its upbeat character certainly has something of Haydn's amiability. In the prologue, the banal interplay of Venus, Cupid and Jealousy ends with the goddess commanding the Pleasures to re-enact the tale of Dardanus. It is not clear whether Leclerc de La Bruère was attempting humour while making a philosophical point about the nature of love. At Venus's command, the Pleasures enchain Jealousy; but the singing of the Pleasures becomes so languorous that Venus and Cupid begin to fall asleep. To bring life back to Cupid's realm Venus releases Jealousy, for 'it is to jealousy that Cupid owes his power'. Rameau never bettered this prologue for sheer invention. Nowhere else in his work does vivacity reign over contemplation for such a length of time. Leclerc de La Bruère's text provided contrasts, solos for Venus and a number of choruses. The four airs for Venus (soprano) are richly expressive and technically audacious, and the chorus 'Nos mains forgent les traits les plus forts qu'Amour lance', sung by the followers of Jealousy, breaches the barriers of 18th century decorum in a glorious outpouring of sound. Then, in the concluding celebrations, two tambourins combine to create the most crazily original dance music composed by Rameau up to this point, an invitation to swirl and stomp in a circle of abandonment and ecstasy that was as striking in the context of its time as Stravinsky's *Rite of Spring* was in its.

Tellingly, there is very little recitative in the first act. Teucer, king of Phrygia, is conducting a devastating war against Dardanus, son of Jupiter. The action takes place before the tombs of the fallen, and begins with a tragic prelude and air for Teucer's daughter Iphise (soprano) – 'Cesse, cruel Amour, de rêgner sur mon âme'. She is suffering because she is in love with her father's enemy. Dardanus is unaware of Iphise's love for him, just as Iphise is unaware of his love for her. Although this air has a sad beauty, it is more voluptuous than its equivalents in Rameau's earlier tragedies. The bassoons' harmonic progression in dotted time, falling away from the strings, is magical. The scene is comparable to the beginning of *Castor et Pollux*, but its mood is more intimate. The following scenes are dominated by the virility of the king and his warriors, and by the joy of the people, but Iphise's distress lingers – she remains on stage, a largely silent and lonely figure, and will be given the last word. She accepts her father's will when he gives her hand in marriage to Anténor, the powerful ally who has joined the fight against Dardanus. In the duo 'Mânes plaintifs, tristes victimes' Teucer and Anténor promise the fallen that they will kill Dardanus: the two bass-baritone voices are backed by chillingly portentous chords in the orchestra. Macabre thoughts of the dead are lifted by the forceful march in D minor that accompanies the arrival of the warriors. In scene three, an intense chorus led by Anténor – 'Mars, Bellone, guidez nos coups' – is introduced and underpinned by accented repeated quavers played *forte* by the orchestra: this passage, even more than the prologue's pair of tambourins, must have rattled its first listeners out of their seats. Its power lies in the simple idea of repetition, and in the way Rameau writes percussively for the strings. Rameau places elegant chord progressions and vocal harmonies on top of the accompaniment to create layers of sound. Following this call to arms, the act ends as it began with Iphise wondering how she can ease her agitated heart. She decides to consult the magician Isménor. The act concludes on a single harpsichord note.

Act two, set in a solitary place before a temple, opens with a vivacious *ritornello*: here Rameau uses repeated notes to convey the power of Isménor (the opera's third bass-baritone). In a long section of recitative, Dardanus (*haute-contre*) tells Isménor that he is in love with Iphise and must see her. He will make peace with Teucer if Iphise returns his love. Isménor commands his followers to cast a spell that will penetrate the gates of Hell. Their chorus, 'Hâtons-nous; commençons nos terribles mystères', is slightly comical; it cannot match the warriors' call to arms in act one. The sun disappears and the only light is thrown by the stars. From this moment on Isménor's music has a disorientating tonal ambiguity. He hands

Dardanus his wand. Possession of the wand will enable Dardanus to take on the appearance of Isménor. As in *Castor et Pollux*, aspects of Masonic ritual can be detected. In scene five, Iphise asks Isménor to cure her of her love-sickness, unaware that he is Dardanus in disguise. During their recitative, Iphise, ashamed, confesses that the person she loves is Dardanus. Dardanus throws away the wand to reveal his true identity. The revelation shocks and angers Iphise, and she flees. But Dardanus is content: 'Should I perish I have at least known her tenderness'.

At the beginning of act three, in Teucer's palace, Iphise is once again alone. A prelude introduces the sorrowful air 'O jour affreux'. Ascending notes in E minor, played by the violas, convey Iphise's misery. Dardanus has been captured, his execution certain. Iphise suffers from the paradox of a double remorse: she hates herself for loving Dardanus, but grieves because their love is impossible. This is one of the places where Leclerc de La Bruère's text may have earned Voltaire's praise. In scene two, Anténor longs for Iphise, but the princess rebukes him: 'Should I promise you my love at an altar drenched in Dardanus's blood?' Anténor realises that Iphise is in love with Dardanus. Rameau skilfully contrasts their different emotional states in the recitative. As the people begin to gather around them, Iphise cannot hide her grief and retreats. In scene three the Phrygians celebrate the peace. An orchestral *air en rondeau* is taken up by the chorus, led by a Phrygian man and woman. The breezy tune is familiar for a reason. It is another self-borrowing from the harpsichord suite of 1724 – the piece *Les Niais de Sologne*. The sweetly lyrical minuets have delightful melodies, and form the basis of the air 'Volez, plaisirs, volez'. The two tambourins are dazzling, but can't quite match their equivalents in the prologue. In scene four, Teucer calls a sudden end to the games. It is at this point that Leclerc de La Bruère's libretto loses its fragile credibility. The king announces that a 'monstre redoubtable, un dragon furieux' has been summoned by Neptune to ravage the coast of Phrygia in revenge for the capture of Dardanus. Teucer and Anténor depart, believing that they will vanquish a monster sent by the gods.

In act four the stage represents a stretch of coast, decimated by the monster. Venus descends in a chariot, with Dardanus lying asleep beside her. He 'suffered a cruel death', but Jupiter sent Venus to bring him back to life. Ignoring the absurdities of his text, Rameau creates ravishing music here, and one wonders how successful the Opéra's orchestra, so regularly accused of only being able to play *forte*, was in delivering the delicate timbres and gently undulating sounds demanded by the composer. In the tender *sommeil* Rameau emulates the deep breathing of someone sleeping. It comes as a surprise to find an 18th century composer creating night music to stand alongside Benjamin Britten's song cycle *Nocturne*. A Dream tells Dardanus about the monster. A second Dream tells him that he is loved. The remarkable orchestral passage 'Calme des sens' is, in its poetry, its ambiguity and its lack of certainty, too intimate for the opera house. Together, the Dreams tell Dardanus that it is time to 'hasten to arms'. Dardanus wakes, and departs to find and fight the monster. Anténor is also searching for the monster. In scene four he has his best moment, the air 'Monstre affreux, monstre redoutable', another forward-looking duet between vocal line and orchestral accompaniment, the latter representing the character's emotional state (the oscillating violin pattern is almost drowned out by the basses beating out the four beats in the bar). The monster rises from the sea in a tempest and is about to overwhelm Anténor when Dardanus arrives and kills it. Dardanus, unrecognised, decides to withhold his identity and to take advantage of his rival's gratitude by making him promise to give Iphise the freedom to refuse his hand. Anténor gives his sword to the stranger.

Leclerc de La Bruère rushes the story towards its inevitable conclusion. On his return to Teucer's palace, in act five, Anténor is greeted as a hero. The Phrygians believe that he has conquered the monster. Anténor is wracked by shame and delays revealing the truth. The arrival of Dardanus causes amazement. It is here that Leclerc de La Bruère's dialogue is at its most risible: 'My surprise is extreme' (Teucer); 'Has he escaped?' (Anténor). Anténor knows that he is undone when Dardanus gives him back his sword. He confesses to Teucer that Dardanus killed the monster. Venus, descending, commands Teucer to 'banish vengeance and hatred forever', and the king, beguiled by 'melodious sounds', obeys. All is now set for the people to celebrate the betrothal of Dardanus and Iphise. Rameau's inspiration remains high. The argument between Anténor and Dardanus, before the sword is passed, is powerfully described, and

Iphise's anxious interjection is all the more telling for consisting of the single word 'Arretez'. In the divertissement, the chorus 'Nous quittons des Plaisirs la demeure chérie' stands out.

The opera is brought to a close by a chaconne. The lilting opening theme, in 3/4 time, climbs gently; but it is the answering fall that lifts the soul. Middle sections divide each return of the main theme, the first for the woodwind, the last consisting of cascading scales played by the violins. At one point the music, enigmatically, almost stops in a moment of haunting suspension; but the chaconne is of a whole. Perhaps Rameau was compensating for his opera's dramatic deficiencies by sending the audience out into the night with this parting gift.

Dardanus was premiered on 19 November. Jélyotte, Albert and Le Page played the roles of Dardanus, Anténor and Teucer; Mlle Pellissier was Iphise, and Mlle Eremans Venus. Dupré, Mlle Sallé and Mlle Barberine led the dancers. Interest was intense, but opinions were too divided to keep the work in the repertoire for more than a month. Mme de Graffigny, who had loved the work in rehearsal, was disappointed when she went to a performance. 'It drags, this opera,' she wrote in a letter to Devaux. 'No beautiful recitative, and it lasts for at least three hours.'[62] The scale of Rameau's achievement was not recognised by the public, who expected operas to be no more ridiculous than they needed to be. *Dardanus* was simply too absurd in its second half. In particular, critics objected to a plot that required the hero to kill a monster summoned by his own father to avenge his capture. The appearance of a supernatural monster was a stock element of French opera, but the monster's part in the plot had to be justified (as it was, for instance, in Rameau's *Hippolyte et Aricie*). *Dardanus* was withdrawn after twenty-six performances and replaced by extra performances of *Les Fêtes d'Hébé*.

Rameau was even more dissatisfied than usual. When the opera was revived five years later he asked Leclerc de La Bruère to re-work the last three acts to make the situations more effective as drama.

In the new act three, Teucer's subjects demand the execution of Dardanus, but Teucer refuses to authorise the murder of a prisoner. Anténor's role is extended: reacting to Iphise's distress over Dardanus, his need for revenge contradicts his sense of honour. Most of the act consists of recitative. Rameau jettisoned nearly all of the original music, including Iphise's great air 'O jour affreux'.

The new act four was even more radically re-written. Dardanus, in prison, expresses his anger and despair. Isménor, Iphise and Anténor arrive in turn. Isménor invokes evil spirits to predict the future. Iphise believes she can help Dardanus to escape, and is willing to die in the attempt. Anténor, who intends to kill Dardanus as he flees, has set a trap; but when he arrives at the prison he is dying from a wound inflicted on the battlefield. Suddenly repentant, he confesses his treachery to Dardanus. In place of the dream music of the original act four, Rameau composed an opening soliloquy for Dardanus, 'Lieux funestes', a love duet for Dardanus and Iphise, 'Frappez! Frappez!' (this duet, greatly admired by Cuthbert Girdlestone for its emotional depth,[63] was subsequently cut), and a death monologue for Anténor.

The new act four has far greater dramatic power than the original, and its music is no less remarkable. Dardanus's soliloquy is among the glories of Rameau's art. When Marc Minkowski recorded the opera in 1998, he chose the 1739 version for its overall musical superiority, but couldn't bear to leave 'Lieux funestes' unrecorded: it was inserted at the beginning of act four. Here, Rameau's orchestral sonorities are at their most individual and haunting. From the opening three-note phrase on unearthly sounding bassoons (throughout, the bassoons are answered by the violins) the music seems suspended; and when the progression of the melody takes its unexpected downward step (from E flat, bar fifteen) it is like a rush of adrenalin that one feels in the throat. In this music defining aspects of Rameau's style achieve their apotheosis: the highly individual harmonic language, in which chromatic modulations and enharmonics[64] are embedded, and the delicate colours of sound create a monologue in music that is as profound as anything in the plays of Racine or even Shakespeare.

Between acts four and five Rameau composed entr'acte music, linked to the plot, for the first time: it describes the ongoing battle and Teucer's defeat. Act five once more wraps things up with the reconciliation of Dardanus and Teucer and the marriage of Dardanus and Iphise. Rameau composed new music for the divertissement, but retained the concluding chaconne.

Dardanus, more than any other of his operas, reveals Rameau's pragmatic and flexible approach to his own art, and the lengths to which he was prepared to go in an attempt to secure success. On this occasion his hard work proved futile: the 1744 *Dardanus* was no more successful than the 1739. This may partly be explained by the decline of interest in tragic operas during the 1740s. *Dardanus*, in its second version, would finally achieve the recognition it deserved when it returned to the repertoire in 1760: 'At the end of the opera,' wrote Jean-Baptiste-André Gautier-Dagoty, ten years later, 'the applause followed Rameau down the stairs.'[65]

vi Hiatus

At the beginning of 1740 Rameau could look back on seven years of concentrated endeavour that had produced five full-scale operas and one major work of music theory, a remarkable feat that must have left him mentally exhausted and in need of a period of recuperation and reflection. We should not be surprised, therefore, that he composed little new music, and published no books or articles, during the next few years. It would seem that most of his time was devoted to fulfilling his duties as La Pouplinière's music director.

Some scholars, seeking a specific cause for these years of near silence, have suggested that Rameau was on bad terms with the management of the Opéra and withdrew his labour. However, Rameau worked at the Opéra on the revival of *Hippolyte et Aricie* in 1741/42 and the new *Dardanus* in 1744. Disputes over fees meant that Rameau was on bad terms with the directors of the Opéra more often than not. During 1740/41 Voltaire hoped that Rameau would take up his libretto *Pandore*; he wrote to Berger to try and make it happen. If Rameau had decided not to create a new work for the Opéra, Berger didn't tell Voltaire (this is a reasonable supposition given the letters we have). Voltaire's letter to Berger of 29 June 1740 implies that Rameau hadn't rejected the offer outright: 'I do not want at all, Monsieur, for M. Rameau to work quickly; on the contrary, I desire that he takes all the time necessary to create a work that puts the finishing touch to his reputation.'[66] Voltaire finally believed that Rameau rejected *Pandore* on the advice of Thieriot (Voltaire's increasingly duplicitous friend), La Pouplinière (whose literary tastes were different from his own) and the abbé de Voisenon.⁶⁷ The likely truth is that Rameau didn't want Voltaire as his librettist.

The only new music released by Rameau prior to *Dardanus* in 1744 was *Pièces de clavecin en concert*, published in 1741. This collection is not one of Rameau's masterpieces and is easily overlooked within the corpus of his work; but it occupies a special place, not simply because it was the composer's only chamber music, but because it was one of his most personal creations. Rameau's five *Concerts* are scored for harpsichord plus two melodic instruments, a violin (or flute) and a viol (or second violin). In this peculiarly French genre, the melodic instruments were expected to accompany the harpsichord, which was an inversion of the Italian trios of Corelli. Rameau was inspired by a recent success, Mondonville's *Pièces de clavecin en sonates avec violon*, but went further. Although he proclaimed in his preface to the published edition that 'these pieces played on the harpsichord alone leave nothing to be desired',⁶⁸ in many of the movements he broke the bounds of the genre and gave the melodic instruments a distinctive voice.

The art of accompaniment was highly technical and required the training of the professional musician. Musicians disagreed over the best method of learning the art. As we have seen, Rameau's dispute with another musician, in 1729/30, led him to write *Dissertation sur les différentes méthodes d'accompagnement pour le clavecin ou pour l'orgue*. The vogue for amateur music-making in private homes, which saw scores of young women strive to master the harpsichord, not least so they could sit *en concert* between professional players from the Opéra, encouraged composers to publish works for keyboard, 'accompanied' by one or more melodic instruments, in which all the parts were written out. The aim was to merge the parts so as to achieve a balance that was appropriate for an intimate setting. In his preface, Rameau emphasised the need for balance, sensitivity and taste:

> It is necessary not only that the three instruments blend together, but that the players hear each other, and above all that the violin and the viol lend themselves to the harpsichord, distinguishing what is accompaniment from what is part of the

subject by playing the former more softly.⁶⁹

Four of the five *Concerts*, the first, third, fourth and fifth, have three movements. The second *Concert* adds to its three movements two minuets. Many of the movements are named after an individual. Rameau's *Concerts*, then, contain musical portraits of people he knew and cared about, and this private aspect adds to their mystery. In considering the named pieces we have to admit that we cannot always be sure that we have understood their meaning.

The curious title of the opening piece of the first *Concert*, 'La Coulicam', may be a reference to Jean-Antoine Du Cerceau's *Histoire de Thamas Kouli-Kam, roi de Perse*, published in 1740. Interest in the Far East was inexhaustible in Paris, and Du Cerceau's book was a bestseller. The character of the music has a regal air, but none of the exoticism the title implies. 'La Livry', marked *rondeau gratieux*, is perhaps linked to Louis Sanguin, comte de Livry (1679-1741), who was Lieutenant Général des Armées. A supporter of the arts, he was the patron of Rameau's first librettist Alexis Piron. Rameau may have met Livry through Piron and frequented his salon at the Château at Raincy. The noble melody suggests that Rameau benefited from Livry's support. Livry died after the publication of the *Concerts*, so 'La Livry' is not a memorial piece. 'Le Vézinet', marked *gaiement*, alludes to another aristocratic soldier and patron of the arts, Adrien-Maurice, duc de Noailles (1678-1766), who was Maréchal de France. He owned the forest and vineyards of Vésinet, on the left bank of the Seine close to Saint-Germain. Rameau may have spent happy summer days at this rural estate, for this unassuming piece evokes breezy sunlit days beside the river.

'La Laborde', the opening piece of the second *Concert*, is a portrait of Jean-Benjamin de La Borde (1734-1794), a child prodigy who studied under Rameau. La Borde hailed from an aristocratic family and grew up to become a tax collector as well as a composer of operas. He would remain a loyal admirer of Rameau all his life. He was guillotined during the Terror. La Borde was only seven in 1741, but given that he began writing music at a very early age it is likely that Rameau was already his teacher. The movement's fast scales indicate precocity and perhaps a sense of mischief. The gracious air 'La Boucon' is the collection's first expression of sadness and longing, and has a depth of feeling that is intriguing. Anne-Jeanne Boucon (1708-1780) was a celebrated harpsichordist and the future wife of the composer Mondonville. She was thirty-two in 1741. It is likely that, as a young woman, she had been taught by Rameau, and had inspired an affection that was still strong. The movement has the intimacy of a love letter. If it contains a message it raises questions about Rameau's marriage, and Rameau's nature, for his wife would have played the keyboard part when the piece was performed at La Pouplinière's after super. The curious title 'L'Agaçante' may simply mean a seductive woman. The music's trills and swirling repetitions seem to satirise a flirtatious *coquette*.

It has traditionally been thought that 'La La Poplinière' was Rameau's portrait of his patron, but surely Thérèse, La Pouplinière's wife, Rameau's student, was the more likely subject? Similarly, in 'La Rameau' perhaps Rameau was not describing himself but his wife Marie-Louise. Neither piece is remarkable, although the former combines three themes to depict someone whose character is mercurial.

The fifth *Concert* is the most substantial. It is dedicated to Rameau's musician friends. 'La Forqueray' was written to celebrate the marriage of the viol player Jean-Baptiste Forqueray and the harpsichordist Marie-Rose Dubois. Jean-Baptiste was the son of Rameau's friend Antoine Forqueray, and one of Rameau's orchestral musicians at La Pouplinière's. It is probable that Marie-Rose was another of Rameau's pupils, and that Rameau was thinking of her when he wrote 'La Forqueray'. The piece is marked *fugue*, but this only meant a melody repeated by different voices in turn. The repeated downward scales are evocatively bell-like. 'La Cupis' has a deep sadness. This gently swinging *berceuse* may have been written to celebrate the birth of Marie Camargo's nephew, while being a portrait of La Camargo herself. The final piece, 'La Marais', was probably written for one of the musician children of the composer Marin Marais, who died in 1728. A charming gavotte, it ends the fifth *Concert* on a joyous note.

6

La Pouplinière

By 1740 Rameau had been working for La Pouplinière for some time, and was settled with Marie-Louise and the children in a house in the rue des Bons Enfants. The contract with La Pouplinière enabled Rameau to continue his creative life without stress or hindrance.

La Pouplinière had transformed his home[1] into a venue for theatrical performances, intellectual exchange and society gossip, a place where aristocrats, artists, members of the connected middle classes, and courtesans, mixed company. La Pouplinière was undoubtedly cultured (he wrote short comedies for private performance), and used his wealth and status to satisfy his passion for music and the theatre; but also to extend his influence. We might think of him as both the chief ringmaster and the first participant in an endless round of hedonistic living. For La Pouplinière, as for the other great men who established private theatres, self-gratification was the primary aim. Maurice Quentin de La Tour's portrait of La Pouplinière[2] in middle age shows a portly, round-faced man whose toothless, self-satisfied smile is anything but welcoming.

La Pouplinière was born Alexandre Le Riche in Chinon in the Loire Valley in 1693. He followed his father into the world of finance, entering the *Ferme générale* in Paris in 1721. The system of tax collecting under the *ancien régime* that allowed the *fermiers généraux* to take a cut of the revenue and to amass immeasurable private wealth as a result, was increasingly associated not only with greed and exploitation but also with inequality and oppression. The *fermiers généraux* were not all exclusively self-serving. Wealth generated from tax farming allowed Pierre-Paul Riquet, the collector for Languedoc in the middle years of the 17th century, to design and build the Canal du Midi; and the great scientist Antoine-Laurent Lavoisier, a member of the consortium in the second half of the 18th, to carry out his experimental work. Jacques-Louis David painted a fine portrait of Lavoisier together with his wife in 1788.[3] Not many years later, during the Terror, David was a member of the committee that issued death warrants. Lavoisier, along with other former tax collectors, was guillotined in 1794. Had he been alive La Pouplinière would have shared their fate.

Portrait de La Pouplinière by Maurice Quentin de La Tour (ca. 1755). Château de Versailles.

What was the nature of Rameau's role at La Pouplinière's? As a newly famous man, the leading composer of the age, his presence enhanced the prestige and influence of the financier's circle. Rameau was much more than an employee; he controlled artistic life. Jean-Jacques Rousseau, for instance, blamed Rameau for his failure to win La Pouplinière's patronage. We should note, though, that La Pouplinière gave Rousseau's opera *Les Muses galantes* an airing. Rameau's critical judgement of the opera was brutally honest.

For artists and intellectuals hoping to make their way in Parisian society, entry into one or more of the leading salons was an obvious goal. Good manners, sociability and a ready acceptance of the unwritten but clearly defined social rules were the prerequisites: 'The first talent of all in company, is to be sociable; and when there are superiors in this company, never to transgress the laws of subordination,' was how the duc de Richelieu put it.[4] Voltaire, for example, found the last requirement a strain, while Rousseau struggled with all three (as a consequence he was never at ease in society and never felt supported). Talent wasn't enough. D'Alembert wrote: 'In England, it was enough for Newton to be the greatest genius of his age: in France he would have been expected also to be agreeable.'[5]

One suspects, therefore, that Rameau, a central figure at La Pouplinière's, had something of value to offer other than his genius, and that he was skilled at judging when it was acceptable to be contrary or sharp in salon company: the cutting down to size of a newcomer like Rousseau was not uncommon. Indeed, the long duration of Rameau's relationship with La Pouplinière suggests that, during the good years, it had meaning for both men and wasn't only a mutually beneficial business arrangement. The close bond between Rameau and La Pouplinière's wife Thérèse Boutinon des Hayes was crucial. Rameau named his second son, born in 1740, after La Pouplinière (La Pouplinière and Thérèse attended the boy's baptism in Saint-Eustache),[6] and asked La Pouplinière to be godfather to his daughter Marie-Alexandrine, born in 1744.[7]

Rameau and his family lived in La Pouplinière's house in the rue de Richelieu from 1746 and spent their summers at his château and estate at Passy, outside the city limits on the right bank of the Seine.[8] The Château de Passy (subsequently called the Château de Boulainvilliers) was purchased in 1722 by the financier Samuel Bernard for his mistress Manon Dancourt, Thérèse's aunt, who owned the château until 1739. It is likely that Thérèse spent time there as a child and influenced La Pouplinière in his decision to acquire the estate when it came up for rent in 1747. Voltaire referred to Thérèse as Polymnie and it is intriguing to consider whether this nickname was used by Rameau and others. Could Rameau have been thinking of Thérèse when, at the end of his life, he wrote profound music for the 'Entrée de Polymnie' in *Les Boréades*?

The writer Jean-François Marmontel knew La Pouplinière well.[9] In his memoirs he left a disappointingly discrete eyewitness account of the 'dangerous temptations' at Passy.[10] We learn that the orchestra included Italian musicians and was of an exceptional quality; and that the most beautiful female performers from the Opéra performed after supper – the ballet master Lany brought along young dancers from the company, including his sister Louise-Madeleine.[11] Rameau composed his operas at Passy and during mass in the private chapel played pieces of 'astonishing wit and brio' on the organ. Did Rameau include in this repertoire works of his own creation? If so he never published them. As for La Pouplinière himself, Marmontel depicts a man of wit and sophistication, amiable if somewhat vain; a figure celebrated in public but mocked in private by the very people who took advantage of his hospitality. Rameau's lawyer Silvain Ballot (a 'strange, grotesque personage' according to Marmontel), remarked: '[La Pouplinière] is drunk with gold, let him sleep it off.' In Marmontel's account, La Pouplinière was outshone by his dazzling wife, and often the victim of fits of jealousy and episodes of melancholy. On discovering, with Ballot's help, the ingenious secret door behind the fireplace that allowed the duc de Richelieu to enter his wife's bedroom from the neighbouring house, La Pouplinière exposed her adultery and banished her from their home (1748). As a rake La Pouplinière wasn't in Richelieu's league. Richelieu's brutal treatment of women was shocking even for the time. La Pouplinière became a laughingstock, mocked in popular street songs such as 'Qu'une bâtarde de catin…';[12] Thérèse was ruined. Rameau must have been devastated by this tragic turn of events. He remained in post at La Pouplinière's, but their relationship began to decline: they parted company in 1753.

La Pouplinière is a more intriguing figure than most men of his type. In 1750, at Passy, he arranged for a work called *Tableaux des mœurs du tems, dans les différens âges de la vie* to be privately printed. Only two copies were produced, for this was a book that only a handful of people would be allowed to read. People within La Pouplinière's circle had seen the dialogues and pornographic images that made up most of the volume, telling the adventures of a young convent girl called Thérèse (note the name), explicitly enacted by some of their own in the private theatre that La Pouplinière had constructed, in a house in the rue de Clichy, for the clandestine performance of erotic plays of his own creation.[13] Also included in the book was a story called *Zaïrette*, about a French girl of quality, kidnapped, raped and placed in an Egyptian seraglio. The manuscript of *Tableaux des mœurs du tems* was seized by the police after La Pouplinière's death and later passed into private hands (it came up for sale at Christie's in Paris in 2006). Both pieces followed very familiar scenarios. It remains unclear whether La Pouplinière was the author of the main work or whether it was written for him by Crébillon fils. This was the belief, unsubstantiated, of the editor of the first published edition of the book in 1865. Works by La Pouplinière that have come down to us, such as *Journal du voyage en Hollande* (1731) and the novel *Daïra* (1760), show that he was an able writer.

As music director, Rameau was charged with organising the delivery of all of the music played in La Pouplinière's establishments, from the very serious to the merely comic. Given his experience, which extended from the church to the fair theatre, he was very well qualified to do so. He may have written instrumental music to accompany performances of the adventures of Thérèse and other plays at the private theatre. For Rameau, though, what mattered most was La Pouplinière's orchestra. It enabled him to rehearse his scores and make any necessary changes in advance of a work's production at the Opéra or at Versailles. An anecdote concerning the creation of the acte de ballet *La Guirlande* in 1751, put down on paper by the composer and critic Adolphe Adam in 1859, is revealing about Rameau's perfectionism and the intolerant demands he made of his players, as well as about their relationship with him. During a rehearsal with the *musiciens de M. de La Pouplinière*, Rameau lost his temper and publicly humiliated both the leader (first violin) and the harpsichordist. He decided to simplify the offending passages, working late into the night to revise the score and calling a final general rehearsal to begin at nine o'clock that morning. The leader was the Italian-born Jean-Pierre Guignon (1702-1774), admired at court, famed for his performances of Vivaldi's concertos and known as the 'roy des violonistes'. He was so wounded that he decided to resign, writing a letter that reached Rameau early in the morning. As one of the most eminent violinists of his time he was not without ego. Adam quotes the letter in full:

> Monsieur,
> It is possible to be both blessed in talent and well mannered. This is what you completely ignore. You told me yesterday that I don't know my job, because I could not execute your music. I could respond in turn that you don't know yours, since you compose baroque music that is impossible to play. But I prefer to accept the hurt you've given me. Therefore, I agree that I am ignorant and unworthy to participate in the performance of your sublime compositions. In consequence, I have the honour to inform you that you'll no longer have to depend on me, or on our regular harpsichordist, who has asked me to send his resignation along with mine.[14]

While the letter's provenance is unknown and its veracity unproven, it reads like an authentic document, for the sentiments ring true. We know from a number of reliable sources that the musicians at the Opéra struggled to play some of Rameau's music, the pain this caused him and the manner in which he lashed out at the culprits; so it's not surprising to learn that his own players were stretched by his scores. Arguments between *maestros* and their musicians were not uncommon, and still aren't, as people who attended the performance of *Die Walküre* given by Daniel Barenboim and the Staatskapelle Berlin at the Proms in 2013 will know, but for Rameau's relationship with his leader to reach such a point of bitterness was a serious matter that must have caused hurt on both sides. Their relationship was repaired, at least partially, for Guignon led the orchestra that premiered some of Rameau's operas at court and at the Opéra during the 1750s.

La Pouplinière was never able to shake off his public notoriety as an accident-prone libertine, easily out-manoeuvred by both cunning young women and his male competitors. It was a view that grew stronger after he parted with Rameau, a falling out caused, as far as the gossips were concerned, by the machinations of his new mistress. In 1759 La Pouplinière entered the pages of Casanova's memoirs. Now in his late sixties, and anxious to sire a legitimate heir, he wanted to marry a beautiful English-Italian girl called Giustiniana Franca Antonia Wynne, recently arrived in Paris from Venice with her mother, Lady Wynne. Lady Wynne was delighted by a match that would have been the making of her family. Unfortunately for La Pouplinière, the girl not only detested him, she was also carrying the child of her Venetian lover and openly flirting with Casanova, who gave her money and organised her secret flight to a convent. Lady Wynne rightly blamed him, and La Pouplinière's latest humiliation was soon the talk of the salons and coffee houses.[15] Shortly afterwards, La Pouplinière's people identified a suitable girl in Toulouse called Thérèse de Mondran, the daughter of a magistrate. She became his wife and gave birth to a boy six months after his death in December 1762.

We are left with the thought that La Pouplinière was, in spite of all the advantages he enjoyed, a troubled and unfulfilled character. In this sense he was a classic playboy. Thieriot left the following summation of his character:

> Capricious, restless, almost neurasthenic, of a ready enthusiasm and easily deceived, liberal when the fit seized him, and, withal, endowed with the keenest sensibility, and a most active imagination, one can see how this intelligent Maecenas,[16] not satisfied with the worldly pleasures which his circumstances could supply, sought in music a distraction and an aliment for his cultured mind.[17]

7

Versailles

The Dauphin's Weddings and the War of the Austrian Succession
1745 to 1749

i Rameau and Voltaire: La Princesse de Navarre

At the beginning of 1745 Rameau began a new phase of his career as a composer at court. This was a natural progression for the leading French composer, and Rameau may have actively sought the position. If he lacked both the sycophantic charm and the ruthless guile to make the most of life at Versailles, he would have felt vindicated by the prestige and financial rewards.

He immediately came across Voltaire. This may have surprised Rameau given the writer's history of offending the establishment. When they last collaborated, on *Samson*, they couldn't get together in Paris because Voltaire was keeping out of sight of the police in Champagne. Voltaire's rehabilitation and re-emergence as a courtier was due to the fact that two of his aristocratic friends, the marquis d'Argenson and the duc de Richelieu (soon to break up La Pouplinière's marriage) had recently been appointed to key positions within the king's inner circle (respectively Foreign Minister and First Gentleman of the King's Chamber, responsible for court entertainments). Voltaire was no less interested in the prestige than Rameau, perhaps more so, but he was aware of the irony of his position, referring to himself as 'a poor devil who finds himself the king's fool at fifty'.[1] Although he could charm and flatter with ease, he couldn't do so without some people suspecting that they heard an undertone of sarcasm or even derision.

Voltaire and Rameau were commissioned by Richelieu to collaborate on the creation of an entertainment to open the celebrations that would mark the marriage of the dauphin, Louis, to the Infanta Maria Teresa Rafaela of Spain, in February 1745.[2] Rameau also provided an opera to close the festivities, *Platée*. The royal wedding was the grandest and most important state occasion for many years, and the accompanying *fête magnifique*, organised by Richelieu, was designed to trumpet the splendour and majesty and culture of France. Its purpose was not only to unite France and Spain, but also to bring the French people together at a time of war.

France and Prussia had been at war with Austria over the succession of Maria Theresa to the Habsburg throne since 1740. Cardinal Fleury, who together with his English counterpart, Walpole, had pursued a policy designed to avoid a Franco-British conflict, died in 1743. The two powers declared war in 1744, the beginning of a period of on and off hostility that wouldn't end until 1815. For the French and the English, so much more was at stake than had been the case during the previous thirty years.

With the death of Fleury, Louis XV was finally his own master. The war provided an opportunity for Louis to demonstrate to the people that the dissolute, weak and remote figure of the Fleury years had been a courageous and commanding ruler in waiting. In 1744 he went to the German front to lead his army. The effect was weakened when it became known that he had taken along his official mistress and her younger sister. Within a few years he would be as remote and as secretive a ruler as before, dependent on his new mistress, Mme de Pompadour, and rarely leaving the palaces and hunting forests of the Paris region. He had no particular liking for the public circus of Versailles, found court etiquette tiresome, and valued the ceremonial aspects of court life only as a means of observing and choosing young women. He was not passionate about music or the theatre. Rameau and Voltaire were unlikely to gain his personal admiration.

Richelieu contacted Voltaire and Rameau months in advance of the wedding in the spring of 1744. He told them to create a play with incidental music, songs and dance, in the style of the masterpieces of Molière and Lully. At a meeting at his house in Versailles,

Richelieu compelled Voltaire to come up with the plot of the play on the spot, something that Voltaire complained about to d'Argental.[3] Voltaire was under pressure because this type of work didn't come easily to him, and he couldn't afford to let his friend down. In tandem with satisfying Richelieu's demands there was the tricky matter of collaborating with Rameau, and Voltaire knew all about that.

The play needed to offer spectacle and entertainment while encapsulating the meaning of the occasion. It needed to flatter France and Spain, and the king and his family. Any ambiguity of meaning would not be acceptable. Voltaire, a master of wit and irony in his writings, found this very hard. He played it safe, writing a conventional comedy about a French duke and a Spanish princess that, once the obstacles have been overcome and the true identity of the disguised duke revealed, ends happily with their betrothal. The action takes place in the garden of the country estate of a Spanish nobleman, the perfect setting for the divertissements that conclude each of the three acts. Rameau's task was to write an overture and the music and songs of the divertissements.

Voltaire called the piece *La Princesse de Navarre*. He wrote frequently to Richelieu, sending his latest drafts, and asking for advice and reassurance and instructions on when to involve Rameau. He complained to d'Argental about the difficulties he was having, both with the writing and with Rameau. The bemused but largely tolerant attitude that Voltaire had shown to Rameau during the *Samson* episode was replaced by bitterness and disdain. This was understandable given that Voltaire had supported Rameau but been rejected by him twice; but it was also a consequence of his anxiety over the commission.

In April Voltaire recommended to Richelieu that Rameau should be sent the text of each act as soon as possible so that he could match his music to the words, and, especially, judge how long the divertissements should last.[4] He was clearly worried that the music would take precedence over his play. This comes over in a letter to d'Argental when, referring to Richelieu, he writes:

> Could we not make [Richelieu] understand that this music, continually intertwined with the declamation of the actors, is a

new genre for which the great edifice of the symphony is not at all appropriate? Could we not make him understand that Rameau should be reserved for a work entirely in music?[5]

Rameau, indeed, would compose almost an hour's music for *La Princesse de Navarre*, perfectly judged for the occasion, and of a quality – elegant, warm-hearted and courtly, with a fragility of balance between joy and melancholy – that the play couldn't sustain. By the end of August Voltaire was calling the composer 'étrange Rameau' and 'le roy des quintes', and telling d'Argental that he had decided to stop replying to Rameau's 'senseless' letters, not least because he was showing the correspondence to others.[6] Voltaire was further angered by the 'petit' Ballot, who was demanding to be sent all the material. Rameau's protectors at La Pouplinière's wanted to ensure that their man's chance of glory at court wasn't scuppered by Voltaire's own ambitions.

By the middle of September Voltaire considered his work on *La Princesse de Navarre* to be done. However, instead of accepting the text Rameau was highly critical and demanded changes. One of the main areas of contention was the structure of the act three divertissement. Voltaire wanted a series of dances to precede a final chorus; but Rameau believed it was better to break up the dances with the chorus and to end the work with a dance. Voltaire gave in but complained to Hénault:[7] '[Rameau] demands that I put in four all that is in eight, and in eight all that is in four; he is crazy.' Voltaire suggested that, if Richelieu didn't bring Rameau into line, the *fête* would fail.[8] By the next day Voltaire had lost all sense of proportion:

> As for Rameau, I believe that his head has turned. It is said that he beats his wife before taking her to bed. It is absolutely necessary that Mme de Tencin has the kindness to write to Monsieur de Richelieu to warn him of the risk he runs. For my part, I expect that the divertissement will fail if he doesn't take measures quickly.[9]

Voltaire was so fearful that Rameau's actions would cause the play to fail that he hoped to engineer his removal from the production, or at least ensure that the composer took the blame. If Richelieu had already started his affair with Thérèse La Pouplinière, one can well understand why he gave the assignment to Rameau and stuck with him despite Voltaire's attempts, via others, to undermine the composer. And one can well understand why Voltaire didn't criticise Rameau directly to Richelieu.

Voltaire had been wounded by Rameau. When he wrote that Rameau was 'a fool governed by faux experts',[10] by which he meant the crowd at La Pouplinière's, he was of course motivated by his disappointment over *Samson* and *Pandore*; and we may agree that, in this respect, the role that La Pouplinière played in Rameau's career was not for the best.

We have no letters or other documents that tell the story from Rameau's point of view. He must have been under serious pressure too. *La Princesse de Navarre* was his comeback as well as his passport to a richer life. Voltaire privately admitted that *La Princesse de Navarre* was mediocre, a farce of the fair. He shouldn't have been surprised that the intelligent, strong-willed and controlling Rameau thought so too. Rameau could afford to delay the work's completion because he knew he could write good music quickly. However, there was pressure. Rameau borrowed two themes from Handel's recent oratorio *Samson*.[11] He finished the music on time.

And so to the premiere of *La Princesse de Navarre* on 23 February 1745, in a specially constructed theatre in the *grand manége* (indoor riding arena) of the Grande Écurie (large stable). The two stables, big and small, were so much more than their name suggested. Constructed in 1682, they were given an architectural grandeur and symmetry, by Jules Hardouin-Mansart, to proclaim Louis XIV's love for his horses, and they housed many of the king's musicians. *La Princesse de Navarre*, conceived on a grand scale, required ten actors, forty-four singers (fourteen of them soloists) and forty-nine musicians. Rameau's regular star performers from the Opéra, the singers Pierre Jélyotte and Marie Fel and the dancer Marie Camargo, led the company. One can imagine Voltaire cringing internally with intellectual embarrassment as his symbolic ending – the collapse of the Pyrenees – was realised in a *coup de théâtre* that was found to be ridiculous. The play was much criticised ('[it] really was not calculated to succeed,'[12] Marmontel wrote pointedly), and the occasion would have misfired miserably had it not been for Rameau's music, which was much applauded. The duc de Luynes left an account in his memoirs:

> The ballet did not end until ten o'clock; it seems that the music was strongly endorsed; the divertissements were found to be very enjoyable. The play was heavily criticised by some, for the immensity of the hall meant that people could not hear the words too well. The story was completely invented, and was just too much to the advantage of France over Spain; and the representation of the Pyrenees was ridiculous. Love settles everything at the end and unites the kingdoms.[13]

It was perhaps fortunate that the spectacle of the play was always going to be secondary to the spectacle of the audience, for this luxurious assembly of France's nobility and the *dames de la cour* was riddled by gossip-provoking liaisons and intrigues. Among the revellers was a young woman, new to court, called Jeanne Antoinette Poisson. She was married to the nephew of her guardian, the *fermier général* Le Normant de Tournehem (rumoured to be her biological father), and known in Parisian society as a woman of charm and taste. Since the sudden death of the duchesse de Châteauroux, in December 1744, the king had been without an official mistress. The powerful men around Jeanne Antoinette, including her father-in-law, saw an opportunity for advancement. They dangled the willing girl in front of the king during the wedding night celebrations and watched him bite. Jeanne had more ambition and flair than a battalion of courtesans. Within a few months she would be in position as the king's official mistress, separated from her husband, living in Versailles and ennobled as the marquise de Pompadour.

Voltaire compared the court to a hive of bees and complained that the courtiers had made more noise than first night groundlings at the Comédie.[14] As the spectators left the Grande Écurie they were delighted by an even more beautiful sight – the façade of the palace illuminated against the night sky.[15] Richelieu had left nothing to chance.

ii Platée, Rameau's Satirical Masterpiece

A little over a month later, on 31 March, Rameau's second work of the celebrations, *Platée*, had its premiere in the Grande Écurie. *La Princesse de Navarre*, performed on the wedding day, had needed to be a work of taste and decorum, measured and conventional. The conditions set down for the final day of the *fête* were much less rigid. Nevertheless, *Platée* was daringly original and inappropriate. It wasn't written for the celebrations. The editor of the printed edition of Jacques Autreau's text, published a few years later in 1749, wrote of the work's origin that 'a comic piece in the manner of *Cariselli* was required at the Opéra, for the carnival season or the slack part of the summer'.[16] This suggests that Richelieu, in need of a work at short notice to conclude the wedding, diverted *Platée* away from the Opéra a few months in advance of its intended premiere.

With this comédie lyrique, or *ballet bouffon*, in three acts and a prologue, Rameau brought the parodies and slapstick of the fairs and the *commedia dell'arte* and *bouffonneries* of the Théâtre Italien into the very heart of official France. It tells us that the irreverent, satirical side of Rameau was very real, that he was as much a man of the fair, embracing the cruelty of comedy, as he was a tragedian and an intellectual.

The painter Jacques Autreau (1657-1745) turned to drama late in life, writing his first farce for the Théâtre Italien, *Le Port à l'Anglais*, when he was around sixty.[17] He enjoyed enough success to be taken on by the Comédie-Française (*Le Chevalier Bayard*, 1731; *La Magie de l'amour*, 1735) and to be befriended by La Pouplinière. Rameau knew him well as a result. But in old age Autreau struggled – as a habitué of the Paris cafés and gambling clubs, he was satirised as a drunk and a misanthrope – and he ended his life in the Hospice des Incurables. At some point Rameau, looking for a comic subject, acquired the rights to Autreau's *Platée, ou Junon Jalouse*. Because the text wasn't quite right for his purposes, Rameau engaged another author, Adrien-Joseph Le Valois d'Orville, to write some additional material, further evidence of the care he took with his libretti. Adrien-Joseph Le Valois d'Orville (1713-1780) was a minor poet and a parodist of the fair theatre. His long poem *Les Nouvelles Lanternes* was published in 1746.

Pierre Jélyotte as Platée. Painting by
Charles-Antoine Coypel (1745). Musée du Louvre.

Autreau lifted the bones of his story from an episode in Pausanias's *Description of Greece*. This epic work of travel literature, written in the 2nd century AD, was translated into French by the abbé Gedoyn as *Pausanias, ou Voyage historique de la Grèce* in the 1730s. The episode in question is found in the volume on the region of Boeotia (Béotie) and the city of Platea (Platées). Juno is angry with Jupiter and rebuffs him when he attempts a reconciliation. To pay her a lesson, and win back her favour, he announces that he is going to marry Platée, the daughter of Asopus. When the jealous Juno rushes to confront Platée, and tears away her veils, she discovers that her rival is a wooden statue. Jupiter has arranged this trick, following advice from the wise Cithéron, ruler of Platées. Juno, charmed by the ploy, and relieved, forgives Jupiter. In Autreau's version the wooden statue is replaced by an ugly and self-deluded marsh nymph, an imaginative leap that transforms a humorous tale into a vicious comedy about vanity and not knowing one's place in the social order on the one hand, and the meanness of mockery and aristocratic disdain on the other. We should not discount Rameau's influence here. Once he became involved he removed the vestiges of dignity that Autreau, in the first version of his libretto, had allowed Platée. Rameau, in fact, is at his most ironic, giving Platée some deep and tender music not to dignify her but to tighten the screw of ridicule. There is an intriguing similarity to Shakespeare's *A Midsummer Night's Dream*. In Shakespeare's play Oberon teaches Titania a lesson by arranging for her to fall in love with a hideous thing, an ordinary man transformed into an ass. Once he's had his fun he lifts the spell and Titania, like Juno, learns good-humour and obedience. Added to this, when Apollo first appears before Platée he does so in the form of an ass. Shakespeare may have been influenced by Pausanias. Was Autreau influenced by Shakespeare? As well as detecting links to *A Midsummer Night's Dream*, one is reminded of the scenes in *Twelfth Night* concerning the humiliation of Malvolio. Like Platée, Malvolio is tricked into believing he is loved by a personage far above his station in life: he makes a fool of himself in public and is cruelly mocked for his vanity and presumption. Shakespeare was not translated into French until later in the century, so if Autreau knew the plays he must have read them in English or seen performances by a touring English company. It is an appealing thought that there might have been a connection between Rameau's *Platée* and Shakespeare.

The stern opening phrase of the overture is immediately mocked by the chatter of vulgar-sounding repeated notes. The pattern is often repeated. Rameau maintains a serious as well as a comedic tone throughout, two parallel lines of thought that help to make the parody so inimitable. The prologue, entitled *La Naissance de la comédie*, sets the scene. In a Greek vineyard, satyrs and maenads mischievously wake Thespis, the creator of acting, from a drunken sleep. Since you've woken me, Thespis responds, I will entertain you by singing a song of autumn, but afterwards I will not spare a single one of you. He praises 'charmant Bacchus, dieu de la liberté, père de la sincérité' for making mortals so comical. Voluptuous harmonies underscore the decorative flourish of the melodic refrain of his song. He reveals to the satyrs that the maenads are unfaithful coquettes. Realising that their prank has backfired, the satyrs and maenads plead with Thespis to go back to sleep. In scene two, Thalie (soprano), the god of satire, and Momus (bass baritone), muse of comedy, commission Thespis to present a play relating how Jupiter dealt with his wife Juno's jealousy, a play that will mock both mortals and the gods – surely Rameau's warning to the king and his courtiers that the opera will target the powerful as well as the weak, should they have been alert enough to notice. The rigaudons and other dances of the divertissement are propelled by exuberant music, refined yet earthy, graceful yet rowdy: they possess that combination of sensuality and wit that is typical of Rameau.

After the overture is reprised, Thepis's play begins. The setting is a watery marsh at the foot of Mount Cithéron. A storm, caused by Juno's jealousy, rages overhead. Mercury (*haute-contre*) has been sent by Jupiter to seek Cithéron's advice. Straight away Cithéron (bass baritone) thinks of Platée and conceives of the plan to dupe Juno. In one of a number of masterstrokes, Rameau decided that a man should play Platée and wrote the role for Jélyotte's *haute-contre* voice. On her first appearance, in scene three, Platée sings the air 'Que ce séjour est agréable'. The vocal line of this lyrical air is deliberately disjointed, cut up into little sobs of music, and Platée constantly stresses the wrong syllables. She believes that Cithéron is in love with her and only ignores her out of shyness. On spotting Cithéron, she summons the inhabitants of the 'tender reeds' and cajoles them into singing her praises. To create this chorus of shrieking cuckoos and croaking frogs Rameau dares to use his flutes and horns inelegantly. The courtiers must have been challenged by this vulgarisation of instruments closely associated with martial glory and royal splendour. Platée, of course, thinks the marsh music is harmonious and sweet. Mercury and Cithéron go to work on Platée and then sit back and watch, incredulously, as she is consumed by vanity. In the ensuing ballet, dissonances, repetitions and multiple glissandos are employed with aplomb, and noble themes, disjointed, are wittily subverted. Rameau gives the nymph Clarine a tender air, 'Soleil, fuis de ces lieux', undiluted by parody and embellished by a weaving counter-melody played by the oboes and bassoons. Clarine's dignity contrasts with Platée's vulgarity. A sudden storm, unleashed by the north wind, forces an end to the festivities.

At the beginning of act two Mercury tells Cithéron that he has successfully tricked Juno into believing that Jupiter is about to marry Platée. Everything is set for the next phase of the plan. Accompanied by Momus, Jupiter (bass baritone) descends, ready to play his part. Platée looks up at a cloud and senses the presence of the god. 'Have I the courage to receive his homage?' she asks herself. The cloud parts and reveals Jupiter disguised as an ass. Platée is allowed a graceful vocal line for once, but her song is immediately interrupted by the ugly braying of the ass, played by *forte* strings. Platée thinks these animal noises are an eloquent expression of love. Jupiter metamorphoses into an owl, and Platée, unflummoxed, summons the birds of the forest to pay homage to the owl. Rameau's scoring here, for violins and flageolets, creates an inharmonious wall of sound. Jupiter disappears. Platée calls after him in vain. The basses rumble, and the nymph sings a tragic air: her despair is real, but undercut once more by the device of disjointed notes. An extended chord announces the third appearance of Jupiter, this time in human form and upon the earth, his hands releasing bolts of lightning. Platée is dazed into silence by the splendour and fury of his fiery entrance. The god, proving himself to be a skilful actor, plays upon the vanity of the star-struck nymph. 'Charmant objet de mes dignes amours,' he begins. Still tongue-tied, Platée lets out a wordless expletive – 'Ouffe'. Jupiter calls for the wedding festivities to begin.

The chorus's seemingly sweet words of homage to Platée – 'Qu'elle est aimable! Qu'elle est belle!' – are immediately followed by derisive laughter ('ah, ah, ah, ah'). The music of the overture is heard within a 'Symphonie extraordinaire'. It is Rameau's way of proclaiming the significance of the character he introduces next, La Folie (Folly). In the form of a glamorous soprano, a diva, La Folie – both demi-goddess and female fool, contrary and truth-telling[18] – gatecrashes the party and takes charge of the divertissement in a brilliantly theatrical manner. The fourth wall is shattered. In modern productions of *Platée* La Folie interacts with the musicians and the conductor, and we can only hope that Mlle Fel was this mischievous during the first performance in March 1745. On one level, Rameau uses La Folie to demonstrate his command of both the Italian and French styles and to parody them affectionately. La Folie steps forward, holding a lyre she has stolen from Apollo, the god of music, and sings the only extended show-stopping coloratura aria in the whole of Rameau's work, 'Aux langueurs d'Apollon Daphné se refusa', a comedic *tour de force* of vocal effects that exploits the whole range and character of the soprano voice; but, this Italianate gigue in 6/8 also manages to be extremely beautiful.[19] It possesses, in concentrated form, the duality of purpose that defines the work as a whole. La Folie is one of Rameau's most erotic creations, and her primary purpose is not to mock but to give pleasure. She relates the story of how Daphne rejected Apollo and was transformed into a tree by Eros, for 'Love is cruel when unrequited'. Next, she demonstrates her range by singing a tragic air in the French style, 'Aimables jeux suivez nos pas', that would cut very deep if placed in a different context. The melody reaches a height of beauty on the words 'si Zéphyr ne badinait pas, Flore lui serait moins fidèle'. There follows a slow dance, built on a single bass note that sounds like a groan. La Folie declares, 'I will finish with a stroke of genius, a masterpiece of harmony'. She instructs Momus, Mercury and Cithéron to follow her lead and the fugal quartet that follows – 'Hymen, Hymen, l'Amour t'appelle' – lives up to her boast. The chorus intervenes with the refrain 'Prépare à Jupiter une chaîne nouvelle, viens couronner sa nouvelle Junon', words that delight poor Platée, who ends this passage of sublime music with a single line: 'Hé, bon, bon, bon, bon'. The 'bon, bon, bon, bon' refrain is taken up by everyone and the act ends.

Act three begins with the arrival of furious Juno, seeking Jupiter and his would-be bride. She is a little early, so Mercury whisks her away. The festivities continue. Nymphs and satyrs dance to a chaconne as Platée, veiled, watches from a chariot drawn by frogs. Rameau calls the sequence a 'Symphonie de danse' and writes music that, although majestic, is a little too pompously so for one to miss the comic intention. Jupiter and Momus walk beside the chariot. Momus needs to delay the mock ceremony a little longer, so he masterminds several interruptions. First, he impersonates Eros, for the god is too busy to attend. Rameau composes exaggerated glissandos to express Platée's heart-dropping disappointment. Next, La Folie returns. She berates 'Eros' for failing to shoot his arrows and then summons the three Graces to dance a loure for Platée. Each interruption frustrates the nymph, and perhaps the audience, for the comic parodies of Eros and the Graces outstay their welcome. Finally, La Folie leads the company in the chorus 'Chantons Platée, égayons-nous, chantons le pouvoir de ses charmes'. Momus tells Jupiter that Juno is nearby: the wedding can begin. Jupiter takes Platée by the hand and starts to say his vows, slowly, listening out for Juno, who arrives a little late for comfort. She attacks her rival, tearing away her veil. 'Que je-vois! O ciel!' Jupiter grins at his wife: 'Vous voyez votre erreur.' Juno is relieved to discover that Jupiter has not betrayed her, but is only having some fun at her expense.

Everyone now turns on Platée, with Cithéron acting as the ringmaster and La Folie leading the charge. The chorus 'Chantons Platée, égayons-nous, chantons le pouvoir de ses charmes' is reprised, and Rameau relishes the irony. He orchestrates this scene of mob cruelty with all the mastery at his disposal, ensuring that Platée's animal cries of 'toi' and 'quoi' cut through the glorious vocal harmonies of the chorus. It would be possible, in performance, to make Platée sympathetic, but Rameau doesn't encourage it. Platée hasn't learned humility or self-awareness from her humiliation. She fights back, threatening retribution, revealing her true nature, and then scurries away into the swamp. Rameau ends his opera with three decisive chords, each separated by a rest.

The audience in the Grande Écurie on 31 March 1745 didn't know what to make of *Platée*, and the king was certainly unimpressed. 'The reaction was not strongly positive,' the duc de Luynes wrote in his journal, before going on to add that

> Rameau's music was found to be singular, and there were some likeable moments, but overall the divertissements were felt to be too long and too uniform. M. de Richelieu proposed to the king that the work should be repeated; he made the proposal three times but the king didn't respond. [...] Besides, the reaction to Wednesday's performance suggested that a second would fare no better. Curiosity had attracted a huge crowd, and we could hardly find a seat in the theatre.[20]

The work's importance would be recognised during the next decade, following its first staging by the Opéra in 1749. Even Rousseau made an exception for *Platée*, for it was neither a tragédie lyrique nor a ballet héroïque but a new type of opera that, for him, shared its aesthetics with the Italian works he loved. At its first performance, though, it was too modern and strange to be fully enjoyed or understood. There were no exact precedents for Rameau's *ballet bouffon*, even at the fair theatres, and the expression of humour and irony through wrong notes, misplaced accents, counter-rhythms and wide apart intervals had not previously been attempted on this scale. Then there was the issue of the opera's subject matter. Even before the Infanta had arrived in France stories concerning her unattractiveness had been widely circulated. There must have been many people in the wedding party, particularly on the Spanish side, who wondered whether the mock ceremony on stage was meant to be read as a grotesque parody of the royal wedding. In public decorum prevailed. The Spanish could not complain without revealing that they thought the Infanta was indeed ugly. People kept their thoughts on the matter to themselves, but the king's refusal to even respond to Richelieu's request for further performances may indicate that he was severely displeased. A man like Richelieu, of course, may have enjoyed the way the mockery in the play spilt out into the room, as long as the intent could not be proven. Rameau had composed the opera independently of the celebrations, so no connection was intended; but he was enough of a provocateur to enjoy the piquancy of coincidence. No blame was attached to Rameau, for that May the king granted him the title Compositeur de la Musique du Cabinet du Roi along with a royal pension of two hundred *livres*.

iii Rameau and Voltaire: Le Temple de la gloire

On 11 May 1745 the French army defeated the English at Fontenoy, a victory that allowed France to capture most of the Austrian Netherlands. The battle was much celebrated. In quick time Rameau composed *Les Fêtes de Polymnie*, his first work with the writer Louis de Cahusac, premiered at the Opéra on 12 October; and *Le Temple de la gloire*, with Voltaire, for Versailles on Richelieu's instructions (27 November). Voltaire, who was trying hard to succeed as a courtier, had gained extra favour by producing *Le Poème de Fontenoy*, a work of patriotism and royal sycophancy that was an instant bestseller.

On this, the last of their collaborations, and the only one to be presented before the Parisian public, Rameau and Voltaire worked without conflict. Richelieu must have asked Voltaire to tolerate Rameau's demands, for Voltaire told him, 'I will be [Rameau's] slave to prove to you that I am yours'.[21] Despite Voltaire's dislike for Rameau's manner and his contempt for Rameau's literary judgement, he never doubted his musical genius; and after *Le Temple de la gloire* was revived at the Opéra, that December, he wrote to Berger to declare that 'Rameau is so superior in his field, and his earnings so inferior to his talents, that it is right for him to receive all of the remuneration'.[22]

Voltaire decided to use the commission to make a serious point. His libretto contained the political message that for a ruler to be worthy of glory he must show clemency to the vanquished and work for the well-being of the people. As with *Samson*, he wanted to change the nature of the opera form, in this case opéra-ballet, by using it to address questions of moral philosophy:

> It was time to see if true courage, moderation and clemency following a victory, and the happiness of the people, were subjects as suited to moving music as the simple dialogues of love that were so often repeated, under different names, in every ballet.[23]

Each of the three acts centres on a conqueror. Bélus, who thinks only of war (act one), and Bacchus, who thinks only of pleasure (act two), are denied entry into the temple of glory. Only the Roman emperor Trajan (act three) is deemed worthy, for, in Voltaire's portrait, he is virtuous, just, merciful and more concerned with securing public happiness than achieving personal glory. Voltaire meant for the courtiers to substitute Louis XV for Trajan. And since few people believed that Voltaire was being serious, the libretto was easily interpreted, not as a tribute, but as a statement on how the king *should* rule.

Indeed, although Louis XV believed in the idea of France, as the great power, acting magnanimously (three years later, at the end of the war, he would give back all of France's gains in the Netherlands, a high-minded policy that his subjects would fail to understand), he did not like Voltaire's libretto: at the banquet that followed the premiere, he spoke to Rameau but ignored the writer.[24] An enquiring, suspicious personality, he may have wondered whether Voltaire while seeming to flatter him as Trajan was actually mocking him as Bacchus. He would not have appreciated Voltaire's presumption in telling him how to rule. Voltaire dared to say to the king as he passed: 'Is Trajan satisfied?' The courtiers present were shocked by Voltaire's disregard for court protocol.[25]

Rameau, responding to the seriousness of Voltaire's theme, created powerful music for *Le Temple de la gloire*. The first and final pages of the opera feature appropriate but subtle scoring for trumpets, piccolos, horns and timpani; in between the score is dominated by Rameau's richly sonorous writing for the strings. In the opening section of the overture, the trumpets soar above the vivacious scales and trills of the strings, flutes and horns to achieve an unexpected turn of melody. However, the two interior sections are in keeping with Rameau's approach throughout the opera: he makes less use of unexpected leaps and falls than in his other opéra-ballets, and doesn't acknowledge court taste by censoring his talent for ambivalence. The harmonies often edge towards dissonance.

Le Temple de la gloire was presented for a second time at Versailles early in December before its transfer to the Opéra. The *parterre* was not impressed, with one wit declaring that 'Rameau must have written the verses and Voltaire the music' and another that 'Voltaire is currently living in rue des Mauvaises Paroles [Bad Words] and Rameau in rue des Petits Chants [Little Songs]'.[26] When the piece returned to the Opéra's repertoire in the spring of 1746, Voltaire and Rameau made some major revisions. The three acts of the original version were bookended by a prologue and an epilogue. Now, to improve the structure of the work and to provide the public with an entertainment that was as much about love as politics, Voltaire and Rameau largely re-wrote the first act, *Bélus*, and subsumed the music of the epilogue into the third act, *Trajan*. Indeed, the female characters, created by Marie-Jeanne Chevalier[27] (Lydie and Plautine) and Marie Fel (Érigone and Glory), carried more weight in the revised work than the heroes, created by Chassé (Bélus), Poirier (Bacchus) and Jélyotte (Trajan). The changes were effective. The reviewer in the *Mercure de France* welcomed the new *Bélus*, writing that 'it is of a great beauty, and [...] worthy of the illustrious author of the poem', and he particularly admired the many orchestral passages by the 'inimitable' Rameau: 'There is nothing more enjoyable than the *musette* that turns into a chorus, the two gavottes in the form of tambourins and the two minuets.'[28] Overall, the new version of *Le Temple de la gloire* was a modest success. It is this version that I discuss below.

In the allegorical prologue, Apollo and the Heroes vanquish Envy and the demons, and Envy is chained to Glory's throne. Envy's chilling invocation 'Profonds abîmes du Ténare', a powerful monologue for the bass, was greatly admired during Rameau's lifetime: 'I have never heard sung *Profonds abîmes du Ténare, nuit, éternelle nuit*,' declares Diderot's fictional Rameau's nephew, 'without telling myself with sorrow: that is what you'll never do.'[29] As so often in Rameau's darkest airs, the strings combine with obbligato bassoons, and the underpinning chords played by the basses rumble ominously. Rapid glides punctuate the vocal line. The tone of the monologue continues in the dramatic 'Air for the Demons and Heroes', a courtly dance for the devil.

At the beginning of *Bélus*, Lydie, princess of Asia, sings a striking *da capo* aria, 'Muses, filles du ciel, la paix règne en vos fêtes', its contrasting sections vividly differentiated, and then expresses her sadness to her friend Arsine. Bélus has not only abandoned her but also the nobility that defined his character before he became a merciless conqueror, a hero unworthy of love. She seeks solace from the Muses, and then from the shepherds and shepherdesses who enter the grove of the Muses to the evocative accompaniment of a *musette en rondeau*. At the end of the dances a flourish on the timpani announces the arrival of Bélus and the warriors. The shepherds and shepherdesses respond by singing an irresistible chorus, 'Les éclairs embrasent les cieux'. The gods, unleashing bolts of lightning, have refused to let Bélus enter the temple of glory with the corpses of his enemies. Fortunately, in this 1746 version, he is beguiled by the singing of the shepherdesses and by Lydie into declaring that he will abandon war and rule by just laws.

Bacchus offers a marked contrast to *Bélus*, for its processionals, dances and choruses form one long divertissement. The dance sequences, for the strings alone, include a vibrant loure (scene one) and an air 'for the followers of Bacchus': they describe Bacchus's reign of pleasure in a style that is deliberately rustic. Rameau's decision to restrict his orchestral palate in this act is curious, but not regrettable, for it means that *Bacchus* has its own contrary style within his œuvre. A Bacchante leads the chorus, and the object of Bacchus's desire, Érigone, is quickly seduced. They sing a fine duet, 'Dans l'heureux cours de nos beaux jours'. Bacchus's attention turns to the temple of glory: 'Let us hasten to this solitary temple. Pleasure makes us the equal of the gods worshipped inside.' Bacchus takes the High Priest's decision to block his entry into the temple in his stride, for he has the whole world in which to export his life of pleasure.

It is in the third act, *Trajan*, that Voltaire and Rameau most fully present their serious theme by embedding it in a situation that has at least some dramatic interest. The action takes place in Armenia, where Trajan is fighting to quell a rebellion against Rome. Trajan's wife Plaudine, waiting for his return from battle, sings the monologue 'Reviens, divin Trajan, vainqueur doux et terrible', one of Rameau's most probing evocations of longing: the vocal line is accompanied by the violins and flutes in a swooning harmonic progression of rises and falls. Trajan returns, but only for a short respite: the decisive battle is about to begin. Trajan's dialogue with his wife is tragic in tone. There is an exquisite moment of pure simplicity, when Plaudine, accompanied by a melodic phrase on the harpsichord, sings the words: 'Quel mot funeste? Un moment! Vous, O ciel! Un seul moment me reste [What fatal words do I hear? A single moment! You, O Heaven! Only a single moment is given to me].' Rameau ignores Voltaire's exclamation marks, and transforms Plaudine's cries into a moment of private grief. Plaudine wants to follow Trajan into battle, and rebukes him bitterly when he refuses to allow her. After he has departed Plaudine summons the Priests of Mars and the Priestesses of Venus to watch over him. In their double chorus, the men and women sing separately and then together. The ballet includes two attractive gavottes; the second's succession of swirling phrases suggests a choreography of fast pirouettes.

The battle over, Trajan enters with the conquered kings in chains; but immediately, in the monologue 'Rois, qui redoutez ma vengeance', he grants them clemency. The chorus 'O grandeur! O clémence!', shared by the kings and the Roman people, is given an intense spirituality by Rameau. Glory descends from the skies to reward Trajan for his deeds and his magnanimity. Voltaire now defies expectations and makes a final point: Trajan asks the gods to transform the Temple of Glory into a Temple of Happiness for the benefit of the people.

In these final pages of the opera, Rameau's organisational sense is at its most elegant. A mysterious *passacaille*, closely related to the great chaconne that closes *Dardanus*, is divided in two by a chorus and an *ariette* sung by Glory to wonderful effect. The flutes depict birdsong while Trajan sings 'Make the air resonate with harmonious sounds'. (The point is made more subtly here than in the 1745 work, which ended with a long divertissement on the theme of the Temple of Happiness.) The piccolos and the horns rejoin the scoring, reminding us of the overture and giving a sense that the music has come full circle.

Voltaire's libretto is of historical importance as an artistic statement that dared to address, provocatively, the king and his ministers. Voltaire stuck to his principles at a time when he was seeking election to the Académie française and knew that a cabal was just as determined to block his entry into the academy as the High Priest in his libretto was determined to block Bacchus's entry into the Temple of Glory. Rameau, with the tastes of the Parisian public in mind, was surely the instigator of changes that made the piece less polemical and more lyrical. In setting Voltaire's words he composed gravely beautiful music. One can only marvel that Rameau was able to create in quick succession two works as different in tone as *Platée* and *Le Temple de la gloire*.

iv Rousseau Enters the Scene

In the 1740s, Jean-Jacques Rousseau had yet to make his name as a thinker and writer, but was known in the Paris salons and cafés as someone eager to succeed. If society paid any attention to Rousseau at this time, it did so with a mocking look – who is this gatecrasher? – or a derisory shrug. His provincial origins (he was from Geneva, the son of a watchmaker) would not have mattered a great deal had he possessed the skills to be amusing in company and to parry the verbal thrusts of those keen to test him. Rousseau's supreme intelligence didn't lend itself to verbal wit; he was a formidable chess player at the café de la Régence, as Diderot would discover, but an awkward conversationalist at the supper table. Unable to afford fine clothes, Rousseau was often unkempt and unshaven. He would later turn his commonplace appearance into a badge of honour, but at this point in his life it was a matter of acute embarrassment, made much worse by the fact that he was the victim of a urinary complaint that made him painfully incontinent. He would remain, not least in his own mind, an outsider.

At this time Rousseau was pursuing music above all other disciplines. When he first arrived in Paris in 1741, with a letter of introduction to Louis-Bertrand Castel, his great hope was to achieve recognition for his new system of musical notation. The members of the Académie Royale des Sciences were polite but unenthusiastic: they were unable to judge its merits either way. Rousseau managed to get to show his notation to Rameau, probably at La Pouplinière's, and it was Rameau who pointed out its fatal flaw.[30] The main requirement of musical notation is to allow complicated music to be read by the musician at speed; Rousseau's system completely lacked this essential readability and was therefore useless in the real world.

Rousseau abandoned the notation, but continued to believe in his future as a composer. He was self-taught, and knew little about practical music-making, but his self-belief was unassailable. Most of Rousseau's knowledge of composition had come from a study of Rameau's theoretical works, and he saw himself as the great master's heir. In only a few months he composed an opera called *Les Muses galantes*. Rousseau wrote the words as well as the music, but persuaded the young musician Philidor (fast becoming a famous chess player[31]) to take on some of the scoring. It wasn't a good sign that Rousseau didn't acknowledge the importance of orchestration as a means of adding harmony, creating style and defining an individual voice.

Rousseau took the opera to La Pouplinière. He craved Rameau's endorsement, and expected it, believing that Rameau would be generous to a disciple. Rameau was unsympathetic and dismissive from the start, unwilling to even look at a score written by an amateur. La Pouplinière persuaded Rameau to attend a performance of extracts, which he arranged. According to Rousseau, who left an account of the episode in his *Confessions*, Rameau, 'grumbling all the while and repeating endlessly that he could not wait to hear the sort of piece a man composed who had not been born into the profession but had learnt his music all by himself', gave a critical commentary of the opera during the performance in front of the invited audience:

> The extravagant praise with which Rameau greeted the overture was clearly meant to imply that it could not have been written by me; thereafter he did not let a single movement go by without displaying signs of impatience; until during one air for counter-tenor, whose melody was virile and sonorous while its accompaniment was very brilliant, he could contain himself no longer, but turned on me with a brutality that scandalised everybody, declaring that part of what he had just heard was the work of a consummate artist and the rest that of an ignoramus who clearly knew nothing about music; and it is true that my work, unequal and careless of the rules, was at times sublime and at times very flat, as must surely be that of anyone whose flights are inspired by genius alone, unsustained by a knowledge of technique.[32]

If this passage reveals Rousseau's egotism and vulnerability, it also portrays Rameau convincingly. It was Rameau's implied accusation that the opera's best moments had been stolen from someone else that made Rousseau understandably bitter, along with his belief that he had been deliberately mocked and humiliated. On the last point, Rousseau came to believe that even his closest friends were against him; on the first, the accomplished Philidor may have been responsible for giving the sections he scored a professional polish. Rameau's view, expressed later in print,[33] was that Rousseau succeeded when presenting melodic airs in the Italian style; but failed when attempting to write the more complicated vocal lines and harmonies of the French style. Rameau would have been fairer if he'd accused Rousseau of imitating rather than stealing. When Rousseau came to accept the basic truth of Rameau's judgement, he blamed the French style of music and became wholly Italian.

The powerful Richelieu wanted to discover whether the novice composer was worth employing. He ordered a try-out performance of the complete opera with full orchestra and chorus conducted by Francœur at the home of the Intendant des Menus-Plaisirs du Roi,

Michel de Bonneval. Rousseau believed that Richelieu was a genuine admirer of his music, but was talked out of this admiration by Thérèse:

> M. le Duc exclaimed and applauded throughout. [...] Mme de la Poplinière, who was present, said not a word. Rameau, although invited, had chosen not to come. The next day Mme de la Poplinière, who was at her toilette, received me coldly, affected to disparage my work, and said that although M. de Richelieu had at first been dazzled by its rather showy brilliance, he had soon got over this.[34]

Richelieu wasn't convinced by *Les Muses galantes* and decided not to select it for performance at Versailles. Instead, he commissioned Rousseau to adapt Voltaire and Rameau's *Princesse de Navarre* into an acte de ballet for the court called *Les Fêtes de Ramire*. Voltaire and Rameau agreed to this, having no desire to do the legwork themselves. Voltaire, in his usual style, wrote a flattering letter to Rousseau, thanking him for undertaking the tedious task of adapting such mediocre material. Rousseau expected rewards to follow, only to find that his status on the project was that of a lackey. Following a rehearsal, he was told that some sections needed more work, and that he would have to consult Rameau.

It is difficult to view Rousseau's conviction that Rameau was jealous of his talent, and determined, through Thérèse, to wreck his chances, as anything other than paranoia. Why would Rameau feel threatened by a young composer of Rousseau's ability? Rousseau became ill and didn't leave his house for six weeks, during which time, in December 1745, the piece was performed at Versailles under Voltaire's name only, Rameau having declined to be associated with it.

The episode would have deep consequences. During the *querelle des bouffons* of the 1750s, Rousseau, emerging as a figure of influence, would position himself as one of Rameau's most powerful enemies. Rameau, tragically, devoted much of his time to defending his position against Rousseau and other members of a younger generation who insisted that the tunefulness and naturalness of Italian opera had made French opera redundant. This was a political as much as a cultural quarrel.

v Rameau's Librettist: Louis de Cahusac

During the last years of the 1740s, Rameau continued to create work for Versailles, but also renewed his interest in tragedy and the public stage of the Opéra. For the first time in his career he formed a partnership with a librettist that would last, Louis de Cahusac.[35]

Cahusac was born in Montauban in Languedoc in 1706. He followed his father into the legal profession, studying in Toulouse and working for some years back in Montauban before making the long journey to Paris to try his luck as a writer. His first tragedy, *Pharamond*, presented at the Comédie-Française in 1736, was admired, repeated at Versailles and parodied at the Théâtre Italien. His second tragedy, *Le Comte de Warwick* (1742), was mocked at its premiere. Cahusac turned things around with his comédie-ballet *L'Algérien, ou Les Muses comediennes*, written to celebrate the king's recovery from grave illness during the 1744 campaign. A reviewer in the *Mercure de France* wrote: 'This comedy does not suffer from the haste of its composition, either in its style, the elegance of its verses or in the delicacy of its homage to the king and the nation. The author has met the expectations of his early work.'[36]

According to the 19th century author of a biographical essay on Cahusac, Rameau saw and admired *L'Algérien*.[37] A police file on Cahusac, kept by Joseph d'Hémery, the official who monitored the book trade, recorded that he was 'very intimate' with La Pouplinière,[38] so it is likely that the financier brought the two men together. In 1745 Cahusac was thirty-nine, more than twenty years younger than Rameau. Charles Collé, writing in his journal, dismissed Cahusac as Rameau's 'valet de chambre'.[39] This was the prevailing opinion of people hostile to Rameau, Cahusac or both. It was wide of the mark. Rameau and Cahusac's partnership was mutually beneficial. Cahusac was able to tolerate Rameau's demands; and Rameau admired Cahusac's writing. The younger man brought new slants and new creativity to familiar forms. Cahusac was passionate about opera and dance and a leading authority on many aspects of the lyric arts.

D'Hémery's description of Cahusac – 'small, blond and always run down'[40] – was not flattering, and yet he had the charisma to attract star actresses and singers. His relationship with Marie Fel provoked much jealousy. It would seem that Cahusac had a vulnerable nature. He was ill-equipped to deal with the spite of his rivals or the jibes of his critics. The letters of Cahusac's friend Mme de Graffigny to Devaux provide a fascinating portrait of this enigmatic figure. Following *Pharamond*, Cahusac enjoyed some influence at the Comédie-Française. Matters were complicated, though, by his habit of becoming involved with more than one of the Comédie's actresses at the same time. The celebrated star Mlle Gaussin, with whom he was having an affair, was outraged when he became infatuated with the fourteen-year-old ingénue Mélanie Laballe, who was protected by the duc d'Aumont (Premier gentilhomme de la Chambre du Roi). The scandal ended Cahusac's hope of writing plays for the Comédie and made him an isolated figure. Mme de Graffigny, who had hoped to use Cahusac to persuade the actors to stage a play written by Devaux, wrote about him with a mixture of distaste and pity. At the time of the failure of *Warwick*, Cahusac was living in the house of the comte de Saint-Florentin and working as his secretary, but his moods and habit of answering back would wreck this arrangement. Cahusac had collapsed emotionally during supper with Mme de Graffigny and Saint-Florentin's mistress, at the latter's home. The two women took him to task for arrogance, smugness and rudeness and then attempted to console him. 'Nothing brought him back, the scene lasted more than two hours,' Mme de Graffigny told Devaux. When Mme de Graffigny got up to leave, Cahusac latched on to her.

> It seemed that I was his refuge, for he was like a frightened child clinging to his mother: I have rarely seen a more pathetic sight. He seemed to be afraid to be alone in his sedan chair. Finally, I took him home in my carriage. I told him that his behaviour was ugly, rough, surly, and without charm; that it was necessary to dress him up in pretty clothes. He played the cynic; I played the philosopher of the world; he was very harsh; I was very calm. I gave him lessons in politeness which, although expressed in a witty tone, should be very useful to him if he takes them on board, but I doubt he will. [...] Here is where I am with Jaco [Cahusac]. As long as I pity him, I will overcome my revulsion, but I doubt that I will ever be able to love him. Even his face is rough and shocking without having any-

thing extraordinary about it. [...] Men are strange machines.[41]

Like many of the men of literary Paris, Cahusac wrote erotic fiction on the side (the novel *Grigri*, published in 1749). He was also an important contributor to Diderot and d'Alembert's *Encyclopédie*, writing dozens of entries on ballet and dance and other aspects of the lyric and fine arts, including 'Comédie-ballet', 'Décoration', 'Divertissement', 'Entrée', and 'Fête'. His interest in dance led him to publish an important study of the art, *La Danse ancienne et moderne, ou Traité historique de la danse* (1754). Cahusac was dismissive of the notion that ballet should merely be an interlude, an exercise in technique for its own sake. He believed in *ballet figuré*, or *danse d'action*, expressive choreography, utilising gesture and mime, which advanced narrative. This chimed with Rameau's own thinking and preferences.

Cahusac's inventive mind was better employed in the opera house than elsewhere. Creating a theatre of frivolous pleasure was a serious business, and Cahusac took it seriously; but his writing had a lightness of touch, an elegance that elevated the genre, as well as a dramatic intelligence and coherence that Rameau found particularly attractive. Emmanuel Soleville made a connection between the imaginative world of Cahusac and Rameau's opéra-ballets and the art of Boucher[42] and Lancret ('if the figures in their paintings came to life they would speak Cahusac's verses'), and went on to write: 'Don't forget that these literary manners were then in all their novelty; let us remember the popularity they enjoyed in a voluptuous and frivolous society, and we will understand why Cahusac was attracted to this genre of literature, and why Rameau, in turn, found in him a poet who was productive and flexible.'[43] Cahusac was a far more serious writer than the above may suggest, motivated by radical ideas as well as by aesthetics, and using his fantastical stories to express a moral code.

Rameau and Cahusac's first collaboration, *Les Fêtes de Polymnie*, dedicated to the king in celebration of Fontenoy, was a moderate success at the Opéra in October 1745. An opéra-ballet of the ballet héroïque kind, containing both mythological and supernatural stories, it begins with an allegorical prologue in which the Arts and Muses honour the victorious Louis XV by erecting his statue, and in which Polymnie, the muse of poetry, announces the three *fêtes* that follow. They are connected by the theme of the transforming power of love. In the first, *La Fable*, Alcide courts Hébé; in the second, *L'Histoire*, King Séleucus of Syria hands over his betrothed, Stratonice, to his love-sick son Anthiocus; and in the third, *La Féerie*, set in a fantasy version of the Orient, Argélie's love for Zimès breaks the evil spell of the fairy Alcine. *Les Fêtes de Polymnie* was Rameau's fourth opera of 1745, following *La Princesse de Navarre*, *Platée* and *La Temple de la gloire*, but there was no falling away of quality. The slow opening of the overture, with its hollow, stacked harmonies, must have sounded strikingly original in 1745; it is followed by a fast section of equal audacity. The reviewer in the *Mercure de France* made special mention of the overture – 'The adagio is of the grandest harmony and the following presto loses nothing in comparison' – and declared that Rameau's ability to create different beginnings for all his operas was 'the most certain sign of his genius and inexhaustible imagination'.[44]

Mme de Graffigny, who attended rehearsals, praised both the score and the words. Marie Fel, playing Argélie, had just returned to work after a very serious illness and was noticeably vulnerable. Mme de Graffigny was moved to tears when Rameau, who had been scolding many of the actresses, complimented Marie Fel:

> My poor little Fel was still very weak, but a gallant remark from Rameau revived her. He was seated in the parterre, facing the stage. My little nightingale sang the line 'Est-ce assez pour charmer d'avoir un cœur tendre et sincere?' ['To charm is it not enough to have a sincere and tender heart?'] and Rameau, crying out, told her, 'To charm, you just have to sing'. Everyone then clapped their hands for a quarter of an hour.[45]

Rameau and Cahusac's next piece, *Les Fêtes de l'Hymen et de l'Amour*, was premiered at the Grande Écurie, Versailles, during the festival marking the wedding of the dauphin to Maria Josepha of Saxony, on 15 March 1747. Cahusac wrote the text during the previous year. In May 1746 he recited extracts to Mme de Graffigny. She found the words 'very pretty' but noticed that most of the lines had been crossed out in the manuscript, for Cahusac had 'erased everything that Rameau did not want, which in truth was almost everything'⁴⁶ – a perceptive observation that adds to our understanding of Rameau as the controlling master of the men who wrote his verses.

Marie Fel by Maurice Quentin de La Tour.
Musée Antoine-Lécuyer, Saint-Quentin.

The premiere was Rameau's greatest night at court. Such was the demand for places that many important people found themselves shut out; and those who got in were crushed together in the narrow confines of the theatre. Thankfully, the performance was enough of a success to justify the fuss. The duc de Luynes recorded that

> Rameau's music, in general, has many supporters, and we must admit that it is filled with harmony. Lovers of Lully find Rameau to be sometimes strange, and consider several of his works to be in the Italian style: this is the judgement of critics of his previous works. However, one has to avow that he is one of the greatest musicians we have. The opera presented last Wednesday was judged following these conflicting views. All the connoisseurs, and Rameau himself, agreed that the overture is

poor, and that he should compose another. Elsewhere, there are some admirable sequences of music, a *musette*, and a chorus that achieves a very beautiful effect. The king seemed happy; he stopped to talk to Rameau, and said that he would perhaps see the piece again, after Easter. He asked Rameau if he had any other operas ready.[47]

The popular appeal of the work was confirmed when it was staged at the Opéra in November 1748. Collé wrote that the opera was a 'great success', adding: 'Nothing better proves the excellence of Rameau's music than the patience of the public for such distasteful words, devoid of substance and detail; even the slightest criticism would honour them too much.'[48] The first and final entrées stayed in the repertoire for many years.

Cahusac took the stories that make up this ballet héroïque from Egyptian mythology. The theme of each of the three entrées is marriage. In the first, a stranger called Osiris wins the hand of the Amazonian queen Orthésie against the wishes of the queen's subject Myrrine. In the second, during a festival by the Nile, the priests plan to sacrifice a virgin called Memphis, but the water god Canope, who has been wooing Memphis in disguise, intervenes by causing the river to flood. Riding in a chariot drawn by crocodiles, Canope reveals his true identity and takes Memphis as his bride. In the last entrée, the nymph Orie loves Aruéris, the god of the arts, and becomes his wife by winning a singing competition held in honour of his mother Isis.

There are seven integrated ballets in *Les Fêtes de l'Hymen et de l'Amour*. Cahusac devised elaborate sequences in which a group of dancers performed movements that complimented, or commented upon, the action of the solo singers. Along with ballet, Cahusac gave new life to the *merveilleux* in French opera. He valued grand stage effects and the machines that created them, but wanted spectacle to flow naturally from the drama. The overflowing of the Nile during the second entrée of *Les Fêtes de l'Hymen et de l'Amour* was one such moment.

The music is splendid throughout. If the recitatives and airs rarely reach the heights achieved by Rameau in his greatest works, the instrumental passages, as typified by the beguiling beginning of the prologue, are the work of a composer who wants his melodies to be both intimate and elusive, forever just out of reach of the casual listener. Wistful is not quite the right word for it is too commonplace.

vi Rameau, Cahusac and Freemasonry

Almost a year separated *Les Fêtes de l'Hymen et de l'Amour* from Rameau and Cahusac's next creation, *Zaïs*, a pastorale héroïque in four acts and a prologue that was premiered at the Opéra on 29 February 1748.

Zaïs wasn't written to fulfil a commission, and it seems that Cahusac invented the fanciful story. The genie Zaïs, disguised as a shepherd, is in love with the shepherdess Zélidie. With the help of his friend Cindor, he tests Zélidie's fidelity. Zélidie, distressed by such cruelty when she learns the truth, proves herself to be worthy, and the king of the Genii makes her immortal so that the two can marry. Was Cahusac thinking about Marie Fel, and fantasising about testing her fidelity, when he created Zélidie, thus drawing a parallel that she would have understood? Marie Fel created the role. Placed under constant pressure, the touchingly vulnerable Zélidie sings the desolate air, 'Coulez mes pleurs' (act three, scene two).

Initiation by trial was one of the central concepts of the Freemasons. In *Zaïs*, Rameau and Cahusac were working on two levels, the second only understood by members of the Brotherhood. Masonic ideas and symbolism can be found not only in the text but also, remarkably, in the music: the overture, a mini tone poem, describes the creation of the world – the emergence out of chaos of the four elements, another Masonic obsession. The hesitant, fragmentary opening gives way to swirling violin and flute runs, the basses and bassoons pulsing beneath. Writing about the work's reception, the abbé Raynal makes special mention of the overture, and from his words we get an insight into its impact:

> The music of this ballet has its critics and its partisans. In general, the airs for violin are very good, and superior to the airs for voices. The overture made people think that they were at the funeral of an *officer suisse*. A thud on a kettledrum covered with

gauze announces the unravelling of chaos. However, it should be admitted that the musician's idea is most natural. This is not a moment for the other instruments; it is only through the succeeding development that Nature will be born and animated. We hear a faint shudder – the zephyr; then the flutes resonate – the warbling of birds; finally, the violins join the flutes, and by various modulations, sometimes vivacious, sometimes slow, we are made to imagine a torrent flowing noisily and a stream flowing slowly, representing the separation of the elements of air and fire. Then, all of a sudden, through more daring sounds, the composer transports us into the air. Here he creates sounds that evoke wind and thunder, and, with a voluptuous harmony, full of majesty, he inspires in us the pleasure of love, and calms our senses by announcing the presence of the gods.[49]

For a time after his arrival in Paris, Cahusac had been secretary to Louis de Bourbon, comte de Clermont, the Grand Master of all the lodges of France. Louis de Bourbon was a prince of the blood. He was a churchman, appointed abbé de Saint-Germain-des-Prés in 1737, but also one of the king's military commanders. Marie Camargo was among his mistresses.

Freemasonry was a new phenomenon in France having been imported into the country by Britons (including Jacobite exiles) in the 1720s. The first grand masters in France were British aristocrats, but the duc d'Antin became master in 1738, followed by Louis de Bourbon in 1743. Freemasonry attracted men from many levels of society – aristocrats, writers, members of the professions, artisans, soldiers, and so on. The lieutenant of police, Hérault, alerted his political masters to the existence of this secret society made up of individuals from all the significant sections of society, as well as Englishmen and other foreigners. Police reports reveal that a dancer at the Opéra, one Mademoiselle Carton, informed on the Freemasons, having been told their secrets by a lover. For a time, innkeepers were forbidden from hosting meetings, and a series of raids took place; but police action was restrained by Hérault's standards, curtailed because the Freemasons were led, and protected, by powerful men like Louis de Bourbon. Louis de Bourbon was able to shield Freemasonry from the political instincts of Fleury to suppress any organisation that attempted to exist outside the control of the state or the church. On reflection, Fleury and his successors decided that Freemasonry was not threatening enough to risk the divisions that could have resulted from its suppression. In 1738 the Paris *Parlement* refused to ratify a papal bull designed to outlaw Freemasonry throughout catholic Europe.

In 1732, the first Paris lodge, located at the sign of the 'Louis d'argent' in Saint-Germain, was officially recognised by the Grand Lodge of England. In the latter's records, we find two different addresses listed for the Paris lodge, the rue des Boucheries and the rue de Bussy (Buci).[50] A 19th century French history of Freemasonry gives the meeting-place as the inn kept by Landelle in the rue de Buci;[51] and a news item in the *St James's Evening News* for 1735 connects Montesquieu and others with a lodge in the rue de Bussy.[52]

If we cannot state definitively that Rameau was a Freemason, the evidence is persuasive. The société des dîners du Caveau used Landelle's establishment. This prompts the thought that Rameau may have had a connection to the Freemasons as early as 1732. Two of Rameau's operas of the 1730s, *Castor et Pollux* and *Dardanus*, contain symbolism that can be interpreted as Masonic. The overture to *Zaïs* clinches the argument.

It wasn't necessary to be a Freemason to understand that *Zaïs* was an allegorical work. Zélidie remains faithful even after Zaïs, disguised as Cindor, tells her that Zaïs is pursuing another woman. When Zaïs finally confesses that it has all been a cruel game, and reveals his true identity, Zélidie is so distressed that he realises that his love for her is the only thing that matters: he renounces his power and his immortality, and the lovers, transported to a barren desert, discover that they only need one another. Zaïs has been educated by the goodness and compassion of a shepherdess into believing that love and virtue must reign over power and selfishness if one is to lead a good life. The fact that a conventional ending was needed to provide a reason for a divertissement that contains some of Rameau's most affecting dance music – two airs and a beautiful *musette en rondeau* flushed with amorous tenderness – does not negate the work's didactic purpose.

Cahusac may have been inspired by one of the most popular books of the time, Richardson's *Pamela, or Virtue Rewarded*, published in French in 1742 and adapted for the stage of the Théâtre

Italien a year later – David Charlton makes the connection in his study *Opera in the Age of Rousseau*.[53] Richardson's virtuous maidservant resists the sexual advances of her master. He forces her to endure a number of trials but eventually grows to love her for her goodness and risks his social position by taking her as his wife. Despite its supernatural setting, *Zaïs* was a work of the 1740s that made contemporary points about good governance – Rameau had already addressed this theme more directly with Voltaire in *Le Temple de la gloire* – and the treatment of women. Cahusac and Rameau would further develop these themes in two greater works, *Zoroastre* and *Les Boréades*.

vii Pygmalion

During the final stages of the War of the Austrian Succession Rameau composed the one-act ballet, *Pygmalion*, premiered at the Opéra on 27 August 1748. The acte de ballet genre had been conceived at court to satisfy Mme de Pompadour's preference for short, self-contained ballets. An entrée from an opéra-ballet could fulfil this function, and did, but an acte de ballet was thought to be better because it was a brand new mini opera. *Pygmalion* – the first piece of this kind to be created for the Opéra – was the greatest work produced by Rameau during the very prolific period between *Platée* in 1745 and *Zoroastre* in 1749.

According to a report in the *Mercure de France*, the management of the Opéra needed a work at very short notice and turned to Rameau, who delivered *Pygmalion* in less than eight days.[54] This reads like journalistic exaggeration, but, given Rameau's ability to work at speed and his habit of drawing upon a store of already written music, it is feasible. The ballet was adapted from Houdar de la Motte's libretto for *La Sculpture*, one of the entrées of Michel de la Barre's ballet *Le Triomphe des arts* (1700), itself inspired by Ovid's *Metamorphoses*. The practice of adapting lines from an existing libretto had always been considered unacceptable in the official theatres, so its use here could indicate that the work was written under pressure.

The writer tasked by Rameau to adapt *La Sculpture* was Ballot de Sauvot (or Sovot), the brother of his lawyer. Ballot de Sauvot was a member of the Paris *Parlement* and the author of *Éloge de M. Lancret, peintre du roi* (1743). Once again Rameau had selected a keen amateur from within La Pouplinière's circle at Passy, a fact that was commented upon once the name of the librettist became known. The story was ideal for Rameau's purposes because music and dancing were essential elements rather than, as was so often the case, decorative add-ons. The libretto was short, well-proportioned and written with the economy of expression, if not the elegance, of a poem. The sculptor Pygmalion shares his studio with one of his creations, the statue of a beautiful woman. He has fallen in love with the statue, to the despair of the rejected Céphise, who understandably believes him to be mad. Venus rewards Pygmalion's expression of true love by bringing the statue to life. Cupid calls on the Graces to teach the statue how to move and dance, and the people celebrate love's victory.

Rameau provided the elegance. All the music stems from the charismatic overture, either directly or indirectly, for Rameau integrates his ideas like never before. The overture begins with a noble theme, played *moderato*; in the vivacious main section, as d'Alembert was first to point out, repeated notes wittily depict the blows of the sculptor's chisel as he creates the statue;[55] and falling intervals the fatal *coup de foudre*. Pygmalion's monologue 'Fatal Amour, cruel vainqueur' is as profound as any in the tragedies. The flutes play the initial note and are prominent throughout. A short but satisfying recitative for Pygmalion and Céphise follows, unaccompanied until Céphise's final outburst. The music of Pygmalion's opening monologue momentarily returns. In scene three, ravishing sounds – extended chords, the separate notes entering one after another to create the harmony – signal the moment the statue comes to life. In scene four, the dances are beautifully differentiated. The minuet repeats the overture's opening melody. The lovely *pantomime*, a variation on the overture, precedes Pygmalion's air 'Règne, Amour, fais briller tes flammes'. Pygmalion's joy is conveyed by the held note on the opening word 'Règne' and by coloratura runs on the word 'lance'; underneath, the strings play circular arpeggios to propel the music forward in a witty gallop.

Pygmalion was well-received despite the feeling that the libretto was a travesty of Houdar de la Motte's original. It was performed alongside a number of different entrées during the run. A review in the *Mercure de France* reveals that on 10 September 1748 the Opéra presented three acts from old ballets: the first entrée, *Soirées d'été*, was taken from Pellegrin and Montéclair's *Les Fêtes de l'été*; and the second, *L'Estime*, from Fuzelier and Bourgeois's *Les Amours déguisés*. The third entrée was an 'event': a re-working of Houdar de la Motte's *La Sculpture* by an unknown author with new music by Rameau. The reviewer felt aggrieved for M. de La Motte, but praised the music:

> The music is new and by M. Rameau, destined to reform the harmonic style, but we doubt that the public will agree that the corrector of M. de la Motte's words shares his vocation. The author of the words has not been revealed, since many people will find that M. de la Motte's Pygmalion has been more mutilated than the Pasquino of Rome. The divertissement is bright and varied, and the sculptor and his charming statue are inimitable.[56]

In the December issue of the *Mercure*, we find *Vers à M. Rameau, sur son Ballet de Pigmalion*, signed C.G.B., in which the poet writes that learned Rameau's 'divine harmony charms our senses and beguiles our minds to the extent that we are not surprised it brings marble to life'.[57]

When the opera was revived three years later it was a huge success. It delighted and moved people in equal measure, and was admired by d'Alembert and the other young intellectuals of Paris because of its perfection of tone and scale – it contained everything that was needed and nothing that wasn't. Friedrich Melchior Grimm's *Lettre sur Omphale* is as much a panegyric to Rameau's *Pygmalion* as a critique of Destouches's *Omphale*. This friend of Rousseau would shortly join him in his campaign against Rameau, but in January 1752 he wrote that the composer of *Pygmalion*

> must have been lit by the divine fire we call genius. […] What pattern in the design, what harmony in the orchestration, what simplicity, what wit in the bass continuo, what nobility in the way the music progresses, what expressiveness in the airs – it is all so touching and true it lifts me out of myself.[58]

Whether Rameau cried for joy, as Collé states in his journal, repeating gossip, or not, he certainly had cause to be very pleased with the reception of *Pygmalion*.

viii The End of the War

On 18 October 1748 eight years of war finally came to an end with the signing of the Treaty of Aix-la-Chapelle. If we see the War of the Austrian Succession as part of a century-long struggle for dominance between England and France, the treaty reinstated the *status quo* and only delayed further warfare. England and France handed back to each other their principal gains beyond Europe (Louisbourg; Madras). In Europe, France withdrew from the Austrian Netherlands, and Austria recognised France's ally Prussia's conquest of Silesia. In drawing up the treaty, the rulers of England and France took a pragmatic decision that made political sense (both countries urgently required a respite from the financial burden of conducting the war, plus they were thinking of the bigger picture as they jostled for position globally); but to the French public the terms looked at best unnecessarily magnanimous and at worse inexplicably foolish.

The perception throughout French society was that the *grande nation* had been out-played by English diplomacy. France had won the decisive battles on the ground but had been out-manoeuvred at the peace table. In the crucial areas of trade and global influence the English had the advantages. Following years of hardship caused by war taxation, the French people had been denied the emotional compensation of a triumphant outcome. Under the terms of the treaty, France agreed to abandon Charles Edward Stuart (Bonnie Prince Charlie). Charles Edward Stuart was the 18th century equivalent of a celebrity, one of those rare figures of the 1740s who had entered the consciousness of the common people. His summary expulsion – he was arrested by soldiers as he tried to enter the Opéra – provoked feelings of national shame and dishonour. Public anger was compounded when instead of abandoning the war tax, as protocol dictated, the king maintained it. As far as the king was concerned, there was no such thing as public opinion. It is no coincidence that the aftermath of the treaty coincided with an increase in risk-taking when it came to the clandestine expression of discontent and the mocking of authority. In Paris, the scornful refrain 'bête comme la paix' ('stupid as the peace') was heard everywhere, along with a plethora of vulgar street songs. The regime filled its prisons with many unfortunates who were caught, or suspected of, writing, publishing or speaking critical words.

The more bitter public opinion became, the more it targeted the king's official mistress, Mme de Pompadour, rather than, directly, the king himself. The authors of songs and pamphlets produced a torrent of cheap but effective misogyny, punning on Mme de Pompadour's unfortunate surname (Poisson/Fish) and portraying her, predictably, as sluttish, dirty and mean. One of the more perceptive poets accused her of subjecting the court to endless operas in which she sang like a goat.[59] This was neither a frivolous nor a random line of attack. Those ministers who despised and resented Mme de Pompadour because of her influence on the king believed that she used opera and performing as a means of demonstrating her power over them. The king ordered the building of the private theatre she wanted at Versailles, the *Théâtre des Petits Appartements*, situated on the *Grand Escalier des Ambassadeurs*, and instructed his ministers to attend the performances. Politics aside, Mme de Pompadour was passionate about the stage and her creation of a theatre company at court was not only an act of personal vanity. All the leading roles were played by courtiers, but the orchestra was led by professionals: Mondonville was the first violinist and Jélyotte played the cello. Mme de Pompadour had the whole of artistic Paris at her disposal, and commanded Rameau to write an opéra-ballet in celebration of the peace treaty. It was around this time, in the autumn of 1748, that La Pouplinière discovered Thérèse's affair with Richelieu and exiled her from his life.

Rameau threw himself into his work at court and at the Opéra as if to escape the trauma of these events. His piece for Mme de Pompadour, *Les Surprises de l'Amour*, consisted of an allegorical prologue, *Le retour d'Astrée*, and two entrées, *La Lyre enchantée* and *Adonis*. The commission reunited Rameau with Mme de Pompadour's friend Gentil-Bernard, the librettist of *Castor et Pollux*. Mme de Pompadour took a leading soprano part in each of the two acts

(Vénus and Uranie). Although Rameau was used to working with amateur singers and dancers at La Pouplinière's, it appears that he tolerated rather than embraced the assignment. The music is, for Rameau, ordinary.[60]

Rameau was also commissioned by the directors of the Opéra to write a celebratory ballet for the Opéra, and, in partnership with Cahusac, created a pastorale héroïque in three acts and a prologue called *Naïs, ou Le Triomphe de la paix*. By the time the work was premiered, on 22 April 1749, public anger over the peace terms was at its height and the subtitle was changed to *L'Opéra pour la paix*.

Cahusac and Rameau's desire to make the form serve the story is more apparent in *Naïs* than in their earlier collaborations. The stormy overture leads directly into the opening chorus; and the divertissements are designed to be integral to the story. Since the story is vacuous little is gained dramatically, but that was not the point: Rameau and Cahusac were being asked to celebrate the peace by producing a spectacular entertainment, and this meant musical and visual enchantment and lots of dancing. In each of the divertissements, a *ballet figuré* is the most important element. As for spectacle, Cahusac asked his engineers to conjure collapsing mountains (prologue) and an underwater palace (act three).

In the allegorical prologue, the Titans and the Giants attack the heavens in a failed attempt to overthrow Jupiter. Jupiter shows magnanimity to his fellow gods Neptune and Pluto by granting them, respectively, the sea and the underworld, retaining the heavens and the earth for himself. People understood that Jupiter represented Louis XV and Neptune George II. The main story, loosely inspired by Greek mythology, concerns Neptune's courtship of the water nymph Naïs. On the Isthmus of Corinth Naïs is presiding over the Isthmian Games. Neptune, in disguise, watches as she gently rejects Télénus, king of the Corinthians, and Astérion, leader of the Isthmian shepherds. In act two, Neptune, still in disguise, declares his love to Naïs. She sends him away. Télénus and Astérion are enraged when Naïs's father, the soothsayer Tiresius, tells them that the stranger will win her heart. In the final act, Télénus and Astérion try to kill the stranger, but Neptune causes the waves to rise and engulf them. He reveals his true identity to Naïs, and takes her to his underwater palace, where the sea divinities dance in honour of their new mistress.

Musically, the opera deserves to be better known. The continuous sequence of the overture and opening chorus, in which ascending phrases depict the Titans and the Giants climbing the mountains to reach the heavens, and trumpets and drums, repeated notes and dissonances, the clamour of battle, is one of Rameau's most audacious openings. The orchestral music is inspired throughout. Melodies that the mind has no hope of predicting emerge from Rameau's harmonic style, one after another. The prologue's second rigaudon is of wider interest because the 'Turkish' episode in the final movement of Mozart's Violin Concerto in A (K219), composed in 1775, is similar enough to make one think that Mozart knew Rameau's *Naïs*, or at least parts of it. Mozart may have heard *Naïs* and other music by Rameau during his visit to Versailles, aged six, in the winter of 1763/64. The *ballet figuré* depicting the Isthmian Games in act one, in which athletes wrestle and girls race, is accompanied by a magnificent chaconne that moves from march-like regularity to syncopated irregularity, from major to minor and back again: as the intricate variations proceed, the scoring and harmonies become ever more seductive. In act two, the recitatives between Naïs and Neptune, and Naïs and Télénus, mostly unaccompanied, are written with Rameau's usual flair without being memorable. Astérion's aria 'Les ennuis de l'incertitude' (scene five) is harmonically striking, and features lyrical writing for the oboes and bassoons. The *musette tendre* of the scene six *ballet figuré*, in which a shepherdess sings the air 'Je ne scai quel ennui me presse', and bassoons and oboes form a trio with the soprano voice, is a fine example of how Rameau's harmonies and phrasing make us *feel* as well as hear his music. Just as seductive is the short instrumental *musette* in scene five, a chain of descending phrases, richly harmonised. The final pages of the third act – including the chorus 'Coulez ondes, melez votre plus doux murmure' and the duo, for Naïs and Neptune, 'Que je vous aime' – are masterly. The chorus has a sorrow that isn't in keeping with the rest of the work; the harmony provided by the bassoons during one falling phrase is exquisite. Perhaps the public's anger over the peace terms was foremost in Rameau's mind. He closes the opera with two restrained tambourins and a *contredanse*.

Across the channel, five days after the premiere of Rameau's *Naïs*, the English celebrated the peace in a different way. The English people were content with the treaty terms. Instead of celebrating at the theatre with the privileged classes, George II ordered a public celebration in Green Park, a concert with music by Handel followed by a fireworks display that would light up the sky for all Londoners. Handel composed a suite for wind band and drums (strings were added later). There was pandemonium on the night. People watched the display from whatever vantage point they could find, including rooftops and river barges, and pedestrians and carriages blocked the narrow roads as thousands of people struggled to gain access to the park. It rained. A rogue rocket landed in one of the pavilions; another hit a girl setting her dress on fire. In Paris, nymphs and mythological gods in an ornate room; in London, a brass band and public pleasure on a rainy night in a park.

ix Zoroastre, Rameau's Opera of Ideas

In August 1749, the *Conseil d'Etat du Roi* signed a decree that fundamentally changed the governance of the Opéra. Before this moment, the finances of the Opéra were controlled by its director, a private individual who was often backed by business associates. It was extremely challenging to make the Opéra work financially because the high costs involved were not recovered at the box office. A deficit had grown to such a level that the Opéra's creditors feared for the security of their loans. The minister in charge, the comte d'Argenson,[61] came up with a single decisive solution – the transfer of the financial management of the Opéra to the *Bureau de la ville de Paris* (the governing body of the town of Paris), led by Louis-Bastide de Bernage, the *Prévôt des marchands*, who became the Opéra's director. The *Bureau de la ville de Paris* had the will and the financial clout to make an immediate difference (although within only a few seasons the Opéra's financial state would be once more precarious, and Bernage would be accused of lacking authority). Although the change was a matter of practical politics, it is tempting to view it as a symptom of a general trend which saw the crown's participation in, and influence over, everyday life diminish to the benefit of an ever greedy Paris.

The *Bureau de la ville de Paris* threw a considerable amount of money at the first major tragédie lyrique of the new era, Rameau and Cahusac's *Zoroastre*.

Platée had shown that Rameau was able to create an opera that was startling in its originality and provocative in its meaning. *Zoroastre* was another radical work, groundbreaking in its subject matter, its structure and its philosophical intent. It was the opera of Cahusac and Rameau most indebted to Freemasonry. More than this, it was a work that contained progressive ideas and a potentially subversive message.

Rameau and Cahusac's first innovation was to create a *tragédie* without a prologue. Up until this moment the prologue had been a sacred part of the tragedy form. As conceived by Lully and Quinault, its function was to pay homage to the king: it was a necessary bow of deference at the beginning of the night's entertainment. After the death of the Sun King, the prologue became less specifically about the glory of the monarch, but some allegorical representation of the gods and goddesses of mythology remained a necessary part of the ritual of opera; and, like all rules of etiquette, it was deemed essential until someone dared to remove it.

Rameau cannot have been the only composer frustrated by the requirement to allocate such a large proportion of an opera's running time to a prologue that, at best, only had tenuous links to the story that followed. He was encouraged by Cahusac, who, as we have seen, had firm ideas about theatrical form. In his preface to the revised text of *Zoroastre*, published in 1756, Cahusac explained that 'le temps est si précieux au théâtre lyrique': a genre made from so many elements – poetry, music, dance, painting, stage machinery – could not afford to waste time on superfluities.[62] Rameau knew that, in *Zoroastre*, more than in any previous work, he had a dramatic theme that deserved to be delivered without any additions or distractions. If he was ever to challenge the traditionalists by changing the form it was now.

Zoroastre had appeared as a supporting character, a magician, in two earlier operas, Destouches's *Sémiramis* (1718) and Rebel and Francœur's *Pyrame et Thisbé* (1726). Cahusac was the first librettist to write an opera text inspired by the founder of Zoroastrianism. His principal sources were the writings of two English scholars, Thomas

Hyde (1636-1703) and Humphrey Prideaux (1648-1724). Hyde was the professor of Arabic and Hebrew at Oxford and also Bodley's Librarian. From his study of Oriental documents, he was able to show, in *Historia religionis veterum Persarum* (1700), that Zoroastre was not the Babylonian magician of Greek and Roman literature, but a religious prophet and philosopher from eastern Persia. Zoroastrianism was a faith that stressed the importance of free will: it was up to each individual to choose between right and wrong, good and evil; the purpose of life was to find truth through good thoughts, words and actions. Fire and water were worshipped as sacred elements, representing wisdom.

Cahusac's interest in Zoroastre pre-dated Abraham Anquetil-Duperron's French translation of the ancient texts of *Avesta*, which included *Gathas*, the sacred text attributed to Zoroastre, by twenty years; and may have influenced Voltaire, who, in his *Essai sur les mœurs et l'esprit des nations* (1756), wrote of Zoroastrianism as a faith that believed in a supreme being and a devil, immortality of the soul and damnation, centuries before Judaism and Christianity, while enshrining rational philosophical ideas such as free will.[63]

One can understand why Cahusac, as a Freemason, was drawn to Zoroastrianism's opposition of good and evil, and why, as a writer, he incorporated the theme of magic from the mythological accounts of the prophet's life. In his libretto, he encapsulated these ideas into a conflict between Zoroastre, religious reformer, councillor to the king of Bactria and magus of white magic, and Abramane, High Priest of a cult of idols and sorcerer of dark magic.[64]

The opera begins in Bactria (part of the ancient Persian empire, present-day north Afghanistan). Following the death of the king, Abramane has prevailed over Zoroastre, forcing him into exile. Zoroastre and Amélite, the king's daughter and rightful heir, are in love. Abramane craves power and wants to restore the old religion. He plans to seize the throne with the princess Érinice. Érinice has been rejected by Zoroastre, and is consumed by hatred and jealousy. Together, Abramane and Érinice form an alliance of darkness against Zoroastre and Amélite. The act ends with the abduction of Amélite.

In act two, on the other side of the mountains, the exiled Zoroastre is living among a tribe of noble savages. He has told them of his religion, not as a ruler, but as a teacher: it is up to them to choose.

Two lovers, Abénis and Cénide, are about to marry, a concept previously unknown to them. They praise the god of Zoroastre as a benevolent god, a bringer of light, motivated by love, truth and happiness, and ask Zoroastre to become their ruler. At this point Rameau set to music the most subversive sentence in all of 18th century French opera: 'Nature and love have inspired your laws; let your laws and your innocence be your only guides and your only kings.' The joyous divertissement that follows is suddenly interrupted by the voice of the king of the Genii (Oromasès), telling Zoroastre of Abramane's tyranny in Bactria, and instructing him to free his people. Zoroastre departs in a chariot of fire.

In act three, Zoroastre arrives in Bactria, and discovers a country tormented by the gods of Abramane and smothered in perpetual darkness. Zoroastre invokes the return of the sun, and tells the Bactrians to rise up against the tyrant, for people who have truth on their side, if they are without fear, must prevail. The city is bathed in beautiful light but the Bactrians are too terrified to act. Zoroastre makes the walls of the palace collapse; inside, suddenly revealed, Érinice is about to attack Amélite with a dagger. The people are momentarily emboldened. Érinice flees; Zoroastre and Amélite are reunited. But Abramane appears as an apparition: he threatens the people and they disperse. The lovers are left alone. To reassure Amélite, Zoroastre summons the spirits. Their arrival allows the divertissement that ends the act. They bring a number of magical talismans, including an ivory wand: these objects will help Zoroastre defeat evil. Following the ballet of the spirits, Zoroastre departs.

Act four is set in Abramane's underground temple. Abramane learns that Zoroastre has defeated his army of spectres: at Zoroastre's command the spectres turned their weapons on themselves. In the presence of Érinice Abramane conducts a black ceremony, an invocation of evil. To summon the devil, Ariman, Abramane sacrifices victims with an axe. Vengeance, Hatred and Despair appear, accompanied by a chorus of furies and demons. Despair hands Érinice a bloody dagger. Vengeance hands Abramane a mace with a pointed tip. The furies and demons dance around a statue of Zoroastre; it disappears in a burst of flames. From below ground, the voice of Ariman is heard – 'Par des torrents de sang venge-toi de tes peines'.

Act five begins with Amélite alone in the garden of her palace. Zoroastre returns and tells her of his victory over Abramane. The people arrive, and call for Amélite to rule over them – 'Cédez à notre amour, et donnez-nous des lois'. The people are happy to be ruled by a queen who reciprocates their love. Amélite is about to be enthroned when Abramane arrives, followed by the priests. He attempts to kill Zoroastre with his mace. The Bactrians and the priests take up positions on either side of the stage. Zoroastre and Abramane invoke their gods. The sky darkens. Lightning strikes Abramane and the priests, and the earth opens to swallow them down into the underworld. Zoroastre's victory is complete. A temple for the worship of the sacred flame appears, commemorating the triumph of light over darkness. The opera ends with the announcement that Zoroastre and Amélite will marry and rule together.

The opera was eagerly anticipated, not least because it was the composer's first new tragedy in ten years. It became a hot topic of conversation, in the days leading up to the premiere, after details of the subject matter and the high expenditure of the production became public knowledge. In the news sheet *Nouvelles littéraires* for December 1749, Pierre Clément reported that he was about to go to the Opéra to see a new work by Cahusac and Rameau, adding

> We expect miracles. [...] The overture will serve as the prologue in two parts: the first will be a terrible and lamentable depiction of the barbarian power of a villainous High Priest, and of the cries of the people he oppresses; the second a vivid and smiling image of the beneficent power of Zoroastre, and of the happiness of the people he delivers. M. the *prévôt des marchands* has authorised an extraordinary expense of forty thousand francs. [...] Everything will be new, costumes, décor, machines; only the actresses won't be entirely so.[65]

Zoroastre challenged spectators, like Clément, who were used to the comforting traditions and repetitions of the tragédie lyrique form, and its strangeness was only partly mitigated by the presence in the cast of everyone's favourite performers – Jélyotte, Chassé, Marie Fel and Marie-Jeanne Chevalier. *Zoroastre* only pretended to be a tragedy; it was, in fact, the first and only work in a new genre that, had it been recognised, might have been termed *opéra philosophique* or *opéra des idées*. Because these ideas drove the plot, the plot itself seemed chaotic, bizarre and even ridiculous to those people who didn't grasp what Cahusac and Rameau were saying. One of these, surprisingly, was Friedrich Melchior Grimm, who wrote: 'In *Zoroastre* it is alternately day and night; but as Cahusac cannot count to five, he gets so tangled in his calculations that, in each act, he is forced to make it day and night two or three times so that it will be day at the end of the opera.'[66] The son of a Bavarian pastor, Grimm arrived in Paris at the beginning of 1749, and first achieved notoriety when he developed an unrequited passion for Marie Fel, perhaps after seeing her performance as the vulnerable, tender Amélite in *Zoroastre*. He took to his bed until the sickness passed. Rousseau acted as his nurse and later told the story in his *Confessions*.

Grimm was not a Freemason; he didn't recognise the Masonic symbols that run through *Zoroastre*. Many of the ideas, though, chimed with the enlightened thinking of the *philosophes*. Cahusac needed a complete act (act two), as well as significant parts of the other four, to fully express the thesis of the opera: the necessity, in personal and public life, of virtue, knowledge and free will, and of just laws derived from natural principles. Men should be free to choose their own religion; and rulers, to be legitimate, must have the consent of the people. These revolutionary ideas were clearly expressed, and yet seem to have been missed by the young radicals who would have embraced them, and by the officials who would have stamped on their authors by issuing a *lettre de cachet*. It would seem that the absurdities of the plot and the lavishness of the spectacle masked the meaning of the text.

How much of this was Rameau? The score is among the most dramatic in all of Rameau's output. It is not believable that a composer as cerebral and as controlling as Rameau was unaware of the opera's message, that, as it were, his librettist was slipping advanced ideas into the work without his blessing; but was Rameau the instigator of the intellectual agenda of the 1749 *Zoroastre* or merely its supporter? Always sensitive to criticism, particularly to the charge of plagiarism, Cahusac wrote a letter to the *Mercure de France*, before the premiere, in which he revealed that *Zoroastre* had been written in the summer of 1747 after a long period of thought and declared: 'This tragedy is by me and only by me.' Cahusac was stating his independence from other writers and not from Rameau.[67]

Rameau's imagination elevates Cahusac's pedestrian poetry and one-dimensional characterisations. Abramane is his most powerful creation for the bass voice. There are fewer obvious highlights than in Rameau's previous tragedies. The opera is mostly dialogue broken by *petit airs* and brief duos and sudden thrilling choruses; but the opera is elevated by its consistency of tone and its fixed dramatic intent. The bass instruments and the harpsichord dominate Rameau's orchestration. The harpsichord's music sounds ironic and sinister in this context. In the overture Rameau portrays the malignity of Abramane through his favourite tropes of repeated notes and cascading scales. The second subject, representing the hero, is a little too jolly. Act four contains the finest music. A superb recitative for Abramane and Érinice includes the duo 'O Dieux! Quelle douleur mortelle'. A startling phrase on the violins introduces the black ceremony that will summon the evil spirits. Abramane sings the monologue 'Suprême auteur des maux et des tristes revers' (scene five), and is joined by the priests on the words 'éclate, venge-toi', one of the most forward-looking choruses in 18th century opera. In a marvellous touch, Rameau gives Érinice tender music on the chilling phrase 'Ah! Je crois voir déjà ma rivale sanglante'. Rameau's writing for the orchestra throughout this act took its original players and their instruments to the limit of what was possible, creating edgy sonorities that must have sounded uncontrolled in 1749 despite being precisely scored in an unholy alliance of strings and bassoons.

The opera ran for twenty-five performances and was initially deemed a success by the neutrals. However, only an unqualified hit would have met the expectations of all concerned. Pierre Clément, having set things up nicely in his news sheet, was quick to review the opera in the next issue:

> I have seen Zoroastre; Monsieur, it is sadder than Mr. de Maupertius's treatise on *Happiness*; not a song pleases the ear. […] I say nothing of the words […] but what dark music, worthy of the High Priest of evil who battles against Zoroastre. What noise, what fracas and what boredom! Everything is in choruses, choruses upon choruses. It is true that, in the fourth act, 'Eclate, venge-toi, ce n'est qu'à la terreur que tu dois l'encens de la terre' is admirable. I am sure that this fourth act is full of beauty of the first order: but this first order is apparently too

high for me. The second act, which forms a contrast with the fourth, and which fills the stage with vivid images [...] is nothing at all. Some beautiful symphonies, most of which the composer has stolen from his own pieces for clavecin, from time to time console the afflicted ear; the pretty air in the fifth act is said to be, not by [Rameau], but by Hasse.[68]

Clément was bemused by the very things that made the work thrilling and unique, such as the dark music for Abramane and the prominent role given to the chorus. His review is revealing in a number of respects: we learn that Clément recognised Rameau's self-borrowings and that some people believed that the melody of an air in the fifth act had been borrowed from the German composer Johann Adolph Hasse. However, it is Clément's confession that the music was beyond his grasp that resonates most strongly.

8

Philosophers and Fools

The Encyclopédie and the Querelle des Bouffons
1749-1762

i Diderot, d'Alembert and Rameau before 1752

Denis Diderot came to Paris at the age of fifteen in 1728, the seemingly dutiful son of a master cutler from the ancient town of Langres in Champagne in eastern France. Langres, occupying a strategic site at the edge of an escarpment overlooking the plain below, was a fortress in Gallo-Roman times and had been a prosperous and influential bishopric since the Middle Ages.

Diderot was another product of the Jesuit education system, and a credit to its humanistic core, having, unlike Rameau, gobbled up every last morsel of its syllabus. Diderot's parents wanted their son to enter the clergy, and as a boy he was for a time swept up by the certainty of the Jesuits. Tonsured by the Bishop of Langres, he became an abbé (ecclesiastical scholar) and moved to the capital to enter one of the religious colleges, probably the Jesuit Louis-le-Grand. Caught up in the great intellectual battle being fought within French Catholicism by the Jesuits and the Jansenists, Diderot switched sides by entering the collège d'Harcourt,[1] a hotbed of Jansenism within the University of Paris. For a young intellectual interested in new ideas, one can easily understand the appeal of Jansenism, a movement close to Calvinism that challenged Papal authority.

Jansenism's interpretation of original sin meant that even the contrite were not guaranteed salvation. Salvation was predetermined, and no degree of good deeds, or, for that matter, clerical intervention, could help those not chosen. The logical conclusion of Jansenist thought was that the church was unnecessary. The movement was implicitly politically subversive but impossible to crush given that its influence had spread throughout the higher levels of society. A majority of the elected magistrates of the Paris *Parlement*, the powerful body of constitutional and financial affairs, embraced Jansenism. Louis XIV's direct attempts to oppress the movement were relaxed by Orléans in the 1720s as a matter of political pragmatism.

If Diderot was hoping that the austere fundamentalism of Jansenism would bolster his faith, the opposite happened. In Paris he discovered the theatre, women and good company. He placed religion under an intellectual microscope and discovered that it could not be rationally explained, and relied upon a manipulative plethora of man-made images and narratives. He graduated in 1734 but abandoned theology for the law, a choice that still satisfied the ambitions of his family. It was another false start. Diderot's chief ambition was to make his name as a serious writer, but, to support his wife (he married against his father's wishes in 1743), he was prepared to work as a hack, translating English publications into French. In 1748 he published, anonymously, *Les Bijoux indiscrets*, a licentious novel that was in part an allegorical portrait of the contemporary scene.

Diderot's outgoing nature, natural authority and ability to talk on any subject (easily verified by his prose style, for he was a brilliantly discursive writer, always willing to go off on a tangent) meant that he was the leader of the young thinkers and artists who gathered at the café de la Régence in the place du Palais-Royal, men such as Rousseau, the composer and chess master Philador and the mathematician Jean le Rond d'Alembert. D'Alembert published an important work on fluid mechanics and refraction, *Mémoire sur la réfraction des corps solides*, and was elected to the Académie Royale des Sciences in 1741, and to the Royal Society in 1748.

D'Alembert was born in Paris in 1717, the illegitimate son of the writer and society hostess Mme de Tencin and the soldier Louis-Camus Destouches, both members of the lower aristocracy. Left by his mother as a foundling on the steps of the Saint-Jean-Lerond chapel at Notre Dame, d'Alembert was adopted by the wife of a glazier but secretly supported by his father's family. He was educated at the Jansenist collège des Quatre-Nations[2] within the University of Paris, where he studied law and medicine before concentrating on mathematics. More reserved and less ebullient than Diderot, d'Alembert was something of a cold fish, easily out-shone by his friend in the company of young actresses in the cafés, but he had the comfort of his genius and enjoyed the protection of his connections. Diderot was proud to make his own way, but suffered for his principles. The illegitimate son of aristocrats enjoyed greater status than the cutler's son from Langres.

In 1747 Diderot and d'Alembert undertook the task of editing an *Encyclopédie ou Dictionnaire universel des arts et sciences*. Beginning as a project to translate into French Ephraim Chambers's *Cyclopaedia* it grew into the biggest and most significant publishing endeavour of the age, a multi-volume dictionary of everything worth describing, from everyday work tools to the highest intellectual concepts. Diderot was initially engaged as a translator, with d'Alembert probably acting as an advisor. Diderot subsequently took on the principal management of the whole project with d'Alembert acting as co-editor. While working to prepare the first volume for publication, Diderot continued to write his own books.

He soon faced the paradox that would mark his life. How, as a writer and philosopher, to be true to his talent and his convictions without being punished by the state? In 1749 he took a risk by publishing his first major work, *Lettre sur les aveugles à l'usage de ceux qui voient* (Letter on the Blind), a meditation on the philosophical implications of blindness that dared, as far as the censor was concerned, to question the existence of God (a blind man would need to touch God to believe in Him; abstract thought is meaningless if it can't be validated by the senses). The book was published anonymously, but Diderot made sure that people knew that he was the author of this ingenious, elegant and cuttingly clever essay. The abbé Raynal, fast becoming a member of Diderot's circle, wrote a considered review in his *Nouvelles littéraires*,[3] and Diderot knew that he had 'arrived' when he received a letter from Voltaire, dispensing praise and offering fellowship. He wrote back: 'The moment that I received your letter, monsieur and dear master, was one of the sweetest of my life.'[4]

This sweetness lasted for less than two weeks. The authorities had been watching Diderot for some time: they detected, rightly, an undertone of seditious irreligious allegory in many of his writings. Now, by addressing metaphysical issues surrounding the nature of belief, the young author had gone too far. A busybody cleric complained to the comte d'Argenson (director of publications as well as minister of war) who issued a *lettre de cachet*. Diderot was arrested in his home in the rue de la Vieille Estrapade and transported through eastern Paris to the Château de Vincennes, a state prison only a little less chilling than the Bastille.

Diderot's only course of action was to write pleading letters to d'Argenson and to the lieutenant of police, Berryer. At first he denied that he was the author of *Letter on the Blind* and the other works cited, and outlined the role he was playing as editor of the *Encyclopédie*, implying that his absence would prove disastrous for the Paris book trade (a significant industry). In a letter to Berryer, dated 10 August 1749, Diderot mentioned Rameau, writing that he had 'given an exposition of M. Rameau's system'. He hoped that his association with Rameau, a famous man thought to be politically sound, would prove advantageous. Such special pleading was not enough, though. On 13 August Diderot confessed his guilt, and undertook in future to only publish with the permission of the censor. It was a bitter promise to make, one that Diderot never dared to break.

To which work was Diderot referring when he wrote that he had 'given an exposition of M. Rameau's system'? The quote prompts us to consider the nature and depth of Diderot and d'Alembert's relationship with Rameau. We know that, at some point, Diderot and d'Alembert received lessons from Rameau on the practice and theory of music that lasted for several months (during his bitter dispute with the two philosophers in 1757 Rameau reminded them of the fact).[5] It is possible that the lessons initiated their friendship.

During a review of Diderot's *Mémoires sur différents sujets de mathématiques* in 1748 the abbé Raynal, who was in a position to know, wrote:

> Diderot is an intimate friend of M. Rameau, whose discoveries

he is shortly going to publish. This sublime and profound musician has previously delivered work in which he explained his ideas with insufficient clarity and elegance. M. Diderot will redraft these ideas, and he is very capable of putting them forward to their best advantage.[6]

A few months later, in 1749, following his review of Diderot's *Letter on the Blind*, Raynal returned to the subject:

Our very illustrious and very celebrated musician, M. Rameau, claims to have discovered the principle of harmony. M. Diderot has lent his pen to ensure that this important discovery is put forward to its best advantage.[7]

We can reasonably conclude that Rameau asked, or commissioned, Diderot to improve and finesse the texts he was working on in 1749. This working relationship must have started after the publication of Diderot's *Mémoires sur différents sujets de mathématiques* in 1748, for in the section of this work entitled *Principes généraux d'accoustique* Diderot wrote glowingly of Rameau's theories before adding:

It is hoped that someone will lift [his admirable system of composition] from the obscurities that envelop it and put it within everyone's reach, less for the glory of its inventor than for the progress of the science of sounds.[8]

Rameau, always quick to check out new writing on a subject he considered to be his property, would have read Diderot's essay on acoustics. Given that Diderot made a specific comment about the need for someone to lift Rameau's ideas from obscurity, it feels right that Rameau's immediate response was to ask him to undertake the task.

In 1749 Rameau presented his theoretical ideas to a panel of experts at the Académie Royale des Sciences. He had long sought the endorsement of France's preeminent scientific body. He felt, acutely, that as a 'mere musician' – Rameau used this phrase to describe himself, and not altogether sarcastically, in his furious open letter to Castel published in *Le pour et contre* in 1738 – he was looked down upon by scholars and scientists. His challenge in entering the sombre halls of the Académie (situated in the Louvre) was to clearly express his ideas in the restricted time of a single lecture, without the aid of practical examples: a tall task. The text of the lecture, *Mémoire où l'on expose les fondements d'un système de musique théorique et pratique*, preserved in the archive of the Opéra, bears the imprint of Diderot: it has a lucidity of expression never previously achieved by Rameau. While Diderot was helping Rameau to write his talk, d'Alembert got himself on the judging panel, and wrote the favourable review. It is clear that the two philosophers were doing all they could to support Rameau. *Mémoire où l'on expose les fondements d'un système de musique théorique et pratique* would, over the following months, be enlarged to form part of Rameau's *Démonstration du principe de l'harmonie*, published in 1750. Subsequently, d'Alembert expanded his review of Rameau's lecture into a book called *Eléments de musique, théorique et pratique, suivant les principes de M. Rameau*. When this work was published, anonymously, in 1752 the police inspector d'Hémery wrongly attributed its authorship to Diderot.

Diderot and d'Alembert greatly admired Rameau's system because they believed it to be the most advanced and persuasive scientific and philosophical explanation of music yet attempted. Music was the most arcane of all the arts, and Rameau had unlocked its mysteries. Diderot valued, in particular, that aspect of Rameau's work that followed Pythagoras in stressing the importance of the relationships of intervals in determining beauty in music, and how these ratios could be expressed in numbers. Diderot explored the idea that music gave pleasure because the listener perceived these hidden relationships – 'Le plaisir musical consiste dans la perception des rapports des sons'. He found this principle of the 'perception of relationships' especially satisfying because it could be applied to poetry, painting, architecture, morality – in fact, to all the arts and all the sciences.[9]

One can clearly see the influence of Diderot's adherence to the philosophy of John Locke (the idea that all knowledge is derived from sensory experience) in the *Démonstration du principe de l'harmonie*. Rameau was still a rationalist by instinct, but, influenced by the Diderot of *Letter on the Blind* and *Letter on the Deaf and Mute*, he re-thought aspects of his theory from a sensualist perspective, and declared that the *corps sonore* was a natural phenomenon that revealed itself to our senses: this governing principle of all music didn't have to be deduced mathematically because one could *hear* the harmonic overtone. In the *Démonstration*, Rameau brought into play both his rationalism and the more popular empiricism of the day without acknowledging any contradiction: and in so doing he was declaring that his system was unchallengeable from whatever angle his detractors might choose to attack it.

In contrast to Diderot, d'Alembert was not troubled by Rameau's earlier over-reliance on abstract, pre-existing principles. In this context, Thomas Christensen has identified a personal motivation for d'Alembert's deep admiration for Rameau at this time. In his own work, d'Alembert often followed a rational approach, believing that truths could be deduced from a fundamental principle. In an intellectual world where Locke was king, this aspect of d'Alembert's philosophy made him unusual and placed him in opposition to many of his fellow scientists. In Rameau he found a thinker whose method of enquiry was intellectually aligned to his own.[10]

At some point in 1749, Diderot and d'Alembert invited Rameau to take on the task of writing the articles on music in the *Encyclopédie*. Here was an opportunity for Rameau to use the *Encyclopédie*, and the editing and writing skills of Diderot and d'Alembert, to present his ideas in the most lucid and most prominent way possible. He declined, but graciously offered to check the articles before publication.[11] We don't know why Rameau declined. The consequences were profound, for Diderot and d'Alembert handed the work to Jean-Jacques Rousseau, a man who was in the process of turning his grudge against Rameau into a polemic against the whole of French music. Diderot and d'Alembert's choice of Rousseau to write articles that were expected to be summaries of Rameau's principles – d'Alembert, as the editor responsible, set firm guidelines which in the initial volumes Rousseau largely followed – suggests that they weren't aware of the extent of Rousseau's personal animosity towards the composer. Diderot and d'Alembert chose not to pass the articles by Rameau before publication, a decision that would rankle with the composer.

Rameau's refusal didn't damage his relationship with the editors. D'Alembert wrote what amounted to an act of homage in the 'Discours préliminaire' of the first volume of the *Encyclopédie* (1751), in effect giving Rameau pride of place alongside Newton and Descartes at the beginning of the first volume of the most anticipated and most prestigious publishing event of the century:

> Music, of all the arts, has perhaps made the most progress among us during the last fifteen years. Thanks to the work of a genius, forceful, brave and prolific, foreigners who suffered our symphonies began to get a taste for them, and the French were finally persuaded that Lully had left much to be done. M. Rameau, by pushing the practice of his art to such a high degree of perfection, has become both the model and the object of jealousy of a great number of artists, who decry him while striving to imitate him. But what distinguishes him most particularly, is that he has reflected with much success on the theory of this same art; that he has discovered in the fundamental bass the principle of harmony and of melody; that by these means he has distilled into more certain laws a science that was thought to have arbitrary rules, or rules that were dictated by blind experience. I seize eagerly the opportunity to celebrate this artist-philosopher, in an essay intended primarily to celebrate the greatest men. His merit, which he has compelled our century to recognise, will be well known only when time has silenced envy; and his name, dear to the enlightened of our nation, cannot offend anyone.[12]

Unambiguously, then, for d'Alembert, Rameau was a genius of both the arts and sciences who had increased France's standing in the world, a revolutionary who, because he had not achieved the standing he deserved (despite d'Alembert's advocacy Rameau was not made a member of the Académie, possibly because most academicians did not consider the theory of music to be an important science), required the special support of the enlightened.

This was the context in which d'Alembert completed the manuscript of *Eléments de musique, théorique et pratique, suivant les principes de M. Rameau*. In the work's foreword he explained that his aim was to propagate Rameau's ideas by making them easily understood by people who were unversed in music theory.[13]

D'Alembert sent his drafts to Rameau asking for comments and suggestions.[14] Rameau suggested some revisions, all of which d'Alembert happily incorporated. D'Alembert's achievement was to extract from Rameau's *Génération harmonique* and *Démonstration du principe de l'harmonie*, the main texts he consulted, a clear organisational structure that showed how the rules of composition, including the fundamental bass, outlined in book two of the *Eléments*, were founded on the principles of harmony, outlined in book one. The result was a work that Rameau proudly endorsed at the time of its publication. He was not worried that some of the details of his theory were smoothed out in d'Alembert's expertly articulated simplification, written, to quote Girdlestone, 'in the most elegant and limpid prose of the century'.[15]

Jean le Rond d'Alembert, after Maurice Quentin de La Tour.

After the publication, in May 1752, Rameau wrote an open letter to the editor of the *Mercure de France* in which he expressed his gratitude to d'Alembert. The letter – one of only a few documents that give an insight into Rameau's complex personality – reveals the extent to which Rameau prized d'Alembert's fellowship, seeing it as his moment of victory over his enemies; it also reveals that his arrogance was closely linked to an inability to dissemble: he could be too honest for his own good. The letter helps to explain why Rameau was so badly hit when, a few years later, d'Alembert, under provocation, withdrew his support.

> Allow me, Monsieur, to express in your journal my thanks to M. d'Alembert for the mark of esteem he has paid me by publishing his *Eléments de musique théorique et pratique*, following my principles. Any publicity I gain from the expression of my deep gratitude will always be less important than the honour I receive. The advancement of my art has been, for me, the first motivation for my hours of work late into the night. The most flattering recompense that I could have wished for is the approval and esteem of scholars. It turned out fortunately for me that in the most celebrated academies these enlightened and just men shone their lights above opposition and placed merit before envy. I was fortunate to gain their votes, and their votes have resulted in those of the multitude. Among those scholars who I have the honour of calling my judges and my masters it is the truthfulness of d'Alembert's style (the elevation of his sentiments and the breadth of his knowledge) that has enhanced my reputation. It is from him, Monsieur, that I have received the most glorious testimony that an author could ever hope to receive. Some writers have tried to make a name for themselves by twisting my principles, sometimes by disputing my discovery of them, sometimes by imagining difficulties that they believe obscure them. They have done nothing for their reputations or against mine; they have neither added nor subtracted from my discoveries [...] The illustrious man to whom I address my gratitude, has found in my works no faults to speak of, but rather truths that he has analysed, simplified, made more familiar and clearer, and therefore more useful for the wider public, in that manner of clarity, order and precision that is so characteristic of his work. He has even considered the reach of children, by the power of a genius that bends and modifies to its will all the matters it considers. Finally, he has given me the consolation of adding to the soundness of my principles a clarity that I

felt they needed and would have only achieved with much effort and perhaps less successfully. Thus, Monsieur, the sciences and the arts [...] would hasten their progress if all authors would choose the pursuit of truth over self-esteem [...] and had the modesty to accept the help that others generously offer. I have the honour to be your obedient servant, Rameau.[16]

One cannot help thinking that a less grandiose, less self-revealing, message of thanks would have served Rameau better.

ii Rameau's Fragile Victory

Diderot and d'Alembert's forceful advocacy elevated Rameau, now in his sixties, to a pinnacle of recognition, allowing him an all too brief period of professional contentment between 1749 and 1751. These years coincided with Rameau's final triumph over his habitual detractors. The *lullistes* had been silenced. Along with the premieres of *Naïs* and *Zoroastre*, four of Rameau's recent works – *Les Fêtes de l'Hymen et de l'Amour, Zaïs, Pygmalion* and *Les Surprises de l'Amour* – were revived at the Opéra in 1749 alone. When Rameau, having only recently recovered from a serious illness, was spotted in one of the rear boxes during a performance of *Pygmalion* in May 1751, spontaneous applause broke out that united the whole house. Even the musicians joined in.[17] Such was Rameau's popularity and dominance that d'Argenson decreed that revivals of his operas should be restricted to two a year, so as to encourage the others.[18] According to Charles Collé, writing in his journal in May 1751, the Opéra, financially-pressed once more, was anxious to secure a major new work from its leading composer (two years had passed since the premiere of *Zoroastre*). Rameau resented the fact that he had been paid modest fees over the years for works that had, collectively, made hundreds of thousands of *livres* for the Opéra, and expected to be awarded a pension in line with those given to Campra and Destouches. This was his condition for handing over a major new work. D'Argenson refused. Rameau asked the abbé de Bernis[19] (poet, future politician and cardinal) to take the matter to his patron Mme de Pompadour. Collé concluded his account of what reads like reasonably well-informed tittle-tattle by stating: 'She'll do nothing for Rameau; she does not like his music, less still his person.'[20] This assertion doesn't ring true where Rameau's music was concerned. We can safely take from Collé's journal that Rameau's relationship with the rulers of the Opéra, Louis-Bastide de Bernage (director) and François Rebel and François Francœur (joint inspectors),[21] was strained because of money matters. The dispute was resolved to the extent that new works were performed later in 1751, *La Guirlande* and *Acante et Céphise*. However, documents concerning *La Guirlande* show that Rameau had to fight to secure what he was due.[22] The Opéra paid Rameau four hundred *livres* for the first fourteen performances of this acte de ballet, but the composer demanded payment for sixteen more. Bernage backed down and accorded Rameau a further six hundred and seventy *livres*.

The tragedy that Rameau was working on in 1750/51, *Linus*, to a libretto by Leclerc de La Bruère, never reached the stage, but this wasn't only because of his dispute with the Opéra. The libretto was probably written after the 1744 revival of Rameau and Leclerc de La Bruère's *Dardanus* and before Leclerc de La Bruère left Paris in 1749 (he was secretary to the duc de Nivernais,[23] the French ambassador in Rome). Leclerc de La Bruère had increased his standing as a librettist collaborating with Mondonville on *Érigone* and Rebel and Francœur on the *Prince de Noisy*, created for Mme de Pompadour's theatre at Versailles in 1748/49, and in *Linus* he provided Rameau with a dramatic subject that mirrored the good versus evil struggle of *Zoroastre*. Linus, son of Apollo, is in love with Queen Cléonice of Thebes. When Cléonice rejects the advances of Gélanor, prince of Thrace, he forms an alliance with his sister Théano, a sorceress in love with Linus. Linus's army is defeated, and Cléonice captured. The lovers escape by taking to the seas. Gélanor and Théano attempt to drown them in a tempest only to be engulfed by the waves themselves.

The circumstances surrounding *Linus* remain mysterious.[24] The opera went into rehearsal in 1751 at the private theatre of Mme de Villeroy, the young wife of Gabriel de Neufville, duc de Villeroy, in their home in the aristocratic rue de Varenne (Faubourg Saint-Germain).[25] This was normal practice for a work being prepared for either the Opéra or Versailles: Rameau's the *Naissance d'Osiras* and

Anacréon would be rehearsed there in 1754.[26] Although the details of Mme de Villeroy's relationship with Rameau are unknown, we know that she remained close to his family: she was one of the witnesses of the contract of marriage between his daughter Marie-Alexandrine and François-Marie de Gaultier in 1764. The scraps of evidence unearthed by Cuthbert Girdlestone suggested that the project was hampered by the onset of the serious illness that threatened Rameau's life at this time. Rameau demanded changes to the libretto, but with Leclerc de La Bruère absent in Rome these could not be addressed to his satisfaction. Two of Nivernais's close friends, the influential comte de Stainville[27] and the abbé de Bernis, someone Rameau seems to have known well and trusted (see above), were acting as intermediaries. Leclerc de La Bruère, Nivernais, Stainville and Bernis had all benefited from the patronage of Mme de Pompadour and we can sense her presence behind the effort to bring *Linus* to the stage.

Joseph de La Porte recorded that a public rehearsal in May had revealed problems in the fifth act.[28] The comte de Stainville felt that its music was weak. Rameau was in partial agreement, but insisted on improvements to the libretto that never materialised. As ever, he wasn't prepared to compromise. Decroix suggested that Rameau abandoned the work because of the attitude of the librettist's intermediaries: 'Who knows if the work's supposed defects were actually things of beauty that Rameau prized, and that the interfering people who sought to make him change them determined him to suppress the whole opera? He was a man to make such sacrifices.'[29] Leclerc de La Bruère and his intermediaries perhaps maintained the hope that Rameau would complete the opera, but the moment had passed. Bernis began his diplomatic career in Venice in 1752. Leclerc de La Bruère died in Rome two years later. Only the first violin part, found in Rameau's papers by his son Claude-François after his death and given to Decroix, has come down to us. Searching elsewhere, Decroix only recovered the libretto.[30]

In March 1751, Rameau presented a revised version of his early motet, *In convertendo*, at the Concert Spirituel. The concerts of the Concert Spirituel, organised during religious holidays when the Opéra was dark, and taking place at the *salle des Suisses* in the Tuileries Palace, had been a feature of Paris's artistic life since 1725.

Rameau's absence from these concerts over the years may be explained in part by his focus on the operatic stage and in part by his contract with La Pouplinière, a contract that required him to organise and provide music for his patron's series of private concerts. Given Rameau's command of the orchestra, it is regrettable that he wasn't inspired, or able, to compose concertos for the Concert Spirituel. The new version of *In convertendo*, performed during Holy Week, was not positively received despite the care Rameau took in preparing the score. People hostile to Rameau believed that he was motivated by jealousy of the musician who, for many years, had been the leading composer of religious works at the Concert Spirituel, Mondonville. Rameau, it was said, wanted to rule over the Concert Spirituel just as he ruled over the Opera. No doubt, rivalry played a part. It was widely publicised that Rameau was dusting off a very old piece: this prejudiced many people against the music before a note was played, meaning that a very beautiful motet was dismissed as dated and mediocre. 'Even Rameau's closest friends,' Grimm wrote, 'were forced to agree that the work was devoid of brilliance or majesty. Mondonville was not dethroned and Rameau's rivalry redoubled the public's esteem for his motets.'[31]

On both *La Guirlande* and *Acante et Céphise* Rameau collaborated with a young writer he knew well at La Pouplinière's, Jean-François Marmontel. *La Guirlande* was premiered in September alongside Rebel and Francœur's *Les Génies tutélaires* and *Les Sauvages* from Rameau's *Les Indes galantes*. Marmontel's text is a hymn to fidelity and forgiveness. In Arcadia, the shepherdess Zélide and her lover Myrtil wear magical garlands of green leaves to symbolise their love. When Myrtil flirts with another woman his garland begins to wither and die. He places it on the altar of Cupid in the hope that the god will restore it to life; but Zélide sees it and learns that her lover has been unfaithful. She decides to trick and test him by exchanging her garland for his. Myrtil returns and Zélide, hiding in the trees, hears his expression of relief at discovering that 'his' garland has been restored to life. The lovers meet, and during the duet that follows Myrtil asks Zélide to show him her garland. She tells him that she has been unfaithful, and invites his anger; but he passes her test by forgiving her, which means she can forgive him.

For an acte de ballet the story is memorable, and Marmontel tells it elegantly. Rameau refuses to be confined by the limited parameters of an acte de ballet pastorale. His music deepens the melancholy that envelops the characters for much of the work. In its lighter moments, though, *La Guirlande* is reminiscent of one of Rameau's earliest pieces, the cantata *Les Amants trahis*.

Acante et Céphise was commissioned, at short notice, to celebrate the birth of the dauphin's first son, the duke of Burgundy, that November. A pastorale héroïque in three acts, it was a large-scale work. The lovers Acante and Céphise are threatened by a wicked genie, Oroès, who wants Céphise for himself. The fairy Zirphile gives them a talisman in the form of a bracelet that allows them to know each other's thoughts and feelings even when apart. In the final act, the genie chains the lovers to rocks in a desert and they are only saved by the intervention Zirphile, who announces the royal birth. A dance ends the opera.

Acante et Céphise is one of Rameau's least well-known operas, the last of his full-scale works to be re-assessed. Sylvie Bouissou and Robert Fajon realised a scholarly edition in 1996, but only the overture and instrumental numbers were recorded. It wasn't until 2020 that the complete opera was recorded and performed. This recording, by the Centre de musique baroque de Versailles (CMBV) and Alexis Kossenko's ensemble Les Ambassadeurs-La Grande Écurie, revealed a major work.

In the superb overture Rameau celebrates the birth of the duke of Burgundy by depicting a fireworks display. A slow introduction, for strings and flutes, gives way to a rapidly repeated single note played *forte* by the double basses and punctuated by the crash of a bass drum, over which the violins and flutes unleash swirling lines of sound. A triumphant fanfare concludes the overture. The descriptive power of this music was much admired. One of its first listeners wrote:

> The overture of *Acante* is a tableau in the grandest manner, it reminds me of the great acts of the imagination of the astonishing Milton. This piece, new and unique, depicts artillery fire: the noise of canons, the explosions of bombs, the speeding rockets, the glittering sky, the tumult, the cries of joy – all are painted with the most vivid colours. Envy itself is obliged to admire the learned fertility of this Raphael of music.[32]

According to the same writer, the words were not received favourably, and Rameau's music only took flight when free of them. Marmontel himself admitted that the text, written in haste, was laboured, and that the work was sustained by some 'grands effets d'harmonie', along with the spectacle of its presentation.[33] This was clearly the view of the reviewer in the *Mercure de France* who found much to admire in Rameau's score. The reviewer commented on the quality of some of the performances as well as on the failure of the musicians to master one section (no doubt this criticism was the only part of the review that Rameau remembered):

> The first act included a very majestic loure, an attractive chaconne danced by M. Dupré with all his nobility, and two lively tambourins danced with real lightness and spirit by Mlle Reix. […] As for the brief instrumental passage that preceded the recitative, ah, it calmed my senses, for it was of a beauty that made one regret that it was so short. The second act's opening monologue was beautiful, and very well interpreted by M. Chassé. The little chorus was very pleasant; I only wish that the accompanying trio had been better executed. The audience greatly enjoyed the *musette* and the two minuets, and, in the 'Festival of the Hunters' that followed, the airs played by the clarinets and the dancing of M. Lany and Mlle Lyonnois. The third act pleased from beginning to end. Nothing made a greater impact than the contrast between the suffering of the two lovers and the chorus sung by the evil spirits tormenting them. […] The *coup de théâtre* that gave the lovers their freedom was universally applauded for both its music and its visual representation.[34]

Rameau had added clarinets to his orchestra in *Zoroastre*, but was using them prominently for the first time. The horns were also given prominence. The players struggled (hence the criticism in the *Mercure de France*), forcing Rameau to make some changes. The opera fulfilled its function as a *pièce d'occasion*, but provoked little lasting passion in either its creators or its audience. It closed after fourteen performances and disappeared from the repertoire.

For the 2020 recording, the CMBV and Kossenko replicated the

Opéra's orchestra of the 1750s. This meant reconstructing the clarinets used at the time and using a continuo consisting of harpsichord, double-bass and three cellos.

iii The Philosophers Dance to an Italian Tune

For all his admiration of Rameau's theoretical work during the 1740s, Diderot was never an unquestioning follower of the composer. He didn't share Rameau's certainties, and trusted his own ideas, which were in transition. Whereas Rameau proclaimed that his principles were absolute and universal, Diderot allowed for contradictions and human factors – the part played by taste and cultural influences in people's appreciation of music. This acceptance of the mundane was already apparent in the opening pages of the *Principes généraux d'accoustique*, where Diderot wrote:

> If we consider only the sounds, their vehicle and the confirmation of our hearing, we would believe that an adagio by Michel, a gigue by Corelli, an overture by Rameau and a chaconne by Lully would have been considered two thousand years ago as today, and in the depths of Tartary as in Paris, admirable pieces of music. However, if we detest the music of the Barbarians, the Barbarians would have no taste for ours… Music is one of those things subject to the caprices of people, the diversity of places and the changes brought about by time.[35]

Diderot must have been aware of, if not yet troubled by, a paradox implied by the ideas he put forward in *Principes généraux d'accoustique*. If harmony was the essence of music as a natural phenomenon, as he proclaimed, after Rameau, why was it absent in the music of primitive societies? Rameau's one practical example – his encounter in the Lyon opera house with an old labourer humming the fundamental bass of an air – was insufficient to challenge the orthodoxy that an appreciation of harmony required learning and refinement, a trained ear. Even in the 1740s, then, we can detect an intellectual basis for Diderot's later rejection of Rameau.[36]

The first three volumes of the *Encyclopédie* appeared between

1751 and 1753. They included articles on 'Accord', 'Accompaniment', 'Basse fondamentale' and 'Cadence'. Rousseau's writing broadly followed Rameau's principles, and where Rameau hadn't been sufficiently acknowledged d'Alembert rectified the omission. It was only on reflection, after battle lines were formed, that Rameau came to the view that the articles either distorted or disparaged his work. Any slight diversion from the true course offended this most self-defensive of characters.

The thin cracks that had started to appear in Rameau's alliance with Diderot and d'Alembert were widened by the controversy that came to be called the *querelle des bouffons* (the quarrel of the fools). In August 1752, between the publication of the second and third volumes of the *Encyclopédie*, a troupe of Italian actors, the Buffoni, managed by Eustachio Bambini, began a season of work at the Opéra (yes, the *Opéra* not the Théâtre Italien) with a performance of Pergolesi's short comic opera *La serva padrona*. The piece had gone unnoticed when first presented in Paris on the stage of the Théâtre Italien six years before. This time it became the talking point of the theatrical year. 'Ma foi, ces maudits bouffons, avec leur *Servante Maîtresse*, nous en ont donné rudement dans le cul,' was how Diderot, in humorous mode, chose to remember its impact ('Lord, these naughty bouffons, with their *Serva padrona*, gave us a real kick up the arse').[37] The Bouffons polarised opinion and ignited one of those passionate intellectual battles so enjoyed by Parisian society. The partisans of Italian music lined up against the partisans of French music, with intellectual terrorists operating for both sides. It was a battle fought out in heated verbal exchanges and little pamphlets that became increasingly political.

Debates over the relative merits of French and Italian music were not new. Fifty years before, the scholar François Raguenet had declared in favour of Italian music in his essay *Parallèle des Italiens et des Français en ce que regarde la musique et les opéras* (1702) prompting Le Cerf de La Viéville's rebuttal *Comparaison de la musique italienne et de la musique française* (1704). The French had long since recognised that their native music, if able to claim some foreign enthusiasts, was not, in contrast to Italian, exportable. In the words of d'Alembert:

> Among the crowd of Englishmen, Spaniards, Germans, and Russians who come running to Paris from every direction, there is scarcely one whom our operas have not bored to distraction. They perceive it either as a deafening racket or as a plainsong that puts them to sleep with its languor, when they are not outraged by its pretension; if they take pleasure in any part of the performance, it is in our dances; but these are not sufficient compensation for three hours of noise and boredom; they leave stopping up their ears, and one will scarcely see them return.[38]

However, it was one thing to be aware of the lack of international appeal of French music, an awareness that actually made many people feel superior to the foreigners who invaded Paris every year, and another to accept an Italian season at the Opéra.

La serva padrona (*The Servant as Mistress*) dated from 1733. It was first performed in Naples as a comic interlude between the acts of Pergolesi's opera seria *Il prigionier superbo*. Pergolesi was an exponent of *opera buffa*, a genre of opera that emerged in Naples at the beginning of the 18th century. Today Pergolesi's operas are much less well known than the *Stabat Mater* he completed shortly before his death at the age of twenty-six in 1736; they deserve to be reassessed. As an *intermezzo*, *La serva padrona* lasts for little more than forty minutes. It concerns the intrigues of a bossy maidservant named Serpina, who tricks her elderly employer, Uberto, into marrying her. All ends well because Uberto realises that he has been in love with the girl all along.

The music was deliberately thinly scored, with the melodic line taking precedence over harmony and counterpoint. The arias – among them Serpina's 'A Serpina, penserete' – are elegant and characterful; they charmed audiences wherever the opera was performed. The music served the text, ensuring that the words were heard and the drama followed; and, together, the music and words encouraged vivid character acting that expressed small changes in emotion while still possessing a naturalism rarely found in French opera.

What made *La serva padrona* so significant, when performed at the Opéra, was the fact that it was a domestic comedy set in the contemporary world featuring character types everyone could recognise. Unlike the most prestigious form of French opera, tragédie lyrique, rooted in history and mythology, a piece like *La serva padrona* had nothing to do with royal power or national glory. The moment a servant girl, rather than Hippolyte, Castor or Dardanus, walked onto the stage of the Académie Royale de Musique something changed; it was a symbol of the multiple small shifts in society that were beginning to challenge the authority of the ruling class.

The masters of the Opéra had missed the work's potential to provoke and divide when, gambling on a much-needed money winner, they'd invited the Bouffons to give a dozen performances on their hallowed stage. They may have expected the experiment to lead to a reanimation of the prestige of French opera. If that was the plan, how badly it misfired; but with Rameau slowing down, and increasingly looking like the last of his kind, the vogue for Italian comic opera was more than convenient.

For the rest of the 1752 season and throughout 1753 comic operas performed by the Italians dominated. A second *intermezzo* by Pergolesi, *Il maestro de musica*, was staged in September, followed by works by Gaetano Latilla (*La finta cameriera*), Rinaldo di Capua (*La donna superba*) and Gioacchino Cocchi (*La scaltra governatrice*). The Opéra tried to readdress the balance as early as October by mounting Dauvergne's ballet héroïque *Les Amours de Tempé*, but the attempt was compromised by the decision to end each performance with an Italian *intermezzo*. A whole-hearted effort to see off the Italians was initiated in January 1753 with the premiere of Mondonville's *Titon et l'Aurore*. This pastorale héroïque was deemed a success, but supporters of the Italians fought back, helped by the first production at the Opéra of Rousseau's *Le Devin du village* in March. Rousseau's Italian-inspired one-act opera had been greatly admired at Fontainebleau the previous October. For Paris, Rousseau's score was re-orchestrated by the Opéra's copyist Lefebvre, who 'added horns and clarinets while respecting as far as possible Rousseau's simple instrumentation'.[39] In August the Opéra revived Rameau's opéra-ballet *Les Fêtes de Polymnie*, but the public didn't respond and the work was withdrawn after fourteen performances.

Because the Italian *intermezzo* genre required few performers, just two singers, Pietro Manelli and Bambini's wife Anna Tonelli, dominated the season. Anna Tonelli was not damaged by a malicious rumour that she was a castrato. The charm of the troupe was enhanced by their continuo player, Bambini's son Felice who was just a boy. In this sense, the vogue for Italian opera in 1752/53 was partly connected to the public's interest in the intimate, family-orientated dynamic of Bambini's troupe.

The proponents of Italian opera, mostly young and middle class, and revelling in this invasion of France's state theatre, formed a boisterous mob beneath the queen's box (*coin de la reine*); the opponents, mostly older and aristocratic, showed their disdain from beneath the king's box (*coin du roi*).[40] The former loved the brevity, colour and informality of the Italian works. The latter made a strong case in proclaiming Rameau's musical superiority over composers such as Latilla, Di Capua and Cocchi, but were wrong to dismiss out of hand a style of opera that would lead directly to Mozart and Da Ponte's masterpieces of the 1780s.

The hot-headed nature of the *querelle* was demonstrated by the case of Ballot de Sauvot, librettist of Rameau's *Pygmalion*, and the temperamental castrato Caffarelli (1710-83). Caffarelli was one of the international stars of Italian music. He was as famous for his bad attitude as for his angelic mezzo-soprano voice, a combination that excited young women in particular. In London in 1738 he created the named roles in Handel's *Faramondo* and *Serse*, but his disruptive antics both on and off the stage (he was known, on occasion, to humiliate his female co-stars and to argue and flirt with audience members during performances) meant that Handel quickly and gladly – Caffarelli's fee was astronomical – cut his losses. Caffarelli's period in France began in the summer of 1753, when Louis XV summoned him to Versailles to amuse Mme la dauphine during her pregnancy. During the mass to celebrate the feast of Saint Louis, in the chapel of the Louvre, Caffarelli sang a motet by Ruranello that was received, according to Grimm, with a degree of rapt attention not given to the mass itself. Grimm raved about Caffarelli in his *Correspondance littéraire*, declaring that it would be 'difficult to give a just idea of the degree of perfection that the singer brings to his art'.[41] When Caffarelli wasn't raking in the money singing Italian airs he was enthusiastically disparaging French music all over Paris. One evening at La Pouplinière's, during supper, Ballot took the castrato to task and the argument became so heated that the men had to be separated. Caffarelli, who was used to settling scores with his rapier, challenged a no doubt dazed and out of his depth Ballot to a duel. Early on a January morning in 1754, probably in the bois de Boulogne, the thrust of Caffarelli's sword pierced Ballot several times. The poet was seriously wounded but survived; the castrato fled the country.[42]

Rameau was not a partisan. He initially distanced himself from the *querelle*. He could see the merits of Pergolesi's music. There was, after all, a certain irony and even a paradox in his position. For most of his career he had been condemned by the *lullistes* for being too Italian. Rameau had worked for the fair theatres, where the ethos was essentially Italian (most of the performers of the Comédie-Italienne had de-camped to the fair theatre following the closure of their theatre in 1697) and anti-establishment. Rameau's satirical comedy *Platée*, revived in February 1749, was far removed from the mainstream of French opera. In his *Code de musique pratique*, published in 1760, Rameau wrote: 'To embrace one national taste rather than another is to prove that one is very much a novice in the art.'[43]

As for Diderot and d'Alembert, they embraced Italian opera as a symbolic declaration of freedom from the tyranny of absolutism. Initially, though, the *querelle* was little more than a distraction. In defending the *Encyclopédie* against the Jesuits and other reactionary forces they were fighting a far greater battle.

In the 'Prospectus' and the 'Discours préliminaire' of the *Encyclopédie*, Diderot and d'Alembert outlined a hierarchical tree of knowledge that was indebted to the well-established principles of the English philosopher Francis Bacon. There was one major divergence, and here Diderot and d'Alembert were making a clear statement of intent: instead of placing Theology at the head of its own independent branch, they made it a sub-branch of Reason. One didn't have to read between the lines to realise that a key purpose of the *Encyclopédie*, as outlined by d'Alembert in the 'Discours préliminaire', was to proclaim the primacy of both sensory experience and reason over faith. This intellectual manifesto was deliberately provocative.

The *Encyclopédie* only survived beyond its first volumes because the enterprise was supported by some powerful people at court and within the ministries, the most important of them by far being Chrétien-Guillaume de Lamoignon de Malesherbes. The appointment in 1750 of the twenty-nine-year-old Malesherbes to the position of *directeur de la librairie*, in charge of censorship, was a stroke of luck for Diderot and d'Alembert. Malesherbes was a fellow scientist and a progressive who wanted the *Encyclopédie* to succeed. The idea that the authorities should suppress and censor publishing to achieve orthodoxy of opinion was anathema to Malesherbes. Because he believed in the printing press as an instrument of progress, advancing knowledge and exposing untruths, he relaxed censorship during his tenure, later writing in his *Mémoire sur la liberté de la presse* (1788): 'It is the entire nation that is the judge; and if this supreme judge has been led to error, as often happens, there is always time to bring it back to the truth. [...] In the end truth prevails.'[44]

There is no more moving a public figure in the history of France in the 18th century than Malesherbes. He came from an important family, and was always loyal to his background and his king, but he had little time for the fopperies of privilege. He owed his rapid advancement to his father, but quickly made a name for himself. He was an advocate in the Paris *Parlement* when his father, as *chancelier de France*, instructed him to oversee the book trade, a role that would dominate his life for the next thirteen years. Malesherbes was later a minister under both Louis XV and Louis XVI. His honesty and courage in defending rights and confronting corruption provoked his dismissal on more than one occasion, but he was always recalled. During the periods when he was out of favour he would return to his country seat in the Loiret and devote his time to the science of botany, creating the finest botanical garden in the kingdom and writing a forty-volume study. In his old age he came out of retirement to defend Louis XVI at his trial. His life ended in the cruellest way possible. The bureaucrats of the Terror ensured that he witnessed the murder of his daughter and granddaughter before his own beheading.[45]

Malesherbes granted the first volume of the *Encyclopédie* a Royal Privilege, officially endorsing the enterprise. This only protected Diderot and d'Alembert up to a point. It was following the publication of the second volume in January 1752 that the Jesuits made their move, rightly accusing the authors of the *Encyclopédie* of inserting into the articles on obscure and difficult secular topics numerous contradictions of doctrine that amounted to an indirect attack on the church and, by extension, royal authority. A bishop at court petitioned the king who immediately demanded the suppression of the work and the seizure of all the documents. Malesherbes issued the command but warned Diderot and hid many of the key papers in his own home.[46] To save the *Encyclopédie*, Malesherbes offered to give the Jesuits authority of censorship over the subsequent volumes. This provoked the most powerful supporter of progressive ideas at court, Mme de Pompadour, into interceding on behalf of the *Encyclopédie*. Control was taken back from the Jesuits and Diderot returned to work.

Having come through this crisis, there was a lull before the publication of volume three in November 1753, during which Diderot and his colleagues enjoyed the Italian season at the Opéra and reflected upon its social and political meaning. Grimm, in a pamphlet that increased his fame as a young provocateur, used satire to make his point.[47] Diderot and d'Alembert considered the issues that lay behind the *querelle* intellectually. They sought a rational basis for their preference for Italian vocal music, and disliked the aggressive posturing of the partisans. In his short essay *Au petit prophète de Boehmischbroda au prophète Monet*, written in response to Grimm's pamphlet, Diderot reflected on the impossibility of reasoned debate in what had become a shouting match dominated, on both sides, by anonymous participants who had little real understanding of music:

> If, from the heart of the *parterre*, I could raise my voice so that both sides could hear [...], perhaps I would take part. Moreover, Messieurs, since your pamphlets are all anonymous I have spoken without having any individual in mind. To address those of you who are ignorant of the two languages and who know next to nothing about music, well it was not necessary.[48]

D'Alembert was also repelled by the confrontational nature of the debate. Why does a preference for French music mean that one has to condemn Italian, or vice versa? Why can't we enjoy their essential difference and accommodate both?

> The majesty of the Opéra, say people of taste, would be gravely offended if street entertainers were to be admitted there. Yet if this *majesty* bores us, I don't see what forces us to hold it in reverence. Moreover, why should the majesty of [Lully's] *Armide* be offended by *La serva padrona*, if that of [Corneille's] *Cinna* is

not offended by [Molière's] *Le Bourgeois gentilhomme*?[49]

Such was d'Alembert's balanced view, expressed in his essay *De la liberté de la musique*. For d'Alembert, the *querelle* was about freedom of choice in music, and freedom in music was, by implication, revolutionary. In an extraordinary passage in the same work, he wrote:

> Freedom in music supposes the freedom to feel, and the freedom to feel supposes the freedom to act, and the freedom to act means the ruin of states. So let us preserve French opera as it is if we wish to preserve the kingdom.[50]

iv Rousseau's Lettre sur la musique française

In November 1753 Jean-Jacques Rousseau published *Lettre sur la musique française*, a frontal attack on French music that forced the tensions that existed between Rameau and his allies Diderot and d'Alembert out into the open.

Rameau was particularly vulnerable that autumn because his relationship with La Pouplinière came to an end. The financier was receptive to the latest fads, and strove to maintain his influence by inviting figures like Caffarelli into his home. There was a woman involved. La Pouplinière's new mistress, Mme de Saint-Aubin, disliked the Rameaus, and no doubt they disliked her. We can't be sure of the exact circumstances of the rupture, but the roots surely go back to the trauma of Thérèse's disgrace and exile. La Pouplinière's desire to break with a past represented by Thérèse may have been a more dominant motivation than the matter of pleasing his new mistress. The Rameaus moved out of the house in the rue de Richelieu and returned to the rue des Bons Enfants. La Pouplinière replaced Rameau with a composer advocated by Mme de Saint-Aubin, Johann Stamitz. La Pouplinière's circle had enveloped Rameau, offering support and protection, for nearly twenty years. For the remainder of his life Rameau was isolated and increasingly professionally lonely. It explains the increasingly anxious and bitter tone of his engagement in public life in general, and the aggrieved aggression he directed at Diderot and d'Alembert in particular, men who, after La Pouplinière, had been the most important champions of his cause.

Since Rousseau's bruising encounter with Rameau in 1745 he had made his name as a philosopher, but he still craved recognition as a composer. He was greatly encouraged by the extravagant success of *Le Devin du village* at Fontainebleau (October 1752) and at the Opéra (March 1753). The king, besieged by an endless barrage of music, was grateful for a work that was short, light and easy to follow, and decided to award Rousseau a state pension; but Rousseau, a nervous wreck at court, mocked for wearing an old wig and the attire of a common man, fled Fontainebleau and missed his audience. More tragically, he came to believe that his success was resented by Diderot and Grimm, and eventually parted with them for good.[51]

In writing *Lettre sur la musique française* Rousseau set out to dismiss French opera in general and Rameau in particular by comparing the French style of vocal music unfavourably with the Italian. It followed an earlier attack, *Lettre à M. Grimm, au sujet des remarques ajoutées à sa lettre sur Omphale*, published in April 1752. In *Lettre sur Omphale* Grimm had proclaimed the superiority of Italian music over French but had acknowledged Rameau's genius, his right to occupy a special place. In his response, Rousseau conceded the importance of *Platée*, calling it the most excellent opera in all of French music, but what followed was a sustained critique of the composer that was the deadlier for granting him some strengths: Rameau is way below Lully in intelligence, but higher in expression; he has learning but not genius; his works contain some good passages, but lack unity.

Rousseau went further in *Lettre sur la musique française*. To paraphrase his argument (I apologise for the over-simplification): the consonant heavy French language, in contrast to the soft syllables of Italian, is not suited to music, therefore French songs are insipid, therefore, to give them vitality, French composers pile on harmonies as if many bad parts could compensate for the lack of a single good one, therefore music becomes noise. Rousseau articulated his thesis in the language and prestige of the philosopher: 'It is for the Poet to write poetry, and for the Musician to compose music: but it belongs only to the Philosopher to speak wisely of them both'.[52] If the tone was smug, the reasoning was widely accepted. Rousseau was at his most persuasive when writing about the French style of recitative. He repeated his argument, succinctly, in his entry on the topic in volume thirteen of the *Encyclopédie*, published in December 1765, stating that

> recitative is a way of singing very much like talking, a musical declamation, during which the musician strives to imitate, as much as this is possible, the inflexions of the voice of the actor. [...] The Italian language is sweet, flexible, and composed of words that are easy to pronounce, and allows the *recitative* all the rapidity of declamation. They insist, though, that nothing foreign should mingle into the simplicity of the *recitative* and that ornaments spoil it. The French, on the other hand, put in as many as they possibly can. Their language, more laden with consonants, harsher, and more difficult to pronounce, demands slower tempi, and it is on these slowed-down notes that they use accents, *portamenti*, and even trills. [...] Foreigners, therefore, can never distinguish in our operas what is recitative and what is song.[53]

D'Alembert and Rousseau were right to single out French recitative as the reason why French opera was, for foreigners, difficult to appreciate. 'I took the whole for recitative,' wrote the Italian dramatist Goldoni after seeing his first opera in Paris. David Garrick fell asleep during a performance in June 1751 and went home with a headache.[54] It must have been frustrating for admirers of Rameau's French opera that the very qualities that helped to make it distinctive, intellectually ambitious and forward-looking – its full exploitation of the orchestra to both accompany and comment on the singer's words, and, especially, its integration of the different elements into a forward moving flow of ideas – for others made it so perplexing and so dissatisfying. French opera did have its foreign champions, among them Telemann, who, in a fascinating letter to his countryman Carl Heinrich Graun, defended Rameau's recitatives. It is rare, in the 18th century, to find evidence of one great composer's opinion of another. Writing to Telemann, in 1751, Graun not only criticised a section from Rameau's *Castor et Pollux*, claiming that the 'false intonations' and unexpected 'changes of metre' made the music difficult to sing and therefore unnatural (the effect, he wrote, is that of the howling of a dog), he also rewrote it in the Italian style (Graun was the leading composer of Italian operas in Germany). In his reply, Telemann enjoyed countering Graun's criticisms, and dismissing his corrections. He provided a line-by-line commentary on the passage, demonstrating how every shift in emotion, as expressed by the words, was precisely rendered by the flexibility of Rameau's style of recitative. You say, Telemann told Graun, that

> French recitatives please nowhere outside France. I do not know, because history books say nothing about it... But I do know that I have met Germans, Englishmen, Russians, Poles and even a couple of Jews who could sing by heart whole scenes of *Atys*, *Bellérophon*, etc. On the other hand, I have not seen one single man who has said anything but this of the Italians: 'It is wonderful, it is matchless, but I couldn't remember anything of it.'[55]

In one section of the *Lettre* Rousseau relates how, in Venice, he observed the reaction of an Armenian who was hearing western music for the first time and therefore had a 'neutral ear'. A singer performed Rameau's 'Temple sacré, séjour tranquille' from *Hippolyte et Aricie* followed by an aria by the Italian Galuppi. The Armenian could not understand the French air, and showed no pleasure, but was visibly enchanted by the Italian. From that moment, Rousseau writes, 'we could no longer make him listen to any French air'.[56] This anecdote is hardly conclusive, but the same could be said of Rameau's Lyon workman singing the fundamental bass. Later on in the *Lettre*, Rousseau dissects Armide's monologue 'Enfin il est en ma puissance' from Lully's opera, and finds that the turmoil of the character's predicament is inadequately expressed by the 'scholastic regularity' of Lully's scoring.[57] He chose Armide's monologue because Rameau had proclaimed its perfection in his *Nouveau système de musique théorique* (1726).

Nowhere did Rousseau mention the key factor that made Italian comic opera subversive when performed in France – its depiction of domestic and contemporary life; and it is noteworthy that the subject matter of *Le Devin du village* was ultra-conservative and typically French – no risqué story here of a maidservant manipulating her betters, but rather a simple pastoral parable about a shepherdess who learns that her love for a lord is inappropriate and impossible.

The *Lettre* enraged many of the most influential proponents of the national music, including members of the Opéra's orchestra, but Rousseau's assertion that the musicians planned to assassinate him in the theatre reads like paranoid fantasy.[58] As for Rameau, he was contemptuous of Rousseau's ideas and felt compelled to issue a rebuttal, *Observations sur notre instinct pour la musique, et sur son principe* (1754), not least because Rousseau was attacking him directly whereas the other champions of Italian music who had gone to print had left him alone, believing that his music was in part inspired by the Italian style.

Rameau opens the *Observations* with a succinct explanation of the key principle of his system:

> Harmony alone stirs the passions; melody derives its strength only from this source, from which it emanates directly… Music is natural to us; the pleasing feeling it gives us results only from pure instinct. That is why the principle of such an instinct should matter to people who cultivate the sciences and the arts. The principle is now known: it exists in the harmony that is produced by the resonance of every sounding body, be it the sound of a voice, of a string, of a pipe, of a bell, etc.[59]

After many pages of detail, Rameau finally turns his attention to Rousseau's *Lettre*. He begins powerfully by stating that the *Lettre* contradicts Rousseau's own work in the *Encyclopédie*, where, guided by d'Alembert, his articles had followed the basic tenets of Rameau's system. He goes on to counter Rousseau's analysis of the passage from Lully's *Armide*, methodically addressing every point and explaining how the subtle musical language of this 'master' perfectly expresses the emotions of the words.

Rameau wasn't wounded by Rousseau's polemic, for, rightly or wrongly, he didn't rate him either as a composer or as a thinker on music. The opinion of d'Alembert was another matter. Rameau took another look at the articles on music in the *Encyclopédie* and decided that they contained hundreds of errors that needed to be exposed in print. Rousseau's writing had been approved by d'Alembert, and Rameau found this hard to bear.

v Rameau versus d'Alembert

Rameau published *Erreurs sur la musique dans l'Encyclopédie* in 1755, followed by a further volume in 1756. He must have spent many tedious hours in his rooms overlooking the garden of the Palais-Royal, surrounded by the heavy folio volumes, systematically going through the articles line by line; and many more brooding on the matter during his lonely morning walks between the trees. The philosopher Alexandre Deleyre told Rousseau: 'I see Rameau every morning walking down the avenue of trees beneath my window, like a shadow.'[60] Deleyre quoted Virgil – 'inceptus clamor frustratur hiantes' – to depict Rameau as a forlorn and grotesque figure, his mouth gaping open as if in agony.

Rameau was never more the pedant than here. He pointed out every unsubstantiated claim and every generalisation, and poured scorn on Rousseau's thesis that musicians of taste have no need for either learning or method. Rameau's contempt for Rousseau enlivens an otherwise tedious exposition. At one point he writes that someone who grew up in Calvinist Geneva, where music was restricted, could not be expected to understand the art. At another, he refers to the performance of Rousseau's *Les Muses galantes* at La Pouplinière's all those years before, putting down in print the points he had made at the time, that the piece contained some pretty Italian airs, plagiarised, and a lot of very bad French music of Rousseau's own invention. Good Italian music is preferable to unremarkable French music, Rameau writes, but Rousseau is too lacking in knowledge and in refinement of taste to be able to tell good from bad.

Rameau's obsessive correcting of the *Encyclopédie* may have looked like curmudgeonly nit-picking on the grandest of scales, and his personal attacks against Rousseau certainly weakened his argument by making him seem more spiteful than scholarly; but the weight and prestige of the *Encyclopédie* as the ark of all knowledge, as the definitive statement offered to posterity by the great thinkers of the age, explains why Rameau was so anxious to set the record straight.

D'Alembert took it very badly and set out to silence the composer.[61] At first we may wonder how d'Alembert could go, in such a short space of time, from placing Rameau on a pedestal of supreme merit in the 'Discours préliminaire' of the first volume of the *Encyclopédie* to treating him so dismissively, but within this paradox lies an answer. Like Voltaire in the 1730s, d'Alembert interpreted Rameau's behaviour as ingratitude. Rameau, by publicly challenging the veracity of the *Encyclopédie*, was aiding the project's many powerful enemies at a time when its survival remained precarious. D'Alembert was acutely sensitive on this issue. He had, after all, invested his own reputation in the *Encyclopédie*.

The argument that followed lasted for the rest of Rameau's life. D'Alembert used an 'Avertissement des Editeurs' at the beginning of volume six of the *Encyclopédie*, published in 1756, to make his initial response. It was a masterly riposte, expressing grievance through the literary device of incredulity. *Erreurs sur la musique dans l'Encyclopédie* had been published anonymously, but no one doubted that Rameau was the author. D'Alembert's argument ran thus: surely the famous musician credited with writing the *Erreurs* cannot actually have been the author, since Diderot and I have always rendered him homage and, at his request, given advice on his own works. Surely he cannot hold such an odd opinion as 'géométrie est fondée sur la musique'?

If d'Alembert hoped that he had found the right words to close the matter he was soon disappointed. Rameau fired back with *Réponse de M. Rameau à MM. les éditeurs de l'Encyclopédie sur leur dernier avertissement* (1757). Rameau's opening words set the tone: 'Vous m'accusez, vous m'attaquez, Messieurs...' He responded to the suggestion of ingratitude by reminding the editors that his association with them had been mutually beneficial:

> You say that I have never turned down the opportunity to consult you; what you should say is that you did me the honour of taking my lessons on music theory and practice for some months, and therefore it is you who have consulted me... And did you not, yourself, add to the title of your *Eléments de musique théorique et pratique* the words *according to the principles of M. Rameau*?[62]

Rameau and d'Alembert were both too proud, too sensitive and too intractable to return to common ground. The editors of the *En-*

cyclopédie decided to adopt, from that moment on, a critical approach to Rameau's ideas, beginning with the articles 'Fondamental' and 'Gamme' (Scale), written mostly by d'Alembert, in volume seven, published in 1757. In the first of the articles, d'Alembert targeted the spot where Rameau was most vulnerable, using the term 'musician' in a derogatory way and implying that he was a *faux* scientist. This was as vicious as an intellectual duel could get. D'Alembert was dismantling the reputation of a man who, in volume one of the same work, he had called a 'genius', and an 'artist-philosopher', and of whom he had written: 'His merit […] will be well known only when time has silenced envy; and his name, dear to the enlightened of our nation, cannot offend anyone.' He must have been aware of the contradiction. Rameau did this to people: it was both his strength and his curse.

The articles 'Fondamental' and 'Gamme' were far more serious for Rameau than Rousseau's attack in *Lettre sur la musique française*. He needed time to respond. His *Code de musique pratique*, published in 1760, included *Lettre à M. d'Alembert, sur ses opinions en musique, insérées dans les articles Fondamental et Gamme de l'Encyclopédie*. The two great men then exchanged open letters in the pages of the *Mercure de France*. D'Alembert's *Lettre à M. Rameau* and Rameau's reply *Réponse à la lettre de M. D'Alembert, qu'on vient de lire*, appeared in April 1761. Rameau's *Suite de la réponse* was published in July of that year.

Although Rameau's claims for the import of the *corps sonore* had become ever more eccentric, the concept itself had not changed. D'Alembert's opinion, though, had shifted. He was prepared to accept Rameau's ideas as speculation, but not as rules that he had demonstrated to be true; and during the exchanges it became clear that he wasn't even prepared to acknowledge, unequivocally, the mathematical basis of music, let alone that a fundamental law of proportions was revealed by the harmonic progression produced by the *corps sonore*, and that this law was given by nature.

Rameau was perplexed by what he believed to be a complete reversal of d'Alembert's earlier position. He wanted to know why d'Alembert had supported his work and endorsed it as a member of the Académie. D'Alembert replied that the paper Rameau had submitted to the Académie had been entitled *Mémoire où l'on expose les fondements d'un système de musique théorique et pratique*, and that Rameau had been wrong to change it on publication to *Démonstration du principe de l'harmonie*, and to declare on the title page that it had been 'Approuvée par Messieurs de l'Académie Royale des Sciences'. Rameau, not unreasonably, pointed to the glowing conclusion of the Académie's report, written by d'Alembert:

> Thus harmony [...] has become, thanks to the work of M. Rameau, a more geometric science, to which mathematical principles can be applied with more usefulness than had previously been the case.[63]

D'Alembert responded, accurately, that nowhere in the report had he agreed that Rameau's ideas had been proven. Nevertheless, one can understand why Rameau felt aggrieved. Rameau's obstinacy had boxed d'Alembert in a corner where he was guilty of the spirit if not the letter of hypocrisy.

In 1762 d'Alembert delivered what he clearly intended to be the *coup de grace*, a new version of his *Eléments de musique, théorique et pratique, suivant les principes de M. Rameau*. A work that had been written to popularise Rameau's theories was significantly revised to become a critical commentary. In the 'Discours préliminaire' d'Alembert accepted that Rameau had 'found in the resonance of the corps sonore the most probable origin of harmony',[64] but in the pages that followed he was not only critical of many of Rameau's conclusions, he also presented his own alternatives. Lacking a music background, d'Alembert's ideas were not always completely convincing as music theory. Jonathan W. Bernard sums up the nature of d'Alembert's contribution by declaring that 'the value of what d'Alembert had to say ultimately arose from the strengths of Rameau's theories'.[65] It is a statement that neither man would have taken issue with before 1753.

Given that most people received Rameau's ideas through d'Alembert, the revised *Eléments* was a serious blow. Rameau had to confront the bitter truth that d'Alembert's little book, translated and frequently reprinted, would take a distorted image of his theoretical ideas to England and Germany, and far into the future. D'Alembert made it known, in his *Réponse à une lettre imprimée de M. Rameau*, published in the *Mercure* in March 1762 and included at the end of the *Eléments*, that he was now done with the quarrel, signing off with one of those devastating sentences, elegant and clear and yet full of subtle meaning, that was so typical of his character:

> I flatter myself, Monsieur, that I have sufficiently answered your criticisms, at least those that I have understood; but I also flatter myself that I have given sufficient proof of my kindness and attachment to you by answering once; and I believe, therefore, that I have earned the right to keep my silence from now on.[66]

Rameau, of course, continued. A pamphlet entitled *Origine des sciences, suivie d'une Controverse sur le même sujet* contained his response to the new edition of the *Eléments*. His self-belief was impregnable; his faith in the *corps sonore* as the key that unlocked all the sciences, unassailable; his need for vindication, unfathomable. As Deleyre recognised, he was like a figure in a classical tragedy, alone on a stage, his mouth gaping open as if words were stuck in his throat.

For neutral followers of this very public argument, Rameau's reputation had not suffered ('I have never claimed that I have a head organised like a Newton, a Rameau. I would never have discovered the fundamental bass or the calculus' wrote Voltaire in 1760);[67] but those concerned for his well-being must have regretted that aspect of his nature that led him to alienate Diderot and especially d'Alembert, men whose sincere friendship he had cause to value. The general view, though, was summed up by Voltaire: 'It is said that Rameau is writing against a philosopher on music; I'd prefer him to compose an opera.'[68]

It is to d'Alembert's credit that, unlike Rousseau, he never turned his sense of personal grievance into an attempt to belittle Rameau's achievements as a composer. His *De la liberté de la musique* was an insightful analysis of the political and cultural implications of the *querelle*, written after the Italians had withdrawn, that contained a fair-minded assessment of the relative merits of French and Italian music. D'Alembert called *Platée* the masterpiece of French music, and went on to deliver a profound summation of Rameau's significance, viewing him as an artist who had to calibrate his genius to the expectations of his country and his century:

> Rameau is more deserving of esteem in that he dared everything he could, and not everything he would have wanted to dare; he had the merit of seeing beyond the place where he took his listeners, and the merit, perhaps also great, of judging just how far they could be taken. He would have missed his aim in going further. He gave us, not the best music of which he was capable, but the best that we were able to receive. It is not only by their works that it is necessary to measure men, it is in comparing them to their century and their nation.[69]

vi Rameau's Nephew

Diderot, like d'Alembert, continued to think deeply about the state of French opera. In *Entretiens sur Le Fils naturel*, written in 1757 to accompany his play *Le Fils naturel*, Diderot used the conceit of a conversation between himself and the leading character of his play, Dorval, to explore the limitations of a theatre dominated by the opposing genres of tragedy and comedy. Both genres, Dorval proclaims, rely on absurdities and are unable to reflect the realities of everyday life, for life is lived somewhere in the middle of these two extremes: 'For a man of taste there is the same absurdity in [Rameau's] Castor being made a god as in [Molière's] bourgeois gentleman being made a mamamushi.'[70] In the third dialogue of the *Entretiens*, Diderot discusses how French opera can be modernised:

> I believe that neither the poets nor the musicians [...] have a real idea of their theatre. If the lyric genre is bad, it is the worst of all genres. If it is good, it is the best. But can it be good if it is unable to imitate nature? [...] Men of genius have reanimated our philosophy of the intelligible world. Cannot someone do the same for lyric poetry, bringing it down from a region of fantasy to the world in which we live?[71]

Diderot seems indifferent to Rousseau's assertion that the French language does not lend itself to music, for in his exposition of a reformed opera he takes one of Clytemnestra's great speeches from Racine's *Iphigénie* as his text and writes: 'In her despair Clytemnestra must wrench from her womb a cry of nature; and the musician must be able to convey all its nuances.'[72]

If Diderot had written the *Entretiens* twenty years earlier he may have viewed Rameau as the genius capable of putting his ideas into practice, for had not Rameau, in *Hippolyte et Aricie*, conveyed Phèdre's despair in all its nuances? But Rameau had never really challenged the overriding artificiality of French opera. Although, in the 1750s and 60s, he was still striving to make the form as truthful and elegant as possible, he never went as far as Diderot wanted.

Diderot did not feel the need to publicly aid d'Alembert in his dispute with Rameau. Instead, he poured his anger over Rameau's attacks on the *Encyclopédie* into his enigmatic literary masterpiece *Le Neveu de Rameau*. The first draft of *Le Neveu* was written during the dispute, in 1760/61. Diderot never published the work: some of its ideas were likely to prove controversial, and he was ever fearful of the promise he made to the censor back in 1749. Given the way Diderot satirises public figures, it seems unlikely that it was circulated to more than a few close friends, Grimm being one. The work was not mentioned by Diderot or anyone else, from Voltaire downwards, in papers or letters. Diderot wrote *Le Neveu* in the belief that it would be published, and admired, after his death. The work is too mysterious, and too open to interpretation, for us to be sure about Diderot's motives, but even if the work is much more than an act of revenge against Rameau, it is certainly that in part.

Le Neveu de Rameau is a fictional philosophical dialogue between the narrator, Diderot, and Rameau's nephew Jean-François, that takes place in the café de la Regence in the place du Palais-Royal. It is likely that Diderot's imagination was fired by an actual encounter. He took aspects of Jean-François's public notoriety, particularly his reputation as a sponger who played the jester in fashionable households to earn his keep, and from these scraps created a comic character worthy of Molière – a self-aware nihilist and cynical truth teller who acts as a commentator on the absurdities of the times. Diderot diminishes the real nephew but also his uncle. In this sense the work was a joke at Rameau's expense.

The narrator's initial comments on Rameau the artist and thinker are not controversial; they are satirical in tone, and lightly expressed. The narrator tells us that the hero of his dialogue

> is a nephew of the famous musician who has delivered us from the plainsong of Lully that we have been chanting for over a hundred years, who has written so many unintelligible visions and apocalyptic truths on the theory of music, not a word of which he or anyone else has ever understood, and from whom we have a certain number of operas in which there is harmony, snatches of song, disconnected ideas, clash of arms, dashings to and fro, triumphs, lances, glories, murmurs and victories to take your breath away, and some dance tunes which will last forever. Having buried the Florentine master [Lully] he will himself be buried by the Italian virtuosi, which he foresaw.[73]

It is when Diderot turns his attention to Rameau's character that the writing's tone contains more bile than wit:

> I (Diderot): Are you still in good health?
> HE (Jean-François): Yes, usually, but not all that good today.
> I: What? And you with a paunch like Silenus and a face –
> HE: A face you would take for his behind. The spleen which has dried up my uncle is apparently fattening his dear nephew.
> I: Speaking of your uncle, do you see him sometimes?
> HE: Yes, going past in the street.
> I: Doesn't he ever do anything for you?
> HE: If he ever did anything for anybody it was without realising it. He is a philosopher in his way. He thinks of nothing but himself, and the rest of the universe is not worth a pin to him. His wife and daughter can just die when they like, and so long as the parish bells tolling their knell go on sounding the intervals of a twelfth and a seventeenth everything will be all right. He's quite happy. That is what I particularly value in men of genius. They are only good for one thing, and apart from that, nothing. They don't know what it means to be citizens, fathers, mothers, brothers, relations, friends.[74]

The theme is developed across several pages before Diderot's thoughts return to Rameau:

> I: Now look, tell me – I won't take your uncle as an example, for he is a hard man, brutal, inhuman, avaricious, he is a bad father, bad husband, bad uncle; but it is not quite certain that he really is a man of genius, that he has taken his art very far or that his work will count ten years from now.[75]

Like d'Alembert, Diderot chose a method of revenge, philosophical and literary, that would stay in print, and therefore remain effective, *indefinitely*.

Let's consider the real nephew. Jean-François was the son of Rameau's younger brother Claude Bernard, a proficient professional musician who, like their father, spent most of his life as a church organist in Dijon. The two brothers remained on excellent terms all their lives. Claude Bernard was godfather to Rameau's eldest son, who was named after him. He was proud of his brother's achievements, and quick to come to his defence when attacks on his theoretical ideas were voiced in Dijon. Jean-François was born in 1716. Also a musician, his early life was even more unsettled than that of his uncle's. He was in the army for a while, and considered a career in the church before arriving in Paris during the late 1730s. From anecdotal accounts, Jean-François emerges as a wayward, temperamental man who Rameau tried to support before realising that the boy was a lost cause.

Jean-François entered the official records in November 1748, following an incident at the Opéra. He had insulted Rebel and Francœur, co-inspectors of the Opéra, probably in support of his uncle, for Rameau's relationship with Rebel and Francœur, as with all the company's managers over the years, was often fractious. Maret recorded that 'Rebel and Francœur often forced Rameau to revise sections of music'.[76] The guards refused to let Jean-François enter the theatre: in the ensuing scuffle punches were thrown. The official who recorded the incident in the *Registres des Ordres du Roi* went so far as to disparage Rameau's nephew as an 'unsociable character, difficult to tame'.[77]

Jean-François was imprisoned in For-l'Evêque for three weeks. The minister of state in charge, Phelypeaux, consulted Rameau, who proposed that his nephew should be ordered to leave for the colonies. It is clear that Rameau was embarrassed by his nephew's behaviour; that he felt he was being held responsible even. His tolerance had been exhausted. This does not excuse the callousness of his actions. Phelypeaux told Rameau that he was happy to make the arrangements, but only if Jean-François agreed to go. Jean-François refused.[78]

Jean-François didn't mend his ways. Five years later, in December 1753, during a rehearsal at the Opéra for a revival of *Castor et Pollux* that marked the end of the *querelle des bouffons*, the *Prévôt des marchands* told the company that Rebel and Francœur were stepping down, at their own request, and were to be replaced by Thuret and Royer. As Rebel and Francœur were being thanked for their long service, Jean-François, listening from the *parterre*, initiated an ironic slow handclap and one of the members of the orchestra started to play a merry air on the violin. This humiliation of Rebel and Francœur caused a minor scandal: the official report of the incident named Jean-François as the ringleader.[79] The incident demonstrated Jean-François's talent as a troublemaker, and his loyalty to his uncle; but also the bad feeling that had built up within the company during the *querelle*: the artists and musicians took the attacks of Rousseau and others very personally, and blamed their directors for programming one Italian comedy after another.

Most of our knowledge of Jean-François comes from his friend Jacques Cazotte, a minor writer who participated in the *querelle* on the pro-French side, writing of Rousseau: 'If contempt for others along with self-esteem make up the philosopher, then Jean-Jacques Rousseau is a very great philosopher.'[80] Cazotte described Jean-François as the most extraordinary man he had ever met, blessed with a natural talent for many genres of music but lacking the discipline to delve very deeply into the art; he was born full of song, and could turn any phrase he was given into music, but lacked the art to go further. Rameau's former librettist Alexis Piron left his own satirical portrait of Jean-François in a letter to Cazotte (the four men were linked by their shared birthplace, Dijon):

> I see him [...] trample on the rich and the great, and cry misery; mock his uncle, and embellish his great name; want to

imitate it, to attain it, to efface it... ; he's a lion in threatening, a hen in action... ; moreover, without contradiction, he is the best child in the world, meriting the goodwill of all those who know him as we do.[81]

If Rameau's relationship with his nephew was often strained, it never completely broke down. Jean-François's own music included a one-act comedy called *Le Calendrier des vieillards*, performed at the fair theatre, and a collection of keyboard suites with descriptive titles. The music is lost, but the pieces were reviewed by Fréron in his *Année littéraire* (1757).[82] The suite entitled *Le Général d'armée* described different stages of a battle, and *Le Génie français* contained a piece called *L'Encyclopédique*. Most intriguing of all, the final suite was called *Les Trois Rameaux*, consisting of Jean-François's musical portraits of his uncle, father and himself. We learn that the portrait of Rameau was to be played 'with beauty, wisdom, depth'. In 1766 Jean-François published a curious autobiographical poem called *La Raméide*. Here, as elsewhere, he wrote admiringly of his uncle.

Diderot was repeating malicious gossip concerning Rameau's family life that the neutral documentary evidence often contradicts. Rameau was diligent as the head of his family, investing money for his wife and children to ensure that they would be comfortable after his death, purchasing the court position of *valet de chambre* for his son Claude-François at the cost of 21,500 *livres*, and supporting his sisters back in Dijon. In a letter to a Dijonnais called Bazin, the buyer of a house belonging to the family, we see that Rameau was a caring brother:

> If you would give my sisters the little treat of giving up to them the rest of the last year which comes to an end on February 15, I should be much obliged to you on my own account; I have already relinquished all the rest to them and would do more if I could.[83]

However, disparaging comments about Rameau, particularly that he was a bad father, were repeated often enough for the topic to remain a difficult and unresolved theme.

The reason may lie in his relationships with his daughters. In August 1751, his daughter Marie-Louise, aged seventeen, entered a convent of the Visitation Order at Montargis in the Loiret, some seventy miles south of Paris. This profound moment in Marie-Louise's life was witnessed by her mother and her uncle, Albert Mangot. Rameau provided a diary but was not present at the clothing,[84] which could suggest that he was unhappy with a decision taken either by his daughter or his wife. From a 21st century perspective, one is inclined to view Marie-Louise's departure as a tragedy for all concerned. Rameau's second daughter, Marie-Alexandrine, born in 1744, remained at home until Rameau's death, but married a young musketeer called François-Marie de Gaultier only two months later, which may indicate, as Cuthbert Girdlestone suggested,[85] that she was prevented from marrying by her father, either because he objected to her suitor or because he wanted to keep her at home. In a play performed in 1763, Charles Collé created a comic character called Dupuis, an old man determined to prevent his daughter from marrying.[86] In his journal, Collé claimed that Rameau had remarked in public: 'I am Dupuis, except I will never be moved to let my daughter marry!'[87] Collé is not a trustworthy source. If on this occasion the circumstances do not contradict him, they are hardly conclusive. Without Collé's claim we would not necessarily view the timing of Marie-Alexandrine's marriage as evidence of her father's tyranny. Rameau could have given his blessing before his death to a match that was socially advantageous: Gaultier was very well connected.

The domestic lives of great men rarely stand up to scrutiny. In his treatise on education, *Émile*, published in 1762, Rousseau wrote of the moral benefits of a mother breastfeeding and nursing her child, and of a father loving his daughter. Rousseau's partner Thérèse bore him five children. He dispatched each baby immediately to the foundling home (L'hôpital des enfants-trouvés). The pain that Thérèse must have felt is incomprehensible. Rousseau kept this aspect of his life from his friends as long as he could, but only, he wrote later in his *Confessions*, out of respect for Thérèse: he could not see the hypocrisy of his actions, let alone the cruelty. As for Diderot, when his daughter Angélique was in her early teens he offered her hand in marriage to one of his friends. The friend was outraged and rejected the offer. A few years later, Diderot arranged a much more appropriate union for Angélique. He would remain a controlling and possessive father. Perhaps Rameau and Diderot were not dissimilar in this respect.

9

The Part-Time Composer

Rameau's Music During and After the Querelle des Bouffons 1753-1760

i In the Forest of Fontainebleau

If Rameau's life during the 1750s was dominated by his theoretical work, he still composed music for the court and, once the vogue for Italian opera had passed, the Paris stage. Rameau's popularity and prestige helped French opera to reclaim temporarily at least some of its glory.

Every autumn the royal court travelled to the Château de Fontainebleau, some thirty-five miles south-southeast of Paris. The palace was smaller and more hospitable than Versailles; and the king loved the vast hunting forests that surrounded it more than any other part of his realm. A lavish programme of entertainments was organised by Richelieu for the 1753 season. Rameau, temporarily exiled from the Paris stage by the *querelle*, provided his first new works since 1751, the one-act ballets *Daphnis et Eglé* and *Les Sybarites*. Rameau was creating work for Fontainebleau for the first time.

The theatre, the *Salle de la comédie*, was situated in the wing of the palace known as the *Cour de la fontaine*. The stage included a partitioned section for an orchestra of thirty players. Because the room was small and rectangular, very similar to a *jeu de paume*, the peninsular stage occupied most of the *parterre*. This was necessary to provide enough performance space for the dancers. The stage machinery was very basic, and the sets needed to be rudimentary and static. Because of these restrictions, large-scale pieces were difficult to stage. The theatre at Fontainebleau was best-suited to an intimate form of opera, with few effects and the skilful integration of the dances.

Charles Collé wrote *Daphnis et Eglé*, and it is here that we discover the probable cause of his contempt for Rameau. It was the only collaboration between these two former members of the Caveau club. They may have met infrequently since the club was dissolved in 1739, and the fact that it took so many years for Rameau to engage Collé suggests that he had limited respect for the writer and only called upon his services because Cahusac was unavailable and time was pressing. Collé was forty-four, and some years away from his first notable success, the aforementioned play *Dupuis et Desronais* staged at the Comédie-Française in 1763. If he is of any interest today, it is because of his journal. In these private pages he criticised Voltaire, Rameau and many of the other great men of his time. Voltaire didn't mention Collé once in his letters, which suggests that he wasn't worth even a passing reference, but also that he never dared to attack Voltaire in public. Similarly, Rameau was probably never aware that Collé held him in such contempt.

Daphnis et Eglé belonged to a genre of opera very popular at court, the pastorale héroïque. The king and his courtiers watched pastoral scenes of idyllic beauty while surrounded by the forest, a domain that was sensibly dreaded by the ordinary men and women who, out of necessity, travelled its roads: the criminal gangs that operated in the forest rarely robbed without raping and murdering their victims, doing so with seeming impunity (the forêt de Fontainebleau and the bois de Boulogne were far more dangerous places than the streets of Paris). Collé's libretto is little more than serviceable: it tells the story of a shepherd and a shepherdess whose friendship is innocent until Cupid tells them that they are in love. Jélyotte and Cahusac's mistress Marie Fel were cast in the title roles. Cahusac's absence may have been down to the fact that his relationship with Mlle Fel was going through one of its rough patches.

Rameau's score is of historical interest. This was the first music composed by Rameau since the outbreak of the *querelle*, and, in the overture, he was clearly trying his hand at writing in the style of the Italians. Here we find unison writing (the doubling of instruments) and less harmonic individuality than normal.[1] The fact that he felt the need to experiment, and did so out of the public eye at Fontainebleau, is revealing.

The dances, over twenty in number, dominated the play, as was the custom at Fontainebleau. Rameau was always adept at judging the occasion, and of delivering a work that fitted the theatre space and the proclivities of the audience. To this end, he gave Collé a hard time, demanding changes and cuts and then more cuts. Given the way Rameau challenged and cajoled Voltaire, we can have no doubt that a journeyman like Collé was made to feel like a lackey.

Daphnis et Eglé was scheduled to be premiered on 30 October after a performance of Nivelle de La Chaussée's play *La Fausse antipathie*. The dress rehearsal on 29 October went very badly and there is reason to believe that the performance was cancelled. Collé's bitterness lasted. After Rameau's death he generalised his own experience, declaring that the composer forced writers to strangle and disfigure their poetry for the sake of his divertissements: 'All those who worked with him were obliged to strangle their subjects, to leave out their verses, to disfigure them, so as to deliver the divertissements he wanted. He bullied lyricists to the point that those of good standing never wanted to work with him again.'[2] Collé could be accused of over-valuing the quality of his verses and expecting them to be given primacy over the music.

Rameau's other pieces for the autumn season at Fontainebleau were composed to texts by Marmontel, the dramatist he had worked with at the Opéra in 1751 to create *Acante et Céphise* and *La Guirlande*. Marmontel had recently been appointed to the court position of *secrétaire des bâtiments royaux*. Their first piece, *Lysis et Délie*, was abandoned at the last minute and replaced by *La Danse* from *Les Fêtes d'Hébé*. The official reason given was that *Lysis et Délie* was too similar to *Daphnis et Eglé*.[3] Both works were concerned with the theme of love disguised as friendship, which may have been considered controversial at court because of the politics surrounding the state of the king's relationship with Mme de Pompadour. Perhaps the cancellation of *Daphnis et Eglé* had little to do with the dress rehearsal. Rameau's difficult time at Fontainebleau was only partially rescued by the ballet *Les Sybarites*, performed on 13 November in honour of the birth of the dauphin's second son. *Les Sybarites* tells the story of two rival cities, Crotona and Sybaris. The king of Crotona leads his army against the Sybarites, who instead of fighting greet their enemy with garlands of flowers. The king falls in love with the queen of the Sybarites, and peace triumphs over war. With tensions growing on the eve of the Seven Years' War, the choice of subject risked being considered political.

Marmontel was a man of letters of distinction, able to collaborate with Rameau on equal terms, and with flexibility. He was a contributor to the *Encyclopédie*, writing articles on literary and theatrical forms, among them 'Comédie', 'Dialogue' and 'Fiction', and his creative work included the stories collected under the title *Contes moraux*. Relations between the two men remained cordial. In his memoirs Marmontel wrote: 'I saw him setting bad poetry, and wanted to give him better.'[4] At this time, in line with his fellow *Encyclopédistes*, Marmontel was falling under the spell of Italian music, and it is in this regard that his remarks on Rameau are of most interest. Having expressed his admiration for the Italians, declaring that their music 'ravished his soul', he went on to write:

> I studied the forms, trying to bend our language so as to accommodate them, and wished that Rameau would undertake with me to bring to our stage all of this rich beauty; but Rameau, already an old man, wasn't disposed to change his manner; and in these Italians he wanted to see only errors and abuses, and pretended to despise them.[5]

Marmontel realised that Rameau's contempt for the Italians was feigned, and had more to do with an acceptance that he was too old to change than with anything else. In his works for Fontainebleau, we find Rameau considering whether the style of the Bouffons had any value, and deciding that its value, for him, was negligible. If he had been of a younger generation perhaps he would have experimented further.

ii Castor et Pollux and the End of the Querelle

While at Fontainebleau, Rameau was working on something far

more important than his ballets for the court: a new version of *Castor et Pollux* for the Opéra. Much was resting on this new production. If any French opera could send the Italians packing it was *Castor*, or so the establishment, finally out of patience with a situation that had been allowed to damage French prestige for too long, hoped. As we have already noted, it was during the rehearsals, in December 1753, that Thuret and Royer replaced the directors who had run the theatre during the *querelle*. The orchestra, clearly relieved to be playing Rameau's music – quite a turnaround, since the master's infernal scores, with their black clusters of notes, had always terrified them – chose this moment, spurred on by Rameau's nephew, to vent feelings that had been growing in intensity during the course of 1753. According to Jean-Benjamin de La Borde, who had studied under Rameau, the musicians of the Opéra considered themselves to be Rameau's children.[6] This rings true for these final years of the composer's life. In contrast, Rameau's relationship with the directors remained difficult. Thuret had previously been the director of the Opéra during Rameau's first great phase of work, 1733 to 1739, but the two men had not always been on good terms, and it seems that any new rapprochement between them was short-lived.

Rameau substantially revised *Castor* for this new production. The prologue was dropped. The sombre and dramatically powerful first act of 1737, depicting Castor's funeral, was moved to become act two. To open the new version Bernard and Rameau wrote an entirely new act: on the day of his wedding to Télaïre, Pollux discovers that she loves his brother; he nobly withdraws in favour of Castor; but their enemy Lyncée arrives and Castor is killed in battle. Act three was 1737's act two; act four contained music from 1737's acts three and four; act five retained the original text but the music was mostly re-written.

What motivated such a radical re-write? The 1754 *Castor* was less original than its predecessor. Following Voltaire's lead, the first version placed the moral dilemma faced by Pollux at the centre of things; in the revised *Castor* there was a shift in favour of more action and greater clarity – events that were part of the back story in 1737 were now depicted on the stage. The 1754 version was more like a typical tragédie lyrique than the original ever was. It seems that Rameau, with the stakes so high, and perhaps influenced by his colleagues, decided to reduce the risks by, this time, starting *Castor* at the beginning and not in the middle. Both versions are commendable; choosing between them poses a dilemma for conductors and producers.

The revival was poignant for the artists of the Opéra in the sense that it showed the passing of time. Claude Chassé, the original Pollux, reprised his role; and Marie Fel, Amour in 1737, sang Télaïre. Chassé's voice was past its best, and Jélyotte, who sang Castor for the first time, was also near the end of his career.

The premiere took place on 8 January. The journalist Élie Fréron, critic of Voltaire – who satirised him as the character Frelon (Hornet) in his comedy *Le Café ou l'Écossaise* – and of the *Encyclopédistes*, reviewed the revised opera in his journal *L'Année littéraire*, declaring it to be a masterpiece of both words and music, and describing, with obvious pleasure, its impact on the pro-Italians, singling out Rousseau *de Genève* (Fréron could indeed be waspish) and likening the scurried departure of the *Bouffonistes* from the theatre to the flight of the citizens of a fallen city after a siege:

> The best response to M. Rousseau of Geneva is this lyric tragedy of *Castor et Pollux*, revived on 8 January of this year, during the greatest heat of musical fermentation. An ordinary man would have perhaps feared the critical circumstances; but a genius such as M. Rameau seizes the moment to triumph even more brightly. [...] If only you had been able, Monsieur, to witness, at the first performance, the unanimous applause ringing throughout the auditorium. You would have seen the *Bouffonistes* leave the corner of the queen, abandoning this important position, wandering about, getting lost in the crowd then rushing to the exits to escape, like the poor unfortunates of a besieged city about to be taken. I confess, Monsieur, that the spectacle moved me. Well, who would not have groaned like me to see these French grieving at the pleasure and success of their compatriots! M. Rameau has deployed in this opera the whole extent of his genius. What power! What energy! What gentleness and what delight! The second and fourth acts achieve the greatest beauty, and are comparable in their genre to what is most sublime in Corneille. I do not believe that one can hear anything that stirs the soul with more vivacity, that fills it with

a sweeter satisfaction. Minds conditioned by subtle sophistry, hearts chilled by icy calculation, I pity you for being insensitive to such masterpieces![7]

There was a sense that, politically, the revival would not be allowed to fail, such was the rediscovered bravado of the pro-French camp; but this bravado would not have lasted beyond a few hours if the work had misfired. Such was the scale of the opera's success that the run of performances was extended. The opera was brought back later in the year, and again in 1755. Recalling the premiere many years later, in 1780, La Borde wrote:

> Never was there a success to compare with this, without contradiction; and more than a hundred performances could not diminish the pleasure that all Paris felt on hearing this beautiful opera, that spoke, all at once, to the soul, the heart and mind, the eyes, the ears and the imagination.[8]

The premiere of the revised *Castor et Pollux* was the moment that the French opera of Lully and Rameau repossessed its own house. The victory was ultimately illusory, for the house itself was doomed. The extent to which *Castor et Pollux* was revelatory, if at all, is difficult to measure. It may well have won over some of the non-partisans, who occupied the middle ground, but the progressive and fashion-conscious young remained overwhelmingly with the Italians. Although Bambini's troupe left Paris, the influence of the Italians and their *intermezzi* was deep and long-lasting, felt at the Opéra and absorbed into the culture of the Comédie-Italienne, under Charles-Simon Favart, and the newly reopened (in 1752) Opéra-Comique, under Jean-Joseph Vadé, to the extent that a new *opéra-comique* emerged.[9] La Borde was exaggerating when he wrote that 'all Paris' loved *Castor*.

An Italian opera, *I Viaggiatori* by Leonardo Leo, had been programmed to follow *Castor*. It was quickly replaced with a revival of the one opera that transcended the national barriers of genre and taste – Rameau's *Platée*. Rameau made only small changes to the score of a work that had been last revived in 1749. The choice of *Platée*, at the moment the Opéra was reaffirming the potency of the tragédie lyrique genre, at first might seem curious. *Platée* was impossible to categorise; it parodied *tragédie*, and disobeyed the key principles of French classical drama in its descriptive sound world of animal noises and vocal effects; and it had been cited by both camps during the *querelle*, often in ways that were contradictory: the opera was sublime, it was vulgar; it had heralded the Italians, it had been obliterated by them. But the choice of *Platée* to follow *Castor* was, in fact, a deliberate means of proclaiming the variety and richness of the French operatic stage.

iii From the Court to the Opéra

In August 1754 the dauphine gave birth to a son, Louis Auguste, duc de Berry – the future Louis XVI. To celebrate Louis's arrival, Rameau was instructed to provide a one-act ballet for performance at Fontainebleau that autumn. Working once more with Cahusac, Rameau adapted a recently written piece to create a *ballet allégorique* (Cahusac's term) called *La Naissance d'Osiris*. The idea was drawn from Egyptian mythology: shepherds pay homage to Jupiter; Jupiter appears from above and announces the birth of the god Osiris; Cupid and the Graces join the shepherds in a celebratory dance. The cast was led by the ubiquitous Marie Fel and Claude Chassé.

There are some self-borrowings, but the music, featuring fine writing for the flutes and especially the oboes, is of a high quality throughout. Rameau's melancholy keeps intruding, but the plentiful melodies carry the work, for Rameau was particularly generous on this occasion. Highlights include an exquisite *air de musette* and the oboe-led *air gracieux* recorded by Marc Minkowski as part of his Rameau *Symphonie imaginaire*. The only surprise is the return of music from the overture at the end. *La Naissance d'Osiris* was performed alongside *Les Incas du Pérou*, from *Les Indes galantes*, and *Pygmalion*. The premiere, on Saturday 12 October, was a success: the king asked to hear the opera again on the following Tuesday.[10]

Less than two weeks later another new ballet by Rameau and Cahusac was presented, *Anacréon*. The venerable poet Anacréon (Chassé) teases two of his young protégés, the lovers Chloé (Fel) and Bathylle (Jélyotte), by pretending that he plans to marry the girl. According to the duc de Luynes the work divided opinion. He attempted a witticism: 'It is not Rameau anymore; but it is still Cahusac.'[11] *Anacréon* would prove to be Rameau's final new work for the court. (During the Seven Years' War, 1756 to 1763, court entertainments were curtailed, with performances at Fontainebleau abandoned altogether from 1757.)

Mystery surrounds the ballets *Nelée et Myrthis* (or, as it should more accurately be called, *Mirthis*) and *Zéphyre*. These works, possibly composed to texts by Cahusac, were abandoned. They may have been written to form two acts of an opéra-ballet called *Les Beaux jours de l'Amour*. *La Naissance d'Osiris* and *Anacréon* may have been originally intended for this work. Other equally fragile suppositions, partly based on scraps of evidence found on the reverse side of *collettes* (pieces of paper with revisions pasted onto the relevant scores), are worth considering. One, that *Zéphyre* was originally written for Mme de Pompadour at the time of *Les Surprises de l'Amour* in 1748 (which could suggest that Gentil-Bernard was the author); two, that the alternative title for *Zéphyre*, *Les Nymphes de Diane*, was, in fact, the name of a planned larger work. The fact that the role of Zéphyre was written, unusually, for a female voice could strengthen the *Les Surprises de l'Amour* theory, for talented amateur *haute-contre* singers were not found at court.

Rameau's autograph score for *Nelée et Myrthis* was rescued by Decroix. He recorded that a number of dances and choruses were missing from the divertissement. Indeed, the opera feels incomplete or at the very least under-developed. There is only one substantial instrumental passage – a chaconne lasting 170 bars. The story is set in ancient Greece. Nelée loves Myrthis, but believes her to be indifferent. To provoke her jealousy he pretends to desire another woman. Myrthis, who has only been feigning indifference, is heartbroken. She sings a tragic air of grave beauty, 'Dieu du bonheur, Dieu des amours'. The ballet ends happily when Nelée, victor of the Argive Games, chooses Myrthis as his prize.

Zéphyre – first performed at Benjamin Britten's Aldeburgh Festival in June 1967 – is quintessential one-act Rameau, as tantalising as a beautiful day in early spring. The story is told within an overriding musical curve of exquisite symmetry. Zéphyre, the god of the West Wind, is in love with one of Diana's nymphs, the chaste Cloris. He secretly watches her dance with her companions in a wooded glade.

As the nymphs depart, Zéphyre reveals himself to Cloris and causes flowers to bloom around her feet. His words of love both charm and frighten her. She is not so innocent as to be unaware of the predatory intent that lies behind his words, but her resolve begins to weaken. When the other nymphs attempt to intervene, Zéphyre orders the zephyrs to block their way. In the ballet, Zéphyre shows Cloris the sensual pleasure that has been denied her. Dancers represent the flowers and a flute-playing zephyr courts and makes love to a nymph. The music perfectly conveys a double meaning, for the sweetness of the two minuets is corrupted by Rameau's harmonies. Zéphyre finally persuades Cloris to abandon her vow of chastity, but only with the help of Cupid. Diana appears to the sound of hunting horns. Because she is in love with Endymion she forgives the seduction of young Cloris and blesses her union to Zéphyre. The lovers sing the poignant duo 'Non, ce n'est qu'en aimant qu'on sent le bonheur de vivre': 'No, it is only by loving that we feel the joy of living, it is sweet to follow a tender desire.' Cloris is transformed to become Flore, the goddess of the spring. The divertissement features a short sarabande and two enchanting gavottes, while the concluding *contredanse* is the opera's only expression of uninhibited joy. In *Zéphyre* Rameau was returning to a theme – the seduction of a young woman – that had already inspired some of his finest music.

No new music by Rameau was performed in 1755, the year he became obsessed with the *Encyclopédie*. However, he was working on a revised version of *Zoroastre*. Following the success of *Castor et Pollux*, both Rameau and the directors of the Opéra were keen to revisit his other tragedies. This formed part of a concerted effort to keep alive what many people still believed to be the true French opera. The baton was passed to a composer thirty years younger than Rameau, Antoine Dauvergne, who composed no less than four tragédie lyriques for the Opéra between 1758 and 1763. *Énée et Lavinie* (1758) and *Canente* (1760) enjoyed decent runs of, respectively, thirty-five and twenty-eight performances. In revising *Zoroastre*, Rameau radically re-thought both the words and the music. Acts two, three and five were re-written. It wasn't simply that Rameau was self-critical; he wanted to make *Zoroastre* work in the theatre for the public, to make the drama tighter and more unified. The daring intellectual agenda of the 1749 work was not abandoned but made much less explicit: its ideas were subsumed into the dramatic story in ways that were more subtle and less polemical. Rameau and Cahusac increased the importance of the female characters, and adjusted Zoroastre's motivation. The new *Zoroastre* opened at the Opéra in January 1756.

Hippolyte et Aricie was revived in February 1757, and in May Rameau presented *Anacréon*, his first wholly new creation for Paris since *Acante et Céphise* in 1751. *Anacréon* was performed as the final entrée of a revival of Rameau and Gentil-Bernard's opéra-ballet for Mme de Pompadour, *Les Surprises de l'Amour*. The two original entrées, *Adonis* (renamed *L'Enlèvement d'Adonis*) and *La Lyre enchantée* were revised and the prologue dropped. In July Rameau decided to replace *La Lyre enchantée* with *Les Sybarites*, first seen at Fontainebleau in 1753. By the time *Les Surprises de l'Amour* returned to the repertoire in October 1758 Rameau had further revised *La Lyre enchantée* and it was reinstated.

Anacréon (not to be confused with the Fontainebleau ballet of 1754) is a significant work. Bernard's libretto is a conceit about love and wine – which of these wonders offers the deeper pleasure? As the opera opens, aged Anacréon (bass-baritone) is hosting a feast. Slaves serve wine and Anacréon's mistress, Lycoris (a non-singing role), dances. A short orchestral introduction leads into an intimate expression of hedonism, the chorus 'Règne, ô divin Bacchus! Enflâme nos esprits'. This hymn to Bacchus, with its infectious descending scale on the words 'enflâme nos esprits', is repeated after Anacréon sings in praise of Lycoris's youth and beauty – she is, he declares, a new Hébé. Lycoris's movements become ever more sensual as she dances to the quick beat of a passepied.

Anacréon's drinking song, 'Point de tristesse, buvons sans cesse', is cut short by the arrival of the Priestess of Bacchus (soprano) and her followers. The priestess is enraged because Anacréon has evoked love: Bacchus will not share this place of pleasure with Cupid. 'Why keep apart two things that belong together?' Anacréon asks. The priestess orders her followers to destroy the statue of Cupid. A *ballet figuré* depicts the battle that ensues between Anacréon's slaves and the Bacchantes. Lycoris tries to escape but finds herself trapped in the circle of dancers. The Bacchantes prevail and destroy the statue. Anacréon angrily renounces Bacchus. Overcome with fatigue and longing for Lycoris, who has disappeared, he lies down to sleep (scene four). Rameau's music, gloriously virile up until this point, slows to a crawl as, above the bass line, extended notes on the violins and flutes convey the coming of sleep, and pizzicato strings, rare in Rameau, emulate drops of rain. These few bars are among the most evocative in Rameau's later work. Graham Sadler has identified a close parallel between Rameau's *sommeil* and the harvest and 'sleeping drunkards' music from the autumn movement of Vivaldi's *The Four Seasons*,[12] one of the rare occasions when Rameau referenced another composer's work deliberately. There are also Vivaldi references in the storm music that presages the arrival of Cupid (soprano) disguised as a slave boy. He tells Anacréon that Lycoris is suffering because her lover has betrayed her. Their exchanges are surprisingly highly charged, for this recitative is a fine example of Rameau's skill at making musical dialogue flow naturally. Cupid sings two limpid airs, 'Avant ce jour' and 'L'infidèle sur ses traces', and Anacréon, accompanied only by the strings, is given a moment of stark truth: 'Perhaps declining age causes [Lycoris's lover] to leave [Cupid's] court; it takes less effort to follow an old man like Silenus than a child such as Cupid.' Surely Rameau was thinking of himself when he gave these words such dark music? At the end of the recitative Anacréon admits that he is Lycoris's shameful lover. He realises that the boy is Cupid and begs to be reunited with Lycoris, promising to give up wine for love. In the divertissement, Lycoris dances once more and Cupid, backed by throbbing strings, sings the showcase air 'Règne avec moi, Bacchus'. The followers of Bacchus come together with those of Cupid, and both sides agree on a truce: 'Bacchus does not forbid loving; and Cupid allows us to drink.'

Anacréon is a companion piece to *Pygmalion*. Both works are about an ageing creative artist in love with an ideal of feminine beauty. The theme inspired Rameau into writing some of his most beautiful music, leading one to think that he saw himself in Pygmalion and Anacréon.

Les Surprises de l'Amour with the new *Anacréon* was another big success for Rameau. The *Mercure de France* found the opening of *Anacréon* brilliantly done,[13] and declared that the scene between Anacréon and Cupid was, of its kind, unsurpassed.[14] People particularly admired the sleep scene and the storm. The opera was revived on a number of occasions during the following few years.

iv Les Paladins

During 1759 Rameau prepared his first full-scale opera since *Acante et Céphise* and *Linus* in 1750/51 – *Les Paladins*, a comédie lyrique in three acts. It was only the second opera Rameau composed in this genre, the first being *Platée*. *Les Paladins* was probably written some years before but revised extensively once the Opéra had finally decided to place it. The author of the libretto cannot be definitively stated. Decroix indicated that Gentil-Bernard was the author. Two other contemporary sources, though, attributed the text to a certain Duplat de Monticourt. Linguistic analysis of the text alongside that of the known libretti of Gentil-Bernard should settle the matter. For now, Duplat de Monticourt is usually given the honour. It is likely that the Duplat de Monticourt in question was Pierre-Jacques (born in 1708) and not his younger brother Jean-François. Pierre-Jacques translated Edward Moore's play *The Gamester* as *Le Joueur*.[15] The text is written in an informal style, with only a limited reliance on recitative: this inspired Rameau, who surely wanted such a libretto, and cajoled his poet into creating it, to compose in an equally free style.

The story, set in Italy, was loosely inspired by one of the tales of La Fontaine, *Le Petit chien qui secoue de l'argent et des pierreries*, itself based on Ariosto's *Orlando furioso*. There are similarities, too, with Molière's play *L'École des maris* (1661), a comedy in which a man plans to marry his young ward but is duped by her. Given the success of the revivals of the highly regarded *Platée*, one can well understand why Rameau decided to compose a second comédie lyrique.

The paladins were the most important knights of Charlemagne's court. They appear in the *Song of Roland* and other *chansons de geste*. The heroine of the opera, Argie, is in love with the paladin Atis; but her guardian, Anselme, wants to marry her himself. He has imprisoned Argie and her friend Nérine in his castle in the forest. Nérine attempts to secure their freedom by seducing the jailor, Orcan. Atis and his companions gain access to the castle disguised as pilgrims.

He easily deals with Orcan, but his attempt to free Argie is foiled by the return of Anselme.

Premiere of *Les Paladins*, 1760. Mlle Arnould as Argie. Costume design by Louis-René Boquet. Bibliothèque nationale de France.

In act two, set in a hamlet not far from the castle, Anselme learns about the pilgrims from Orcan. Argie tells him of her love for Atis. Anselme gives his permission, but as soon as Argie has departed he instructs Orcan to kill her. The paladins make their second appearance, this time disguised as demons. They easily wrestle Argie from Orcan.

The paladins are celebrating when Anselme arrives with his warriors (act three). Argie, Atis and the paladins retreat into the castle. The miraculous intervention of the fairy Manto – she transforms the castle into a Chinese palace and seduces Anselme – saves the day. Atis and Argie are now free to marry and the opera concludes with the celebrations.

There is, in the libretto, a muddle of unrelated elements. Archetypal ideas from the age of the troubadours – imprisoned damsel, rescuing knight – could have provided Rameau with a wonderful subject, a Baroque *Pélleas et Mélisande* or *Written on Skin*. Instead, he wrote a curious entertainment, in which he parodied both French and Italian vocal styles (most notably in act two, scene one). It is not the kind of work one would expect a great master to produce in his old age, but Rameau was singular and original to the end. In *Les Paladins* we find him almost abandoning recitative, surely a recognition of the preferences of younger commentators and theatregoers, brought into sharp focus during the *querelle des bouffons*, and instead making his characters converse in solo songs, duets and trios.

Les Paladins lacks the bite of *Platée*, but it has its own contrary spirit. The opening monologue for Argie (soprano), 'Triste séjour, solitude ennuyeuse', could easily belong in one of Rameau's tragedies, but the mood is lightened immediately by the coquettish Nérine (soprano), who sings a bravura parody of Italian vocalising, 'L'amant, peu sensible et volage', and then easily deludes Orcan (baritone) into believing that she loves him. Wise Rameau gives the ridiculous Orcan serious music as well as exaggerated vocal mannerisms, such as the sobbing way he declaims and repeats Nérine's name. The sound of a musette announces the arrival of Atis (tenor) and the paladins, dressed as pilgrims. This theme permeates the rest of the opera's musical structure. 'Quels concerts insolents osent se faire entendre?' cries the tone-deaf Orcan. The dances that follow are written to appeal to the most jaded of operagoers. Rameau's orchestration is richer than before, with clarinets and horns added to his usual palate, but the naive charm of this music lies in the feeling of community spirit it evokes, inviting everyone to pick up a tambourine and dance. The unease that so often in Rameau's music lurks beneath and between the notes is mostly absent. Nérine and Orcan, drawn from *opera buffa*, are more involving characters than Argie and Atis, drawn from French tragedy, since, inevitably, they have the best lines (Nérine is a precursor of the maid Despina in Mozart's *Cosi Fan Tutte*); but in act two Argie tells Anselme (bass) that she loves a paladin and the story darkens. Anselme seems to accept that Argie can only love him as a father, but two half-spoken asides – 'un homme!' and 'le monstre!' – reveal his jealousy. As Orcan contemplates the knife that Anselme, ordering Argie's murder, has handed him, he sings a remarkable monologue, in which the line separating tragedy and parody moves in and out of focus. Here Rameau parodies the music he wrote for Abramane in *Zoroastre*, but in a manner that is droll and unforced. Nérine teases Orcan for a second time, initiating a superb comedy duo. Orcan threatens violence and Nérine summons the demons, the cue for a magnificent sequence of descriptive orchestral writing during which the chorus reprises Atis's plaintive 'Vengeurs des beautés qu'on outrage'.

Dramatic interest effectively ends here. The last act is dominated by its vibrant dances. Argie's extended air 'Je vole, Amour, où tu m'appelles', though, along with a tender duo for the lovers, interrupts the hectic razzle-dazzle of rushing music and quick steps with an expression of true feeling. Anselme threatens to lead a revenge chorus, but is instantly enchanted by Manto. The fairy is played by a man (*haute-contre*), but Rameau writes serious music and doesn't heighten the comedy. There is a ferocious trio for Anselme, Manto and Argie in which counterpoint is used to express three points of view. In this act, as nowhere else in his work, Rameau writes long sequences of dance movements, conceiving them as an integrated whole, the music growing ever more complex. He ends the opera, though, with a return to the naivety of the opening act, composing a catchy little refrain in 6/8 – to the words 'Let's sing and laugh in the face of the jealous' – that is as preposterous as it is beautiful.

Les Paladins opened at the Opéra on 12 February 1760. For the first time in over twenty-five years a major opera by Rameau was created without at least one of the three artists who had served the composer so faithfully – Jélyotte, Chassé and Marie Fel. In their place a new generation stepped forward: Nicolas Gélin,[16] as Anselme; Marie-Jeanne Lemière,[17] as Nérine; and twenty-year-old Sophie Arnould,[18] creating her first role for Rameau, as Argie. In its subtle parodies, *Les Paladins* was surely Rameau's response to the *querelle des bouffons*; his way of proclaiming that he could master all styles in the creation of a new form of comic opera. Most people in the audience weren't persuaded, and the appearance of Mlle Arnould didn't distract them. The opera was withdrawn on 20 March and never revived.

10

The Solitary Walker

Rameau's Last Years
1761 to 1764

i Les Boréades

Now in his late seventies, Rameau was still working long hours, driven on by his dispute with d'Alembert. Rameau's ability to write so many words and so many musical notes in old age was the triumph of his mind over his ailing body. In a letter to a would-be thinker who was trying to initiate a correspondence with him, Rameau wrote: 'I have neither time to write nor health to think, to reflect; forgive me, Monsieur, I am old, you are young, and I am your very humble and very obedient servant.'[1] In another equally poignant confession, made to an organist of Dijon called Balbastre, and recorded by La Borde, we find Rameau reflecting that

> music is perishing; taste is changing every second. I wouldn't know how to manage if I had to work as I did in the past; only Daquin has had the courage to resist the torrent; he has always preserved for the organ the majesty and grace it deserves.[2]

It would seem that Rameau's mood justified Diderot's view that the success of the Italians had left him feeling sad and surly, for 'nobody has less humour, not even a pretty woman who wakes to find a pimple on her nose, than an author threatened with outliving his fame'.[3] And yet, one of the striking things about Rameau's last years was that he never succumbed to nostalgia or complacency. When Rameau was not working he went for long walks in the garden of the Palais-Royal. Rameau walking between the trees – like a ghost – was part of the rhythm of life in the Palais-Royal, only a little less reliable than the tolling of the bells. Although lost in thought, and not seeking out company, Rameau was courteous when Chabanon wished him good day; given the depth of his reverie, he sometimes needed several moments to recognise the young man. After the premiere of a revival of *Castor et Pollux* at Fontainebleau, Chabanon came across Rameau

> in an anteroom, very poorly lighted. As I went up to kiss his cheeks he started to flee, only turning back when I gave my name. He told me that he shunned compliments because they embarrassed him and he didn't know how to respond. On the subject of revising his opera, he said, 'My friend, I have better taste than before but my genius is spent'.[4]

Maret is strong on this theme too, relating how Rameau had confessed that 'imagination is used up in my old head, and it is not wise at my age to endeavour to work on arts that rely entirely on invention'.[5] This may partly explain why he gave preference to his theoretical work. However, Rameau's creativity wasn't worn out before the summer of 1763. During his solitary walks he wasn't only reflecting on his dispute with d'Alembert; he was also conceiving the vibrant art that would materialise into his final opera, the tragédie lyrique *Les Boréades*.

One should note that there was no significant decline in the popularity of Rameau's operas. *Castor et Pollux* wasn't the only tragedy by Rameau revived in Paris and at court during the early 1760s. Following the fire that destroyed the theatre of the Palais-Royal in April 1763, *Dardanus* was staged at court; then, in January 1764, *Castor et Pollux* inaugurated the Opéra's new temporary home in Paris, the Salle des Machines in the Palais des Tuileries. In November 1763 the six-year-old Mozart arrived in Paris with his father and older sister. Rameau may have been present when Mozart performed for the king at Versailles. If Mozart attended performances of *Castor et Pollux* and *Dardanus*, perhaps he thought of Rameau when he composed the French-inspired *Idomeneo* sixteen years later.

Rameau by Frédéric-Désiré Hillemacher (ca. 1850). Bibliothèque nationale de France.

The global conflict with England that became known as the Seven Years' War was in a final phase that would see England take control of the whole of New France (Canada) and France sue for peace, a calamity for French prestige. A British blockade, high taxation and high prices meant that everyone felt the strain of the war. For the first time since the assassination of Henri IV in 1610 a French king and the absolute state he represented looked human, fallible and vulnerable. There is no reason to think that Rameau was unconcerned by these events but given that time was running out and he had his own artistic priorities he must have been relieved that the war precluded frivolous court entertainments. During these years Rameau's sense of his mortality was heightened by the deaths of many of the people who had been important in his life. His brother Claude Bernard died in Autun, where he was organist at the cathedral, in May 1761, and his last surviving sibling, Marie-Claude, died in Dijon just over a year later. Thérèse Boutinon des Hayes never recovered her reputation or her equilibrium. We don't know whether Rameau had any contact with her following her separation from La Pouplinière. She died at the age of forty-two in 1756. Following the revival of *Zoroastre* in 1756, Cahusac started work on the text of *Les Boréades*,[6] setting the opera in the same ancient kingdom, Bactria, and once more incorporating Masonic references. Sadly, this vulnerable man started to lose his reason and was incarcerated in the asylum at Charenton. The *libelliste* François-Antoine Chevrier wrote that the failure of his relationship with Marie Fel was the cause.[7] Cahusac died in June 1759, possibly at his own hand. La Pouplinière, increasingly a figure of public scorn, died in 1762, shortly after his arranged marriage to a young girl.

During the previous decade Rameau had created revised versions of *Castor et Pollux* and *Zoroastre*, but he had not composed a new tragedy since *Linus*, mysteriously unperformed in 1750/51. He now returned to the form, taking up the libretto of *Les Boréades* that he must have had in his possession since Cahusac's death. The subject, provocative in the extreme, was individual liberty – the right of a ruler to abdicate for personal reasons and of a woman to make her own choices. The opera's heroine, Alphise, the young queen of Bactria, is obliged by the laws of her country to marry one of the descendants of Borée, the god of the north wind. The Boread princes Calisis and Borilée compete for her hand, but Alphise is in love with a stranger of unknown heritage, Abaris, and determined to make him king.

The opera begins in a forest, where the royal party is on a hunt. Rameau makes effective use of horns and clarinets in an overture that sets the scene with a succession of fanfares. Alphise (soprano) breaks away from her retinue, followed by her confidante Sémire (soprano). They discuss the agonising predicament faced by the queen. Alphise yearns for Abaris. Sémire reminds her of the law. Borilée (baritone), stern and formal, and Calisis (*haute-contre*), ebullient and charming, approach the queen. It has been decreed that Apollo will decide Alphise's fate. In scene four, the Pleasures and Graces depict Calisis's desire for Alphise. Trilling flutes lead the dances (two gavottes and a fast rondeau); hollowed out strings leave a space for the oboes and bassoons. The air 'Un horizon serein, le doux calme des airs', with its haunting opening and closing theme and dramatic changes of tone, is the opera's first striking statement. It is curious that Rameau indicates that it can be sung by either soprano when the sentiment of the words strongly suggests Alphise. Rameau, at his most subversive, immediately deflates the serious and refined tone achieved by this air with a marvellous *contredanse en rondeau* that launches with an impudent two-chord phrase in C minor.

Act two, set in the vestibule of the temple of Apollo, introduces Abaris (*haute-contre*). The air 'Charmes trop dangereux, malheureuse tendresse' establishes his gentle nature. It is one of those lyrical arias of Rameau that, in melody and style, reveal his shared nationality with later masters of French songwriting. Adamas (baritone), the High Priest of Apollo, has protected Abaris since his infancy. He knows the truth about Abaris's parentage, but won't reveal it, believing that Abaris must prove himself through the pursuit of honour. Abaris confesses that he loves the queen and asks for guidance. The High Priest is non-committal. In scene five, Abaris and Alphise meet in the temple and exchange declarations of love. The act concludes with a divertissement in which Borilée and Calisis lead the celebrations in honour of Apollo, the god of light, and a nymph declares 'it is liberty that we must love, the highest good is liberty'. The orchestral sequences, fragile and mysterious, are among the most personal in all of Rameau's work. The beguiling melodies take unexpected paths and the harmonies are like musical shadows. Rameau adds to his art new timbres and cadences. Between these passages Calisis is joined by the chorus in the sensual, enigmatic refrain 'Écoutez, l'amour qui vous presse'. Eros descends in a chariot and hands

Alphise an enchanted arrow. The Masonic symbolism is at its least subtle here.

In the monologue 'Songe affreux, image cruelle', at the beginning of act three, Alphise commits her future to Abaris despite her fear of the consequences. A brief love duet, during which the queen's anxiety lingers, is interrupted by the arrival of the two suitors. Rameau composes a rousing theme for the strings to accompany the 'Entrée des peuples' (scene three), through which the bassoons play a lyrical counter-melody. Borilée and Calisis court the queen in turn. The assertive Calisis has the best lines, leading the chorus in the magnificent 'Jouissons, jouissons de nos beaux ans'. This episode begins, remarkably, as a sung tambourin, but concludes with a passage of vocal runs reminiscent of the final chorus in Rameau's early motet *In convertendo*. At the beginning of scene four, before Adamas, her suitors and the people, Alphise reveals her love for Abaris and renounces the throne. She hands Abaris Eros's arrow. The people entreat their queen to reconsider. Borilée and Calisis call for vengeance and the god of the north wind responds by unleashing a terrifying storm. Alphise's vulnerability in the face of the rage of the implacable god makes the scene dramatically gripping as well as spectacular. A whirlwind sweeps her into the air and away.

As the fourth act begins the storm is still raging and the people are crying out for help. The High Priest tells Abaris that only he can save Alphise and the people. Abaris believes that to do this he must kill himself with the arrow, but the priest tells him that the arrow is a magical device that will transport him to the place where Alphise is being held captive. Abaris appeals to Apollo to aid him in his mission, and to Polymnie, the muse of dance.

Throughout these scenes Rameau's inspiration is at its most questioning and original. The music he composed next was revelatory. Beginning with the succession of a descending phrase from the bassoons, leading the way (a masterstroke), to unison violins and flutes, a bar behind, the 'Entrée de Polymnie' has, in its seeming simplicity, a pure beauty: transparent yet profound; sensual yet soulful. It is both transfixing and consoling. It stops time. Rameau may have been remembering Thérèse Boutinon des Hayes when he composed this music, for she was referred to as Polymnie by Voltaire (who had recognised her importance to the composer as a muse) in his letters to Thieriot of the 1730s, and the nickname may have been used more widely within La Pouplinière's circle.

For John Eliot Gardiner, the 'Entrée de Polymnie' is 'perhaps the most melting and gravely sensual writing for orchestra to emerge from the entire Baroque era'.[8] The beauty of Polymnie infects all the music that follows. A sequence of charming gavottes and rigaudons is followed by the great chorus 'Parcourez la terre', closely related to the 'Entrée'; and Abaris's impassioned 'Fuyez, reprenez vos chaînes' is one of the highpoints of Rameau's writing for the *haute-contre* voice. A second air, 'Je vole, amour, où tu m'appelles', in which Abaris declares that he will save Alphise or die, contains some of Cahusac's most heartfelt verses, inspired perhaps by Marie Fel.

At the beginning of the final act, a strange orchestral passage introduces Borée (bass). The instruments, entering in turn, play stabbing notes, each cluster separated by a pause, to create a sound world that is unlike anything else in Rameau's work. Borée commands the subterranean winds to terrorise the universe. In scene two, Alphise disobeys Borée by refusing to marry either Borilée or Calisis. She would rather die. Borée orders his henchmen to bind and torture her. His chilling words are followed by the second great surprise of the opera after the 'Entrée de Polymnie', a thrillingly syncopated *air vif* that conveys Borée's malign elation as he watches Alphise. The theme of the *air vif* underpins Borée's monologue, the answering chorus and Alphise's courageous response. However, the dramatic potential is not realised. Abaris arrives with his arrow and Borée is subdued. The barren landscape is bathed in light and Apollo descends to reveal that Abaris is the son of a nymph of Borée's blood and therefore allowed to marry Alphise. Rameau creates an ethereal sound by writing extended chords for the violins and flutes. The setting changes, and Abaris and Alphise, at last united, sing the tender duo 'Que ces moments sont doux'. The dances are lyrical but mischievous. Abaris sings a final air, 'Que l'amour embellit la vie', then Rameau signs off with a vivacious *contredanse*, music better suited to the revelry of the fair than the values of the Académie Royale de Musique.

In *Les Boréades* Cahusac and Rameau integrated the various elements of the tragédie lyrique form into a cohesive whole more successfully than ever before. There is very little superfluous material. With no prologue and with the overture thematically linked to the opening scene, the dramatic situation upon which the plot turns is placed before the audience without distractions, and the divertissements and moments of spectacle advance the narrative without contrivance. Dialogue, solos and choruses flow seamlessly. There is an elegance to the storytelling that must have satisfied Rameau.

Les Boréades went into rehearsal in April 1763.[9] Performances were planned at Mme de Pompadour's royal château at Choisy, on the Seine some six miles south-east of the capital, to mark the end of the Seven Years' War. The destruction of the Opéra's home at the Palais-Royal prevented performances in Paris. Rameau attended rehearsals in the Opéra's store room and at Versailles later that month. Shortly afterwards, the court body that oversaw entertainments, the Menus-Plaisirs du Roi, decreed against *Les Boréades* and the work was withdrawn. Given the nature of the peace terms forced on France by the Treaty of Paris, signed on 10 February, a sombre opera like *Les Boréades* was more appropriate than the usual court fare; but the message of the work, its plea for freedom and individual rights, proved unacceptable to the authorities. As a result, this supreme masterpiece of Rameau's life was not publicly performed and soon forgotten. It was thanks to the efforts of Decroix, after Rameau's death, that the manuscript score and parts were preserved, eventually finding their way into the collections of the Bibliothèque Nationale. *Les Boréades* would finally be premiered on the stage two hundred and twenty years later, in 1982, at Aix-en-Provence, one of the great French cultural events of the latter half of the 20th century and arguably the finest achievement of John Eliot Gardiner's career.

The suppression of *Les Boréades* must have caused Rameau a profound hurt. The work was a grand statement, the last of his life, rich in invention and advances in orchestral sonorities. It was also an act of defiance. In the extraordinary modernity of much of the score Rameau was defying old age and all the mediocre musicians of his time. At the end of his pioneering work to bring *Les Boréades* before the public, John Eliot Gardiner wrote:

> Prolonged acquaintance with this score leads one to the inescapable conclusion that Rameau has resolved for once in his lifetime to write the music he wanted to write (perhaps he even

guessed that the work was unlikely to be performed in his absence, being too difficult for the Opéra orchestra of the time to play and too subtle for the Parisian public to appreciate) – and that in the spirited final *contredanse* he is cocking a snook at his detractors.[10]

ii The End

During the final year of his life Rameau was working on a new essay entitled *Vérités également ignorées et intéressantes tirées du sein de la nature*. The manuscript was found among his papers after his death. Rameau had long since extracted everything of practical worth from his principles, and was now claiming that the phenomenon of the *corps sonore* was the source of all enlightenment. A reader of the essay can be forgiven for thinking that its author was the inmate of an asylum scribbling 'unintelligible visions and apocalyptic truths'[11] on the walls of his cell. There was method in Rameau's madness, but one cannot avoid the feeling that, in old age, he had lost his way. He had started his journey as a kind of Cartesian and was ending it as a kind of Pantheist, which shows just how difficult it is to come to an understanding of Rameau's ideas. His theories had always been somewhat knotted, and in endlessly attempting to unravel them he actually made the knots ever tighter.

It wasn't enough for Rameau that the fundamental bass was widely used in the teaching of music, and he couldn't have known that his ideas on tonal harmony would remain central to the study of music theory. For Thomas Christensen

> [Rameau] almost single-handedly […] redirected the focus of music to questions involving chordal generation, harmonic coherence, and tonal identity, questions that still resonate today. Moreover, he offered a convincing analytic method and vocabulary informed by contemporaneous science by which these questions could be answered. […] To this day, much of the discourse related to tonal harmony is still carried out in the scientific terms and perspectives first articulated by Rameau, however much our own cultural rhetoric has transformed

them.[12]

It is likely that the last music Rameau wrote was for a revival of *La Princesse de Navarre* at Bordeaux in November 1763. The duc de Richelieu had been Governor of Guyenne and Intendant of Bordeaux since the late 1750s. Setbacks on the German front during his command of the army had temporarily damaged his standing at court, and precipitated his departure from Paris. To invigorate Bordeaux's cultural life, and to satisfy his own passion for the arts, Richelieu formed a new opera company. He must have been feeling nostalgic for the old days because he decided to mount a production of *La Princesse de Navarre*. Voltaire wrote a new prologue, and it is likely that Rameau updated the score. The score and instrumental parts used by the Bordeaux company, discovered in Bordeaux's municipal library in 1983, reveal that three dances – an air and two tambourins – were added to act three and that the orchestration throughout the piece was revised. In 1745 Voltaire had lost an argument with Rameau over the number and placement of the dances in the final act. Voltaire wanted a continuous sequence of dances but Rameau, with his greater understanding of the need for contrast in music, insisted on fewer dances separated by a chorus. In revising the final act for Bordeaux, Voltaire restored his original design. We don't know whether the three dances had been written and discarded in 1745 or whether Rameau, in a conciliatory frame of mind, wrote them in 1763. The suggestion that another musician composed the new music is not credible. Rameau always reconsidered his works on revival. Lionel Sawkins has shown that the changes to the orchestration – the upper viola parts were transposed down an octave and given to the bassoons and horns feature prominently – are consistent with Rameau's late style: for instance, similar scoring for horns is present in *Les Paladins*.[13]

Voltaire's letters give no clues as to whether he was in direct contact with Rameau over the new version, but do reveal that his own opinion of a work that had originally caused him so much anxiety had softened. In 1769, when the final divertissement was performed at Fontainebleau, Voltaire wrote to Richelieu that 'the music is delightful, and in truth there are some nice touches in the words'.[14]

La Princesse de Navarre opened on 26 November in a theatre near the Porte Dauphine (Bordeaux's Grand Théâtre, commissioned by Richelieu, had yet to be built). An account of the performance was published in the *Mercure de France*.[15] It is unlikely that Rameau travelled to Bordeaux, a journey that took a week. The nature of Richelieu's relationship with Rameau and his family is intriguing. When, two months after Rameau's death, his daughter Marie-Alexandrine married François-Marie de Gaultier, a king's musketeer from Mazan who was lodging in the Hôtel d'Orléans in the rue des Bons Enfants, Richelieu was one of the witnesses. This was no ordinary wedding, but rather a lavish gathering of ministers of state, senior soldiers and other aristocrats. Among the names of the wedding guests one notices M. le comte de Sade, *lieutenant général* of the province of Bresse and the father of the writer and libertine Donatien-Alphonse-François de Sade, who was twenty-four years old in 1764 and already of interest to the Paris police because of his mistreatment of prostitutes. The comte de Sade owned the château that dominates the small town of Mazan and was lord of the domain, hence his presence at the wedding. Gauthier and the young Sade were the same age. Patterns tend to emerge when one opens a door onto aristocratic society during the 18th century. Sade liked to drug and arouse his young victims by feeding them pastilles soaked in aniseed and laced with Spanish fly. It was Richelieu who established this practice. Was Richelieu at the wedding for the groom or the bride or both? Richelieu didn't take Voltaire's side during his disputes with Rameau. His presence at the wedding may suggest an intimate connection to Rameau and his family.

Rameau had lived with his wife, son and youngest daughter in the same apartment in the rue des Bons Enfants since 1752. It was a reasonable size and in a good location, but it was not an extravagant abode for a man of Rameau's standing. Most of the ten rooms, including the bedrooms of Rameau and Mme Rameau, overlooked the courtyard; but Rameau's office had a view of the garden of the Palais-Royal. The kitchen and dining room were situated on the second floor, and the maid lived in a small room on the third. Another genius lived in the house, Antoine-Laurent Lavoisier. Lavoisier's father, a wealthy lawyer, was the property's primary tenant. Lavoisier was in his teens during these years but since his understanding of mathematics and science was already advanced he would have been able to discuss complex ideas with his elderly neighbour. We know from Chabanon and La Borde that Rameau was willing to engage with the young.

The Palais Royal during Rameau's lifetime. Rameau and his family lived in one of the houses on the left-hand side. *Vûe et Perspective du Palais Royal du côté du Jardin* by A. Aveline. Bibliothèque nationale de France.

Carlo Goldoni also lived in a house beside the garden, on the rue de Richelieu side. The great playwright arrived in Paris in May 1762, to take up the management of the Théâtre Italien, with a letter of introduction to Rameau written by Padre Martini of the Accademia delle Scienze dell'Instituto di Bologna. Since 1759 Rameau had been corresponding with Martini in the hope that the academy would endorse his ideas (Bologna proved no more accommodating than Paris or London). Rameau must have been helpful and hospitable, for Goldoni declared in his *Memoirs*: 'I was very intimate with that celebrated composer, for whose talents and science I had the highest consideration.'[16] Goldoni shared the opinion of most Italians, and of many young Frenchmen, that French opera was all recitative ('it is a paradise for the eyes, and a hell for the ears'), but *Castor et Pollux* caused him to revise his opinion a little: 'I soon perceived the difference between the music of Rameau and that which had given me so much displeasure. [...] Rameau distinguished himself, and produced a great revolution in France in instrumental music.'[17] Goldoni's workroom overlooked the garden, and he described the kind of scene that Rameau contemplated from his own window:

> The breakfasts at the Café de Foy were taken under my window. People of every description resorted there, to repose and refresh themselves. I overlooked also the famous chestnut tree, called the tree of Cracow, round which the newsmongers used to flock with their news, and to trace trenches, camps, military positions, and divide Europe as their fancy led them, with their canes on the sand.[18]

Perhaps Rameau shared Goldoni's sentiment that 'these voluntary abstractions were sometimes useful to me; they afforded an agreeable repose to my mind, and I returned to my labour with more vigour'.[19] Back in Venice Goldoni had written libretti for Baldassare Galuppi, including *L'Arcadia in Brenta* (1749) and *Il filosofo di campagna* (1752). If Rameau had been ten or more years younger, perhaps Goldoni would have been the man to interest him in *opera buffa*, initiating a partnership to place beside that of Mozart and Da Ponte.

Rameau was now a rich man, worth around two hundred thousand *livres*. He had learned through necessity during the first sixty years of his life to be careful with money, and the instinct remained after the need was no longer there. His clothes were old and threadbare, and his rooms sparsely furnished. His loyalty to his home region was revealed by his wine cellar – it only contained barrels from a Burgundy vineyard, Hérissé. The only instrument he owned was an old harpsichord, and he kept few books in his home.[20] It comes as a surprise to discover that Rameau did not have a library of either scores or books, beyond the printing plates and hard copies of his own works and runs of the *Mercure de France* and the *Journal de*

Trévoux. In contrast, Handel collected hundreds of scores by other composers, among them Rameau's operas and keyboard suites. Handel also owned copies of Rameau's theoretical works.[21] How can it be that Rameau, a man engaged in learned study, didn't have a collection of relevant texts? He would have had access to the books he needed at La Pouplinière's house, but not after 1753. It is equally perplexing that he didn't own a violin, the instrument he was said to use when he was composing, and that his harpsichord was old and in a very poor condition. Because of a handwritten receipt signed by Rameau, we know that he received two keyboards from the harpsichord maker Christophe Chiquelier in April 1753.[22] Perhaps he sold or passed books on after he'd finished with them; perhaps he gave his violin and his books to his son not long before his death.

One can understand how easily Rameau's frugality was turned into avarice by men who disliked him and were capable of a sharp turn of phrase, especially Diderot and Diderot's friend Grimm, whose vicious lines on Rameau became common currency: 'Rameau's nature was hard and wild; he was a stranger to all feelings of humanity. [...] His ruling passion was greed. He was indifferent to reputation, honours and glory; he wanted money, and he died rich.'[23]

At the beginning of 1764 Rameau was ennobled by the king as knight of the *Ordre de Saint-Michel*. The honour had been long in coming, perhaps because certain figures at court, including Mme de Pompadour, were ambivalent about a man who was not naturally deferential. Mme de Pompadour died that April. In choosing a coat of arms, Rameau incorporated his name: a silver dove holding a golden *rameau d'olivier* (olive branch) in its beak.

Rameau was struck down by a 'putrid fever' in late August and died in his apartment on 12 September. He was interred the next day in his parish church, Saint-Eustache. Our knowledge of Rameau's last hours comes from an entry in a salon news diary maintained by the art critic Bachaumont. Bachaumont was wrong to claim that Rameau had refused, out of avarice, to pay to register his letters of nobility. However, Rameau's deathbed dismissal of a pest of a priest, as related by Bachaumont, is so piquant, and so in character, that one wishes it to be true: 'What the devil are you singing to me, M. le curé? Your voice is out of tune.'[24] One can only hope that Voltaire came to hear of it, for it would have greatly pleased him. Rameau said farewell to life not with a noble chaconne but with an acidic little *contredanse*.

A memorial service was held at the church of the Pères de l'Oratoire in the rue Saint-Honoré on 27 September. This grand occasion was organised and financed by the directors of the Opéra, Rebel and Francœur. Mme Rameau sent out fifteen hundred invitations, and one hundred and eighty musicians and singers from the Opéra assembled to remember Rameau. The *chef d'orchestre*, Berton, conducted Jean Gilles's *Messe des morts*. The *Kyrie eleison* was sung to the music of Rameau's 'Que tout gémisse' from *Castor et Pollux*. Then, at the end of the mass, Rebel conducted his own *De Profundis*.[25] This formidable act of homage and gesture of fraternity from the musicians of Paris was genuine. Voltaire wrote to an acquaintance: 'I hear that all of Rameau's fellow musicians attended his funeral and that they sang a very beautiful *De Profundis*. When I die my fellow poets will mock me with epigrams. In the meantime I commend myself to you and the philosophers.'[26]

Rameau had dominated the musical life of his country for three decades. A new form of tragedy, Italian-inspired in its recitatives and arias and freed from the constraints of the *merveilleux*, would emerge in the years immediately following Rameau's death, Philidor's *Ernelinde* (1767) being the key representative work, a form that would lead directly to the success of Gluck's reformed opera in Paris; but at the time of his death Rameau was still the solitary genius of French opera, something that the men and women who performed Rameau's music, gathering to remember him in the church of the Pères de l'Oratoire, knew only too well. Diderot was wrong to believe that Rameau had outlived his fame, and d'Alembert right when he declared that *Platée* was the work against which all new music should be measured. As for Rameau, he took his greatness as a composer for granted. He believed that the musician was inferior to the scientist or philosopher. Above all things, he had wanted to be acknowledged by d'Alembert and by d'Alembert's peers by being admitted into the Académie Royale des Sciences and the Royal Society. Rameau's tragedy was not that he failed in this ambition, but that he wanted it so badly.

Epilogue

In 1770 the Opéra's new theatre at the Palais-Royal, designed by Pierre-Louis Moreau-Desproux, was completed and the company returned home. Just over ten years later, on the evening of 8 June 1781, as the players and crew were preparing to leave the theatre after a performance of Gluck's *Orphée et Eurydice*, a candle flame ignited a gauze backdrop and the building was destroyed in a matter of hours. Eleven dancers, trapped in their dressing room, perished. Other members of the company only escaped by climbing onto the rooftops. The dressing rooms of the principal players were not close to the origin of the blaze, giving time for their occupants to escape. It was said that the star dancer Marie-Madeleine Guimard, still undressed as panic struck, was paralysed by a fit of modesty and had to be carried to safety by a stagehand.[1]

Understandably, many people decided that the Opéra was jinxed. Others, though, believed that the gods were on the side of the great masters: 'After the last work of Rameau, so, one may say, after that of Gluck, the fire was determined to prevent that vaulted roof still echoing to the sublime chords of the master from being long profaned by the vulgar and paltry airs of his unworthy rivals.'[2] A new theatre was rapidly constructed at the Porte-Saint-Martin.

In the years following Rameau's death his ballets were performed alongside new one-act pieces: *Pygmalion* and *La Musique* from *Les Fêtes d'Hébé* were among the most popular. *Platée*, the piece by Rameau most admired by younger connoisseurs because of its modernity and vitality, was ignored after the composer's death. In contrast, Rameau's tragedies remained current up until the mid-1780s. *Hippolyte et Aricie* was revived in 1767; *Dardanus* in 1768; and *Zoroastre* opened the new theatre at the Palais-Royal in 1770. In truth, only *Castor et Pollux* remained popular enough to be performed with high regularity. The last revival was in 1784. After this, with Rameau's prestige finally fading, the directors of the Opéra only risked staging *Dardanus* and *Castor et Pollux*, and only in reworked versions. *Dardanus*, re-composed by Antonio Sacchini, failed in 1784. *Castor et Pollux*, in an adaptation by Pierre Candeille ('Tristes apprêts' and 'Que tout gémisse' survived Candeille's cuts, additions and re-orchestrations), returned to the repertoire during the first phase of the Revolution, in June 1791, just a week before the royal family's flight to Varennes. The king, captured and taken back to Paris, subsequently agreed to sign the new Constitution. It seemed to some that the Revolution was over. In this climate of false hope Louis XVI and Marie Antoinette attended a performance of *Castor et Pollux* at the Opéra on 20 September 1791. This proved to be the king's final visit to the Opéra.

Mme Rameau went to live with her daughter Marie-Alexandrine and son-in-law François de Gaultier in Andrésy, some twenty miles north of Paris. She died in Andrésy in 1785. It appears that subsequently Gaultier inherited the family estate in Mazan, for Marie-Alexandrine died there in 1808. Rameau's other daughter, Marie-Louise, died in the convent at Montargis in 1777.

Rameau's son Claude-François, *valet de chambre* to the king, married Marie-Françoise Dubois in 1772; their son Louis-Antoine was born in 1773. Claude-François wrote music, but never professionally. He died in Versailles in 1788. He inherited Rameau's papers, scores and publishers' plates, and sent copies of scores to Decroix.

A letter written by Claude-François to Decroix in 1777 has survived.[3] Claude-François comes across as a warm and affable person as well as an able writer. The letter gives an insight into his character as both a son and a father. Therefore, I close this account of Rameau's life and work with the words of his son:

> Monsieur,
>
> Deaf though I am in one ear, with the other I very clearly hear you heave a sigh and say: 'Ah! word at last from M. Rameau, to whom I have written several letters since 31 August 1776 and who at last deigns to honour me with a reply. He might well have deferred writing until next month, to round off the year. Yet it does seem to me that I have shown him sufficient consideration and even evinced towards him a good deal

more friendship than he deserved.' 'Eh! rightly said,' responds M. Rameau; 'it is precisely this friendship, on which I rely, that is in part the cause of my negligence.'

In consequence of this, Monsieur, you may well feel that after all my wrongs towards you I should need at least a ream of paper to make my excuses; you might even say, with reason, that the best [of excuses] would not be acceptable, since your letters are dated 31 August, 9 September and 30 December 1776 and 4 April 1777, all entreating the same friendship with which you have had the kindness to honour me hitherto. I dare to flatter myself that you will overlook all [this] and thus that all my sins may be forgiven me… *Amen.*

I begin by thanking you a thousand times for the consignment of motets and cantatas which you were so kind as to send me and which I received with the greatest pleasure.

I now send you the following works – though it has been impossible to [find] for you as many as I should have wished – with a note as to which of them I should ask you to return to me during the course of next December, since I scarcely expect to be in Paris until around that time.

[A list of works follows.]

With regard to the other [items] you request of me, I much regret being unable to satisfy you at present. Please be assured of my ambition to be able to do so in due course.

As for the violin part of *Linus*, I am in the same position. But do not worry; you may have it earlier that you expect. Meanwhile, I hope that while you are waiting you will give me the pleasure of receiving a copy of the words of this work you have discovered.

When I am not with the king this year I shall be at Marly, where I have been lent an apartment. So if you come to Paris, Monsieur, I invite you to come there. I shall be there from 3 August until the 25th, and from the 25th intermittently, but my wife will always be there. She has asked me when I write to send you her compliments. If you come before the 25th I shall even be in a position to offer you a bed. My little lad has been suffering from childhood ailments. Since last September he has been having trouble with his teeth. But I am told that no action is necessary, and he grows apace.

I greatly look forward to having the honour of making the

acquaintance of Madame Decroix. Until I have that pleasure I ask you to present to her my very humble respects and to believe me, Monsieur, with the most sincere friendship,

Your ever very humble and very obedient servant
Rameau.[4]

Appendices

Appendix I

Chronology of Rameau's Life, Work and Times

1683 Birth of Rameau on 24 September in Dijon
   Lully: *Phaëton* (Opéra, Paris)
1684 Death of Corneille in Paris
   Birth of Watteau in Valenciennes
   Lully: *Amadis* (Opéra, Paris)
1685 Revocation of the Edict of Nantes
   Birth of Bach in Eisenach
   Birth of Handel in Halle
   Lully: *Roland* (Opéra, Paris)
1686 Lully: *Armide* (Opéra, Paris)
1687 Death of Lully in Paris
   Campra: *L'Europe galante* (Opéra, Paris)
1688 Glorious Revolution in England; James II deposed
   Charpentier: *Te Deum*
   Purcell: *Dido and Aeneas* (Josias Priest's School for Girls, London)
1689 Bill of Rights in England: William and Mary ascend to the throne
   Birth of Montesquieu at the Château de la Brède
1691 Purcell: *King Arthur* (Queen's Theatre, London)
1692 Purcell: *The Fairy Queen* (Queen's Theatre, London)
   Purcell: *Ode to St Cecilia*
1693 Charpentier: *Médée* (Opéra, Paris)
1694 Death of Queen Mary; William III sole sovereign of England
   Birth of Voltaire in Paris
   Purcell: *Timon of Athens*
1695 Death of Purcell in London
   Rameau studies at the Jesuit collège des Godrans in Dijon
   Purcell: *The Indian Queen*
   Purcell: *The Tempest*
   Purcell: *Music for the Funeral of Queen Mary*
1697 Birth of Hogarth in London

Death of Rameau's mother
Vanbrugh: *The Provoked Wife*
1699 Birth of Chassé in Rennes
Death of Racine in Paris
1700 Death of Charles II; Louis XIV's grandson becomes Philip V of Spain
Death of Le Nôtre
1701 Beginning of the War of the Spanish Succession: the English led Grand Alliance against France and Spain (ends 1713)
Rameau travels to Italy
1702 Death of William III; Anne ascends to the throne of England
Beginning of the revolt of the Camisards in the Cévennes
Rameau is temporarily engaged as organist of Notre-Dame des Doms in Avignon; he then accepts the position of maître organiste at the cathedral in Clermont-Ferrand
Campra: *Tancrède* (Opéra, Paris)
1704 Battle of Blenheim (Bavaria)
Death of Charpentier in Paris
Death of Locke in Essex
Newton: *Opticks*
Swift: *A Tale of a Tub*
1705 Handel's first opera *Almira, Königin von Castilien* premiered in Hamburg
1706 Death of Bayle in Rotterdam
Rameau travels to Paris; he takes up the position of organist at the Jesuit collège Louis-le-Grand
Rameau: *Premier livre de pièces de clavecin*
Marais: *Alcyone* (Opéra, Paris)
Farquhar: *The Recruiting Officer* (Drury Lane, London)
Locke: *Of the Conduct of the Understanding*
1707 Kingdom of Great Britain created by the Act of Union
Birth of Marie Pélissier
Death of Vauban in Paris
Bach: Cantata *Christ lag in Todes Banden*
Scarlatti: *Il Mitridate Eupatore* (Venice)
1708 Death of Hardouin-Mansart at Marly-le-Roi
1709 Rameau returns home to Dijon and succeeds his father as organist at Notre-Dame
1710 Birth of Pergolesi in Jesi
Birth of Marie Camargo in Brussels

Campra: *Les Fêtes vénitiennes* (Opéra, Paris)
Berkeley: *A Treatise Concerning the Principles of Human Knowledge*
1711 Birth of Mondonville in Narbonne
Handel: *Rinaldo* (Queen's Theatre, London)
Pope: *An Essay on Criticism*
Shaftesbury: *Characteristics of Men, Manners, Opinions, Times*
1712 Unigenitus bull outlawing Jansenism issued by Pope Clement XI
Birth of Rousseau in Geneva
Rameau travels to Lyon to take up the position of maître organiste at the convent of the Jacobins
During his time in Lyon Rameau writes the motets *In convertendo, Deus noster refugium* and *Quam dilecta*
Handel settles in England
Campra: *Idoménée* (Opéra, Paris)
Pope: *The Rape of the Lock*
Watteau: *Les Acteurs de la Comédie-Française*
1713 Treaty of Utrecht ends the War of the Spanish Succession
Birth of Diderot in Langres
Birth of Jélyotte in Lasseube
Birth of Marie Fel in Bordeaux
Couperin: *Premier livre de pièces de clavecin*
Berkeley: *Three Dialogues between Hylas and Philonou*
1714 Death of Queen Anne; the Elector of Hanover ascends to the throne of Great Britain and Ireland as George I
Birth of Gluck in Erasbach
Death of Rameau's father
Corelli: *12 Concerti grossi*
Couperin: *Leçons de ténèbres*
Vivaldi: *Orlando finto pazzo* (Venice)
1715 Death of Louis XIV; Philippe d'Orléans becomes Regent
Birth of Helvétius in Paris
Rameau leaves Lyon for Clermont, where he takes up his former job as organist
During his second sojourn in Clermont Rameau composes the cantatas *Medée, L'Absence, L'Impatience, Aquilon et Orithie, Téthis, Orphée* and *Les Amants trahis*
Bach: *English Suites*
Handel: *Amadigi di Gaula*, based on the tragédie lyrique by Destouches and Houdar de la Motte (King's Theatre, London)
1716 Birth of Capability Brown in Northumberland

Death of Leibniz in Hanover
Vivaldi: *Arsilda, regina di Ponto* (Venice)
1717 Birth of d'Alembert in Paris
Birth of Garrick in Hereford
Handel: *Water Music*
1718 Handel: *Acis and Galatea*
Defoe: *Continuation of Turkish Letters Writ by a Turkish Spy in Paris*
Watteau: *La Gamme d'amour*
1719 Foundation of the Royal Academy of Music (London)
Defoe: *Robinson Crusoe*
Watteau: *Pierrot* (*Gilles*)
1720 Bach: *Partitas* for violin (completed)
1721 Robert Walpole becomes prime minister of Great Britain
Birth of Malesherbes in Paris
Bach: *Brandenburg Concertos*
Scarlatti: *Griselda* (Rome)
Montesquieu: *Lettres persanes*
1722 Rameau settles in Paris
Rameau: *Traité de l'harmonie reduite à ses principes naturels*
Bach: *Well-Tempered Clavier*
Bach: *French Suites*
Defoe: *A Journal of the Plague Year*
Defoe: *Moll Flanders*
1723 Death of Philippe d'Orléans; Louis XV reaches maturity; Louis Henri, duc de Bourbon, becomes first minister
Death of Wren in London
Rameau: *L'Endriague* (Foire St-Germain)
Bach: *Cello Suites* (completed)
Campra: *Requiem*
1724 Bach: *St John Passion* (Leipzig)
Rameau: *Pièces de clavecin*
Handel: *Giulio Cesare* (King's Theatre, London)
Handel: *Tamerlano* (King's Theatre, London)
Defoe: *A Tour Thro' the Whole Island of Great Britain*
Defoe: *Roxana, the Fortunate Mistress*
1725 Death of Scarlatti in Naples
Handel: *Rodelina* (King's Theatre, 1725)
Vivaldi: *The Four Seasons*
1726 Fleury exiles Bourbon from court and begins his long period of power as *de facto* first minister

Voltaire begins his years of exile in England
Rameau marries Marie-Louise Mangot
Rameau: *Nouveau Système de musique théorique*
Rameau: *L'Enrôlement d'Arlequin* (Foire St-Germain)
Rameau: *Le P., ou La Rose* (Foire St-Laurent) (Banned by the censor)
Rameau: *La Robe de dissension, ou Le Faux-prodige* (Foire St-Laurent)
Bach: *Partitas* for keyboard
Couperin: *Les Nations*
Swift: *Gulliver's Travels*

1727 Death of George I; accession of George II to the British throne;
Handel composes *Zadok the Priest* for the coronation
Handel becomes a naturalised citizen of England
Death of Newton in London
Bach: *St Matthew Passion* (Leipzig)

1728 Gay: *The Beggar's Opera* (Lincoln's Inn Fields Theatre, London)
Rameau: cantata *Le Berger fidèle* (Concert spirituel)
Pope: *The Dunciad*
Prévost: *Mémoires et aventures d'un homme de qualité qui s'est retiré du monde* (vol.1-4)
Chardin: *La Raie*

1729 Theoretical dispute between Rameau and another composer whose identity is unknown
Rameau: *Nouvelles Suites de pièces de clavecin*
Swift: *A Modest Proposal*

1730 Handel: *Partenope* (King's Theatre, London)
Telemann: *Quadri* ('Paris Quartets' I)
Marivaux: *Le Jeu de l'amour et du hasard* (Théâtre Italien)

1731 Marivaux: *La Vie de Marianne* (pt.1)
Prévost: *Manon Lescaut* (*Mémoires et aventures d'un homme de qualité*, vol.7)
Prévost: *Le Philosophe anglais* (vol.1)
Hogarth: *A Harlot's Progress*

1732 Birth of Haydn in Rohrau
Rameau: *Dissertation sur les différentes méthodes d'accompagnement pour le clavecin ou pour l'orgue*
Montéclair: *Jephté* (Opéra, Paris)
Marivaux: *Le Triomphe de l'amour* (Théâtre Italien)
Voltaire: *Zaïre* (Comédie-Française)

1733 Beginning of the War of the Polish Succession: France and Spain against Russia, the Habsburg monarchy, Prussia and Poland (ends

1738)
Death of Couperin in Paris
Thuret becomes director of the Opéra
Rameau: *Hippolyte et Aricie* (Opéra, Paris)
Handel: *Orlando* (King's Theatre, London)
Pergolesi: *Il prigionier superbo*, containing *La serva padrona* (Naples)
Voltaire: *Letters Concerning the English Nation*

1734 With John Rich Handel establishes a company at the Covent Garden Theatre, and writes the opéra-ballet *Terpsicore* for Marie Sallé, performed as a prologue to his opera *Il pastor fido* (Covent Garden Theatre, London)
Voltaire's *Lettres philosophiques*, the French version of *Letters Concerning the English Nation*, is banned and Voltaire flees to Champagne
Rameau and Voltaire: *Samson* (abandoned)
Rameau: *Les Courses de Tempé* (Comédie-Française)
Pope: *An Essay on Man*

1735 Rameau becomes music director of La Pouplinière's private orchestra, probably in 1735 but perhaps during the previous year
Rameau: *Les Indes galantes* (Opéra, Paris)
Bach: *Overture in the French Style* for keyboard
Bach: *Italian Concerto* for keyboard
Handel: *Ariodante*, with dance sequences in the French manner for Marie Sallé (Covent Garden Theatre)
Handel: *Alcina* (Covent Garden Theatre)
Hogarth: *A Rake's Progress*

1736 Death of Pergolesi in Pozzuoli
Rameau and Voltaire: 2nd version of *Samson* (abandoned)
Handel: *Alexander's Feast*
Pergolesi: *Stabat Mater*

1737 Birth of Tom Paine in Thetford
Death of Montéclair in Domont
Rameau establishes a school of composition at his home in the rue des Bons Enfants
Rameau: *La Génération harmonique, ou Traité de musique théorique et pratique*
Rameau: *Castor et Pollux* (Opéra, Paris)
Telemann: *Nouveaux quatuors* ('Paris Quartets' II)
Marivaux: *Les Fausses confidences* (Théâtre Italien)
Hume: *A Treatise of Human Nature*

1739 Rameau: *Les Fêtes d'Hébé* (Opéra, Paris)

Rameau: *Dardanus* (Opéra, Paris)
1740 Frederick the Great becomes King of Prussia
Beginning of the War of the Austrian Succession: France, Spain and Prussia against Great Britain, the Habsburg monarchy and Russia (ends 1748)
Birth of Sade in Paris
Mondonville: the motet *Venite exultemus domino*
D'Alembert: *Mémoire sur la réfraction des corps solides*
Richardson: *Pamela*
1741 Death of Vivaldi in Vienna
Rameau: *Pièces de Clavecin en concert*
Bach: *Goldberg Variations*
Handel's last opera *Deidamia* premiered at the Lincoln's Inn Fields Theatre.
Chardin: *La Fillette au volant*
1742 Bach: *Well-Tempered Clavier* Book Two
Handel: *Messiah* (Dublin)
Fielding: *Joseph Andrews*
1743 Death of Fleury in Issy-les-Moulineaux
Handel: *Samson*
D'Alembert: *Traité de dynamique*
1744 Death of Campra
Rameau: *Le P., ou La Rose* (Foire St-Germain)
Rameau: new version of *Dardanus* (Opéra, Paris)
1745 Jacobite Rising in Great Britain ('The Forty-five')
Battle of Fontenoy (Belgium)
Death of Walpole in London
Rameau becomes Compositeur de la Musique du Cabinet du Roi and receives a royal pension
Rameau and Voltaire: *La Princesse de Navarre* (Versailles)
Rameau: *Platée, ou Junon jalouse* (Versailles)
Rameau: *Les Fêtes de Polymnie* (Opéra, Paris)
Rameau and Voltaire: *La Temple de la gloire* (Versailles)
Rameau and Voltaire: *Les Fêtes de Ramire* (Versailles)
Diderot: translation of Shaftesbury's *Inquiry concerning Virtue and Merit*
Voltaire: *Eléments de la philosophie de Newton*
Hogarth: *Marriage à-la-mode*
1746 Death of Philip V of Spain
Battle of Culloden (Scotland)

Rameau and Voltaire: *La Temple de la gloire* (Opéra, Paris)
1747 Rameau: *La Dauphine* for keyboard
Rameau: *Les Fêtes de l'Hymen et de l'Amour, ou Les Dieux d'Égypte* (Versailles)
Goldoni: *I due gemelli veneziani*
Voltaire: *Zadig*
1748 Treaty of Aix-la-Chapelle ends the War of the Austrian Succession
Birth of David in Paris
Rameau: *Zaïs* (Opéra, Paris)
Rameau: *Pygmalion* (Opéra, Paris)
Rameau: *Les Surprises de l'amour* (Versailles)
Diderot: *Les Bijoux indiscrets*
Diderot: *Mémoires sur différents sujets de mathématiques*
Montesquieu: *De l'Esprit des Lois*
Hogarth: *The Gate of Calais*
Richardson: *Clarissa*
1749 Death of Destouches in Paris
Death of Marie Pélissier in Paris
Diderot is imprisoned in the Château de Vincennes following the publication of his *Lettre sur les aveugles*
Rameau presents a paper (finessed by Diderot) at the Académie royale des Sciences: *Mémoire où l'on expose les fondements du système de musique théorique et pratique de M. Rameau*
Rameau: *Naïs* (Opéra, Paris)
Rameau: *Zoroastre* (Opéra, Paris)
Bach: Mass in B Minor
Handel: *Music for the Royal Fireworks*
Mondonville: *Le Carnaval du Parnasse* (Opéra, Paris)
Diderot: *Lettre sur les aveugles*
Fielding: *The History of Tom Jones, a Foundling*
Johnson: *The Vanity of Human Wishes*
1750 Death of Bach in Leipzig
Rameau: *Démonstration du principe de l'harmonie*
Rameau: *Zéphyre* (abandoned, ca.1750, exact date unknown)
Rousseau: *Discours sur les sciences et les arts*
Gainsborough: *Mr and Mrs Robert Andrews*
1751 Publication of the first volume of Diderot and d'Alembert's *Encyclopédie* ('A-Azymites')
Rameau: revised version of the motet *In convertendo* (Concert spirituel)
Rameau: *La Guirlande* (Opéra, Paris)

Rameau: *Acante et Céphise* (Opéra, Paris)
Rameau: *Linus* (abandoned)
Bach: *Art of Fugue* (published)
Handel: *Jephtha*
D'Alembert: *Discours préliminaire de l'Encyclopédie*
Lessing: *Kleinigkeiten*

1752 An Italian troupe (the Buffoni) begin a season at the Opéra with Pergolesi's *La serva padrona*, initiating the 'Querelle des Bouffons'
Rameau: *Nouvelles réflexions de M. Rameau sur sa Démonstration du principe de l'harmonie*
Rousseau: *Le devin du village* (Fontainebleau)
Haydn: *Der krumme Teufel* (Vienna)
Diderot and d'Alembert: *Encyclopédie*, vol.2, 'B'
D'Alembert: *Eléments de musique, théorique et pratique, suivant les principes de M. Rameau*
Grimm: *Lettre de M. Grimm sur Omphale*
Rousseau: *Lettre à M. Grimm, au sujet des remarques ajoutées à sa lettre sur Omphale*

1753 Rameau's long association with La Pouplinière comes to an end
Thuret and Royer replace Rebel and Francœur as directors of the Opéra
Rameau: *Daphnis et Églé* (Fontainebleau)
Rameau: *Les Sybarites* (Fontainebleau)
Rousseau: *Le devin du village* (Opéra, Paris)
Diderot and d'Alembert: *Encyclopédie*, vol.3, 'Cha-Consécration'
Goldoni: *Il servitore di due padroni*
Grimm: *Le petit prophète de Boehmischbroda*
Rousseau: *Lettre sur la musique française*

1754 Rameau: *Observations sur notre instinct pour la musique et sur son principe*
Rameau: new version of *Castor et Pollux* at the Opéra marking the end of the 'Querelle des Bouffons'
Rameau: *La Naissance d'Osiris* (Versailles)
Rameau: *Anacréon* (Fontainebleau)
Diderot and d'Alembert: *Encyclopédie*, vol.4, 'Conseil-Dizier'

1755 Death of Montesquieu in Paris
Rameau: *Erreurs sur la musique dans l'Encyclopédie*
Diderot and d'Alembert: *Encyclopédie*, vol.5, 'Do-Esymnete'
Johnson: *A Dictionary of the English Language*
Kant: *Allgemeine Naturgeschichte und Theorie des Himmels*
Lessing: *Miss Sara Sampson*

1756 Beginning of the Seven Years' War: Great Britain and Prussia against France, Austria, Spain and Russia (ends 1763)
  Birth of Mozart in Salzburg
  Birth of William Godwin in Wisbech
  Rameau: *Suite des Erreurs sur la musique dans l'Encyclopédie*
  Rameau: new version of *Zoroastre* (Opéra, Paris)
  Diderot and d'Alembert: *Encyclopédie*, vol.6, 'Et-Fne'
  Gainsborough: *The Painter's Daughters Chasing a Butterfly*
1757 Louis XV survives an assassination attempt
  Rameau: *Réponse de M. Rameau à MM. les éditeurs de l'Encyclopédie sur leur dernier avertissement*
  Rameau: new version of *Les Surprises de l'amour* (Opéra, Paris)
  Haydn begins to compose his first symphonies
  Diderot and d'Alembert: *Encyclopédie*, vol.7, 'Foang-Gythium'
1758 Rousseau: *Lettre à d'Alembert sur les spectacles*
  Birth of Robespierre in Arras
  Rameau: new entrée *Anacréon* added to *Les Surprises de l'amour* (Opéra, Paris)
  Helvétius: *De l'esprit*
1759 Death of Handel in London
  Birth of Danton in Arcis-sur-Aube
  Birth of Mary Wollstonecraft in London
  D'Alembert: *De la liberté de la musique*
  Smith: *The Theory of Moral Sentiments*
  Sterne: *The Life and Opinions of Tristram Shandy*
  Voltaire: *Candide*
1760 Death of George II; accession of George III to the British throne
  Rameau: *Code de musique pratique ou Méthodes pour apprendre la musique*
  Rameau: *Les Paladins* (Opéra, Paris)
  Diderot: *La Religieuse*
1761 Rousseau: *Julie, ou la nouvelle Héloïse*
  Diderot: *Le Neveu de Rameau*
1762 Catherine the Great becomes Empress of Russia
  Gluck: *Orfeo ed Euridice* (Vienna)
  Haydn: *Acide e Galatea*
  D'Alembert: new edition of *Eléments de musique*
  Kant: *Die falsche Spitzfindigkeit der vier syllogistischen Figuren erwiesen*
  Rousseau: *Émile, ou de l'éducation*
  Rousseau: *Du contrat social*

1763 Treaty of Paris ends the Seven Years' War
  The Opéra's theatre at the Palais-Royal is destroyed by fire; a temporary home is created in the Palais des Tuileries; a revival of *Castor et Pollux* opens the new theatre
  Mozart, aged six, performs before the king at Versailles
  Rameau: *Les Boréades* (abandoned)
  Rameau and Voltaire: *La Princesse de Navarre* (Bordeaux)
1764 Death of Mme de Pompadour
  Rameau ennobled by the king
  Rameau dies in Paris on 12 September

Appendix II

Rameau's Theoretical Writings

Chronology

1722-31

Traité de l'Harmonie réduite à ses principes naturels (Paris: Ballard, 1722)

'De la mécanique des doigts sur le clavecin', in *Pieces de clavecin* (Paris: Hochereau, Boivin, l'Auteur, 1724)

Nouveau Système de musique théorique (Paris: Ballard, 1726)

'Remarques sur les pièces de ce livre et sur les différents genres de musique', in *Nouvelles suites de pièces de clavecin* (Paris: l'Auteur, Boivin, Leclerc, [1729])

Dispute with another musician, possibly Michel Pignolet de Montéclair or François Campion:

  Other musician: 'Conférence sur la musique', in *Mercure de France* (June 1729)

  Rameau: 'Examen de la conférence sur la musique', in *Mercure de France* (October 1729)

  Rameau: 'Observations sur la méthode d'accompagnement pour le clavecin qui est en usage', in *Mercure de France*, (February 1730)

  Rameau: 'Plan abrégé d'une méthode nouvelle d'accompagnement pour le clavecin', in *Mercure de France* (March 1730)

Other musician: 'Réponse du second musicien au premier musicien, sur les deux écrits qui concernent l'accompagnement', in *Mercure de France* (June 1730, t. 1)

Rameau: 'Réplique du premier musicien à la réponse du second', in *Mercure de France* (June 1730, t. 2)

Rameau: 'Lettre de M. à M. sur la musique', in *Mercure de France* (September 1731)

1732-39

Dissertation sur les différentes méthodes d'accompagnement pour le clavecin ou pour l'orgue (Paris: Boivin, 1732)

Dispute with Louis-Bertrand Castel:

Castel: 'Suite et seconde partie des nouvelles expériences sur l'optique', in *Journal de Trévoux* (August 1735)

Rameau: 'Lettre de M. Rameau au R. P. Castel', in *Journal de Trévoux* (July 1736)

Castel: 'Remarques du P. Castel sur la lettre de M. Rameau', in *Journal de Trévoux* (September 1736)

Génération harmonique, ou Traité de musique théorique et pratique (Paris: Prault, 1737)

'Remarques de M. Rameau sur l'extrait qu'on a donné de son livre intitulé Génération harmonique', in *Pour et Contre* (1738)

1740s

Mémoire où l'on expose les fondements du système de musique théorique et pratique de M. Rameau (ms., 1749)

1750s

Démonstration du principe de l'harmonie (Paris: Durand, 1750)

'Lettre de M. Rameau à l'auteur du Mercure', in *Mercure de France* (May 1752)

Nouvelles Réflexions de M. Rameau sur sa Démonstration du principe de l'harmonie (Paris: Durand, 1752)

'Réflexions de M. Rameau sur la manière de former la voix', in *Mercure de France* (October 1752)

Extrait d'une réponse de M. Rameau à M. Euler sur l'identité des octaves (Paris: Durand, 1753)

Observations sur notre instinct pour la musique et sur son principe (Paris: Prault fils, 1754)

Erreurs sur la musique dans l'Encyclopédie (Paris: Jorry, 1755)

Suite des Erreurs sur la musique dans l'Encyclopédie (Paris: Jorry, 1756)

Réponse de M. Rameau à MM. les éditeurs de l'Encyclopédie sur leur dernier avertissement (London: Jorry, 1757)

Prospectus où l'on propose au public par voie de souscription un Code de musique pratique composé de sept methods (Paris, 1757)

1760s

Code de musique pratique ou Méthodes pour apprendre la musique... avec de nouvelles réflexions sur le principe sonore (Paris: Imprimerie royale, 1760)

Dispute with d'Alembert:

> Rameau: *Lettre à M. d'Alembert sur ses opinions en musique* (Paris, 1760)

D'Alembert: 'Lettre à M. Rameau', in *Mercure de France* (April 1761)

Rameau: 'Réponse de M. Rameau à la lettre de M. d'Alembert', in *Mercure de France* (April 1761)

Rameau: 'Suite de la réponse de M. Rameau à la lettre que M. d'Alembert lui a adressée', in *Mercure de France* (July 1761)

D'Alembert: new edition of *Eléments de musique…* (Lyon: Bruyset, 1762)

D'Alembert: 'Réponse à une lettre imprimée de M. Rameau', in *Mercure de France* (March 1762)

'Source où vraisemblablement on a dû puiser la première idée des proportions', in *Mercure de France* (April 1761)

'Origine des modes et du temperament', in *Mercure de France* (June 1761)

Origine des sciences suivie d'une controverse sur le même sujet (Paris: Jorry, 1762)

'Lettre de M*** à M. D**** sur un ouvrage intitulé l'Origine des sciences', in *Mercure de France* (April 1762)

'Seconde lettre de M*** à M***', in *Mercure de France* (April 1762)

'Observations de M. Rameau sur son ouvrage intitulé Origine des sciences', in *Mercure de France* (June 1762)

'Conclusions sur l'origine des sciences', in *Journal encyclopédique* (July 1762)

'Lettre de Monsieur Rameau aux Philosophes', in *Journal de Trevoux* (August 1762)

Vérités également ignorées et intéressantes tirées du sein de la nature (1763/64)

Date unknown

L'Art de la Basse fondamentale (found among d'Alembert's papers, attributed to Rameau)

Appendix III

Rameau's Compositions

[A] Chronology

1706-07: Paris

Organ pieces (ca.1706). Music lost.
Premier Livre de pièces de clavecin (1706). Harpsichord.
Lucas, pour se gausser de nous (ca.1707). Air for two voices. Published in *Recueil d'Airs sérieux et a boire de différents auteurs*, 1707.

1713-15: Lyon

Concert de la feste de la publication de la paix (1713). Music lost.
Deus noster refugium (ca.1713-14). Grand motet.
In convertendo (ca.1713-15). Grand motet.
Quam dilecta (ca.1713-15). Grand motet.
Exultet caelum laudibus (1715). Motet without choir. Music lost.
Concert pour l'intronisation de Monseigneur de Villeroi (1715). Music lost.

1715-22: Clermont

Medée (ca.1715). Cantata. Music lost.
L'Absence (ca.1715). Cantata. Music lost.
L'Impatience (ca.1715). Cantata.
Aquilon et Orithie (ca.1715). Cantata.
Thétis (ca.1718). Cantata.
Avec du vin, endormons-nous (1719). Canon. Published in Rameau's *Traité de l'harmonie*, 1722.
Réveillez-vous dormeurs sans fin (ca.1719). Canon. Published in Rameau's *Traité de l'harmonie*, 1722.
Mes chers amis (ca.1720). Canon. Published in La Borde's *Essai sur la musique ancienne et modern*, 1780.
Frère Jacques (ca.1720). Canon. Attributed to Rameau by Sylvie

Bouissou.
Grégoire est mort (ca.1720). Canon. Attributed to Rameau by Sylvie Bouissou.
Si tu ne prends garde à toi (1720). Canon. Attributed to Rameau by Sylvie Bouissou.
L'Épouse entre deux draps (1720). Canon. Attributed to Rameau by Sylvie Bouissou.
Je suis un fou Madame (1720). Canon. Attributed to Rameau by Sylvie Bouissou.
Orphée (ca.1721). Cantata.
Les Amants trahis (ca.1721). Cantata.
Laboravi (ca.1722). Motet without choir. Published in Rameau's *Traité de l'harmonie*, 1722.
Ah! Loin de rire (ca.1722). Canon. Published in Rameau's *Traité de l'harmonie*, 1722.

1723-44: Paris

L'Endriague (1723). Opéra-comique. Music lost.
Pièces de clavecin (ca.1724). Harpsichord.
L'Enrôlement d'Arlequin (1726). Opéra-comique. Music lost.
Le P., ou La Rose (ou *Les Jardins de l'Hymen*) (1726). Opéra-comique. Banned. Music lost.
La Robe de dissension, ou Le Faux-prodige (1726). Opéra-comique. Music lost.
Le Berger fidèle (ca.1729). Cantata.
La Diatonique enharmonique (ca.1729). Harpsichord. Music lost.
Nouvelles Suites de pièces de clavecin (ca.1729). Harpsichord.
Hippolyte et Aricie (1733). Tragédie lyrique.
Samson (1734-36). Tragédie lyrique. Abandoned. Music lost.
Les Courses de Tempé (1734). Pastorale.
Les Indes galantes (1735-36). Ballet héroïque.
Fille du ciel, ô charmante harmonie (1735). Ode (Voltaire). Music lost.
Castor et Pollux (1737). Tragédie lyrique.
Les Fêtes d'Hébé, ou Les Talents lyriques (1739). Ballet héroïque.
Dardanus (1739). Tragédie lyrique.
Pièces de Clavecin en concert (1741). Trio.
Hippolyte et Aricie 2nd version (1742). Tragédie lyrique.
Le P., ou La Rose (ou *Les Jardins de l'Hymen*) (1744). Opéra-comique. Music lost.
Dardanus 2nd version (1744). Tragédie lyrique.

1745-55: Paris, Versailles and Fontainebleau

Io (ca.1745). Acte de ballet. Unfinished and abandoned. Possibly connected to *Platée*.
La Princesse de Navarre (1745). Comédie-ballet. Versailles.
Platée, ou Junon jalouse (1745). Comédie-lyrique. Versailles.
Cantate pour le Jour de la Saint-Louis (1745). Cantata (Voltaire). Paris.
Les Fêtes de Polymnie (1745). Ballet héroïque. Paris.
Le Temple de la Gloire (1745-46). Ballet héroïque. Versailles and Paris.
Les Fêtes de Ramire (1745). Acte de ballet, reworking of *La Princesse de Navarre* (Rousseau). Versailles.
La Dauphine (1747). Harpsichord. Paris.
Les Fêtes de l'Hymen et de l'Amour, ou Les Dieux d'Égypte (1747). Ballet héroïque. Versailles.
Zaïs (1748). Pastorale héroïque. Paris.
Pygmalion (1748). Acte de ballet. Paris.
Les Surprises de l'Amour (1748). Ballet héroïque. Versailles.
L'Amante préocupée (ca.1749). Air. Paris.
Naïs (1749). Pastorale héroïque. Paris.
Zoroastre (1749). Tragédie lyrique. Paris.
Zéphyre, ou Les Nymphes de Diane (ca.1750-53). Acte de ballet. Paris. Abandoned.
La Guirlande (1751). Acte de ballet. Paris.
Acante et Céphise, ou La Sympathie (1751). Pastorale héroïque. Paris.
Linus (1751). Tragédie lyrique. Paris. Abandoned. Music Lost.
Les Petits Marteaux (1753). Harpsichord. Paris.
Daphnis et Églé (1753). Acte de ballet. Fontainebleau.
Lisis et Délie (1753). Acte de ballet. Fontainebleau.
Les Sybarites (1753). Acte de ballet. Fontainebleau.
Castor et Pollux 2nd version (1754). Tragédie lyrique. Paris.
Nélée et Myrthis (ca.1754). Acte de ballet.
La Naissance d'Osiris (1754). Acte de ballet. Versailles.
Anacréon (1754). Acte de ballet. Fontainebleau.

1756-64: Paris

Zoroastre 2nd version (1756). Tragédie lyrique.
Non, non, le dieu qui sait aimer (ca.1757). Air.
Hippolyte et Aricie 3rd version (1733). Tragédie lyrique.
Les Surprises de l'Amour 2nd version (1757-58). Ballet héroïque.
Le Procureur dupe sans le savoir (1759). Opéra-comique. Abandoned.

Music lost.
Les Paladins (1760). Comédie lyrique.
Les Boréades (1763). Tragédie lyrique. Abandoned.
La Princesse de Navarre 2nd version (1763). Comédie-ballet. Bordeaux.

[B] By Genre

Instrumental Music

Premier Livre de pièces de clavecin (1706).
Pièces de clavecin (1724).
Nouvelles Suites de pièces de clavecin (ca.1729).
Pièces de Clavecin en concert (1741). Harpsichord; violin or flute; viol or second violin.
La Dauphine (1747). Harpsichord.
Les Petits Marteaux (1753). Harpsichord.

Stage Works

Tragédie lyrique

Hippolyte et Aricie (1733)
Samson (1734)
Castor et Pollux (1737)
Dardanus (1739)
Zoroastre (1756)
Linus (1751)
Dardanus 2nd version (1744)
Castor et Pollux 2nd version (1754)
Zoroastre 2nd version (1756)
Les Boréades (1763)

Ballet héroïque

Les Indes galantes (1735)
Les Fêtes d'Hébé, ou Les Talents lyriques (1739)
Les Fêtes de Polymnie (1745)
Le Temple de la Gloire (1745)
Le Temple de la Gloire 2nd version (1746)

Les Fêtes de l'Hymen et de l'Amour, ou Les Dieux d'Égypte (1747)
Les Surprises de l'Amour (1748)
Les Surprises de l'Amour 2nd version (1757)

Pastorale héroïque
Zaïs (1748)
Naïs (1749)
Acante et Céphise, ou La Sympathie (1751)

Comédie lyrique
Platée, ou Junon jalouse (1745)
Les Paladins (1760)

Acte de ballet
Les Fêtes de Ramire (1745)
Io (ca.1745)
Pygmalion (1748)
Zéphyre, ou Les Nymphes de Diane (ca.1750-53)
La Guirlande (1751)
Lisis et Délie (1753)
Daphnis et Églé (1753)
Les Sybarites (1753)
Nélée et Myrthis (ca.1754)
La Naissance d'Osiris (1754)
Anacréon (1754)

Comédie-ballet
La Princesse de Navarre (1745)

Pastorale
Les Courses de Tempé (1734)

Opéra comique
L'Endriague (1723)
L'Enrôlement d'Arlequin (1726)
Le P., ou La Rose (ou *Les Jardins de l'Hymen*) (1726)
La Robe de dissension, ou Le Faux-prodige (1726)

Le Procureur dupé sans le savoir (1759)

Vocal Music

Airs for one or two voices

Lucas, pour se gausser de nous (ca.1707)
L'Amante préocupée (ca.1749)
Un Bourbon ouvre sa carrière (1751)
Non, non, le dieu qui sait aimer (ca.1757)

Canons

Avec du vin, endormons-nous (1719)
Réveillez-vous dormeurs sans fin (ca.1719)
Mes chers amis (ca.1720)
Frère Jacques (ca.1720)
Grégoire est mort (ca.1720)
Si tu ne prends garde à toi (1720)
L'Épouse entre deux draps (1720)
Je suis un fou Madame (1720)
Ah! Loin de rire (ca.1722)

Cantatas

Medée (ca.1715)
L'Absence (ca.1715)
L'Impatience (ca.1715). Tenor; viol and basso continuo.
Aquilon et Orithie (ca.1715). Bass baritone; violin or flute and basso continuo.
Thétis (ca.1718). Bass baritone; violin and basso continuo.
Orphée (ca.1721). High voice; flute, violin and basso continuo.
Les Amants trahis (ca.1721). Two voices (*haute-contre* and bass); viol and basso continuo.
Le Berger fidèle (ca.1729). Tenor; two violins and basso continuo.
Cantate pour le Jour de la Saint-Louis (1745). Violin and basso continuo.

Motets

Deus noster refugium (ca.1713-14). Solo voices; choir in four parts; orchestra.
In convertendo (ca.1713-15, 1751). Solo voices; choir in five parts;

orchestra.
Quam dilecta (ca.1713-15). Solo voices; choir in five parts; orchestra.
Laboravi (ca.1722). Solo voices; basso continuo.

Appendix IV

Rameau's Stage Works

Chronology with Performance History

A list of professional productions of Rameau's operas. Please note that the list is not exhaustive.

L'Endriague
Opéra comique in three acts. Music lost.
Libretto: Alexis Piron.
1723/Feb. Paris: Saint-Germain fair (Dolet's company).
Pettipas (Grazinde).

L'Enrôlement d'Arlequin
Opéra comique in one act. Music lost.
Libretto: Alexis Piron.
1726/Feb. Paris: Saint-Germain fair (Théâtre d'Honoré).

Le P., ou La Rose (ou *Les Jardins de l'Hymen*)
Opéra comique in one act. Music lost.
Libretto: Alexis Piron.
1726 Paris: Saint-Laurent fair. Banned by censor.
1744 Paris: Saint-Germain fair (Théâtre de l'Opéra Comique).

La Robe de dissension, ou Le Faux-prodige
Opéra comique in two acts. Music lost.
Libretto: Alexis Piron.
1726/Sep. Paris: Saint-Laurent fair (Théâtre d'Honoré et Francisque).

Hippolyte et Aricie
Tragédie lyrique in five acts and a prologue.
Libretto: Simon Joseph Pellegrin, after Racine's *Phèdre*.
1733/Oct. Paris: Opéra.
  Tribou (Hippolyte), Pélissier (Aricie), Chassé (Thésée), Antier (Phèdre), Petitpas (Matelotte), Jélyotte (Parque).
1741/Dec. Paris: Opéra.
  Antoine (Hippolyte), Perrin (Aricie), Cuvillier (Thésée), Clement (Phèdre), Bastide (Matelotte), Dutilly (Parque).
1742/Sep. Paris: Opéra.
  Jélyotte (Hippolyte), Le Maure (Aricie), Chassé (Thésée), Eeremans (Phèdre), Fel (Matelotte), Cuvillier (Parque), Chevalier (Diane).
1743/Feb. Paris: Opéra.
1750/Feb. Paris: Opéra.
1757/Feb. Paris: Opéra.
  Poirier (Hippolyte), Fel (Aricie), Chassé (Thésée), Chevalier (Phèdre), Lemière (Matelotte), Person (Parque).
1767/Mar. Paris: Opéra.
1908 Paris: Opéra (Garnier).
1964 Paris: Hôtel de Soubise.
1964 Paris: Théâtre des Champs-Élysées. Concert performance.
  Pierre Boulez (musical direction).
  Orchestre national de France.
1972 Nantes: Grand Théâtre.
1974 Marseilles: Opéra municipal.
1974 Strasbourg: Opéra du Rhin.
1978 Versailles: Opéra royal.
1980 London: Royal Opera.
  English Bach Festival production.
  Charles Mackerras (musical direction).
1983 Aix-en-Provence: Festival.
  Aler (Hippolyte), Yakar (Aricie), Van Dam (Thésée), Norman (Phèdre).
  John Eliot Gardiner (musical direction).
  Pier Luigi Pizzi (production).
  English Baroque Soloists.
1985 Paris: Opéra Comique.
  William Christie (musical direction).
  Ensemble Baroque.
1996 Paris: Opéra (Garnier).

Padmore (Hippolyte), Panzarella (Aricie), Naouri (Thésée), Hunt (Phèdre).
William Christie (musical direction).
Jean-Marie Villégier (production).
Les Arts Florissants.

2009 Toulouse: Théâtre du Capitole.
Antoun (Hippolyte), Gillet (Aricie), Degout (Thésée), McHardy (Phèdre).
Emmanuelle Haïm (musical direction).
Ivan Alexandre (production).
Le Concert d'Astrée.

2010 Aix-en-Provence: Festival (Grand Théâtre de Provence). Extracts.
William Christie (musical direction).
Trisha Brown (production).

2012 Paris: Opéra (Garnier).
Lehtipuu (Hippolyte), Gillet (Aricie), Degout (Thésée), Connolly (Phèdre).
Emmanuelle Haïm (musical direction).
Ivan Alexandre (production).
Le Concert d'Astrée.

2013 Glyndebourne: Festival
Lyon (Hippolyte), Karg (Aricie), Degout (Thésée), Connolly (Phèdre).
William Christie (musical direction).
Jonathan Kent (production).
Orchestra of the Age of Enlightenment.

2020 Paris: Opéra comique.
Van Mechelen (Hippolyte), Benoit (Aricie), Degout (Thésée), Brunet-Grupposo (Phèdre).
Raphaël Pichon (musical direction).
Jeanne Candel (production).
Ensemble Pygmalion.

Les Courses de Tempé

Pastorale in one act by Alexis Piron. Final divertissement by Rameau.
Music lost.
1734/Aug. Paris: Comédie-Française.

Samson
Tragédie lyrique in five acts and a prologue. Music lost.
Libretto: Voltaire.
1734 Abandoned.
2024 Aix-en-Provence: Festival (Théâtre de l'Archevêché).
  Ott (Samson), Desandre (Timna), Stucker (Dalila), Di Pierro (Achisch).
  Raphaël Pichon (musical direction).
  Claus Guth (production).
  Pygmalion.
  Not an attempt to recreate Rameau and Voltaire's *Samson*. A new libretto was written and matched with appropriate music from Rameau's operas.

Les Indes galantes
Ballet héroïque in four acts and a prologue.
Libretto: Louis Fuzelier.
Entrée 1: Le Turc généreux.
Entrée 2: Les Incas du Pérou.
Entrée 3: Les Fleurs.
Entrée 4: Les Sauvages.
1735/Aug. Paris: Opéra. Revived 1735, 1736.
  Jélyotte (Valère/Carlos), Antier (Phani), Pélissier (Émilie), Chassé (Huascar), Petitpas (Amour), Eeremans (Hébé).
1743/May Paris: Opéra.
1749/Aug. Paris: Opéra.
1751/Jun. Paris: Opéra.
1761 Paris: Opéra.
1765 Versailles.
1770 Paris: Opéra.
1773 Paris: Opéra.
1925 Paris: Opéra Comique.
1952 Paris: Opéra (Garnier). Revived 1953, 1954, 1955, 1958, 1959.
  Maurice Lehmann (production).
1978 Bordeaux: Grand Théâtre.
1983 Paris: Théâtre du Châtelet / Dijon: Théâtre de Dijon.
1990 Aix-en-Provence: Festival (Théâtre de l'Archevêché).
  William Christie (musical direction).
  Les Arts Florissants.

1999 Paris: Opéra. Revived 2003.
  Beuron (Valère), Paton (Carlos), Hortelius (Phani), Dessay (Hébé/Fatime/Zima), Grant Murphy (Émilie/Zaïre), Agnew (Tacmas).
  William Christie (musical direction).
  Andrei Serban (production).
  Les Arts Florissants.
2012 Toulouse: Théâtre du Capitole / 2014 Bordeaux: Grand Théâtre.
  Tarver/Dahlin (Valère/Tacmas), Auvity/Dahlin (Carlos/Damon), Guillemette/Brahim-Djelloul (Hébé/Phani/Fatime), Van Wanroij/Van Wanroij (Émilie/Atalide).
  Christophe Rousset (musical direction).
  Laura Scozzi (production).
  Les Talens Lyriques.
2016 Munich: Bayerische Staatsoper.
  Auvity (Valère/Tacmas), Vidal (Carlos/Damon), Oropesa (Hébé/Zima), Prohaska (Phani/Fatime), Benoit (Émilie), Lis (Huascar), Nazmi (Osman/Ali), Quintans (Amour).
  Ivor Bolton (musical direction).
  Sidi Larbi Cherkaoui (production).
  Münchner Festspielorchester.
  Balthasar-Neumann-Chor, Freiburg.
  Tänzer der Compagnie Eastman, Antwerpen.
2025 Hampshire: Grange Festival
  Leonardo García-Alarcón (musical direction).
  Bintou Dembélé (production).

Castor et Pollux

Tragédie lyrique in five acts and a prologue.
Libretto: Pierre-Joseph Bernard.
1737/Oct. Paris: Opéra.
  Tribou (Castor), Chassé (Pollux), Pélissier (Télaïre), Antier (Phébé), Fel (Amour), Petitpas (Plaisir céleste).
1754/Jan. Paris: Opéra. New version.
  Jélyotte (Castor), Chassé (Pollux), Fel (Télaïre), Chevalier (Phébé).
1763 Fontainebleau.
1764/Jan. Paris: Opéra.
1765/Feb. Paris: Opéra.
1770 Versailles.
1771 Cassel, Nord.

1772/Jan. Paris: Opéra.
1773/Jan. Paris: Opéra.
1777 Versailles.
1778/Oct. Paris: Opéra.
1780/May. Paris: Opéra.
1781/Jan. Paris: Opéra.
1782/Jun. Paris: Opéra.
1784/Jun. Paris: Opéra.
1903 Paris: Schola Cantorum.
1981 London: Royal Opera (1754 version).
  English Bach Festival production.
  Charles Farncombe/Roger Norrington (musical directors).
1991 Aix-en-Provence: Festival (Théâtre de l'Archevêché) (1737 version).
  William Christie (musical direction).
  Pier-Luigi Pizzi (production).
  Les Arts Florissants.
2011 London: ENO (1754 version).
  Clayton (Castor), Williams (Pollux), Bevan (Télaïre), Tatulescu (Phébé).
  Christian Curnyn (musical direction).
  Barrie Kosky (production).
2024 Oxford: Sheldonian Theatre (1737 version). The Rameau Project, University of Oxford.
  Carver (Castor), Lawrence-Jones (Pollux), Cronin (Télaïre), Averina (Phébé).
  Jonathan Williams (musical direction).
  Guido Martin-Brandis (production).
  Rameau Project Orchestra.
2025 Paris: Opéra (1737 version).
  Van Mechelen (Castor), Mauillon (Pollux), De Bique (Télaïre), D'Oustrac (Phébé).
  Teodor Currentzis (musical direction).
  Peter Sellars (production).

Les Fêtes d'Hébé, ou Les Talents lyriques

Ballet héroïque in three acts and a prologue.
Libretto: Antoine Gautier de Montdorge and others.
Entrée 1: La Poésie.
Entrée 2: La Musique.

Entrée 3: La Danse.
1739/May Paris: Opéra.
  Fel (Hébé), Jélyotte (Theleme/Mercure), Eeremans (Sapho), Pélissier (Iphise), Mariette (Eglé), Le Page (Tirtée).
1740 Paris: Opéra.
1747 Paris: Opéra.
  Fel (Hébé/Iphise), Poirier (Theleme), Jélyotte (Mercure), Romainville (Sapho), Pélissier (Iphise), Camargo (Eglé), Chassé (Tirtée).
1749 Paris: Opéra.
1756 Bordeaux.
1756 Paris: Opéra.
1764 Versailles.
1764 Paris: Opéra.
1765 Versailles.
1770 Paris: Opéra.
1950 Versailles: Trianon.
1964 Lyon: Théâtre romain de Fourvière.
1966 Angoulême: Théâtre du Jardin Vert.
  Orchestre du Théâtre de Nancy.
2017 Paris: Opéra (Amphithéâtre Bastille) / London: Britten Theatre, Royal College of Music.
  Co-production: The Rameau Project (University of Oxford), Académie de l'Opéra national de Paris, Centre de musique baroque de Versailles, Royal College of Music (London).
  Texier (Hébé/Eglé), Dios Mateos (Theleme/Mercure), Gonzalez (Iphise/Sapho), Timoshenko (Tirtée/Hymas), Kumiega (Alcée), Poissonnier (Amour), Penfold (Naïade), Marras (Lycurgue/Momus).
  Jonathan Williams (musical direction).
  Thomas Lebrun (production).
  Chanteurs de l'Académie de l'Opéra national de Paris.
  Les Chantres du Centre de musique baroque de Versailles.
  Royal College of Music Baroque Orchestra.
2024 Paris: Opéra comique.
  Negri (Hébé), Desandre (Iphise/Eglé/Sapho), Rondepierre (Theleme), Mauillon (Momus/Mercure), Dolcini (Tirtée/Hymas), Auvity (Lycurgue), Leite (Love/The Stream), Walendzik (The River).
  William Christie (musical direction).
  Robert Carsen (production).
  Les Arts Florissants.

Dardanus

Tragédie lyrique in five acts and a prologue.
Libretto: Charles-Antoine Leclerc de la Bruère.
1739/Nov. Paris: Opéra.
  Jélyotte (Dardanus), Pélissier (Iphise), Albert (Antenor), Le Page (Teucer/Isménor), Eeremans (Vénus), Fel (Songe).
1744/Apr. Paris: Opéra. New version.
  Jélyotte (Dardanus), Le Maure (Iphise), Le Page (Antenor), Chassé (Teucer/Isménor), Fel (Vénus).
1760 Paris: Opéra.
  Pillot (Dardanus), Arnould (Iphise), Gélin (Antenor), Larrivée (Teucer/Isménor), Dubois (Vénus).
1768 Paris: Opéra.
1771 Paris: Opéra.
1907 Dijon.
1980 Paris: Opéra.
  Jorge Lavelli (production).
2009 Lille: Opéra / Caen: Théâtre / Dijon: Opéra.
  Dahlin (Dardanus), Perruche (Iphise), Gleadow (Antenor), Lis (Teucer), Foster-Williams (Isménor).
  Emmanuelle Haïm (musical direction).
  Claude Buchvald (production).
  Le Concert d'Astrée.
2012 Versailles: Opéra royal (1744 version). Concert performance.
  Richter (Dardanus), Arquez (Iphise), Arnould (Antenor), Buet (Teucer), Fernandes (Isménor), Devieilhe (Venus), De Negri (Amour).
  Raphaël Pichon (musical direction).
  Ensemble Pygmalion.
2015 Bordeaux: Grand Théâtre / Versailles: Opéra royal (1739 version, with later additions).
  Van Mechelen/Vidal (Dardanus), Arquez (Iphise), Sempey (Antenor), Di Pierro (Teucer/Isménor), Gauvin (Venus), Watson (Amour).
  Raphaël Pichon (musical direction).
  Michel Fau (production).
  Ensemble Pygmalion.
2017 London: Hackney Empire/UK Tour: English Touring Opera (1744 version). The Rameau Project, University of Oxford/English Touring Opera co-production.
  Gregory (Dardanus), Averina (Iphise), Nelson (Antenor), Doyle

(Teucer), Long (Isménor), Penfold (Venus).
Jonathan Williams (musical direction).
Douglas Rintoul (production).
The Old Street Band.

La Princesse de Navarre

Comédie-ballet in three acts.
Text: Voltaire.
1745/Feb. Versailles.
   Clairon, Dangeville, Gaussin, Grandval, Poisson (from the Comédie-Française), Fel, Jélyotte, Chassé, Camargo, Sallé (from the Opéra).
1763 Bordeaux. With a new prologue by Voltaire.
1977 London: Royal Opera.
   English Bach Festival production.

Platée, ou Junon jalouse

Comédie lyrique in three acts and a prologue.
Libretto: A.-J. Levallois d'Orville, from the play by Jacques Autreau.
1745/Mar. Versailles.
   Jélyotte (Platée), Chevalier (Junon), Fel (Folie), Chassé (Jupiter).
1749/Feb. Paris: Opéra.
   La Tour (Platée), Jacquet (Junon), Fel (Folie), Person (Jupiter).
1750 Paris: Opéra.
1754 Paris: Opéra.
   La Tour (Platée), Jacquet (Junon), Fel (Folie), Person (Jupiter).
1901 Munich (German version by Hans Schilling-Ziemssen).
1917 Monte Carlo.
1956 Aix-en-Provence: Festival (Théâtre de l'Archevêché).
   Michel Sénéchal (Platée).
   Hans Rosbaud (musical direction).
   Jean-Pierre Grenier (production).
   Orchestre de la Société des Concerts du Conservatoire.
1957 Lyon: Opéra.
1964 Versailles: Théâtre de la Montansier / Lyon: Opéra.
   Orchestre de la RTF.
1972 Lyon: Théâtre romain de Fourviere.
   Orchestre Philharmonique Rhône-Alpes.
1977 Paris: Opéra Comique.
   Orchestre de l'Opéra de Paris.

1981 Paris: Opéra (Garnier)
1983 Versailles: Opéra royal / London: Sadler's Wells.
  English Bach Festival production.
  Jean-Claude Malgoire (musical direction).
1989 Paris: Opéra Comique/Tour
  Ensemble du Centre national d'Art Lyrique de Marseille.
1997 London: Royal Opera at the Barbican
  Fouchécourt (Platée), Montague (Junon), Tibbels (Folie), Leroux (Jupiter), Padmore (Thespis).
  Nicholas McGegan (musical director).
  Mike Morris (production).
  Mike Morris Dance Group.
1999 Paris: Opéra (Garnier). Revived 2002, 2006, 2009, 2015.
  Fouchécourt/Agnew/Talbot (Platée), Gubisch/Lemprecht/Legay (Junon), Massis/Delunsch/Fuchs (Folie), Le Texier/Lis (Jupiter), Agnew/Beuron/Antoun (Thespis).
  Marc Minowski (musical director).
  Laurent Pelly (production).
  Musiciens du Louvre, Grenoble.
2010 Toulouse: Théâtre Jules-Julien.
  Orchestre à Bout de Souffle.
2010 Strasbourg: Opéra du Rhin.
  Christophe Rousset (musical direction).
  Mariame Clément (production).
  Les Talens Lyriques.
2012 Blagnac: Odyssud.
  Orchestre à Bout de Souffle.
2013 Versailles: Opéra royal.
  Agnew (Platée), Legay (Junon), Devieilhe (Folie/Amour), Arnould (Jupiter), Auvity (Thespis).
  Jean Claude Malgoire (musical direction).
  François Raffinot (production).
  Ensemble vocal de l'Atelier Lyrique de Tourcoing.
2014 Paris: Opéra Comique.
  Beekman (Platée), Renard (Junon), Kermes (Folie), Crossley-Mercer (Jupiter).
  William Christie (musical direction).
  Robert Carsen (production).
  Les Arts Florissants.
2024 Wormsley Estate, Buckinghamshire: Garsington Opera.

Boden (Platée), Kennedy (Junon), Asselin (Folie), Huskinson (Jupiter).
Paul Agnew (musical direction).
Louisa Muller (production).
The English Concert.

Les Fêtes de Polymnie
Ballet héroïque in three acts and a prologue.
Libretto: Louis de Cahusac.
Entrée 1: La Fable.
Entrée 2: L'Histoire.
Entrée 3: La Féerie.
1745/Oct. Paris: Opéra.
  Jélyotte (Alcide/Antiochus), Chassé (Seleucus/Zimès), Le Page (Jupiter), Fel (Hébé/Argelie), Chevalier (Stratonice/Mnémosine), Romainville (Oriade/Victoire), Bourbonnois (Polymnie), Coupée (Syrienne), La Tour (Chef des Arts).
1753/Aug. Paris: Opéra.
  Poirier (Alcide/Antiochus), Chassé (Seleucus/Zimès), Gélin (Jupiter), Fel (Hébé/Argelie), Chevalier (Stratonice), Jacquet (Mnémosine/Oriade), Chefdeville (Victoire), Dubois (Polymnie/Syrienne), La Tour (Chef des Arts).
1754/Apr. Paris: Opéra.
2014 Budapest: Orfeo Foundation (Palais des Arts de Budapest).
Concert performance.
  Vidal (Alcide/Antiochus/Chef des Arts), Dolié (Seleucus/Zimès/Jupiter), Gens (Stratonice/Oriade), Legay (Mnémosine/Hébé/Argelie), Stefanik (Victoire), Barath (Polymnie/Syrienne).
  György Vashegyi (musical direction).
  Orfeo Orchestra.
  Purcell Choir.

Le Temple de la gloire
Ballet héroïque in three acts and a prologue.
Libretto: Voltaire.
Entrée 1: Bélus.
Entrée 2: Bacchus.
Entrée 3: Trajan.

1745/Nov. Versailles.
  Jélyotte (Trajan/Apollo), Chassé (Bélus), Poirier (Bacchus), Fel (Erigone/Gloire), Chevalier (Lydie/Plaudine), Le Page (Envie/Grand prêtre).
1746/Apr. Paris: Opéra. New version.
2014 Versailles: Opéra royal. Concert performance (1746 version).
  Vidal (Trajan/Apollo/Bacchus), Buet (Bélus/Envie/Grand prêtre), Santon-Jeffery (Erigone/Gloire), Van Wanroij (Lydie/Plautine), Velletaz (Junie).
  Guy van Wass (musical direction).
  Les Agrémens.
  Chœur de Chambre de Namur.
2017 Berkeley, Ca.: Zellerbach Hall (1745 version).
  Co-production: Philharmonia Baroque Orchestra, Cal Performances and Centre de musique baroque de Versailles.
  Sheehan (Trajan/Apollo), Sargsyan (Bacchus), Martin (Bélus), Labonnette (Envie/Grand prêtre), Ortiz-Lafont (Erigone), Santon-Jeffery (Lydie/Gloire), Philiponet (Plautine/Arsine).
  Nicholas McGegan (musical direction).
  Catherine Turocy (production).
  Philharmonia Baroque Orchestra and Chorale.
  New York Baroque Dance Company.

Les Fêtes de Ramire

Acte de ballet (re-working, by Rousseau, of *La Princesse de Navarre*).
Libretto: Voltaire.
1745/Dec. Versailles.

Les Fêtes de l'Hymen et de l'Amour, ou Les Dieux d'Egypte

Ballet héroïque in three acts and a prologue.
Libretto: Louis de Cahusac.
Entrée 1: Osiris.
Entrée 2: Canope.
Entrée 3: Aruéris, ou Les Isies.
1747/Mar. Versailles.
  Jélyotte (Osiris), Fel (Orie), Chevalier (Orthésie), Metz (Memphis), Romainville (Hymen), Coupée (Amour).
1748/Nov. Paris: Opéra.
1753/Nov. Fontainebleau.

1754/Jul. Paris: Opéra.
1755 Paris: Opéra.
1762 Choisy-le-Roi: Théâtre royal.
1776 Paris: Opéra.
1772 Paris: Opéra.
2014 Versailles: Opéra royal. Concert performance.
  Van Mechelen (Osiris), Santon (Orie/Orthésie), Sampson (Memphis/Amour), Staskiewcz (Hymen), Borghi (Myrrine), Vidal (Agéris/Aruéris), Christoyannis (Canope), Buet (Grand prêtre).
  Hervé Niquet (musical direction).
  Chœur et orchestre du Concert Spirituel.
  Centre de musique baroque de Versailles.

Zaïs

Pastorale héroïque in four acts and a prologue.
Libretto: Louis de Cahusac.
1748/Feb. Paris: Opéra.
  Jélyotte (Zaïs), Fel (Zélide), Romainville (Amour), Albert (Oromasés), Le Page (Cindor), Poirier (Sylphe).
1761/May Paris: Opéra.
1769 Paris: Opéra.
2014 Beaune: Festival (Basilique Notre-Dame). Concert performance.
  Prégardien (Zaïs), Arnet (Zélide), Bennani (Amour), Wolff (Oromasés), Arnould (Cindor), Brahim-Djelloul (Sylphe).
  Christophe Rousset (musical direction).
  Les Talents Lyriques.
  Chœur de Chambre de Namur.
2014 London: Queen Elizabeth Hall.
  The Rameau Project, University of Oxford/OAE co-production.
  Budd (Zaïs), Alder (Zélide), Riches (Cindor).
  Jonathan Williams (musical direction).
  Choir of the Enlightenment.
  Orchestra of the Age of Enlightenment.

Pygmalion

Acte de ballet.
Libretto: Ballot de Sauvot after Antoine Houdar de la Motte.
1748/Aug. Paris: Opéra.
  Jélyotte (Pygmalion), Romainville (Céphise), Coupée (Amour),

Puvignée (Statue).
1751/Mar. Paris: Opéra.
1979 Versailles.
  Orchestre de l'Opéra du Nord.
1983 Paris: Théâtre de Paris.
  La Chapelle royale.
  Comediens-Danseurs du Théâtre du Nombre d'Or.
2004 Nancy: Opéra.
  Le Concert Spirituel.
2005 Paris: Théâtre du Châtelet.
  Le Concert Spirituel.
2010 Aix-en-Provence: Festival (Grand Théâtre de Provence).
  Ed (Pygmalion), De Negri (Statue), Blixt (Céphise), Karthäuser (Amour).
  William Christie (musical direction).
  Trisha Brown (production).
  Les Arts Florissants.

Les Surprises de l'amour
Opéra-ballet initially in two acts and a prologue (1748).
Libretto: Pierre-Joseph-Justin Bernard.
Entrée 1: Adonis (renamed L'Enlèvement d'Adonis in 1757).
Entrée 2: La Lyre enchantée.
Entrée 3: Anacréon (added in 1757).
1748/Oct. Versailles.
  Pompadour (Uranie).
1757/May Paris: Opéra. New version.
1758/Oct. Paris: Opéra.
  Chevalier (Uranie), Fel (Parthénope)
  Larrivée (Apollon), Lombard (Linus).
1769 Paris: Opéra.
1781 Brunoy: Petit Château.
1985 Versailles: Opéra royal. 1757 version.
  William Christie (musical direction).
  Les Arts Florissants.

Naïs, ou l'Opéra pour la paix
Pastorale héroïque in three acts and a prologue.
Libretto: Louis de Cahusac.

1749/Apr. Paris: Opéra.
1764/Aug. Paris: Opéra.
1980 Versailles: Opéra royal.
  English Bach Festival production.
  English Bach Festival Baroque Orchestra and Dancers.

Zoroastre

Tragédie lyrique in five acts.
Libretto: Louis de Cahusac.
1749/Dec. Paris: Opéra.
  Jélyotte (Zoroastre), Chassé (Abramane), Fel (Amélite), Chevalier (Érinice).
1752 Dresden.
1756 Paris: Opéra. New version.
  Poirier (Zoroastre), Chassé (Abramane), Fel (Amélite), Chevalier (Érinice).
1770 Paris: Opéra.
  Legros (Zoroastre), Gélin (Abramane), Lemière (Amélite), Dubois (Érinice).
1903 Paris: Schola Cantorum.
1979 London: Queen Elizabeth Hall (1756 version).
  English Bach Festival production, semi-staged.
  Andrew Parrott (musical director).
2006 Drottningholm, Sweden: Drottningholm Court Theatre (1756 version)
  Dahlin (Zoroastre), Alexiev (Abramane), Bundgaard (Amélite), Panzarella (Érinice).
  Christophe Rousset (musical direction).
  Pierre Audi (production).
  Drottningholm Court Theatre Orchestra/Les Talens Lyriques.
2016 Aix-en-Provence: Festival (Grand Théâtre de Provence). Concert performance (1756 version).
  Van Mechelen (Zoroastre), Courjal (Abramane), Watson (Amélite), De Negri (Érinice).
  Raphaël Pichon (musical direction).
  Ensemble Pygmalion.
2017 Berlin: Komische Oper (1756 version).
  Walker (Zoroastre), Dolié (Abramane), Watson (Amélite), Mchantaf (Érinice).
  Christian Curnyn (musical direction).

Tobias Kratzer (production).

Zéphyre, ou Les Nymphes de Diane
Acte de ballet.
Libretto: Unknown, possibly Louis de Cahusac.
Ca.1750-53. Abandoned.
1967 Aldeburgh: Festival (Jubilee Hall). Concert performance.
　Woodland (Zéphyre), Vyvyan (Cloris).
　George Malcolm (musical direction).
1976 Albi: Festival (Palais de la Berbie).
　Langridge (Zéphyre), Pena (Cloris), Garcisanz (Diane).
　Jean-Pierre Wallez (musical direction).
　Michel Odin (production).
　Ensemble instrumental de France.
　Ballet de l'Opéra de Paris.
　Maîtrise Gabriel Fauré.
　Chœur Élisabeth Brasseur.
2008 Vienna: Kammeroper.
　Gerber (Zéphyre), Shilova (Cloris), Higbee (Diane).
　Bernhard Klebel (musical direction).
　Giorgio Madia (production).

Linus
Tragédie lyrique in five acts. Music lost.
Libretto: Charles-Antoine Leclerc de la Bruère
1751 Paris. Rehearsed but not performed.

La Guirlande, ou Les Fleurs enchantées
Acte de ballet.
Libretto: Jean-François Marmontel.
1751/Sep. Paris: Opéra.
　Jélyotte (Mirtil), Fel (Zélide), Person (Hilas).
1763/Dec. Versailles.
1903 Paris: Schola Cantorum.
1983 Strasbourg: Opéra du Rhin.
　Orchestre du Théâtre de Drottningholm.

Acante et Céphise, ou La Sympathie
Pastorale héroïque in three acts.
Libretto: Jean-François Marmontel.
1751/Nov. Paris: Opéra.
   Jélyotte (Acante), Fel (Céphise), Chassé (Oroès), Chevalier (Zirphile), Poirier (Coryphée), Coupée (Fée), Romainville (Grande prêtresse).
2012 London: University College Opera (Bloomsbury Theatre).
   Charles Peebles (musical direction).
2021 Paris: Théâtre des Champs-Elysées. Concert performance without audience, streamed on the internet.
   Devieilhe (Céphise), Dubois (Acanthe), Witczak (Oroès), Van Wanroij (Zirphile), Amzal (La Grande Prêtresse).
   Alexis Kossenko (musical direction).
   Chantres du Centre de Musique Baroque de Versailles.
   Les Ambassadeurs.

Daphnis et Eglé
Acte de ballet.
Libretto: Charles Collé.
1753/Oct. Fontainebleau.
   Jélyotte (Daphnis), Fel (Eglé), Gélin (Grand prêtre), Riancourt (Amour).
2014 Caen: Théâtre de Caen. Performed with *La Naissance d'Osiris*.
   Van Mechelen (Daphnis), Fonnard (Eglée), Léger (Amour).
   William Christie (musical director).
   Sophie Daneman (production).
   Les Arts Florissants.

Lysis et Délie
Acte de ballet. Music lost.
Libretto: Jean-François Marmontel.
1753/Nov. Fontainebleau. Not performed.

Les Sybarites
Acte de ballet.
Libretto: Jean-François Marmontel.
1753/Nov. Fontainebleau.
   Chevalier (Hersilide), Chassé (Astole), Poirier (Agis).

La Naissance d'Osiris, ou La Fête Pamilie
Acte de ballet [Ballet allégorique].
Libretto: Louis de Cahusac.
1754/Oct. Fontainebleau.
  Fel (Pamilie), Chassé (Jupiter), Poirier (Berger), Gélin (Grand prêtre de Jupiter).
2014 Caen: Théâtre de Caen. Performed with *Daphnis et Eglé*.
  Léger (Pamilie).
  William Christie (musical director).
  Sophie Daneman (production).
  Les Arts Florissants.

Anacréon
Acte de ballet.
Libretto: Louis de Cahusac.
1754/Oct. Fontainebleau.
2012 Oxford: Sheldonian Theatre.
  The Rameau Project, University of Oxford/OAE co-production.
  Jonathan Williams (musical direction).
  Orchestra of the Age of Enlightenment.

Nélée et Myrthis
Acte de ballet.
Libretto: Unknown, possibly Louis de Cahusac.
Ca.1754. Abandoned.
  1974 Melbourne, Australia: Victoria State Opera.

Les Paladins
Comédie lyrique in three acts.
Libretto: Jean François Duplat de Monticourt.
1760/Feb. Paris: Opéra.
  Arnould (Argie), Lemière (Nérine), Lombard (Atis), Gélin (Anselme), Larrivée (Orcan), Pillot (Manto).
1967 Lyon: Théâtre romain de Fourvière.
2004 Paris: Théâtre du Châtelet.
  William Christie (musical direction).
  José Montalvo (production).
  Les Arts Florissants.

Compagnie Montalvo-Hervieu.

Les Boréades

Tragédie lyrique in five acts.
Libretto: Louis de Cahusac.
1763 Paris: Opéra. Rehearsed but not performed.
1964 Paris: Maison de la Radio. Concert performance.
  Michel Le Conte (musical direction).
1975 London: Queen Elizabeth Hall. Concert performance.
  Langridge (Abaris), Smith (Alphise), Rodde (Sémire), Beverly (Polymnie/Amour), Orliac (Calisis), Herincx (Borée), Duesing (Borilée), Hemsley (Adamas/Apollon).
  John Eliot Gardiner (musical direction).
1982 Aix-en-Provence: Festival (Théâtre de l'Archevêché).
  Langridge (Abaris), Smith (Alphise), Rodde (Sémire), Bourdy (Polymnie), Aler (Calisis), Lafont (Borée), Cachemaille (Borilée), Le Roux (Adamas), Varcoe (Apollon), Priday (Amour).
  John Eliot Gardiner (musical direction).
  Jean-Louis Martinoty (production).
  English Baroque Soloists/Monteverdi Choir.
1985 London: Royal Academy of Music.
  Dyer (Abaris), Hetherington (Alphise), Ventris (Calisis), Mayor (Borilée), Britton (Apollon).
  Roger Norrington (musical direction).
  Stephen Lawless (production).
1999 Salzburg: Festival.
  Workman (Abaris), Bonney (Alphise), Murphy (Sémire/Polymnie/Amour), Francis (Calisis), Wilson-Johnson (Borée), Bruan (Borilée), Scaltriti (Adamas/Apollon).
  Simon Rattle (musical direction).
  Ursel and Karl-Ernst Herrmann (production).
  Orchestra of the Age of Enlightenment/European Voices.
2003 Paris: Opéra.
  Agnew (Abaris), Bonney (Alphise), Panzarella (Sémire), Azzaretti (Polymnie), Spence (Calisis), Naouri (Borée), Degout (Borilée), Rivenq (Adamas/Apollon), Joulia-Demoury (Amour).
  William Christie (musical direction).
  Robert Carsen (production).
  Les Arts Florissants/La La La Human Steps.
2005 Strasbourg: Opéra du Rhin.

Agnew (Abaris), Sollied (Alphise), Gillot (Sémire), Laporte (Calisis), Foster Williams (Borée), Cavallier (Borilée), Dolié (Adamas/Apollon), Bendi Merad (Amour).
Emmanuelle Haïm (musical direction).
Laurent Laffargue (production).
Le Concert d'Astrée.

2014 Aix-en-Provence: Festival (Grand Théâtre de Provence). Concert performance.
Boden (Abaris), Fuchs (Alphise), Briot (Sémire/Amour/Polymnie), Nuñez-Camelino (Calisis), Pass (Borée), Saint-Martin (Borilée).
Marc Minowski (musical direction).
Ensemble Aedes.
Musiciens du Louvre, Grenoble.

2019 Dijon: Opéra de Dijon
Vidal (Abaris), Guilmette (Alphise), De Negri (Sémire/Polymnie), Droy (Calisis), Purves (Borée), Dubruque (Borilée).
Emmanuelle Haïm (musical direction).
Barrie Kosky (production).
Le Concert d'Astrée.

Appendix V

Rameau and His Contemporaries

Works Premiered at the Opéra During Rameau's Career

Includes works initially seen at court. Does not include revivals of works already performed at the Opéra. Includes the Italian operas performed by Bambini's company during the Querelle des Bouffons.

Rameau (Pellegrin): *Hippolyte et Aricie*
Tragédie lyrique. 1 October 1733.

Duplessis (Massip): *Les Fêtes nouvelles*
Opéra-ballet. 22 July 1734.

Campra (Danchet): *Achille et Déidamie*
Tragédie lyrique. 24 February 1735.

Mouret (Roy): *Les Graces*
Ballet héroïque. 5 May 1735.

Rameau (Fuzelier): *Les Indes galantes*
Ballet héroïque. 23 August 1735.

Rebel/Francœur (La Motte/La Serre): *Scanderberg*
Tragédie lyrique. 27 October 1735.

Rameau (Fuzelier): *Les Sauvages*
New entrée added to *Les Indes galantes*. 11 March 1736.

Boismortier (Leclerc de La Bruère): *Les Voyages de l'Amour*
Opéra-ballet. 3 May 1736.

Niel (Bonneval): *Les Romans*
Ballet héroïque. 23 August 1736.

Duval (Fleury): *Les Genies*
Opéra-ballet. 18 October 1736.

Grenet (Le Franc de Pomignan): *Le Triomphe de l'harmonie*
Ballet héroïque. 9 May 1737.

Rameau (Bernard): *Castor et Pollux*
Tragédie lyrique. 24 October 1737.

Blamont (Ferrand/Tannevot/Pellegrin): *Les Caracteres de l'amour*
Ballet héroïque. 15 April 1738.

Rebel/Francœur (Roy): *Le Ballet de la paix*
Opéra-ballet. 29 May 1738.

Rameau (Gautier de Mondorge): *Les Fêtes d'Hébé*
Ballet héroïque. 21 May 1739.

Royer (La Marre): *Zaïde, reine de Grenade*
Ballet héroïque. 3 September 1739.

Rameau (Leclerc de La Bruère): *Dardanus*
Tragédie lyrique. 19 November 1739.

Mion (La Serre): *Nitétis*
Tragédie lyrique. 14 April 1741.

Mouret (Bellis/Roy): *Le Temple de Gnide*
Pastorale in one act. 14 October 1741.

Mouret (Néricault Destouches): *Les Amours de Ragonde*
Comédie lyrique. 31 January 1742.

Mondonville (La Rivière): *Isbé*
Pastorale héroïque. 10 April 1742.

Boismortier (Favart): *Don Quichotte chez la duchesse*
Ballet comique. 12 February 1743.

Royer (Lefebvre de Saint-Marc): *Le Pouvoir de l'amour*
Ballet héroïque. 23 April 1743.

De Bury (Duclos): *Les Caractères de la Folie*
Opéra-ballet. 20 August 1743.

Niel (Fuzelier): *L'École des amants*
Opéra-ballet. 11 June 1744.

Rebel/Francœur (Roy): *Les Augustales*
Divertissement. 14 November 1744.

Rebel/Francœur (Moncrif): *Zelindor, roi des Sylphes*
Opéra-ballet. 10 August 1745.

Rameau (Cahusac): *Les Fêtes de Polymnie*
Ballet héroïque. 12 October 1745.

Rameau (Voltaire): *Le Temple de la gloire*
Ballet héroïque. 7 December 1745.

Leclair (D'Albaret): *Scylla et Glaucus*
Tragédie lyrique. 4 October 1746.

Mion (Roy): *L'Année galante*
Opéra-ballet. 11 April 1747.

Boismortier (Laujon): *Daphnis et Chloé*
Pastorale. 28 September 1747.

Rameau (Cahusac): *Zaïs*
Ballet héroïque. 29 February 1748.

Rameau (Ballot de Sovot): *Pygmalion*
Acte de ballet. 27 August 1748.

Rameau (Cahusac): *Les Fêtes d'l'Hymen et de l'Amour*
Ballet héroïque. 25 November 1748.

Rameau (Autreau): *Platée*
Comédie lyrique. 4 February 1749.

Rameau (Cahusac): *Naïs*
Pastorale héroïque. 22 April 1749.

Mondonville (Fuzelier): *Le Carnaval du Parnasse*
Ballet héroïque. 23 September 1749.

Rameau (Cahusac): *Zoroastre*
Tragédie lyrique. 5 December 1749.

Brassac (Le Franc de Pompignan): *Léandre et Héro*
Tragédie lyrique. 5 May 1750.

Royer (Moncrif): *Almasis*
Acte de ballet. 28 August 1750.

Rebel/Francœur (Moncrif): *Ismène*
Pastorale héroïque. 28 August 1750.

De Bury (Roy): *Titon et l'Aurore*
Acte de ballet. 18 February 1751.

Lagarde (Laujon): *Aeglé*
Ballet héroïque. 18 February 1751.

Rameau (Marmontel): *La Guirlande*
Acte de ballet. 21 September 1751.

Rameau (Marmontel): *Acante et Céphise*
Pastorale héroïque. 18 November 1751.

*Pergolesi: *La serva padrona*
Intermezzo in two parts. 1 August 1752.
Beginning of the Querelle des Bouffons: works performed by Bambini's company during this phase, August 1752 to February 1754, marked *

*Orlandini: *Il giocatore*
Intermezzo in three parts. 22 August 1752.

*Pergolesi: *Il maestro de musica*
Intermezzo in two parts. 19 September 1752.

Dauvergne (Cahusac): *Les Amours de Tempé*
Ballet héroïque. 7 November 1752.
An Italian intermezzo was performed at the end of the evening.

*Latilla: *La finta cameriera*
Intermezzo. 30 November 1752.

*Di Capua: *La donna superba*
Intermezzo in two parts. 19 December 1752.

Mondonville (La Marre): *Titon et l'Aurore*
Pastorale héroïque. 9 January 1753.

*Cocchi: *La scaltra governatrice*
Opéra burlesque in three acts. 25 January 1753.

*Blavet: *Le Jaloux corrigé*
Opéra bouffon in one act. 1 March 1753.
Music lifted from the above works by Pergolesi.

Rousseau: *Le Devin du village*
Intermède in one act. 1 March 1753.

*Pergolesi: *Tracollo, medico ignorante*
Intermezzo in two parts. 1 May 1753.

*Sellitti: *Il cinese rimpatriato*
Divertimento. 19 June 1753.

*Di Capua: *La zingara*
Intermezzo in two parts. 19 June 1753.

*Latilla: *Gli artigiani arrichiti*
Intermezzo in two parts. 25 September 1753.

*Jomelli: *Il paratajo*
Intermezzo in two parts. 25 September 1753.

*Ciampi: *Bertoldo in corte*
Intermezzo in two parts. 9 November 1753.
Libretto by Goldoni.

*Léo: *I viaggiatori*
Intermezzo in three parts. 12 February 1754.
End of the residence of Bambini's company at the Paris Opéra.

Mondonville: *Daphnis et Alcimadure*
Pastorale languedocienne. 29 December 1754.

Giraud/Montan Berton (Saint-Foix): *Deucalion et Pyrrha*
Acte de ballet. 30 September 1755.

Herbain (Chennevières): *Célime*
Acte de ballet. 28 September 1756.

Rameau (Bernard): *Les Surprises de l'amour*
Opéra-ballet. 31 May 1757.

Dauvergne (Fontenelle): *Énée et Lavinie*
Tragédie lyrique. 14 February 1758.

Mondonville (Collé/Leclerc de La Bruère): *Les Fêtes de Paphos*
Ballet héroïque. 9 May 1758.

Dauvergne (Moncrif and others): *Les Fêtes d'Euterpe*
Opéra-ballet. 8 August 1758.

Iso (Fuzelier): *Phaëtuse*
Acte de ballet. 20 July 1759.

Rameau (Duplat de Monticourt): *Les Paladins*
Comédie lyrique. 12 February 1760.

Rebel/Francœur (Leclerc de La Bruère): *Le Prince de Noisy*
Ballet héroïque. 16 September 1760.

Dauvergne (La Motte): *Canente*
Tragédie lyrique. 11 November 1760.

Dauvergne (Marmontel): *Hercule Mourant*
Tragédie lyrique. 3 April 1761.

De Bury (Duclos): *Hylas et Zélis*
Fragment. 6 July 1762.

Giraud (Gautier de Mondorge): *L'Opéra de société*
Acte de ballet. 1 October 1762.

Dauvergne (Joliveau): *Polyxène*
Tragédie lyrique. 11 January 1763.

Works Cited

Adolphe Adam, *Derniers souvenirs d'un musicien* (Paris: Lévy frères, 1859)
Jean le Rond d'Alembert, 'De la liberté de la musique', in *Melanges de litterature, d'histoire, et de philosophie*, t.4 (Amsterdam, 1759)
Jean le Rond d'Alembert, *Eléments de musique, théorique et pratique, suivant les principes de M. Rameau* (Paris, 1752)
Jean le Rond d'Alembert, *Eléments de musique, théorique et pratique, suivant les principes de M. Rameau.* Nouvelle ed. (Lyon: Bruyset, 1762)
Jean le Rond d'Alembert, 'Extrait des registres de l'Académie Royale des Sciences, du 10 décembre 1749', in Rameau, *Démonstration du principe de l'harmonie* (Paris: Durand, 1750)
Jean le Rond d'Alembert, 'Lettre à M. Rameau', in *Mercure de France* (April 1761)
Jean le Rond d'Alembert, 'Reponse à une lettre imprimée de M. Rameau', in *Mercure de France* (March 1762)
Nicholas Anderson, 'Rameau's *Platée*: Burlesque or Grotesque?', in *Early Music*, vol.11, n.4 (October 1983)
James R. Anthony, *French Baroque Music from Beaujoyeulx to Rameau* (Portland: Amadeus Press, 1997)
Pierre Louis d'Aquin de Château-Lyon, *Siècle littéraire de Louis XV, ou Lettres sur les homes célèbres* (Amsterdam: Duchesne, 1754)
Jaques Autreau, *Chef-d'œuvres dramatiques de d'Autreau* (Paris: Bureau général des Chef-d'œuvres dramatiques, 1791)
Louis Petit de Bachaumont, *Mémoires secrets de Bachaumont, de 1762 à 1787* (Paris: Brissot-Thivars, 1830)
Pierre-Yves Beaurepaire, 'Sociability', in *The Oxford Handbook of the Ancien Régime* (Oxford: Oxford University Press, 2011)
Philippe Beaussant (ed.), *Rameau de A à Z* (Paris: Fayard/IMDA, 1999)
Hector Berlioz, 'Castor et Pollux: la partition', in *Revue et gazette musicale de Paris*, n.46 (1842)
Hector Berlioz, 'De Rameau et de quelques uns de ses ouvrages', in *Revue et gazette musicale de Paris*, n.32 (1842)

Jonathan W. Bernard, 'The Principle and the Elements: Rameau's Controversy With d'Alembert', in *Journal of Music Theory*, vol.24/1 (1980)

Philipp Blom, *Encyclopédie: the Triumph of Reason in an Unreasonable Age* (London: Fourth Estate, 2004)

Sylvie Bouissou, 'Les Boréades de J.-Ph. Rameau: un passé retrouvé', in *Revue de Musicologie*, t.69, n.2 (1983)

Sylvie Bouissou, *Jean-Philippe Rameau: Musicien des Lumières* (Paris: Fayard, 2014)

Nicolas Bricaire de la Dixmerie, *Les Deux ages du goût et du génie français sous Louis XIV et sous Louis XV* (La Haye: Lacombe, 1769)

Charles Burney, *A General History of Music from the Earliest Ages to the Present Period*, vol.4 (London: The Author, 1789)

Louis de Cahusac, *Anacréon* (Paris: Ballard, 1754)

Louis de Cahusac, *La Danse ancienne et moderne, ou Traité historique de la danse* (The Hague: Neaulme, 1754)

Louis de Cahusac, *Les Fêtes de l'Hymen et de l'Amour* (Paris: Ballard, 1747)

Louis de Cahusac, *Les Fêtes de Polymnie* (Paris: Ballard, 1745)

Louis de Cahusac, 'Lettre à M. Remond de Sainte Albine', 18 November 1749, in *Mercure de France* (December, 1749)

Louis de Cahusac, *Naïs* (Paris: Delormel et fils, 1749)

Louis de Cahusac, *La Naissance d'Osiris* (Paris: Ballard, 1754)

Louis de Cahusac, *Zaïs* (Paris: Delormel et fils, 1748)

Louis de Cahusac, *Zoroastre* (Paris: Aux depéns de l'Académie royale de musique, 1749)

Louis de Cahusac, *Zoroastre: opéra représenté pour la première fois par l'Académie royale de musique le 5 décembre 1749 et remis au théâtre le mardi 20 janvier 1756* (Paris, 1756)

Giacomo Casanova, *Histoire de ma vie*. Livre 3. Paris, Bibliothèque Nationale de France, ms. NAF 28604 (3)

Louis-Bertrand Castel, 'Suite et seconde partie des nouvelles expériences sur l'optique', in *Journal de Trévoux* (August 1735)

Louis-Bertrand Castel, 'Remarques du P. Castel sur la lettre de M. Rameau', in *Journal de Trévoux* (September 1736)

Jacques Cazotte, *Observations sur la lettre de Jean-Jacques Rousseau au sujet de la musique française* (1753)

Centre de musique baroque de Versailles, *Rameau 2014* (2014-), online at http://www.rameau2014.fr (last accessed 10/1/15)

Michel Paul Guy de Chabanon, *Éloge de M. Rameau* (Paris: M. Lambert,

1764)

David Charlton, *Opera in the Age of Rousseau: Music, Confrontation, Realism* (Cambridge: Cambridge University Press, 2015)

David Charlton and Sarah Hibberd, 'My Father Was a Poor Parisian Musician: a Memoir (1756) concerning Rameau, Handel's Library and Sallé', in the *Journal of the Royal Musical Association*, vol.128, n.2 (2003)

Nick Childs, 'Jacques Autreau', in *The Burlington Magazine*, vol.109, n.771 (June 1967)

Nick Childs, *A Political Academy in Paris, 1724-1731* (Oxford: Voltaire Foundation, 2000)

Thomas Christensen, *Rameau and Musical Thought in the Enlightenment* (Cambridge: Cambridge University Press, 1993)

William Christie, 'A Faithful Travelling Companion' [Liner notes], in *Hippolyte et Aricie* [CD] (Erato, 1997)

Pierre Clément, *Les Cinq années littéraires, ou Nouvelles, des années 1748, 1749, 1750, 1751 et 1752*, t.2 (La Haye: Ant. De Groot, 1754)

Richard Cobb, *Paris and its Provinces, 1792-1802* (London: Oxford University Press, 1975)

Christine Coquillat-Horvallis, *Rameau: Le Site* (2003-), online at http://jp.rameau.free.fr (last accessed 10/1/15)

Charles Collé, *Journal et mémoires de Charles Collé sur les hommes de letters, les ouvrages dramatiques et les événements les plus mémorables du règne de Louis XV (1748-1722)*, ed. H. Bonhomme, nouvelle éd. (Paris: Librairie de Firmin Didot, 1868)

Georgia Cowart, 'Of women, sex and folly: Opera under the Old Regime', in *Cambridge Opera Journal*, vol.6, iss.3 (1994)

Georges Cucuel, *La Pouplinière et la musique de chambre au XVIIIe siècle* (Paris: Fischbacher, 1913)

Robert Darnton, *The Devil in the Holy Water* (Philadelphia: University of Pennsylvania Press, 2010)

Robert Darnton, *A Literary Tour de France* (Sep 1, 2014), online at http://www.robertdarnton.org

Robert Darnton, *Poetry and the Police: Communication Networks in 18th Century Paris* (Cambridge, Mass.: Harvard University Press, 2010)

Ian Davidson, *Voltaire: a Life* (London: Profile Books, 2010)

Claude Debussy, 'Le bilan musical en 1903', in *Gil Blas* (28 June 1903)

Claude Debussy, 'Musique', in *Gil Blas* (2 February 1903)

Jacques Joseph Marie Decroix, *L'Ami des arts, ou Justification de plusieurs grands hommes* (Amsterdam, 1776)

Pierre Desfontaines (ed.), *Observations sur les écrits modernes* (Paris: Chez Chaubert, 1735)

Denis Diderot and Jean Le Rond d'Alembert (eds.), *Encyclopédie, ou Dictionnaire raisonné des sciences, des arts et des métiers*, 17 t. (Paris: Chez Briasson [and others], 1751-1765)

Denis Diderot, *Au petit prophète de Boehmischbroda au grand prophète Monet* (Paris, 1753)

Denis Diderot, *Les Bijoux indiscrets* (Paris: Garnier, 1965)

Denis Diderot, *Correspondance générale* (Paris: Garnier, 1875)

Denis Diderot, *Écrits sur la musique*, ed. Béatrice Durand-Sendrail (Paris: Lattès, 1987)

Denis Diderot, *Lettre sur les aveugles à l'usage de ceux qui voient* (Paris: Gallimard, 2004)

Denis Diderot, *Mémoires sur différents sujets de mathématiques* (Paris, 1748)

Denis Diderot, *Le Neveu de Rameau* (Paris: Gallimard, 1972)

Denis Diderot, *Œuvres complètes de Diderot: revues sur les éditions originales*, t.7 (Paris: Garnier, 1875)

Denis Diderot (trans. Leonard Tancock), *Rameau's Nephew* (London: Penguin, 1966)

Pierre Dubois, 'From Rameau to Avison: Discord or Concord?', in Frédéric Ogée (ed.), *Better in France?: the Circulation of Ideas Across the Channel in the Eighteenth Century* (Cranbury, NJ: Associated University Presses, 2005)

Simon Henri Dubuisson, *Mémoires secrets du XVIIIe siècle: lettres du commissaire Dubuisson au Marquis de Caumont, 1735-1743* (Paris: Arnould, 1882)

Béatrice Durant-Sendrail, 'Diderot et Rameau: archéologie d'une polémique', in *Diderot Studies*, vol.24 (1991)

Élie Fréron, *L'Année littéraire: annee 1754*, t.2 (Amsterdam, 1754)

Louis Fuzelier, *Les Indes galantes, ballet heroique représenté par l'Academie royale de Musique; pour la premiere fois, le mardy 23. aoust 1735* (Paris: Ballard, 1736)

John Eliot Gardiner, 'Les Boréades' [Liner notes], in *Les Boréades* [CD] (Erato, 1990)

David Garrick (ed. Ryllis Clair Alexander), *The Diary of David Garrick, Being a Record of His Memorable Trip to Paris in 1751* (New York: Oxford University Press, 1928)

Jean-Baptiste-André Gautier-Dagoty, *Galerie Françoise, ou Portraits des hommes et des femmes célèbres qui ont paru en France* (Paris: Hérissant le

fils, 1770)
Gazettes à la main, F-Pbhvp, ms. 617
Cuthbert Girdlestone, *Jean-Philippe Rameau: His Life and Work* (New York: Dover, 1969)
Carlo Goldoni (trans. John Black), *Memoirs of Goldoni, Written by Himself*, vol.2 (London: Hunt and Clarke, 1828)
Mme de Graffigny, *Correspondance de Madame de Graffigny*, ed. J.A. Dainard et al. (Oxford: Voltaire Foundation, 1985-)
Friedrich Melchior Grimm, *Lettre de M. Grimm sur Omphale, tragédie lyrique, reprise par l'Académie royale de musique le 14 janvier 1752* (Paris, 1752)
Friedrich Melchior Grimm, *Le petit prophète de Boehmischbroda* ([Paris], 1753)
Friedrich Melchior Grimm, *Correspondance littéraire, philosophique et critique de Grimm et de Diderot depuis 1753 jusqu'en 1790*, Nouvelle éd., 16 vol. (Paris: Furne, 1829)
Grimm, Diderot, Raynal, Meister (ed.), *Correspondance littéraire, philosophique et critique* (Paris: Garnier, 1877-1882)
Eric Hazan (trans. David Fernbach), *The Invention of Paris: a History in Footsteps* (London: Verso, 2010)
Journal de Trévoux (1722-1765)
Jean-Benjamin de La Borde, *Essai sur la musique ancienne et moderne*, t.3 (Paris: P.D. Pierres, 1780)
Théodore Lajarte (ed.), *Bibliothèque musicale du Théâtre de l'Opéra: catalogue historique, chronologique, anecdotique*, t.1 (Paris: Librairie des Bibliophiles, 1878)
Joseph de La Porte, *Les Spectacles de Paris, ou Suite du calendrier historique et chronologique des théatres*, pt.12 (Paris: Duchesne, 1754-94)
Pierre Laujon, *Œuvres choisies de P. Laujon*, t.4 (Paris: L. Collin, 1811)
L. de La Laurencie, 'Quelques documents sur Jean-Philippe Rameau et sa famille', in *Mercure musical et S.I.M.* (June 1907)
Antoine de Léris, *Dictionnaire portatif historique et littéraire des théatres*. 2nd ed. (Paris: Jombert, 1763)
Charles Philippe d'Albert Luynes, *Mémoires du duc de Luynes sur la cour de Louis XV (1735-1758)* (Paris: Firmin Didot Frères, 1860-1865)
Colin Jones, *The Great Nation: France from Louis XV to Napoleon* (London: Penguin Books, 2003)
Colin Jones, *Paris: Biography of a City* (London: Allen Lane, 2004)
Antoine Louis Le Brun, 'La théâtre lyrique', in *Le Journal des sçavans, pour l'année 1712* (Paris, 1712)

Albert G. Mackey and William R. Singleton, *History of Freemasonry*, pt.4 (The Masonic History Co., 1898)

Albert G. Mackey and H.L. Haywood, *Encyclopaedia of Freemasonry*, pt.3 (The Masonic History Co., 1909)

André Magnan, *Rameau le neveu: texts et documents* (Paris: CNRS, 1993)

Hugues Maret, *Éloge historique de Mr. Rameau* (Dijon: Causse, 1766)

Jean-François Marmontel, *Mémoires de Marmontel*, t.1 (Paris: Librairie des Bibliophiles, 1891)

Jean-François Marmontel, *Memoirs of Marmontel, Written by Himself*, vol.1 (London: Whittaker, Treacher and Arnot, 1830)

Paul-Marie Masson, *L'Opéra de Rameau* (Paris: Laurens, 1930)

Mercure de France (1724-1790)

Leta E. Miller, 'Rameau and the Royal Society of London: New Letters and Documents', in *Music and Letters*, vol.66, n.1 (1985)

[Antoine Gautier de Montdorge], 'Extrait d'une lettre, écrite à M. Rameau', in *Les Fêtes d'Hébé, ou Les Talents lyriques* (Paris: Ballard, 1739).

Montesquieu, *De l'esprit des lois* (Paris: Gallimard, 1995)

Montesquieu, *Persian Letters* (Oxford: Oxford University Press, 2008)

Joachim Christoph Nemeitz, *Le Séjour de Paris* (Leyden: J. van Abcoude, 1727)

Jean-Georges Noverre, *Lettres sur la danse, et sur les ballets* (Lyon: chez Aimé Delaroche, 1760)

Edward Nye, *Mime, Music and Drama on the Eighteenth-Century Stage: the Ballet d'Action* (Cambridge: Cambridge University Press, 2011)

Jean-Jacques Pauvert (ed.), *Théâtre érotique français au XVIIIe siècle* (Paris: Terrain Vague, 1993)

Simon-Joseph Pellegrin, *Hippolyte et Aricie* (Paris: Ballard, 1733)

Alexis Piron, *Œuvres complètes d'Alexis Piron*, ed. Rigoley de Juvigny, t.2-3 (Paris: Lambert, 1776)

Nicolas Poisson, *Traité de la mechanique, composé par Monsieur Descartes. De plus l'Abrégé de musique du mesme autheur mis en françois* (Paris, 1688)

J.-G. Prod'homme (trans. Theodore Baker), 'A French Maecenas of the Time of Louis XV: M. de La Pouplinière', in *The Musical Quarterly*, vol.10, n.4 (1924)

Gunnar von Proschwitz (ed.), *Alexis Piron, épistolier: choix de ses lettres* (Göteborg: Université de Göteborg, 1982)

Jean-François Rameau, *La Raméide* (Petersbourg: Aux Rameaux couronnés, 1766)

Jean-Philippe Rameau, *Code de musique pratique, ou Méthodes pour apprendre la musique… avec de nouvelles réflexions sur le principe sonore* (Paris: Imprimerie royale, 1760)

Jean-Philippe Rameau, 'Conclusions sur l'origine des sciences', in *Journal encyclopédique* (July 1762)

Jean-Philippe Rameau, 'De la mécanique des doigts sur le clavecin', in *Pieces de clavecin* (Paris: Hochereau, Boivin, l'Auteur, 1724)

Jean-Philippe Rameau, *Démonstration du principe de l'harmonie* (Paris: Durand, Pissot, 1750)

Jean-Philippe Rameau, *Dissertation sur les différentes méthodes d'accompagnement pour le clavecin ou pour l'orgue* (Paris: Boivin, Le Clair, 1732)

Jean-Philippe Rameau, *Erreurs sur la musique dans l'Encyclopédie* (Paris: Jorry, 1755)

Jean-Philippe Rameau, 'Examen de la conférence sur la musique', in *Mercure de France* (October 1729)

Jean-Philippe Rameau, *Extrait d'une réponse de M. Rameau à M. Euler sur l'identité des octaves* (Paris: Durand, 1753)

Jean-Philippe Rameau, *Les Fêtes d'Hébé, ou Les Talents lyriques* (Paris: l'Auteur, [1745])

Jean-Philippe Rameau, *Génération harmonique, ou Traité de musique théorique et pratique* (Paris: Prault, 1737)

Jean-Philippe Rameau, *Les Indes galantes, ballet réduit à quatre grands concerts avec une nouvelle entrée complette* (Paris: Boivin, Leclair, l'Auteur, 1735)

Jean-Philippe Rameau (ed. Erwin R. Jacobi), *Jean-Philippe Rameau: Complete Theoretical Writings* (American Institute of Musicology, 1967-1972)

Jean-Philippe Rameau, *Lettre à M. d'Alembert sur ses opinions en musique* ([Paris], 1760)

Jean-Philippe Rameau, 'Lettre de M. à M. sur la musique', in *Mercure de France* (September 1731)

Jean-Philippe Rameau, 'Lettre de M*** à M. D**** sur un ouvrage intitulé l'Origine des sciences', in *Mercure de France* (April 1762)

Jean-Philippe Rameau, 'Lettre de M. Rameau à l'auteur du Mercure', in *Mercure de France* (May 1752)

Jean-Philippe Rameau, 'Lettre de Monsieur Rameau aux Philosophes', in *Journal de Trevoux* (August 1762)

Jean-Philippe Rameau, 'Lettre de M. Rameau au R. P. Castel', in *Journal de Trévoux* (July 1736)

Jean-Philippe Rameau, *Mémoire où l'on expose les fondements du système de musique théorique et pratique de M. Rameau* (ms., 1749)

Jean-Philippe Rameau, *Nouveau système de musique théorique* (Paris: Ballard, 1726)

Jean-Philippe Rameau, *Nouvelles réflexions de M. Rameau sur sa Démonstration du principe de l'harmonie* (Paris: Durand, Pissot, 1752)

Jean-Philippe Rameau, 'Observations de M. Rameau sur son ouvrage intitulé Origine des sciences', in *Mercure de France* (June 1762)

Jean-Philippe Rameau, 'Observations sur la méthode d'accompagnement pour le clavecin qui est en usage', in *Mercure de France* (February 1730)

Jean-Philippe Rameau, *Observations sur notre instinct pour la musique et sur son principe* (Paris: Prault fils, 1754)

Jean-Philippe Rameau, 'Origine des modes et du temperament', in *Mercure de France* (June 1761)

Jean-Philippe Rameau, *Origine des sciences suivie d'une controverse sur le même sujet* (Paris: Jorry, 1762)

Jean-Philippe Rameau, *Pièces de clavecin en concerts, avec un violon ou une flute, et une viole ou un deuxième violin* (Paris: Boivin; Le Clair, 1741)

Jean-Philippe Rameau, 'Plan abrégé d'une méthode nouvelle d'accompagnement pour le clavecin', in *Mercure de France* (March 1730)

Jean-Philippe Rameau, *Prospectus où l'on propose au public par voie de souscription un Code de musique pratique composé de sept methods* ([Paris], 1757)

Jean-Philippe Rameau, 'Réflexions de M. Rameau sur la manière de former la voix', in *Mercure de France* (October 1752)

Jean-Philippe Rameau, 'Remarques de M. Rameau sur l'extrait qu'on a donné de son livre intitulé Génération harmonique', in *Le Pour et Contre* (1738)

Jean-Philippe Rameau, 'Remarques sur les pièces de ce livre et sur les différents genres de musique', in *Nouvelles suites de pièces de clavecin* (Paris: l'Auteur, Boivin, Leclerc, [1729])

Jean-Philippe Rameau, 'Réplique du premier musicien à la réponse du second', in *Mercure de France* (June 1730)

Jean-Philippe Rameau, 'Réponse de M. Rameau à la lettre de M. d'Alembert', in *Mercure de France* (April 1761)

Jean-Philippe Rameau, *Réponse de M. Rameau à MM. les éditeurs de l'Encyclopédie sur leur dernier avertissement* (London: Jorry, 1757)

Jean-Philippe Rameau, 'Seconde lettre de M*** à M***', in *Mercure de France* (April 1762)

Jean-Philippe Rameau, 'Source où vraisemblablement on a dû puiser la première idée des proportions', in *Mercure de France* (April 1761)

Jean-Philippe Rameau, 'Suite de la réponse de M. Rameau à la lettre que M. d'Alembert lui a adressée', in *Mercure de France* (July 1761)

Jean-Philippe Rameau, *Suite des Erreurs sur la musique dans l'Encyclopédie* (Paris: Jorry, 1756)

Jean-Philippe Rameau, *Traité de l'Harmonie réduite à ses principes naturels* (Paris: Ballard, 1722)

Jean-Philippe Rameau (trans. Philip Gossett), *Treatise on Harmony* (New York: Dover, 1971)

Jean-Philippe Rameau, *Vérités également ignorées et intéressantes tirées du sein de la nature* (ms., 1763/64)

Emmanuel Rebold, *Histoire des trois grandes loges de francs-maçons en France* (Paris: Collignon, 1864)

Toussaint Rémond de Saint-Mard, *Réflexions sur l'opéra* (La Haye: J. Neaulme, 1741)

Nicolas Rétif de la Bretonne, *Les Nuits de Paris* (Paris: Gallimard, 1986)

Paul F. Rice, 'The Fontainebleau Operas of Jean-Philippe Rameau', in *The Journal of Musicology*, vol.6, n.2 (Spring 1988)

Daniel Roche, *The People of Paris: an Essay in Popular Culture in the 18th Century* (Berkeley: University of California Press, 1987)

Jean-Jacques Rousseau, *Les Confessions* (Paris: Gallimard, 1995)

Jean-Jacques Rousseau, *Correspondance complète de Jean Jacques Rousseau: 1758*, ed. R.A. Leigh (Geneva: Institut et Musée Voltaire, 1969)

Jean-Jacques Rousseau, *Dictionnaire de musique* (Paris: Duchesne, 1768)

Jean-Jacques Rousseau, *Lettre sur la musique française* ([Paris], 1753)

Christophe Rousset, *Jean-Philippe Rameau* (Arles: Actes Sud, 2007)

Graham Sadler, 'A Letter from Claude-François Rameau to J.J.M. Decroix', in *Music and Letters*, vol.59, n.2 (April 1978)

Graham Sadler, Shirley Thompson and Jonathan Williams (eds.), *The Operas of Rameau: Genesis, Staging, Reception* (London: Routledge, 2022)

Graham Sadler, 'Patrons and Pasquinades: Rameau in the 1730s', in *Journal of the Royal Musical Association*, vol.113, n.2 (1988)

Graham Sadler, 'Rameau', in *The New Grove French Baroque Masters* (London: Macmillan, 1986)

Graham Sadler, *The Rameau Compendium* (Woodbridge: Boydell Press, 2014)

Toussaint Rémond de Saint-Mard, *Réflexions sur l'opéra* (La Haye: J. Neaulme, 1741)

Lionel Sawkins, 'Rameau's Last Years: Some Implications of Re-Discovered Material at Bordeaux', in *Proceedings of the Royal Musical Association*, vol.111 (1984/85)

Joseph Sauveur, *Principes d'acoustique et de musique, ou Système général des intervalles des sons…* (Geneva: Minkoff, 1973)

Simon Schama, *Citizens: a Chronicle of the French Revolution* (London: Penguin Books, 1989)

Eyre Massey Shaw, *Fires in Theatres* (London: Spon, 1876)

Emmanuel Soleville, 'Louis de Cahusac, poète dramatique', in Émerand Forestié, *Biographie de Tarn-et-Garonne: études historiques et bibliographiques* (Montauban, 1860)

[Jules Taschereau (ed.)], *Revue rétrospective, ou Bibliothèque historique, contenant des mémoires et documens authentiques, inédits et originaux…* , t.5 (Paris, 1834)

Paul Tillit, 'Zoroastre (1749) de Rameau: droit et utopies dans un opéra franc-maçon du siècle des Lumières', in *Droit et cultures*, n.52 (2006)

Léon Vallas, *La Musique à l'Académie de Lyon au dix-huitième siècle* (Lyon: Editions de la Revue Musicale de Lyon, 1908)

Voltaire (trans. John Butt), *Candide or Optimism* (London: Penguin Classics, 1947)

Voltaire, *Candide et autres contes* (Paris: Gallimard, 1992)

Voltaire, *Correspondence and related documents*, ed. Th. Besterman, in *Œuvres complètes de Voltaire*, vol.85-135 (Geneva, Banbury, Oxford, 1968-1977)

Voltaire, *Œuvres complètes de Voltaire: Essai sur les mœurs et l'esprit des nations*, t.1 (Paris: A.-A. Renouard, 1819)

Voltaire, *Œuvres complètes de Voltaire avec des notes et une notice historique sur la vie de Voltaire*, t.1 (Paris: Furne, 1835)

Voltaire, *La Princesse de Navarre* (Paris: Ballard, 1745)

Voltaire, *Samson* (Paris: Le Mercier, 1750)

Voltaire, *Le Temple de la gloire* (Paris: Ballard, 1745)

Notes

PREFACE

[1] Quoted in James R. Anthony, *French Baroque Music from Beaujoyeulx to Rameau* (Portland: Amadeus Press, 1997), p.122.

[2] Quoted in Enrico Fubini, *Music and Culture in Eighteenth-Century Europe: a Source Book* (Chicago: University of Chicago Press, 1994), p.90.

INTRODUCTION

[1] Jean-Baptiste-André Gautier-Dagoty, *Galerie Françoise, ou Portraits des hommes et des femmes célèbres qui ont paru en France* (Paris: Hérissant le fils, 1770), 'Rameau', p.4.

[2] 'Lettre de M*** à Mlle*** sur l'origine de la musique', in *Mercure de France* (May, 1734), p.868-69. The French word 'baroque' is derived from the Portuguese 'barroco', meaning a misshapen pearl.

[3] See Claude V. Palisca, 'Baroque', in *Grove Music Online* (Oxford University Press), http://www.oxfordmusiconline.com.

[4] See Yves Florenne, 'Platée', in *Le Monde*, 25 July 1956.

[5] 'Rameau's *Platée* Lives Again', in *The Times*, 27 July 1956.

[6] Marc Minkowski with Antone Boulay, *Chef d'orchestre ou centaure: Confessions* (Paris, 2022), p.193.

[7] Edward Greenfield, 'Les Boréades on Radio 3', in *The Guardian*, 21 April 1975.

[8] See Sylvie Bouissou, *Jean-Philippe Rameau: Musicien des Lumières* (Paris: Fayard, 2014), p.153-56.

[9] Rupert Christiansen, '*Castor et Pollux*', in the *Daily Telegraph* (25 October, 2011).

[10] In the unpublished *Le Neveu de Rameau*.

[11] Entry for 4 October 1742 in 'Chronique de règne de Louis XV, 1742-43', in [ed. Jules Taschereau], *Revue rétrospective, ou Bibliothèque historique, contenant des mémoires et documens authentiques, inédits et originaux...* , t.5 (Paris, 1834), p.48-9.

[12] Michel Paul Guy de Chabanon, *Éloge de M. Rameau* (Paris: Lambert, 1764), p.5.

¹³ Chabanon, *Éloge de M. Rameau*, p.6.
¹⁴ *Gil Blas* (28 June, 1903).

1 EARLY LIFE

¹ Rameau was fifteen years younger than Couperin; five and a half years younger than Vivaldi; and two and a half years younger than Telemann. He was one and a half years older than Bach and Handel. At the time of Rameau's birth, the great active composers were Lully (d. 1687), Purcell (d. 1695), Charpentier (d. 1704) and Corelli (d. 1713).

² The vineyards were destroyed by the phylloxera epidemic at the end of the 19th century. The Demartinécourt family home survives, at 27 rue de Jean-Philippe Rameau.

³ See Sylvie Bouissou, *Jean-Philippe Rameau: Musicien des Lumières*, p.27.

⁴ Five girls and six boys. Four daughters were born before the first son: his arrival must have been celebrated with some relief. Jean-Philippe was the second son.

⁵ 3-7 rue Vaillant, in the very centre of the city. Today an estate agency and a pharmacy occupy the lower parts of the building. The city of Rameau's childhood can still be seen in Dijon's old centre of 17th and 18th century buildings. Dijon flourished economically and politically in the Middle Ages as the capital of the duchy of Burgundy, and remained prosperous and independent-minded after Burgundy fell to the French crown in the late 15th century. By the time of Rameau's birth the importance of the wine trade had given rise to an affluent merchant class. As a consequence, many elegant town houses were built, and the new parishes needed churches. Burgundy remains a sparsely-populated region of ancient landscapes and small towns and villages. The tolling of a bell and the barking of a dog are the only significant sounds one is likely to hear during a day of walking.

⁶ Today the building, in the rue de l'École de Droit, is home to the municipal library.

⁷ Hugues Maret, *Éloge historique de Mr. Rameau* (Dijon: Causse, 1766), p.44. 'Le Père Gauthier, Religieux Carme, condisciple de Rameau, m'a assuré qu'il se distinguoit dans le collège par une vivacité peu commune; mais que pendant les classes il chantoit ou écrivoit de la musique, et qu'il ne passa pas la quatrième.'

⁸ See Bouissou, *Jean-Philippe Rameau: Musicien des Lumières*, p.40.

⁹ Rameau to Mongeot, 29 May 1744, published in *Mercure de France* (June, 1765), p.54-6.

¹⁰ See Bouissou, *Jean-Philippe Rameau: Musicien des Lumières*, p.39.

¹¹ Michel Paul Guy de Chabanon, *Éloge de M. Rameau*, p.7.

¹² Hugues Maret, *Éloge historique de Mr. Rameau*. Maret was the Secretaire Perpétuel of the Académie des Sciences, Arts et Belles-Lettres de Dijon. He

interviewed a number of people who had known Rameau.

[13] [Rameau], 'Réplique du premier musicien à la réponse du second', in *Mercure de France* (June, 1730), p.1337-38. Maret refers to the organist as Delacroix (p.44).

[14] It still is. Today's lycée Louis-le-Grand (LLG) prepares students for entry into the *grande écoles*. Georges Pompidou, Valéry Giscard d'Estaing and Jacques Chirac all attended LLG.

[15] Joachim Christoph Nemeitz, *Le Séjour de Paris* (Leyden: J. van Acoude, 1727), p.107-109, quoted in Anthony, *French Baroque Music from Beaujoyeulx to Rameau*, p.62-63.

[16] The convent buildings still stand (no. 45); the church was on the site of no. 47.

[17] James R. Anthony, *French Baroque Music from Beaujoyeulx to Rameau*, p.318.

[18] Decroix was a lawyer and writer from Lille who, in the 1780s, co-edited the Kehl edition of Voltaire's works. In his book *L'Ami des arts* (1776) he wrote passionately about both Rameau and Voltaire. He collected Rameau's scores for posterity, determined to track down even the most obscure examples.

[19] Quoted in Bouissou, *Jean-Philippe Rameau: Musicien des Lumières*, p.58.

[20] See Maret, *Éloge historique de Mr. Rameau*, p.44-45.

[21] The organ played by Rameau was replaced in the 19th century.

[22] Jean-François Rameau, *La Raméide* (Petersbourg: aux rameaux couronnés, 1766), p.17.

[23] Today's place des Jacobins. The church was demolished in 1808.

[24] See Bouissou, *Jean-Philippe Rameau: Musicien des Lumières*, p.75.

[25] Rameau to Jean-Pierre Christin, 3 November 1741. Quoted in Bouissou, *Jean-Philippe Rameau: Musicien des Lumières*, p.77.

[26] *Inventaire de la Bibliothèque du Concert de l'Académie des Beaux-Arts de la Ville de Lyon*. Reproduced in Léon Vallas, *La Musique à l'Académie de Lyon au dix-huitième siècle* (Lyon: Editions de la Revue Musicale de Lyon, 1908), p.149-68.

[27] Maret, *Éloge historique de Mr. Rameau*, p.62.

[28] Jacques Joseph Marie Decroix, *L'Ami des arts ou Justification de plusieurs grands hommes* (Amsterdam, 1776), p.179.

[29] See Rameau, *Démonstration du principe de l'harmonie* (Paris: Durand, 1750), p.110. '[J'étais] conduit, dès ma plus tender jeunesse, par un instinct mathématique dans l'étude d'un Art pour lequel je me trouvais destiné, et qui m'a toute ma vie uniquement occupé, j'en ai voulu connaître le vrai principe, comme seul capable de me guider avec certitude, sans égard pour les habitudes ni les règles reçues.'

[30] Rameau told the story himself in the *Mercure de France* (October, 1752).

[31] See Maret, *Éloge historique de Mr. Rameau*, p.61-62.

[32] Jean-Philippe Rameau (trans. Philip Gossett), *Treatise on Harmony* (New

[33] Rameau (trans. Gossett), *Treatise on Harmony*, p.5.
[34] Rameau used Nicolas Poisson's French translation of Descartes's *Compendium Musicae, Traité de la mechanique, composé par Monsieur Descartes. De plus l'Abrégé de musique du mesme autheur mis en françois* (Paris, 1688).
[35] Rameau (trans. Gossett), *Treatise on Harmony*, p.3.
[36] 'Consonance' is defined by Rameau as 'an interval the union of whose sounds is very pleasing to the ear'.
[37] Rameau (trans. Gossett), *Treatise on Harmony*, p.8.
[38] Rameau (trans. Gossett), *Treatise on Harmony*, p.152.
[39] Rameau (trans. Gossett), *Treatise on Harmony*, p.xxii.
[40] Denis Diderot (trans. Leonard Tancock), *Rameau's Nephew* (London: Penguin, 1966), p.35.
[41] *Journal de Trévoux* (October/November, 1722). Louis-Bertrand Castel (1688-1757), b. Montpellier, taught at Louis-le-Grand.
[42] For a detailed analysis of Rameau's theoretical ideas, see Thomas Christensen's *Rameau and Musical Thought in the Enlightenment* (Cambridge: Cambridge University Press, 1993).

2 BEGINNING AGAIN IN PARIS

[1] Rétif de la Bretonne in *Les Nuits de Paris* (nuit 61): 'Ce quartier, qui est comme le cerveau de la capitale, c'est la rue Saint-Honoré, unie au quartier du Palais-Royal. La rue Saint-Honoré ne paraît composée que de marchands: mais il est une infinité de gens de goût dans les étages supérieurs, et surtout dans les rues adjacentes. Il est même des étrangers, qui ne vivent que là, sans y demeurer.'
[2] Chabanon, *Éloge de M. Rameau*, p.51.
[3] Piron to Hugues Maret, 18 May 1765, in Gunnar von Proschwitz (ed.), *Alexis Piron, épistolier: choix de ses lettres* (Göteborg: Université de Göteborg, 1982), p.193.
[4] While it cannot be stated definitively that the painting is of Rameau, the circumstantial evidence is strong. The portrait hangs in the Musée de Beaux-Arts de Dijon.
[5] The Marché Saint-Germain occupies the site today.
[6] A market, mostly of luxury items traded by Portuguese merchants, had thrived in the fortified enclave of the Abbey since the Middle Ages. Until the 17th Century the Abbey quarter lay outside the city walls.
[7] The Saint-Germain Fair was abolished in 1789.
[8] The Saint-Laurent fair took place in August and September in today's 10th arrondissement between rue du Faubourg-Saint-Denis and rue du Faubourg-Saint-Martin.
[9] Piron to Maret, quoted in Cuthbert Girdlestone, *Jean-Philippe Rameau:*

His Life and Work (New York: Dover, 1969), p.514.

[10] See L. de La Laurencie, 'Quelques documents sur Jean-Philippe Rameau et sa famille', in *Mercure musical et S.I.M.* (June 1907), p.543.

[11] *Éloge historique de Mr. Rameau*, p.74.

[12] Claude-François, b. 1727; Marie-Louise, b. 1732 (at the age of seventeen, Marie-Louise entered a convent of Visitandines at Montargis); Alexandre, b. 1740 (died in infancy); and Marie-Alexandrine, b. 1744.

[13] The building was destroyed at the end of the 18th century.

[14] I recommend Alexandre Tharaud's recording of Rameau's *Nouvelles suites* (Harmonia Mundi, 2001).

[15] Rameau, 'Remarques sur les pièces de ce livre, et sur le differens genres de musique', in *Nouvelles suites de pièces de clavecin* (Paris: The Author; Boivin, [1729]).

[16] Rameau to Houdar de la Motte, 25 October 1727. Quoted in Girdlestone, *Jean-Philippe Rameau: His Life and Work*, p.9-10.

[17] 'Je tâche de cacher l'art par l'art même.'

[18] A notice of the concert was published in *Mercure de France* (November, 1728). Rameau would prefer Catherine-Nicole Le Maure's rival Marie Pélissier during his first decade at the Opéra, but the fact that the mercurial Mlle Le Maure often absented herself from the stage was also a factor. During the 1740s she would sing the leading soprano roles in the revivals of *Hippolyte et Aricie*, *Les Indes galantes* and *Dardanus*.

[19] Rameau, *Nouveau système de musique théorique* (Paris: Ballard, 1726), p.viii. Quoted in Girdlestone, *Rameau: His Life and Work*, p.515.

[20] 'Conference sur la musique', in *Mercure de France* (June, 1729), p.1281-89.

[21] [Rameau], 'Examen de la conférence sur la musique, insérée dans le deuxiéme volume du Mercure de juin 1729', in *Mercure de France* (October, 1729), p.2369-77.

[22] [Rameau], 'Réplique du premier musicien à la réponse du second', in *Mercure de France* (June, 1730), p.1337-38.

[23] [Rameau], 'Réplique du premier musicien à la réponse du second', p.1339.

[24] See Girdlestone, *Jean-Philippe Rameau: His Life and Work*, p.486.

[25] See Maret, *Éloge historique de Mr. Rameau*, p.25-6.

[26] See Christensen, *Rameau and Musical Thought in the Enlightenment*, p.57.

[27] Pierre Laujon, *Œuvres choisies de P.Laujon*, t.4 (Paris: L. Collin, 1811), p.225-30.

[28] Simon-Joseph Pellegrin (1663-1745).

[29] Alexandre Jean Joseph Le Riche de La Pouplinière (1693-1762).

[30] Today's rue des Petits Champs, near the Palais-Royal.

[31] See Girdlestone, *Jean-Philippe Rameau: His Life and Work*, p.11.

[32] *Éloge historique de Mr. Rameau*, p.64.

[33] See Graham Sadler, 'Patrons and Pasquinades: Rameau in the 1730s', in *Journal of the Royal Musical Association*, vol.113, n.2 (1988), p.314-33.

[34] Thérèse Boutinon des Hayes (1714-1756).

[35] Victor Amadeus I, Prince de Carignan (1690-1741).

[36] See Girdlestone, *Jean-Philippe Rameau: His Life and Work*, p.11.

[37] The house was demolished after the prince de Carignan's death. The Bourse de Commerce de Paris now occupies the site.

[38] Sadler, 'Patrons and Pasquinades: Rameau in the 1730s', p.322-23.

3 INTERLUDE

[1] Later fictionalised in James Fenimore Cooper's bestseller *The Last of the Mohicans* (1826).

[2] Voltaire (trans. John Butt), *Candide, or Optimism* (Penguin Classics, 1947), p.111.

[3] See Colin Jones, *The Great Nation: France from Louis XV to Napoleon* (Penguin Books, 2003), p.82-124.

[4] Voltaire, *The Embellishments of Paris* (1739). Quoted in Eric Hazan (trans. David Fernbach), *The Invention of Paris: a History in Footsteps* (London: Verso, 2010), p.17.

[5] Quoted in Daniel Roche, *The People of Paris: an Essay in Popular Culture in the 18th Century* (Berkeley: University of California Press, 1987), p.9.

[6] Quoted in Colin Jones, *Paris: Biography of a City* (London: Allen Lane, 2004), p.204.

[7] For a detailed analysis of France's musical life up until 1733 see James R. Anthony, *French Baroque Music from Beaujoyeulx to Rameau* (Portland: Amadeus Press, 1997).

[8] Built for Cardinal Richelieu, the Palais-Royal was designed by Jacques Lemercier (1629). Its theatre was located in the south-east wing of the building, facing the place du Palais-Royal. It was occupied by Molière's troupe from 1660.

[9] Antoine Louis Le Brun, 'La théâtre lyrique', in *Le Journal des sçavans, pour l'année 1712* (Paris, 1712), p.436.

[10] Quoted in James R. Anthony, *French Baroque Music from Beaujoyeulx to Rameau*, p. 95.

4 THE OPÉRA

[1] Rameau to Mongeot, 29 May 1744, published in *Mercure de France* (June, 1765), p.54-6.

[2] Rameau to Mongeot, 29 May 1744.

[3] Montesquieu (trans. Margaret Mauldon), *Persian Letters* (Oxford: Oxford University Press, 2008), p.37-8.

⁴ For a fascinating analysis of the role of women at the Opéra, see Georgia Cowart, 'Of women, sex and folly: Opera under the Old Regime', in *Cambridge Opera Journal*, vol.6, iss.3 (1994), p.205-220.

⁵ In the rue des Bons Enfants. This street ran between the rue Saint-Honoré and the rue des Petits Champs, along the eastern edge of the garden. As part of the site's redevelopment in the 1780s, a new street and new houses were constructed between the rue des Bons Enfants and the garden, reducing the latter's size; and the later construction of the rue du Colonel Driant removed the northern stretch of the rue des Bons Enfants.

⁶ See the beginning of Diderot's *Le Neveu de Rameau*.

⁷ Jean-Barthélemy Lany (1718-1786) worked at the Opéra from 1740, as dancer, choreographer and, eventually, ballet master. He choreographed a number of Rameau's operas, including *Platée* and *Zoroastre* in 1749, and *Les Paladins* in 1760.

⁸ Marie Fel (1713-1794), b. Bordeaux, made her debut at the Opéra in 1734. She was thirty-seven when Casanova met her: 'Mademoiselle Le Fel n'était pas effrontée, elle était franche, et supérieure à tous les prejugés.'

⁹ Giacomo Casanova, *Histoire de ma vie*, livre 3. Paris, Bibliotheque Nationale de France, MS NAF 28604 (3), chap.12.

¹⁰ *Factum pour Mlle Petit, danseuse de l'Opéra révoquée, complaignante au public*. Quoted in Émile Campardon, *L'Académie royale de musique au XVIIIe siècle: documents inédits découverts aux Archives nationales* (Paris: Berger-Levrault, 1884), p.233-34.

¹¹ See Campardon, *L'Académie royale de musique au XVIIIe siècle: documents inédits découverts aux Archives nationales*, p.238-39.

¹² The rue Saint-Nicaise ran between the rue Saint-Honoré and the riverside Galleries du Louvre. The place du Carrousel occupies the location of the road today.

¹³ See Graham Sadler, *The Rameau Compendium* (Woodbridge: Boydell Press, 2014), p.123.

¹⁴ See Maret, *Éloge historique de Mr. Rameau*, p.72-73.

¹⁵ Governance of the Opéra during Rameau's career – Minister of State: Jean-Frédéric Phélypeaux, comte de Maurepas (1723-49), Marc-Pierre de Voyer de Paulmy, comte d'Argenson (1749-57); Inspector-General: Prince de Carignan (1730-40), François Rebel and François Francœur (1740-53), Joseph Royer (1753-55), post abolished 1757; Director: Louis-Armand Eugène de Thuret (1733-44), Jean-François Berger (1744-47), Joseph Guénot de Tréfontaine and others (1748-49), Ville de Paris (1749-53), Thuret (1753-57), Rebel and Francœur (1757-67).

¹⁶ See David Charlton, *Opera in the Age of Rousseau: Music, Confrontation, Realism* (Cambridge: Cambridge University Press, 2013), p.71.

¹⁷ Mme de Graffigny (1695-1758), novelist and playwright.

¹⁸ Pierre de Jélyotte (1713-1797), b. Lasseube (Aquitaine), moved from

Toulouse, where he was a chorister, to Paris in the early 1730s. He entered the company of the Opéra in 1733. Rameau wrote most of his leading *haute-contre* roles for Jélyotte. The singer retired from the Opéra during the 1750s but continued to sing at court.

[19] Mme de Graffigny to François-Antoine Devaux, [9 November 1739], in *Correspondance de Madame de Graffigny*. Electronic Enlightenment Scholarly Edition of Correspondence, ed. Robert McNamee et al. Vers. 3.0. University of Oxford. 2022.

[20] Rameau, *La Génération harmonique, ou Traité de musique theorique et pratique* (Paris: Chez Prault fils, 1737), p.154-55.

[21] Rameau, *Démonstration du principe de l'harmonie*, p.94. 'Je regrette à ce sujet, le Trio des Parques de mon Opéra d'Hyppolite & Aricie, dont l'essai m'avoit réussi avec d'habiles Musiciens de bonne volonté, & dont l'effet passe l'idée qu'on peut s'en faire, eû égard à la situation. Il me l'a fallu cependant abandonner pour l'exécution théatrale.'

[22] In 1751 Casanova translated the libretto of *Zoroastre* into Italian at the request of the Polish ambassador. Years later, in the preface of his memoirs, he wrote: 'Everyone, in the era of Lully, held the same view of his music; then Rameau came along and changed it.'

[23] Carlo Goldoni (trans. John Black), *Memoirs of Goldoni, Written by Himself*, vol.2 (London: Hunt and Clarke, 1828), p.118.

[24] Louis Dupré (1690-1774), dancer, choreographer and ballet master. He made his debut at the Paris Opéra in 1714 and became its ballet master in 1739. He also worked in London.

[25] Marie-Anne Cupis de Camargo (1710-70) trained at the Paris Opéra from the age of ten and became a star on her debut there in 1726. She enthralled the public, and was the mistress of a succession of noblemen.

[26] Casanova, *Histoire de ma vie*, livre 3, chap.10.

[27] Jean-Georges Noverre, *Lettres sur la danse, et sur les ballets* (Lyon: chez Aimé Delaroche, 1760), p.163-64.

[28] Antoine de Léris, *Dictionnaire portatif historique et littéraire des théatres*. 2nd ed. (Paris: Jombert, 1763), p.653.

[29] Quoted in *Rameau de A à Z*, p.256.

[30] Quoted in Bouissou, *Jean-Philippe Rameau: Musicien des Lumières*, p.310.

[31] The anecdote is told in Joseph de La Porte, *Les Spectacles de Paris, ou Suite du calendrier historique et chronologique des théatres*, pt.12 (Paris: Duchesne, 1763), p.36.

[32] Maret, *Éloge historique de Mr. Rameau*, p.28-29.

[33] James R. Anthony, *French Baroque Music from Beaujoyeulx to Rameau*, p.163-64.

[34] William Christie, 'A Faithful Travelling Companion', in the sleeve notes accompanying his recording of *Hippolyte et Aricie* (Erato, 1997), p.18.

[35] William Christie, 'A Faithful Travelling Companion', in the sleeve notes

accompanying his recording of *Hippolyte et Aricie*, p.16.

[36] Claude-Louis-Dominique de Chassé de Chinais (1699-1786), b. Rennes, made his debut at the Opéra in 1720.

[37] Marie Pélissier (1707-1749) made her debut in 1722. A major star during the 1720s and 30s, she was Rameau's favourite actress up to her early retirement in 1741.

[38] Nemeitz, *Le Séjour de Paris*, p.105, quoted in Anthony, *French Baroque Music from Beaujoyeulx to Rameau*, p.35.

[39] Charles Burney, *The Present State of Music in France and Italy* (London: T. Becket and Co., 1773), p.30. Burney was writing of the 1760s when, after the fire of 1763, the Opéra was temporarily based at the Palais des Tuileries.

[40] *Mercure de France* (October, 1733), p.2248.

[41] Voltaire to Le Cornier de Cideville, [2 October 1733] (D661), in Voltaire, *Correspondence and related documents*, ed. Th. Besterman, in *Œuvres complètes de Voltaire*, vol.85-135 (Geneva, Banbury, Oxford, 1968-1977), vol.2, p.402-403. 'J'assistay hier à la première représentation de l'opéra d'Aricie et d'Hipolite. Les paroles sont de l'abbé Pellegrin, et dignes de l'abbé Pellegrin. La musique est d'un nommé Rameau, homme qui a le malheur de savoir plus de musique que Lully. C'est un pédant en musique. Il est exact et ennuyeux.'

[42] Maret, *Éloge historique de Mr. Rameau*, p.64.

[43] *Mercure de France* (October, 1733), p.2249.

[44] D'Alembert, 'De la liberté de la musique', in *Melanges de litterature, d'histoire, et de philosophie*, t.4 (Amsterdam, 1759), p.516-17.

[45] *Éloge historique de Mr. Rameau*, p.25-6.

[46] Voltaire to Rameau, [December 1733] (D690), in Voltaire, *Correspondence and related documents*, vol.2, p.436-37.

[47] Voltaire to Rameau, [December 1733] (D690), in Voltaire, *Correspondence and related documents*, vol.2, p.436-37.

[48] Louis François Armand de Vignerot du Plessis, duc de Richelieu (1696-1788), libertine, soldier and courtier, was the great-nephew of Cardinal Richelieu. Voltaire met Richelieu at Louis-le-Grand. In 1734 he helped to arrange Richelieu's marriage to the daughter of another of his aristocratic friends, the Prince de Guise.

[49] Voltaire to Rameau, [15 April 1734] (D719), in Voltaire, *Correspondence and related documents*, vol.2, p.462-63.

[50] Alexis Piron, *Œuvres complètes d'Alexis Piron*, t.2 (Paris: M. Lambert, 1776), p.25.

[51] Charles-Augustin de Ferriol d'Argental (1700-1788).

[52] Voltaire to d'Argental, [September 1734?] (D786), in Voltaire, *Correspondence and related documents*, vol.3, p.62-64.

[53] See, for example, Voltaire to Thieriot, 25 [December 1735] (D971), in Voltaire, *Correspondence and related documents*, vol.3, p.293-95.

[54] Jean Baptiste Nicolas Formont to Cideville, 20 November 1733 (D682),

in Voltaire, *Correspondence and related documents*, vol.2, p.429-30.

55 Mme de Châtelet to Louis Touissaint de Brancas de Forcalquier, 14 [September] 1762 (D784), in Voltaire, *Correspondence and related documents*, vol.3, p.59-60.

56 Mme de Châtelet to Maupertius, 23 October 1734 (D797), in Voltaire, *Correspondence and related documents*, vol.3, p.74-76.

57 Jacques Hardion, Deputy Keeper of Books at the Bibliothèque du roi.

58 Voltaire to Rameau, [December 1733] (D690), in Voltaire, *Correspondence and related documents*, vol.2, p.436-37. 'Je n'ai point du tout à ce que je crois le talent des vers lyriques, c'est une harmonie particulière que j'ai peur de n'avoir point saisie. Je suis surtout incapable de faire un prologue passable. [...] Je voudrais pouvoir vous abandoner toute la rétribution de cet opéra et je vous croirais encore bien mal payé. D'ailleurs, vous etes l'unique maitre de tout.'

59 Voltaire to Chabanon, 18 January 1768 (D14685), in Voltaire, *Correspondence and related documents*, vol.33, p.53-54. 'Working on *Eudoxie* must make you think of this bawdy Samson and this whore Delilah... Do you know that Rameau created delightful music for *Samson*, both astounding and graceful. He used part of it in *Castor et Pollux*.'

60 Quoted in Anthony, *French Baroque Music from Beaujoyeulx to Rameau*, p.168.

61 James R. Anthony dates the first phase of the opéra-ballet genre as lasting from 1697 to 1719. Nine such works were presented at the Opéra. Four were by Campra (*L'Europe galante*, with La Motte; *Les Muses* and *Les Fêtes vénitiennes*, with Danchet; and *Les Ages*, with Fuzelier). The others were by La Barre and La Motte (*Le Triomphe des Arts*); Bourgeois and Fuzelier (*Les Amours déguisés*); Mouret and La Font (*Les Fêtes de Thalie*); Montéclair and Pellegrin (*Les Fêtes de l'été*); and Bertin de La Doué and Pellegrin (*Les Plaisirs de la compagne*). The second, ballet héroïque phase, included, in the period before Rameau's *Indes galantes*, operas by Destouches and Roy (*Les Eléments* and *Les Stratagèmes de l'Amour*), Mouret and Fuzelier (*Les Amours des Dieux*), and de Brassac and Moncrif (*L'Empire de l'Amour*).

62 Louis Fuzelier, *Les Indes galantes, ballet heroique représenté par l'Academie royale de Musique; pour la premiere fois, le mardy 23. aoust 1735* (Paris: Ballard, 1736), p.vii.

63 See *Mercure de France* (September, 1725), p.2276.

64 The claim is found in the *Journal de Paris* (5 January, 1777). See Girdlestone, *Jean-Philippe Rameau: His Life and Work*, p.347.

65 See Nicolas Bricaire de la Dixmerie, *Les Deux ages du goût et du génie français sous Louis XIV et sous Louis XV* (La Haye: Lacombe, 1769), p.523.

66 David Garrick (ed. Ryllis Clair Alexander), *The Diary of David Garrick, Being a Record of His Memorable Trip to Paris in 1751* (New York: Oxford University Press, 1928), p.8-9.

⁶⁷ Noverre, *Lettres sur la danse, et sur les ballets*, p.143-44.

5 AN ARGUMENT IN THE COURTYARD OF THE LOUVRE

¹ *Observations sur les écrits modernes* (Paris: Chez Chaubert, 1735), Lettre 25, 9 Septembre 1735, p.238-39.

² Voltaire to Thieriot, 11 September 1735 (D911), in Voltaire, *Correspondence and related documents*, vol.3, p.196-97.

³ Quoted in Girdlestone, *Jean-Philippe Rameau: His Life and Work*, p.483.

⁴ Toussaint Rémond de Saint-Mard, *Réflexions sur l'opéra* (La Haye: J. Neaulme, 1741), p.45-6. Quoted in Girdlestone, *Jean-Philippe Rameau: His Life and Work*, p.144-45.

⁵ Denis Diderot, *Les Bijoux indiscrets* (Paris: Garnier, 1965), p.33-34.

⁶ Rameau, 'Préface', in *Les Indes galantes, ballet réduit à quatre grands concerts avec une nouvelle entrée complette* (Paris: Boivin, Leclair, l'auteur, 1735). 'Comme on n'a point encore entendu la Nouvelle Entrée des Sauvages que j'ajoûte ici aux trois premieres, je me suis hasardé de la donner complete: heureux si le succès répond à mes soins. Toûjours occupé de la belle déclamation, et du beau tour de Chant qui regnent dans le Récitatif du grand LULLY, je tâche de l'imiter, non en Copiste servile, mais en prenant, comme lui, la belle et simple nature pour modéle.'

⁷ See Graham Sadler, 'Patrons and Pasquinades: Rameau in the 1730s', p.324-27, 334-37.

⁸ Quoted in Sadler, 'Patrons and Pasquinades: Rameau in the 1730s', p.337.

⁹ Pierre-Charles Roy (1683-1764) wrote a number of libretti for André Destouches, including *Callirhoé* (1712), *Les Elémens* (1721) and *Les Stratagèmes de l'Amour* (1726).

¹⁰ See Voltaire to Jean-Baptiste Rousseau, [1 March 1719] (D72), in Voltaire, *Correspondence and related documents*, vol.1, p.79-80. 'J'ai été si malheureux sous le nom d'Arouet que j'en ai pris un autre surtout pour n'être plus confondu avec le poète Roy.'

¹¹ Christensen, *Rameau and Musical Thought in the Enlightenment*, p.140.

¹² Mairan to Gabriel Cramer, 16 September 1749, quoted in Christensen, *Rameau and Musical Thought in the Enlightenment*, p.14.

¹³ Rameau, *La Génération harmonique*, p.225.

¹⁴ Rameau, *Démonstration du principe de l'harmonie*, p.111-12.

¹⁵ Rameau, *Nouveau Système de musique théorique*, p.106.

¹⁶ Rameau, *Code de musique pratique, ou Méthodes pour apprendre la musique, même à des aveugles, pour former la voix et l'oreille* (Paris: Imprimerie royale, 1760), p.93.

¹⁷ Quoted in Leta E. Miller, 'Rameau and the Royal Society of London: New Letters and Documents', in *Music and Letters*, vol.66, n.1 (1985), p.20.

¹⁸ Quoted in Leta E. Miller, 'Rameau and the Royal Society of London:

New Letters and Documents', p.26.

[19] Rameau to the Royal Society, 26 February 1750, quoted in Leta E. Miller, 'Rameau and the Royal Society of London: New Letters and Documents', p.27.

[20] Rameau to the Royal Society, 18 November 1750.

[21] *Observations sur les écrits modernes* (Paris: Chez Chaubert, 1737), Lettre 89, 31 Août 1737, p.73-86.

[22] Jean-Jacques Rousseau, *Les Confessions* (Paris: Gallimard, 1995), p.270.

[23] *Journal de Trévoux* (December, 1737), p.2142-67.

[24] See Christensen, *Rameau and Musical Thought in the Enlightenment*, p.192-93.

[25] *Le pour et contre*, t.14 (1738), p.74-78. Quoted in Girdlestone, *Jean-Philippe Rameau: His Life and Work*, p.488.

[26] Voltaire, *Lettre à Mr Rameau*, 21 June 1738 (Letter D.app.50), in Voltaire, *Correspondance and related documents*, vol.5, p.505-508.

[27] Zoilus (ca.400 BC-320 BC), a Greek writer infamous for his severe criticisms of Homer and others. According to some accounts, Zoilus was crucified.

[28] Voltaire to Thieriot, 10 April 1738 (D1480), in Voltaire, *Correspondance and related documents*, vol.5, p.82-84.

[29] Charles Burney, *A General History of Music from the Earliest Ages to the Present Period*, vol.4 (London: The Author, 1789), p.612-13.

[30] Quoted in Charles Philippe d'Albert Luynes, duc de, *Mémoires du duc de Luynes sur la cour de Louis XV (1735-1758)*, t.1 (Paris: Firmin Didot Frères, 1860), p.401.

[31] Rameau, *Observations sur notre instinct pour la musique, et sur son principe* (Paris: Prault, 1754), p.67.

[32] Rameau, *Code de musique pratique*, p.168.

[33] Hector Berlioz, 'Castor et Pollux: la partition', in *Revue et gazette musicale* (1842), p.442. 'Ici l'harmonie, la mélodie, le rhythme, et l'expression concourent également à émouvoir l'auditeur. Chaque note a son importance, parce que chaque note est précisément celle que l'expression demande; et l'explosion finale "Non, je ne veux plus que vos clartés funèbres" est préparée de loin avec une égale habileté.' Berlioz's analysis of the rest of the opera was not entirely complementary.

[34] *Gil Blas* (2 February, 1903). The 1903 performance took place in Paris at the Schola Cantorum. Only the first two acts were performed.

[35] The Hébé music was particularly admired by Debussy, who, in his *Gil Blas* review of the 1903 performance, wrote: 'Jamais la sensation d'une volupté calme et tranquille n'a trouvé de si parfaite traduction; cela joue si lumineusement dans l'air surnaturel qu'il faut toute l'énergie spartiate de Pollux pour échapper à ce charme, et penser encore à Castor.'

[36] Edward Nye, *Mime, Music and Drama on the Eighteenth-Century Stage:*

the Ballet d'Action (Cambridge: Cambridge University Press, 2011), p.155.

[37] Gautier-Dagoty, *Galerie Françoise, ou Portraits des hommes et des femmes célèbres qui ont paru en France*, 'Rameau', p.4.

[38] Charles Philippe d'Albert Luynes, duc de, *Mémoires du duc de Luynes sur la cour de Louis XV (1735-1758)*, t.1, p.401.

[39] *Mercure de France* (December, 1737), p.2657.

[40] Voltaire to Thieriot, 3 November 1737 (D1383), in Voltaire, *Correspondence and related documents*, vol.4, p.390-92.

[41] *Mercure de France* (December, 1737), p.2648.

[42] See Nick Childs, *A Political Academy in Paris, 1724-1731* (Oxford: Voltaire Foundation, 2000), p.9.

[43] Guillaume-Thomas-François Raynal, *Nouvelles littéraires* in *Correspondance littéraire, philosophique et critique*, t.1 (Paris: Garnier, 1877), p.80. Raynal's *Nouvelles littéraires* was a hand-copied newsletter on French life and letters sent to distinguished subscribers abroad. Because it by-passed the censor Raynal was able to express himself freely. He kept it going until 1751, at which point Friedrich Melchior Grimm took it over and renamed it *Correspondance littéraire*.

[44] Montdorge (1707-1768) was born in Lyon. He held the important position of Treasurer to the king (Maître à la Chambre aux Deniers du Roi). A passionate supporter of the arts, particularly the fine arts, he wrote the articles 'Gravure en couleurs, à l'imitation de la Peinture' and 'Gravure en maniere noire' in volume seven of the *Encyclopédie* (1757).

[45] Simon Henri Dubuisson's *Lettres au Marquis de Caumont* (Lettre VI, 8 June, 1739) and *Le Postillon français* (30 June, 1739) are key sources cited by Girdlestone.

[46] Louis Petit de Bachaumont, *Mémoires secrets de Bachaumont, de 1762 à 1787*, t.2 (Paris: Brissot-Thivars, 1830), p.352-53. 'C'était un financier, qui, dans son temps, avait eu des prétentions au bel esprit.'

[47] 'Extrait d'une lettre, écrite à M. Rameau', in *Les Fêtes d'Hébé, ou Les Talents lyriques* (Paris: Ballard, 1739).

[48] Mme de Graffigny to Devaux, [20 July 1739], in *Correspondance de Madame de Graffigny*. Electronic Enlightenment Scholarly Edition of Correspondence, ed. Robert McNamee et al. Vers. 3.0. University of Oxford. 2022.

[49] See Bouissou, *Jean-Philippe Rameau: Musicien des Lumières*, p.458.

[50] Rameau, *Les Fêtes d'Hébé, ou Les Talents lyriques* (Paris: L'Auteur, [1745]). 'La protection dont votre Altesse Sérénissime a honoré mes premiers ouvrages, me fait prendre la liberté de lui présenter celui-cy: s'il peut mériter son approbation, mon ambition est satisfaite.'

[51] Girdlestone, *Rameau: His Life and Work*, p.353.

[52] Mme de Graffigny to Devaux, [20 July 1739], in *Correspondance de Madame de Graffigny*. Electronic Enlightenment Scholarly Edition of

Correspondence, ed. Robert McNamee et al. Vers. 3.0. University of Oxford. 2022.

[53] Mme de Graffigny to Devaux, [22 August 1739], in *Correspondance de Madame de Graffigny*. Electronic Enlightenment Scholarly Edition of Correspondence, ed. Robert McNamee et al. Vers. 3.0. University of Oxford. 2022.

[54] Marie Sallé (1707-1756) made her debut at the Opéra at the age of fourteen. She collaborated with her former teacher Michel Blondy to create the choreography of *Les Fêtes d'Hébé*.

[55] *Mercure de France* (January, 1732), p.146.

[56] Mme de Graffigny to Devaux, [20 July 1739], in *Correspondance de Madame de Graffigny*. Electronic Enlightenment Scholarly Edition of Correspondence, ed. Robert McNamee et al. Vers. 3.0. University of Oxford. 2022.

[57] Voltaire to Berger, 5 April 1736 (D1054), in Voltaire, *Correspondence and related documents*, vol.3, p.424-25.

[58] François Berger would later become director of the Opéra (1744-47).

[59] Voltaire to Berger, [10 April 1738] (D1481), in Voltaire, *Correspondence and related documents*, vol.5, p.84-85.

[60] Voltaire to Thieriot, [10 December 1738] (D1684), in Voltaire, *Correspondence and related documents*, vol.5, p.420-21.

[61] Girdlestone, *Rameau: His Life and Work*, p.238.

[62] Mme de Graffigny to Devaux, 6 December [1739], in *Correspondance de Madame de Graffigny*. Electronic Enlightenment Scholarly Edition of Correspondence, ed. Robert McNamee et al. Vers. 3.0. University of Oxford. 2022.

[63] See Girdlestone, *Jean-Philippe Rameau: His Life and Work*, p.266.

[64] Writing about enharmonics, Rameau cited 'Lieux funestes' in his *Observations sur notre instinct pour la musique, et sur son principe*, p.65-66.

[65] Gautier-Dagoty, *Galerie françoise, ou Portraits des hommes et des femmes célèbres qui ont paru en France*, 'Rameau', p.5.

[66] Voltaire to Berger, 29 June 1740 (D2252), in Voltaire, *Correspondence and related documents*, vol.7, p.225-26.

[67] Voltaire to d'Argental, [15 April 1744] (D2957), in Voltaire, *Correspondence and related documents*, vol.9, p.91.

[68] Rameau, *Pièces de clavecin en concerts, avec un violon ou une flute, et une viole ou un deuxième violin* (Paris: Boivin; Le Clair, 1741), p.[iii].

[69] Rameau, *Pièces de clavecin en concerts*.

6 LA POUPLINIÈRE

[1] La Pouplinière's main residence was in the rue Neuve-des-Petits-Champs until 1739; after this date it was in the rue de Richelieu. He had a secret

property near the Palais-Royal, where he took women; and a private theatre in the rue de Clichy.

² Collections du château de Versailles.

³ Jacques-Louis David, *Portrait d'Antoine-Laurent Lavoisier et de sa femme* (Metropolitan Museum of Art, New York).

⁴ Richelieu to Mme Favart, 30 August 1768, quoted in Pierre-Yves Beaurepaire, 'Sociability', in *The Oxford Handbook of the Ancien Régime* (Oxford: Oxford University Press, 2011), p.377.

⁵ Quoted in Pierre-Yves Beaurepaire, 'Sociability', in *The Oxford Handbook of the Ancien Régime*, p.378.

⁶ See Georges Cucuel, *La Pouplinière et la musique de chambre au XVIIIe siècle* (Paris: Fischbacher, 1913), p.114.

⁷ See J.-G. Prod'homme (trans. Theodore Baker), 'A French Maecenas of the Time of Louis XV: M. de La Pouplinière', in *The Musical Quarterly*, vol.10, n.4 (1924), p.518.

⁸ Today the quarter of Passy forms part of the 16th arrondissement.

⁹ Jean-François Marmontel (1723-1789), playwright, librettist, historian. During the 1750s he wrote the texts for three works by Rameau: *La Guirlande*, *Acante et Céphise*, and *Les Sibarites*.

¹⁰ See Jean-François Marmontel, *Mémoires de Marmontel*, t.1 (Paris: Librairie des Bibliophiles, 1891), p.227-246; and, in English translation, Jean-François Marmontel, *Memoirs of Marmontel, Written by Himself*, vol.1 (London: Whittaker, Treacher and Arnot, 1830), p.153-66.

¹¹ Louise-Madeleine Lany (1733-1777).

¹² 'That a bastard whore…' See Robert Darnton, *Poetry and the Police: Communication Networks in 18th Century Paris* (Cambridge, Mass.: Harvard University Press, 2010), p.68.

¹³ See Jean-Jacques Pauvert (ed.), *Théâtre érotique français au XVIIIe siècle* (Paris: Terrain Vague, 1993), p.13.

¹⁴ Adolphe Adam, *Derniers souvenirs d'un musicien* (Paris: Lévy frères, 1859), p.155. Quoted in Bouissou, *Jean-Philippe Rameau*, p.293.

¹⁵ See Casanova, *Histoire de ma vie*, vol.5, chapters 8-9.

¹⁶ Maecenas was one of Voltaire's nicknames for La Pouplinière; the other was Pollion.

¹⁷ Quoted in J.-G. Prod'homme (trans. Theodore Baker), 'A French Maecenas of the Time of Louis XV: M. de La Pouplinière', in *The Musical Quarterly*, vol.10, n.4 (1924), p.523.

7 VERSAILLES

¹ Voltaire to Cideville, 31 January 1745 (D3073), in Voltaire, *Correspondence and related documents*, vol.9, p.209-10.

² Maria Teresa Rafaela died in childbirth the following year. The dauphin

married Maria Josepha of Saxony in 1747. He never became king because he died before his father. His son was crowned Louis XVI in 1774.

[3] See Voltaire to d'Argental, 4 [August 1744] (D3010), in Voltaire, *Correspondence and related documents*, vol.9, p.155-56.

[4] See Voltaire to Richelieu, 24 April 1744 (D2964), in Voltaire, *Correspondence and related documents*, vol.9, p.98-99.

[5] Voltaire to d'Argental, 11 July [1744] (D2999), in Voltaire, *Correspondence and related documents*, vol.9, p.139-41.

[6] See Voltaire to d'Argental, 18 [July 1744] (D3004) and Voltaire to d'Argental, 27 [July 1744] (D3008), in Voltaire, *Correspondence and related documents*, vol.9, p.146-47, 153-54.

[7] Charles-Jean-François Hénault (1685-1770), writer, superintendent of the Queen's household.

[8] Voltaire to Hénault, 14 September 1744 (D3029), in Voltaire, *Correspondence and related documents*, vol.9, p.209-10.

[9] Voltaire to d'Argental, 15 September [1744] (D3030), in Voltaire, *Correspondence and related documents*, vol.9, p.172-73.

[10] Voltaire to Mme Denis, [15 April 1745] (D3100), in Voltaire, *Correspondence and related documents*, vol.9, p.228.

[11] From the aria 'Honour and arms'. See Sadler, *The Rameau Compendium*, p.105.

[12] Marmontel, *Memoirs of Marmontel, Written by Himself*, vol.1, p.191.

[13] *Mémoires du duc de Luynes sur la cour de Louis XV (1735-1758)*, t.6, p.320.

[14] Voltaire to d'Argental, [25 February 1745] (D3076), in Voltaire, *Correspondence and related documents*, vol.9, p.211-12. 'La cour de France ressemble à une ruche d'abeilles, on y bourdonne au tour du roy. Il y avait plus de bruit à la premiere représentation qu'au parterre de la Comédie. Cependant le roy a été très content.'

[15] See 'Avertissement' to *La Princesse de Navarre* in Voltaire, *Œuvres complètes*, vol.9 ([Paris]: La Société Littéraire Typographique, 1784), p.49-52.

[16] Quoted in Nicholas Anderson, 'Rameau's Platée: Burlesque or Grotesque?', in *Early Music*, vol.11, n.4 (October, 1983), p.506.

[17] See Jacques Autreau, *Chef-d'œuvres dramatiques de d'Autreau* (Paris: Bureau général des Chef-d'œuvres dramatiques, 1791). For biographical information on Autreau, and an examination of his work as a painter, see Nick Childs, 'Jacques Autreau', in *The Burlington Magazine*, vol.109, n.771 (June 1967), p.335-39.

[18] The source of the character of Folly is Erasmus's *The Praise of Folly* (1509). Folly appears in Destouches's *Le Carnaval et la Folie* (1704) and Campra's *Les Fêtes vénitiennes* (1710).

[19] See the clip of the young French soprano Sabine Devieilhe recording the aria on the 'Château de Versailles Spectacles' YouTube channel

(www.youtube.com/VersaillesSpectacles).

[20] *Mémoires du duc de Luynes sur la cour de Louis XV (1735-1758)*, t.6, p.381-82.

[21] Voltaire to Richelieu, 20 June [1745] (D3152), in Voltaire, *Correspondence and related documents*, vol.9, p.278-80.

[22] Voltaire to Berger, 13 June [1746] (D3417), in Voltaire, *Correspondence and related documents*, vol.10, p.43.

[23] Voltaire, *Le Temple de la Gloire*, in *Œuvres complètes de Voltaire avec des notes et une notice historique sur la vie de Voltaire*, t.1 (Paris: Furne, 1835), p.511.

[24] See *Mémoires du duc de Luynes sur la cour de Louis XV (1735-1758)*, t.7, p.132.

[25] See *Correspondance de Madame de Graffigny*, t.7, p.185; and *Memoirs of Marmontel, Written by Himself*, vol.1, p.191.

[26] See Mme de Graffigny to Devaux, [10 December 1745], in *Correspondance de Madame de Graffigny*. Electronic Enlightenment Scholarly Edition of Correspondence, ed. Robert McNamee et al. Vers. 3.0. University of Oxford. 2022. 'On dit du balet de la *Gloire* que Rameau a fait les vers et Voltaire la musique.'

[27] Marie-Jeanne Fesch, dite Mlle Chevalier (1722-1789). For Rameau, she played Phani-Palla in *Les Indes galantes* (1743), Junon in *Platée* (1745), Stratonice in *Les Fêtes de Polymnie* (1745), Orthésie in *Les Fêtes de l'Hymen et de l'Amour* (1747), Érinice in *Zoroastre* (1749 and 56), Zirphile in *Acante et Céphise* (1751), and Phèdre in *Hippolyte et Aricie* (1757).

[28] *Mercure de France* (May, 1746), p.142.

[29] Diderot, *Le Neveu de Rameau* (Paris: Gallimard, 2005), p.42.

[30] See Jean-Jacques Rousseau (trans. Angela Scholar), *Confessions* (Oxford: Oxford University Press, 2000), p.277.

[31] François-André Danican Philidor (1726-1795). See Diderot, *Le Neveu de Rameau* (Paris: Gallimard, 2005), p.[31]: 'Si le temps est trop froid, ou trop pluvieux, je me réfugie au café de la Régence; là je m'amuse à voir jouer aux échecs… C'est chez Roy que font assaut Légal le profond, Philidor le subtil, le solide Mayot…'

[32] Rousseau (trans. Angela Scholar), *Confessions*, p.324. [In French: Rousseau, *Les Confessions* (Paris: Gallimard, 1995), p.410-12.]

[33] Rameau, *Erreurs sur la musique dans l'Encyclopédie* (1755), p.41-42.

[34] Rousseau (trans. Angela Scholar), *Confessions*, p.325.

[35] The texts of nearly all of Rameau's major works from 1747 onwards were written by Cahusac: *Les Fêtes de l'Hymen et de l'Amour* (1747); *Zaïs* (1748); *Naïs* (1749); *Zoroastre* (1749); *La Naissance d'Osiris* (1754); *Anacréon* (1754); and *Les Boréades* (1762).

[36] *Mercure de France* (September, 1744), p.2066.

[37] Emmanuel Soleville, 'Louis de Cahusac, poète dramatique', in Émerand

Forestié, *Biographie de Tarn-et-Garonne: études historiques et bibliographiques* (Montauban, 1860), p.212.

[38] See Robert Darnton, *A Literary Tour de France*, published Sep 1, 2014, http://www.robertdarnton.org. Joseph d'Hémery kept files on hundreds of authors.

[39] Charles Collé (ed. H. Bonhomme), *Journal et mémoires de Charles Collé sur les hommes de letters, les ouvrages dramatiques et les événements les plus mémorables du règne de Louis XV (1748-1722)*, nouvelle éd., t.2 (Paris: Librairie de Firmin Didot, 1868), p.375.

[40] Robert Darnton, *A Literary Tour de France*, http://www.robertdarnton.org. 'Petit, blond et l'air toujours délabré.'

[41] Mme de Graffigny to Devaux, [11 December 1742], in *Correspondance de Madame de Graffigny*. Electronic Enlightenment Scholarly Edition of Correspondence, ed. Robert McNamee et al. Vers. 3.0. University of Oxford. 2022.

[42] François Boucher (1703-1770) was a member of the Caveau. He designed sets and costumes at the Opéra.

[43] Soleville, 'Louis de Cahusac, poète dramatique', in *Biographie de Tarn-et-Garonne: études historiques et bibliographiques*, p.214-15.

[44] *Mercure de France* (October, 1745), p.136.

[45] Mme de Graffigny to Devaux, [10 October 1745], in *Correspondance de Madame de Graffigny*. Electronic Enlightenment Scholarly Edition of Correspondence, ed. Robert McNamee et al. Vers. 3.0. University of Oxford. 2022.

[46] Mme de Graffigny to Devaux, [15 May 1746], in *Correspondance de Madame de Graffigny*. Electronic Enlightenment Scholarly Edition of Correspondence, ed. Robert McNamee et al. Vers. 3.0. University of Oxford. 2022.

[47] *Mémoires du duc de Luynes sur la cour de Louis XV (1735-1758)*, t.18, p.144-45.

[48] Collé, *Journal et mémoires de Charles Collé*, t.1, p.22.

[49] Raynal, *Nouvelles littéraires* in *Correspondance littéraire, philosophique et critique*, t.1, p.144-45.

[50] See Albert G. Mackey and William R. Singleton, *History of Freemasonry*, pt.4 (The Masonic History Co., 1898), p.1028. The rue des Boucheries and the rue de Buci ran parallel to each other. The rue de Buci survives; the rue des Boucheries was swallowed up by the boulevard Saint-Germain.

[51] Emmanuel Rebold, *Histoire des trois grandes loges de francs-maçons en France* (Paris: Collignon, 1864), p.44.

[52] See Albert G. Mackey and H.L. Haywood, *Encyclopaedia of Freemasonry*, pt.3 (The Masonic History Co., 1909), p.1312.

[53] Charlton, *Opera in the Age of Rousseau: Music, Confrontation, Realism*, p.112.

[54] *Mercure de France* (April, 1751). 'Cet acte, représenté pour la première fois le 27 août 1748, fut demandé par la Direction dans une circonstance pressante, et il fut mis en musique dans mois de huit jours par M. Rameau.'

[55] D'Alembert, 'De la liberté de la musique', in *Melanges de litterature, d'histoire, et de philosophie*, t.4, p.460.

[56] *Mercure de France* (September, 1748), p.222.

[57] *Mercure de France* (December, 1748), p.82. 'Sçavant Rameau, telle est l'illusion que fait sur nous ta divine harmonie; elle charme nos sens, et séduit nos esprits, au point de n'être pas surpris qu'au marbre elle ait donné la vie.'

[58] Friedrich Melchior Grimm, *Lettre de M. Grimm sur Omphale, tragédie lyrique, reprise par l'Académie royale de musique le 14 janvier 1752* (Paris, 1752), p.43-5.

[59] Quoted in Darnton, *Poetry and the Police: Communication Networks in 18th Century Paris*, p.186. 'La folle indécence/De son opera/Où par bienséance/Tout ministre va./Il faut qu'on y vante/Son chant fredonné/Sa voix chevrotante/Son jeu forcené.'

[60] When the work was revived at the Opéra in 1757, the prologue was abandoned, *Adonis* was revised and renamed *L'Enlèvement d'Adonis*, a new *entrée*, *Anacreon*, was added and, later in the run, *La Lyre enchantée* was replaced by a new version of *Les Sibarites*, Rameau and Marmontel's acte de ballet from 1753.

[61] Marc-Pierre de Voyer de Paulmy d'Argenson (1696-1764), minister of state in charge of the Opéra, 1749-57.

[62] Louis de Cahusac, *Zoroastre: opéra représenté pour la première fois par l'Académie royale de musique le 5 décembre 1749 et remis au théâtre le mardi 20 janvier 1756* (Paris, 1756), p.7. 'C'est le premier Opéra représenté sans Prologue. On se récria en 1749 contre cette nouveauté. L'expérience l'a justifiée. Le temps est si précieux au Théâtre lyrique, une grande action exige dans ce local une si grande quantité de moyens, la Poésie, la Peinture, la Machine, la Musique & la Danse doivent y être enchaînées par des mouvements si rapides et si variés, qu'on ne peut y ménager les moments avec trop d'économie, ni en retrancher les superfluités avec trop de sévérité.'

[63] Voltaire, *Œuvres complètes de Voltaire: Essai sur les mœurs et l'esprit des nations*, t.1 (Paris: A.-A. Renouard, 1819), p.47-51.

[64] See Paul Tillit's essay 'Zoroastre (1749) de Rameau: droit et utopies dans un opéra franc-maçon du siècle des Lumières', in *Droit et cultures*, n.52 (2006), p.85-119.

[65] Pierre Clément, 'Lettre XLIV', in *Les Cinq années littéraires, ou Nouvelles littéraires, des années 1748, 1749, 1750, 1751 et 1752*, t.2 (La Haye: Ant. De Groot, 1754), p.16-17.

[66] Friedrich Melchior Grimm, *Correspondance littéraire, philosophique et critique de Grimm et de Diderot, depuis 1753 jusqu'en 1790*, Nouvelle éd., t.1 (Paris: Furne, 1829), p.464. Grimm was writing following the 1756 revival.

⁶⁷ Cahusac, 'Lettre à M. Remond de Sainte Albine', 18 November 1749, in *Mercure de France* (December, 1749), p.202-203. More of the letter: 'Nous le passâmes à la campagne M. Rameau et moi, j'eus pour témoin de mon travail et du sien plusieurs personnes très estimables, avec lesquelles j'ai l'honneur de vivre, et j'aurai pour défenseurs sur cet article tous ceux qui savent discerner la manière, la coupe et le style des auteurs qui travaillent pour le Théâtre Lyrique.'

⁶⁸ Clément, 'Lettre XLV', in *Les Cinq années littéraires, ou Nouvelles littéraires, des années 1748, 1749, 1750, 1751 et 1752*, t.2, p.18-20.

8 PHILOSOPHERS AND FOOLS

¹ Today's lycée Saint-Louis in the boulevard Saint-Michel, a prestigious school preparing students for entry into the *grandes écoles*. It was founded in the 13th century by Robert d'Harcourt as a residence for hard-up university students; it later became a teaching college. Closed down during the Revolution, it was reconstituted as the collège Saint-Louis, specialising in science subjects, in 1820.

² Also known as collège Mazarin after its founder, Cardinal Mazarin. The fine building on the left bank was designed by Louis le Vau, who also designed the south wing of the Cour Carrée across the river. It opened in 1688. The college was closed during the Revolution. Since 1805 the building has housed the Institut de France.

³ Raynal, *Nouvelles littéraires* in *Correspondance littéraire, philosophique et critique*, t.1, p.311-13.

⁴ Diderot to Voltaire, 11 June 1749, in Diderot, *Correspondance générale* (Paris: Garnier, 1875), p.419.

⁵ See Rameau, *Réponse de M. Rameau à MM. les éditeurs de l'Encyclopédie sur leur dernier avertissement* (London: S. Jorry, 1757), p.25.

⁶ Raynal, *Nouvelles littéraires* in *Correspondance littéraire, philosophique et critique*, t.1, p.202.

⁷ Raynal, *Nouvelles littéraires* in *Correspondance littéraire, philosophique et critique*, t.1, p.313.

⁸ Diderot, *Mémoires sur différents sujets de mathématiques* (Paris, 1748), p.77.

⁹ Diderot, *Mémoires sur différents sujets de mathématiques*, p.51-52.

¹⁰ See Christensen, *Rameau and Musical Thought in the Enlightenment*, p.266.

¹¹ The source of this information is Rameau himself. In *Réponse de M. Rameau à MM. les editeurs de l'Encyclopédie sur leur dernier avertissement* (1757) he wrote: 'You could have avoided [these errors] by sending me your manuscripts to examine, as I offered after excusing myself from undertaking all the work.'

¹² [Jean le Rond D'Alembert], 'Discours préliminaire' in *Encyclopédie, ou*

dictionnaire raisonné des sciences, des arts et des métiers, t.1 (Paris, 1751), p.xxxii-xxxiii.

[13] Jean le Rond D'Alembert, *Eléments de musique, théorique et pratique, suivant les principes de M. Rameau* (Paris, 1752), p.[v]. 'From my reading of the excellent treatise in which M. Rameau has explained his art, I have composed this little work, at the request of a few friends who, unversed in music, desired to gain an understanding of the discoveries and principles of this illustrious artist.'

[14] One letter survives, probably dating from the latter half of 1751. See D'Alembert, 'Lettre à M. Rameau', in Rameau (ed. Erwin R. Jacobi), *Jean-Philippe Rameau: Complete Theoretical Writings* (American Institute of Musicology, 1967-72), vol.6, p.233-34.

[15] Girdlestone, *Jean-Philippe Rameau: His Life and Work*, p.493.

[16] Rameau, 'Lettre à l'auteur du Mercure', in *Mercure de France* (May, 1752).

[17] See *Mercure de France* (May, 1751), p.186. 'À la représentation du Mercredi, M. Rameau, qui relevoit d'une longue et dangereuse maladie, parut a l'Opéra dans une des loges du fond. Sa présence excita d'abord dans l'Amphithéâtre un murmure qui se répandit rapidement dans toute l'assemblée. Il partit alors tout à coup un applaudissement universel, et ce qu'on n'avoit point vû encore, l'Orchestre, qui étoit rassemblé, mêla avec transport ses acclamations à celles du Parterre.'

[18] See Girdlestone, *Jean-Philippe Rameau: His Life and Work*, p.483.

[19] François-Joachim de Pierre de Bernis (1715-1794).

[20] Collé, *Journal et mémoires de Charles Collé*, t.1, p.321.

[21] François Rebel and François Francœur, co-inspectors of the Opéra from 1739 to 53, and co-directors from 1757 to 67.

[22] See L. de La Laurencie, 'Quelques documents sur Jean-Philippe Rameau et sa famille', in *Mercure musical et S.I.M.* (June 1907), p.559-60.

[23] Louis-Jules Mancini-Mazarini, duc de Nivernais (1716-1798).

[24] For the latest research see Marie Demeilliez, 'New Light on the Genesis of the Ill-fated Opera *Linus* by La Bruère and Rameau', in Graham Sadler, Shirley Thompson and Jonathan Williams (eds.), *The Operas of Rameau: Genesis, Staging, Reception* (London: Routledge, 2022), p.113-26.

[25] Mme de Villeroy, née Jeanne Louise Constance d'Aumont (1731-1816). Today the Hôtel Villeroy is the home of the Ministry of Agriculture.

[26] See Sadler, *The Rameau Compendium*, p.219.

[27] Étienne François de Choiseul, comte de Stainville (1719-1785).

[28] Joseph de La Porte, *L'Observateur littéraire* (1760). Quoted in Bouissou, *Jean-Philippe Rameau: Musicien des Lumières*, p.809.

[29] Quoted in Bouissou, *Jean-Philippe Rameau: Musicien des Lumières*, p.809. 'Qui sait si ces prétendus défauts n'étaient pas des beautés particulières auxquelles Rameau était attaché, et si les importuns qui vouliaent les lui faire

changer, ne l'ont pas déterminé à suprimer l'opéra entier? Il était homme à faire de pareils sacrifices.'

[30] See Girdlestone, *Jean-Philippe Rameau: His Life and Work*, p.308-309.

[31] Grimm, *Correspondance littéraire, philosophique et critique*, t.2 (Paris: Garnier, 1877), p.46.

[32] Pierre Louis d'Aquin de Château-Lyon, *Siècle littéraire de Louis XV, ou Lettres sur les homes célèbres* (Amsterdam: Duchesne, 1754), p.75-6.

[33] Marmontel, *Mémoires de Marmontel*, t.1, p.274.

[34] *Mercure de France* (December, 1751), p.163.

[35] Diderot, *Mémoires sur différents sujets de mathématiques*, p.1-2.

[36] For a detailed analysis see Béatrice Durant-Sendrail's essay 'Diderot et Rameau: archéologie d'une polémique', in *Diderot Studies*, vol.24 (1991), p.85-104.

[37] Diderot, *Le Neveu de Rameau* (Paris: Gallimard, 2005), p.103.

[38] D'Alembert, *De la liberté de la musique*, quoted in Enrico Fubini, *Music and Culture in Eighteenth-Century Europe: a Source Book*, p.87.

[39] Théodore Lajarte (ed.), *Bibliothèque musicale du Théâtre de l'Opéra: catalogue historique, chronologique, anecdotique*, t.1 (Paris: Librairie des Bibliophiles, 1878), p.228. 'Lefebvre, le copiste de l'Académie, a réorchestré cette version, et y a ajouté des cors et des clarinettes, tout en respectant, autant que possible, l'instrumentation naïve de J.J. Rouseau.'

[40] The 'querelle des bouffons' was also known as the 'guerre des coins'.

[41] Grimm, *Correspondance littéraire, philosophique et critique de Grimm et de Diderot, depuis 1753 jusqu'en 1790*, Nouvelle éd., t.1 (Paris: Furne, 1829), p.48.

[42] See Georges Cucuel, *La Pouplinière et la musique de chambre au XVIIIe siècle*, p.302-303.

[43] Rameau, *Code de musique pratique*, p.xvi. Quoted in Girdlestone, *Rameau: His Life and Work*, p.502.

[44] Quoted in Robert Darnton, *The Devil in the Holy Water* (Philadelphia: University of Pennsylvania Press, 2010), p.97.

[45] See Simon Schama, *Citizens: a Chronicle of the French Revolution* (London: Penguin Books, 1989), p.96-103, 822-27.

[46] See Schama, *Citizens: a Chronicle of the French Revolution*, p.99.

[47] *Le petit prophète de Boehmischbroda* ([Paris], 1753).

[48] Diderot, *Au petit prophète de Boehmischbroda au grand prophète Monet* (Paris, 1753).

[49] D'Alembert, *De la liberté de la musique*, quoted in Enrico Fubini, *Music and Culture in Eighteenth-Century Europe: a Source Book*, p.85.

[50] D'Alembert, 'De la liberté de la musique', in *Melanges de litterature, d'histoire, et de philosophie*, t.4, p.391.

[51] See Rousseau (trans. Angela Scholar), *Confessions*, p.377.

[52] Rousseau, *Lettre sur la musique française* (1753), p.3.

[53] Quoted in Philipp Blom, *Encyclopédie: the Triumph of Reason in an Unreasonable Age* (London: Fourth Estate), p.123.
[54] See *The Diary of David Garrick, Being a Record of His Memorable Trip to Paris in 1751*, p.30.
[55] Quoted in Girdlestone, *Jean-Philippe Rameau: His Life and Work*, p.207.
[56] Rousseau, *Lettre sur la musique française*, p.28-29.
[57] Rousseau, *Lettre sur la musique française*, p.79.
[58] See Rousseau (trans. Angela Scholar), *Confessions*, p.375.
[59] Rameau, *Observations sur notre instinct pour la musique, et sur son principe*, p.vi, p.1-2.
[60] Alexandre Deleyre to Rousseau, 25 January 1758, in Rousseau, *Correspondance complète de Jean Jacques Rousseau: 1758*, ed. R.A. Leigh (Geneva: Institut et Musée Voltaire, 1969), vol.5, p.25.
[61] For a detailed analysis of Rameau's relationship with d'Alembert, see Jonathan W. Bernard, 'The Principle and the Elements: Rameau's Controversy With d'Alembert', in *Journal of Music Theory*, vol.24/1 (1980), p.37-62.
[62] Rameau, *Réponse de M. Rameau à MM. les éditeurs de l'Encyclopédie sur leur dernier avertissement*, p.25-26.
[63] D'Alembert, 'Extrait des registres de l'Académie Royale des Sciences, du 10 décembre 1749', in Rameau, *Démonstration du principe de l'harmonie*, p.xlv-xlvi.
[64] D'Alembert, *Eléments de musique, théorique et pratique, suivant les principes de M. Rameau*, Nouvelle ed. (Lyon, 1762), p.vii.
[65] Bernard, 'The Principle and the Elements: Rameau's Controversy With d'Alembert', in *Journal of Music Theory*, vol.24/1 (1980), p.54.
[66] D'Alembert, *Eléments de musique, théorique et pratique, suivant les principes de M. Rameau*, Nouvelle ed., p.231.
[67] Voltaire to Thieriot, 22 December 1760 (D9489), in Voltaire, *Correspondence and related documents*, vol.22, p.399-400.
[68] Voltaire to Etienne Damilaville, 6 April 1761 (D9726), in Voltaire, *Correspondence and related documents*, vol.23, p.147-48.
[69] D'Alembert, 'De la liberté de la musique', in *Melanges de litterature, d'histoire, et de philosophie*, t.4, p.388. 'Rameau est d'autant plus digne d'estime, qu'il a osé tout ce qu'il a pu, et non tout ce qu'il aurait voulu oser; il a eu le mérite de voir au-delà du terme où il a conduit ses auditeurs, et le mérite peut-être aussi grand, de juger jusqu'où ils pouvaient être conduits. Il eût manqué son but en allant plus loin; il nous a donné, non la meilleure musique dont il fût capable, mais la meilleure que nous pussions recevoir. Ce n'est pas seulement par leurs ouvrages qu'il faut mesurer les hommes, c'est en les comparant à leur siècle et à leur nation.'
[70] Diderot, *Œuvres complètes de Diderot: revues sur les éditions originales*, t.7 (Paris: Garnier, 1875), p.136.
[71] Diderot, *Œuvres complètes de Diderot*, t.7, p.156-57.

⁷² Diderot, *Œuvres complètes de Diderot*, t.7, p.163.
⁷³ Diderot (trans. Leonard Tancock), *Rameau's Nephew*, p.35-6.
⁷⁴ Diderot (trans. Leonard Tancock), *Rameau's Nephew*, p.37-8.
⁷⁵ Diderot (trans. Leonard Tancock), *Rameau's Nephew*, p.40.
⁷⁶ Maret, *Éloge historique de Mr. Rameau*, p.36.
⁷⁷ Quoted in Beaussant (ed.), *Rameau de A à Z*, p.286.
⁷⁸ See André Magnan, *Rameau le neveu: texts et documents* (Paris: CNRS, 1993), p.45-47.
⁷⁹ Magnan, *Rameau le neveu*, p.57-58.
⁸⁰ Jacques Cazotte, *Observations sur la lettre de Jean-Jacques Rousseau au sujet de la musique française* (1753), quoted in *Rameau de A à Z*, p.90. Jacques Cazotte (1719-92) was born in Dijon. An admirable figure, he remained true to his faith and his values and was guillotined during the Terror.
⁸¹ Letter to Jacques Cazotte, in Gunnar von Proschwitz (ed.), *Alexis Piron, épistolier: choix de ses lettres*, p.186-87.
⁸² See Girdlestone, *Jean-Philippe Rameau: His Life and Work*, p.510-11.
⁸³ Quoted in Girdlestone, *Jean-Philippe Rameau: His Life and Work*, p.507.
⁸⁴ The *acte d'ingression*, dated 22 August 1751, is included in L. de La Laurencie, 'Quelques documents sur Jean-Philippe Rameau et sa famille', in *Mercure musical et S.I.M.* (June 1907), p.526.
⁸⁵ See Girdlestone, *Jean-Philippe Rameau: His Life and Work*, p.507-508.
⁸⁶ *Dupuis et Desronais*, a hit at the Comédie-Française.
⁸⁷ Collé, *Journal et mémoires de Charles Collé*, t.2, p.375.

9 THE PART-TIME COMPOSER

¹ See Paul F. Rice, 'The Fontainebleau Operas of Jean-Philippe Rameau', in *The Journal of Musicology*, vol.6, n.2 (Spring 1988), p.227-244.
² Collé, *Journal et mémoires de Charles Collé*, t.2, p.375.
³ See Charlton, *Opera in the Age of Rousseau*, p.24.
⁴ Marmontel, *Mémoires de Marmontel*, t.1, p.273.
⁵ *Mémoires de Marmontel*, t.1, p.275.
⁶ See Jean-Benjamin de La Borde, *Essai sur la musique ancienne et moderne*, t.3 (Paris: P.D. Pierres, 1780), p.465. 'Les musiciens du roi et ceux de l'Académie royale de musique qui se regardaient tous comme ses enfants.'
⁷ Élie Fréron, *L'Année littéraire: année 1754*, t.2 (Amsterdam, 1754), p.45-49.
⁸ La Borde, *Essai sur la musique ancienne et moderne*, t.3, p.465.
⁹ See Charlton, *Opera in the Age of Rousseau*, chapter 11.
¹⁰ See *Mémoires du duc de Luynes sur la cour de Louis XV (1735-1758)*, t.13, p.375.
¹¹ *Mémoires du duc de Luynes sur la cour de Louis XV*, t.13, p.381.
¹² See Graham Sadler, 'A cluster of allusions to Vivaldi's *Le quattro stagioni*

in Rameau's *Anacréon* (1757)' in *The Operas of Rameau*, p.129-40.

[13] *Mercure de France* (August, 1757), p.187.

[14] *Mercure de France* (October, 1758), p.181.

[15] See Bouissou, *Jean-Philippe Rameau*, p.815-17.

[16] Nicolas Gélin (1726-1810) had previously played Oromasès in *Zoroastre* (1749) and the title role in *Anacréon* (1757).

[17] Jeanne Lemière (1733-1786).

[18] Sophie Arnould (1740-1802) went on to sing Iphise in *Dardanus* (1760), Télaïre in *Castor et Pollux* (1763) and Iphise in *Les Fêtes d'Hébé* (1764). She would have played Alphise in *Les Boréades* had the opera not been withdrawn.

10 THE SOLITARY WALKER

[1] Rameau to Ducharger, 13 June 1754. Quoted in Girdlestone, *Jean-Philippe Rameau: His Life and Work*, p.496.

[2] La Borde, *Essai sur la musique ancienne et moderne*, t.3, p.377.

[3] Diderot, *Le Neveu de Rameau*, p.34.

[4] Chabanon, *Éloge de M. Rameau*, p.53-54.

[5] Maret, *Éloge historique de Mr. Rameau*, p.71-72.

[6] Authorship cannot be definitively stated; however, the themes and style of the text clearly suggest Cahusac. Decroix, who rescued the work for posterity, stated that the libretto was by Cahusac.

[7] See François-Antoine Chevrier, *Le Colporteur, histoire morale et critique* (La Haye, 1761). 'Elle rendit fou le tendre Cahusac qui vient de mourir dans les loges de Charenton.'

[8] John Eliot Gardiner, in the sleeve notes accompanying his recording of *Les Boréades* (Erato, 1990), p.35.

[9] When John Eliot Gardiner mounted the first production of *Les Boréades*, in 1982, it was thought that the piece dated from 1764, and was in rehearsal at the Opéra at the time of Rameau's death in September of that year. An analysis of relevant documents by Sylvie Bouissou showed that the piece was in fact delivered and rehearsed in the spring of 1763. See Sylvie Bouissou, 'Les Boréades de J.-Ph. Rameau: un passé retrouvé', in *Revue de Musicologie*, t.69, n.2 (1983), p.[157]-85.

[10] Gardiner, in the sleeve notes accompanying his recording of *Les Boréades*, p.35.

[11] Diderot's summation of Rameau's ideas, as expressed in *Le Neveu de Rameau*.

[12] Christensen, *Rameau and Musical Thought in the Enlightenment*, p.306.

[13] For a detailed analysis of the Bordeaux score and parts, see Lionel Sawkins, 'Rameau's Last Years: Some Implications of Re-Discovered Material at Bordeaux', in *Proceedings of the Royal Musical Association*, vol.111 (1984/85), p.66-91.

[14] Voltaire to Richelieu, 4 September 1769 (D15872), in Voltaire, *Correspondence and related documents*, vol.35, p.211-12.
[15] See *Mercure de France* (January, 1764).
[16] Carlo Goldoni (trans. John Black), *Memoirs of Goldoni, Written by Himself*, vol.2, p.119.
[17] *Memoirs of Goldoni*, p.119-20.
[18] *Memoirs of Goldoni*, p.109.
[19] *Memoirs of Goldoni*, p.109.
[20] The information on Rameau's apartment, assets and possessions is taken from legal documents drawn up after his death. See L. de La Laurencie, 'Quelques documents sur Jean-Philippe Rameau et sa famille', in *Mercure musical et S.I.M.* (June 1907), p.579-99.
[21] See David Charlton and Sarah Hibberd, 'My Father Was a Poor Parisian Musician: a Memoir (1756) concerning Rameau, Handel's Library and Sallé', in the *Journal of the Royal Musical Association*, vol.128, n.2 (2003), p.197.
[22] See L. de La Laurencie, 'Quelques documents sur Jean-Philippe Rameau et sa famille', p.564. Chiquelier, *Garde des Instruments de la Musique du Roi*, was the court official in charge of musical instruments.
[23] Friedrich Melchior Grimm, *Correspondance littéraire, philosophique et critique de Grimm et de Diderot depuis 1753 jusqu'en 1790*, Nouvelle éd., t.4 (Paris: Furne, 1829), p.83.
[24] Louis Petit de Bachaumont, *Mémoires secrets de Bachaumont, de 1762 à 1787*, t.1, p.315. 'Rameau [...] est mort aujourd'hui d'une fièvre putride, accompagnée de scorbut. [...] Le roi lui avait accordé des lettres de noblesse pour le mettre en état d'être reçu chevalier de Saint-Michel; mais il était si avare qu'il n'avait pas voulu les faire enregistrer, et se constituer en une dépense qui lui tenait plus à cœur que la noblesse. Il est mort avec fermeté. Différens prêtres n'ayant pu en rien tirer, M. le curé de Saint-Eustache s'y est présenté, a péroré long-temps, au point que le malade ennuyé s'est écrié avec fureur: "Quel diable venez-vous me chanter là, M. le curé? Vous avez la voix fausse".'
[25] See L. de La Laurencie, 'Quelques documents sur Jean-Philippe Rameau et sa famille', in *Mercure musical et S.I.M.* (June 1907), p.574-75.
[26] Voltaire to Claude Germain Le Clerc de Montmerci, 8 October 1764 (D12130), in Voltaire, *Correspondence and related documents*, vol.28, p.151-52.

EPILOGUE

[1] See Eyre Massey Shaw, *Fires in Theatres* (London: Spon, 1876), p.31-40.
[2] *Dwight's Journal of Music*, vol.18, n.25 (23 March, 1861), p.409.
[3] See Sadler, 'A Letter from Claude-François Rameau to J.J.M. Decroix', in *Music and Letters*, vol.59, n.2 (April 1978), p.139-147.

[4] Claude-François Rameau to Decroix, 27 July 1777, quoted in Sadler, 'A Letter from Claude-François Rameau to J.J.M. Decroix', in *Music and Letters*, vol.59, n.2 (April 1978), p.141-143.

Index

Absence, L'
  (Rameau), 34, 272, 286, 291
Académie des Sciences, Belles-Lettres
  et Arts, Lyon, 30
Académie Royale de Musique, Paris,
  15, 16, 42, 64, 209, 255
Académie Royale des Sciences, Paris,
  163, 191, 194, 263, 353
Acante et Céphise
  (Rameau), 201, 203, 204, 234,
  242, 244, 278, 288, 290, 309,
  345, 347
Accademia delle Scienze, Bologna, 260
Adam, Adolphe, 141
Ages, Les
  (Campra), 93
Aix-en-Provence Festival, 17, 18, 256,
  294, 295, 296, 298, 301, 306,
  307, 311, 312
Aldeburgh Festival, 240
Alembert, Jean le Rond d', 13, 14, 21,
  87, 106, 110, 139, 168, 176, 177,
  190, 191, 192, 193, 195, 196,
  197, 198, 199, 200, 207, 211,
  212, 214, 218, 219, 220, 221,
  222, 223, 227, 249, 250, 263,
  273, 276, 277, 278, 279, 283,
  284, 285, 339, 349, 350, 351,
  352, 353
Alexander, Ninon, 17
Algérien, L'
  (Cahusac), 166
Amants trahis, Les
  (Rameau), 34, 35, 204, 272, 287,
  291
Ambassadeurs-La Grande Écurie, Les,
  204

Amours de Tempé, Les
  (Dauvergne), 209
Amours déguises, Les
  (Bourgeois), 177
Anacréon
  (1754) (Rameau), 239
  (1757) (Rameau), 242, 243
Andrésy, 265
Année littéraire
  (Fréron), 229, 237, 354
Anquetil-Duperron, Abraham, 184
Antier, Marie, 55, 85, 99, 117, 294,
  296, 297
Aquilon et Orithie
  (Rameau), 17, 34, 48, 49, 272,
  286, 291
Arcadia in Brenta, L'
  (Galuppi), 261
Argenson, Marc-Pierre de Voyer de
  Paulmy d', 182, 193, 200
Argenson, René Louis de Voyer de
  Paulmy d', 144
Argental, Charles-Augustin de Ferriol
  d', 91, 146, 147
Ariosto, Ludovico, 244
Arlequin Deucalion
  (Piron), 45
Armide
  (Lully), 30, 65, 217, 218, 270
Arnould, Sophie, 247, 248, 300, 310,
  355
Arts Florissants, Les, 18
*Au petit prophète de Boehmischbroda au
  prophète Monet*
  (Diderot), 213
Aubert, Pauline, 17
Aumont, duc d', 167

Autreau, Jacques, 150, 301, 346
Aved, Joseph, 42
Avignon, 26, 271
Bach, Johann Sebastian, 46, 96, 114,
    270, 271, 272, 273, 274, 275,
    276, 277, 278, 294, 298, 301,
    302, 307, 332
Bachaumont, Louis Petit de, 120,
    262, 343, 356
Bacon, Francis, 211
Ballet figuré, 99, 168, 180, 181, 242
Ballet héroïque, 95, 156, 168, 171
Ballot de Sauvot, 175, 210, 305
Ballot, Silvain, 140
Bambini, Eustachio, 207
Barenboim, Daniel, 142
Bastille, 61, 193
Beaux jours de l'Amour, Les, 240
Berger fidèle, Le
    (Rameau), 49
Berger, François, 126, 133, 158, 274,
    287, 291, 310, 344, 347
Bergiron de Briou, Nicolas-Antoine,
    31
Berlioz, Hector, 113, 342
Bernage, Louis-Bastide de, 182, 201
Bernard, Jonathan W., 222
Bernard, Pierre-Joseph-Justin, 111,
    112, 115, 117, 118, 119, 120,
    179, 236, 242, 244, 297, 306, 353
Bernis, François-Joachim de Pierre,
    abbé de, 200, 202
Bibliothèque Nationale, 50, 256
Bijoux indiscrets, Les
    (Diderot), 101, 191, 277, 341
Boismortier, Joseph Bodin de, 126
Borciani, Paolo, 17
Bordeaux, 258, 259, 272, 280, 296,
    297, 299, 301, 337, 355
Bordes, Charles, 17
Boréades, Les
    (Rameau), 15, 58, 61, 140, 175,
    249, 250, 252, 255, 256, 280,
    289, 311, 347, 355
Boucher, François, 168, 348
Boucon, Anne-Jeanne, 136
Bouissou, Sylvie, 13, 25, 204, 331,
    332, 333, 338, 343, 345, 355
Boulanger, Nadia, 17

Boulez, Pierre, 18
Bourbon, Louise Françoise de, 121
Bourbon-Condé, Louis Henri de, 59,
    121, 273
Boutinon des Hayes, Thérèse, 53, 92,
    108, 139, 140, 141, 179, 252,
    254, 336
Brasseur, Elisabeth, 18
Britten, Benjamin, 130, 240
Brossard, Sébastien de, 38
Buffoni, The, 207
Bureau de la ville de Paris, 182, 183
Burney, Charles, 86, 110, 339, 342
Cadmus et Hermione
    (Lully), 65
Caens, Thierry, 19
Café de la Regence, 225
Café Procope, 52, 102
Caffarelli, 210, 214
Cahusac, Louis de, 94, 99, 118, 157,
    166, 167, 168, 171, 172, 173,
    180, 183, 184, 186, 187, 188,
    233, 239, 240, 242, 252, 255,
    304, 305, 306, 307, 308, 310,
    311, 347, 348, 349, 350, 355
Camargo, Marie-Anne Cupis de, 75,
    76, 125, 136, 148, 173, 271, 299,
    301, 338
Cambert, Robert, 64
Campanini, Barbara, 125
Campion, François, 50, 281
Campra, André, 28, 34, 48, 65, 74,
    87, 93, 94, 200, 270, 271, 272,
    273, 276, 346
Canal du Midi, 138
Candeille, Pierre, 265
Candide
    (Voltaire), 58, 279, 336
Canente
    (Dauvergne), 241
*Cantates françoises à voix seule avec
    symphonie, livre premier*
    (Rameau), 49
Capua, Rinaldo di, 209, 210
Carignan, Victor Amédée, prince de,
    55, 73, 126, 336, 337
Cariselli, 102, 150
Cartaud de La Vilate, François, 101
Casadesus, Robert, 17

Casanova, Giacomo, 69, 70, 74, 75, 143, 337, 338
Castel, Louis-Bertrand, 41, 108, 109, 110, 163, 194, 282, 334
Castor et Pollux
  (Rameau), 19, 93, 103, 105, 111, 113, 114, 117, 118, 119, 128, 129, 174, 179, 228, 235, 236, 237, 238, 241, 250, 252, 261, 263, 264, 275, 278, 280, 287, 289, 297, 331, 340, 342, 355
Caveau club, 51, 52, 93, 112, 126, 174, 233, 348
Cazotte, Jacques, 228, 354
Centre de musique baroque de Versailles, 204
Chabanon, Guy de, 21, 26, 42, 93, 250, 260, 331, 332, 334, 340, 355
Chaconne, 92, 97, 98, 123, 131, 132, 155, 162, 181, 206, 263
Chapelle Royale, Versailles, 31, 32
Charenton asylum, 252
Charlemagne, 244
Charpentier, Marc-Antoine, 28, 31, 65, 270, 271, 332
Chassé de Chinais, Claude Louis Dominique de, 85, 99, 117, 186, 237, 239, 247, 271, 294, 296, 297, 299, 300, 301, 304, 307, 309, 310, 339
Château de Passy
  (Paris), 139
Châtelet, Émilie du, 91, 92, 340
Chevalier, Marie-Jeanne, 150, 159, 186, 294, 297, 301, 304, 306, 307, 309, 347
Chevrier, François-Antoine, 252
Chinon, 137
Chiquelier, Christophe, 262, 356
Chœur du Conservatoire
  (Paris), 18
Christensen, Thomas, 50, 104, 196, 257, 334, 335, 341, 342, 350
Christiansen, Rupert, 19, 331
Christie, William, 18, 19, 294, 295, 296, 297, 298, 302, 306, 309, 310, 311
Christin, Jean-Pierre, 31, 333
Chromaticism, 15, 33, 105, 113, 132

Clément, Pierre, 186, 188, 189, 302, 349, 350
Clermont-Ferrand, 27, 34, 271
Cocchi, Gioacchino, 209, 210
Code de musique pratique
  (Rameau), 211, 221, 279, 283, 341, 342, 352
Collé, Charles, 51, 52, 166, 171, 178, 200, 201, 230, 233, 234, 309, 348, 351, 354
Collège des Godrans, Dijon, 25
Collège Mazarin, Paris, 192
Collet, Jean, 27
Comédie-Française, 44, 45, 48, 52, 77, 88, 92, 93, 126, 150, 166, 233, 272, 274, 275, 336, 354
Comparaison de la musique italienne et de la musique française
  (Le Cerf de La Viéville), 207
Compendium Musicae
  (Descartes), 38, 334
Comte de Warwick, Le
  (Cahusac), 166
Concert Spirituel, Paris, 32, 49, 202, 305, 306
Confessions
  (Rousseau), 163, 187, 230, 342, 347, 352, 353
Contes moraux
  (Marmontel), 235
Corelli, Arcangelo, 134, 206, 272, 332
Corps sonore, 104, 221, 222, 223, 257
Correspondance littéraire, 210, 343, 348, 349, 350, 352, 356
Cosi Fan Tutte
  (Mozart), 247
Courses de Tempé, Les
  (Rameau), 90
Crébillon, Claude Prosper Jolyot de, 51, 52, 141
Curnyn, Christian, 19, 298
Da Ponte, Lorenzo, 210, 261
Danchet, Antoine, 94
Dancourt, Manon, 139
Danse ancienne et moderne, La
  (Cahusac), 168
Daphnis et Eglé
  (Rameau), 232, 233, 309, 310
Daquin, Louis-Claude, 46, 249

Dardanus
   (Rameau), 16, 73, 119, 120, 126,
      127, 128, 129, 130, 131, 132,
      133, 134, 162, 174, 201, 250,
      264, 276, 287, 289, 300, 335,
      355
Dauvergne, Antoine, 209, 241
David, Jacques-Louis, 138
De la liberté de la musique
   (D'Alembert), 14, 214, 223, 279,
      339, 349, 352, 353
Debussy, Claude, 17, 114, 342
Decroix, Jacques Joseph Marie, 29,
   34, 244, 256, 265, 333, 355
Delalande, Michel-Richard, 28, 32
Deleyre, Alexandre, 219, 353
Demartinécourt, Claudine, 23, 332
Démonstration du principe de
   l'harmonie, 195, 333
   (Rameau), 41, 55, 105, 106, 107,
      198, 222, 277, 283, 341
Descartes, René, 38, 197, 334
Desfontaines, Pierre, 100, 107, 108
Destouches, André Cardinal, 48, 77,
   177, 183, 200, 272, 277, 341, 346
Deus noster refugium
   (Rameau), 31, 32, 272, 291
Devieilhe, Sabine, 346
Devin du village
   (Rousseau), 209, 215, 217
Diderot, Denis, 13, 20, 21, 28, 40,
   41, 61, 101, 163, 168, 190, 191,
   192, 193, 194, 195, 196, 200,
   206, 207, 211, 212, 213, 214,
   215, 220, 223, 225, 227, 229,
   230, 249, 262, 263, 272, 276,
   277, 278, 279, 334, 337, 341,
   347, 349, 350, 352, 355, 356
Dijon, 19, 23, 26, 27, 30, 33, 36,
   227, 228, 229, 249, 252, 270,
   271, 296, 300, 332, 334, 354
Dissertation sur les différentes méthodes
   d'accompagnement pour le clavecin
   ou pour l'orgue
   (Rameau), 51, 134, 274, 282
Divertissement, 45, 64, 82, 83, 94,
   112, 115, 116, 122, 123, 124,
   131, 132, 146, 147, 149, 153,
   154, 156, 177, 180, 185, 234,
   243, 253, 256, 258, 295
Don Carlo
   (Verdi), 113
Du Cerceau, Jean-Antoine, 135
Du contrat social
   (Rousseau), 279
Du Mont, Henry, 31
Dubois, Guillaume, 59
Dubois, Marie-Rose, 136
Dubos, Jean-Baptiste, 14
Dubuisson, Simon Henri, 119, 343
Duplat de Monticourt, Pierre-Jacques,
   244, 310
Dupré, Louis, 75, 76, 99, 131, 338
Dupuis et Desronais
   (Collé), 230, 233, 354
Dussurget, Gabriel, 17, 18, 19
École des maris, L'
   (Molière), 244
Eléments de musique, théorique et
   pratique, suivant les principes de M.
   Rameau
   (D'Alembert), 195, 197, 222, 278,
      351, 353
Éloge historique de Mr. Rameau
   (Maret), 53, 332, 333, 335, 338,
      339, 354, 355
Émile
   (Rousseau), 230
Encyclopédie
   (Diderot and d'Alembert), 21,
      168, 190, 192, 193, 196, 206,
      207, 211, 212, 213, 218, 219,
      220, 221, 235, 241, 277, 278,
      279, 283, 343, 347, 350, 353
Endriague, L'
   (Rameau), 44, 45, 124, 273, 287,
      290, 293
Énée et Lavinie
   (Dauvergne), 241
Enfant prodigue, L'
   (Voltaire), 92
English Bach Festival, 18
English Baroque Soloists, 18
English National Opera, 19
English Suites
   (Bach), 272
English Touring Opera, 20, 300
Enharmony, 47, 48, 74, 132, 344

Enrôlement d'Arlequin, L'
   (Rameau), 45, 274, 287, 290, 293
Entretiens sur Le Fils naturel
   (Diderot), 224
Érigone
   (Mondonville), 201
Erlo, Louis, 18, 19
Ernelinde
   (Philidor), 263
Erreurs sur la musique dans l'Encyclopédie
   (Rameau), 219
Essai sur les moeurs et l'esprit des nations
   (Voltaire), 184, 349
Euripides, 77
Europe galante, L'
   (Campra), 48, 94, 270
Examen de la conférence sur la musique
   (Rameau), 50, 281, 335
Fagon, Louis, 91
Fajon, Robert, 204
Faramondo
   (Handel), 210
Fauré, Gabriel, 35
Fel, Marie, 69, 148, 154, 167, 169, 172, 186, 187, 233, 237, 239, 247, 252, 272, 337
Fêtes d'Hébé, Les
   (Rameau), 49, 118, 119, 120, 121, 123, 125, 126, 131, 264, 275, 287, 289, 298, 343, 344, 355
Fêtes de l'été, Les
   (Montéclair), 177
Fêtes de l'Hymen et de l'Amour, Les
   (Rameau), 169, 171, 172, 200, 277, 288, 290, 304, 347
Fêtes de Polymnie, Les
   (Rameau), 57, 157, 168, 169, 276, 288, 289, 347
Fêtes de Ramire, Les
   (Rameau), 165, 276, 288, 290, 304
Fêtes vénitiennes, Les
   (Campra), 74, 94, 272, 346
filosofo di campagna, Il
   (Galuppi), 261
Fils ingrats, Les
   (Piron), 45
Fils naturel, Le
   (Diderot), 224
Fleury, André-Hercule de, 59, 91, 108, 121, 145, 173, 174, 273, 276
Fontainebleau, 215, 232, 233, 234, 235, 239, 240, 242, 250, 258, 278, 297, 304, 308, 309, 310, 354
Fontenoy (battle), 57, 157, 168, 276
For-l'Evêque, 227
Forqueray, Antoine, 136
Forqueray, Jean-Baptiste, 136
Four Seasons, The
   (Vivaldi), 243, 273
Francoeur, François, 183, 201, 203, 227, 228, 263, 278
Freemasons, 21, 118, 129, 172, 173, 174, 184, 187, 252, 254, 348
French Suites
   (Bach), 273
Frère Jacques, 19
Fréron, Élie Catherine, 229, 237, 354
Fundamental bass, 35, 39, 45, 49, 50, 105, 197, 198, 206, 217, 223
Fuzelier, Louis, 93, 95, 97, 98, 177, 296
Gardiner, John Eliot, 18, 19, 255, 256, 294, 311, 355
Garrick, David, 99, 216
Gaultier, François-Marie de, 202, 230, 259
Gaussin, Mlle, 167
Gazettes à la main, 103
Gedda, Nicolai, 18
Gedoyn, Nicolas, 151
Gélin, Nicolas, 247, 300, 307, 309, 310, 355
Gemeaux, 23, 25
Génération harmonique, La
   (Rameau), 41, 103, 104, 105, 106, 107, 108, 109, 198, 275, 282, 338, 341
Génies tutélaires, Les
   (Rebel and Francoeur), 203
George II, 180, 182, 274, 279
Gilles, Jean, 26, 263
Giovannetti, Julien, 17
Girdlestone, Cuthbert, 13, 50, 121, 127, 132, 198, 202, 230, 334, 335, 336, 340, 343, 344, 351, 352, 354, 355

Gluck, Christoph Willibald, 113, 263, 264, 272, 279
Glyndebourne Festival, 20, 85, 295
Goldoni, Carlo, 75, 216, 260, 261, 277, 278, 338, 356
Gossett, Philip, 40, 333, 334
Graffigny, Françoise de, 73, 120, 123, 125, 131, 167, 169, 337, 338, 343, 344, 347, 348
Grenier, Jean-Pierre, 18
Grenoble, 111, 302, 312
Grigri
 (Cahusac), 168
Grimm, Friedrich Melchior, 177, 187, 203, 210, 213, 215, 225, 262, 278, 343, 349, 352, 356
Guignon, Jean-Pierre, 142
Guimard, Marie-Madeleine, 264
Guirlande, La
 (Rameau), 141, 201, 203, 234, 277, 288, 290, 308, 345
Gulliver's Travels
 (Swift), 107, 274
Haïm, Emmanuelle, 19
Handel, George Frideric, 47, 123, 148, 182, 210, 262, 270, 271, 272, 273, 274, 275, 276, 277, 278, 279, 332, 356
Hardion, Jacques, 92, 340
Hardouin-Mansart, Jules, 148
Harmony, 15, 32, 33, 35, 38, 39, 40, 48, 49, 79, 82, 87, 97, 98, 100, 101, 104, 123, 124, 128, 132, 155, 163, 170, 173, 176, 177, 181, 194, 197, 198, 206, 208, 218, 221, 222, 234
Hasse, Johann Adolph, 189
Haydn, Joseph, 127, 274, 278, 279
Hémery, Joseph d', 166, 195, 348
Hénault, Charles-Jean-François, 147, 346
Henry IV, 252
Hérault, René, 173
Hippolyte et Aricie
 (Rameau), 18, 19, 53, 55, 60, 72, 74, 76, 78, 85, 87, 88, 89, 117, 118, 131, 133, 217, 225, 242, 264, 275, 287, 288, 289, 294, 335, 347

Historia religionis veterum Persarum (Hyde), 184
Houdar de la Motte, Antoine, 34, 48, 94, 98, 175, 176, 177, 272, 305
Huc-Santana, André, 18
Hyde, Thomas, 184
I Viaggiatori
 (Leo), 238
Idomeneo
 (Mozart), 113, 251
Impatience, L'
 (Rameau), 34, 272, 286, 291
In convertendo
 (Rameau), 31, 32, 202, 254, 272, 277, 286, 291
Indes galantes, Les
 (Rameau), 19, 47, 58, 76, 92, 93, 95, 100, 203, 239, 275, 287, 289, 296, 335, 347
Iphigénie
 (Racine), 225
Isis
 (Lully), 30, 171
Jansenism, 190, 191, 192, 272
Jélyotte, Pierre de, 74, 99, 131, 148, 153, 186, 233, 237, 239, 247, 272, 294, 296, 297, 299, 300, 301, 304, 305, 307, 308, 309, 337, 338
Jephté
 (Montéclair), 50, 53, 88, 274
Jesuits, 25, 190, 211, 212
Journal de Trévoux, 41, 108, 262, 282, 334, 342
Kent, Jonathan, 85, 295
Kosky, Barrie, 19, 298
Kossenko, Alexis, 204
La Borde, Jean-Benjamin de, 135, 236, 238, 249, 260, 354, 355
La Fontaine, Jean de, 244
La Pouplinière, Alexandre-Jean-Joseph Le Riche de, 21, 52, 53, 55, 59, 92, 108, 110, 112, 118, 119, 133, 136, 137, 138, 139, 140, 141, 142, 143, 144, 147, 148, 150, 163, 176, 179, 180, 203, 210, 214, 215, 219, 252, 255, 262, 275, 278, 335, 344, 345, 352
Laballe, Mélanie, 167

Lalandi, Lina, 18, 19
Lancret, Nicolas, 168, 176
Landelle, Nicolas-Alexis, 52, 174
Lany, Louise-Madeleine, 140, 337, 345
Latilla, Gaetano, 209, 210
Laujon, Pierre, 52, 335
Lavoisier, Antoine-Laurent, 138, 259, 345
Le Cerf de La Viéville, Jean-Laurent, 65, 207
Le Maure, Catherine-Nicole, 49, 294, 300, 335
Le Valois d'Orville, Adrien-Joseph, 150
Leclerc de La Bruère, Charles-Antoine, 126, 127, 129, 130, 131, 201
Lemière, Marie-Jeanne, 247
Lennon, John, 98
Letters Concerning the English Nation (Voltaire), 60, 275
Lettre à M. d'Alembert (Rameau), 221
Lettre à M. Grimm (Rousseau), 215
Lettre à M. Rameau (D'Alembert), 221, 284, 351
Lettre sur la musique française (Rousseau), 214, 215, 221, 278, 352, 353
Lettre sur les aveugles à l'usage de ceux qui voient (Diderot), 192
Lettre sur Omphale (Grimm), 177, 215
Lettres persanes (Montesquieu), 68, 336
Lettres philosophiques (Voltaire), 60, 61, 88, 91, 275
Lettres sur la danse (Noverre), 99
Linus (Rameau), 201, 244, 252, 266, 278, 288, 289, 306, 308
Livry, Louis Sanguin, comte de, 135
Locke, John, 38, 195, 196, 271
London, 58, 60, 106, 182, 210, 260, 270, 271, 272, 273, 274, 275, 276, 279, 283, 294, 298, 301, 302, 307, 311, 336, 338, 339, 342, 345, 350, 352
Lorin, Esmilian, 30
Louis XIV, 31, 42, 58, 60, 63, 64, 77, 87, 93, 121, 191, 271, 272, 340
Louis XV, 42, 57, 59, 121, 145, 158, 168, 180, 210, 212, 273, 279, 331, 336, 340, 342, 343, 345, 346, 347, 348, 352, 354
Louis XVI, 212, 239, 265, 346
Louis-le-Grand, Paris, 27, 28, 88, 190, 271, 333, 334, 339
Louvre, 42, 46, 62, 100, 103, 195, 210, 302, 312
Lucas, pour se gausser de nous (Rameau), 29
Lully, Jean-Baptiste, 30, 31, 63, 64, 65, 66, 69, 76, 79, 87, 93, 94, 95, 100, 101, 103, 145, 170, 183, 197, 206, 213, 215, 217, 218, 226, 238, 270, 332, 338
Luynes, Charles Philippe d'Albert de, 118, 149, 156, 239, 342, 343, 346, 347, 348, 354
Lyon, 30, 31, 32, 34, 35, 46, 206, 217, 272, 284, 295, 299, 301, 310, 333, 343, 352, 353
Mairan, Jean-Jacques Dortous de, 104
Malclès, Jean-Denis, 18
Malesherbes, Guillaume-Chrétien de Lamoignon de, 211, 212, 213, 273
Manelli, Pietro, 209
Mangot, Marie-Louise, 46, 274
Marais, Marin, 28, 46, 48, 65, 136, 271
Marchand, Louis, 27, 28, 29
Maret, Hughes, 26, 34, 37, 45, 46, 53, 55, 72, 78, 88, 250, 332, 333, 334, 335, 337, 338, 339, 354, 355
Marie Antoinette, 265
Marivaux, Pierre de, 63, 94, 274, 275
Marmontel, Jean-François, 140, 148, 159, 203, 205, 234, 235, 308, 309, 345, 346, 347, 349, 352, 354
Marseille, 53, 55, 59, 63, 77, 302
Marsias allegori, ou le nouveau Carizelly (Roy), 102, 103
Masson, Charles, 38
Masson, Paul-Marie, 13

Mazan, 259, 265
McCartney, Paul, 98
Medée
  (Rameau), 34
Mémoire où l'on expose les fondements d'un système de musique théorique et pratique
  (Rameau), 195, 222
Mémoire sur la liberté de la presse
  (Malesherbes), 212
Mémoire sur la réfraction des corps solides
  (Diderot), 191, 276
Mémoires sur différents sujets de mathématiques
  (Diderot), 193, 194, 277, 350, 352
Mercure de France, 26, 49, 86, 87, 93, 118, 119, 159, 166, 175, 177, 187, 198, 221, 243, 259, 261, 281, 282, 283, 284, 332, 333, 335, 336, 339, 340, 343, 344, 347, 349, 350, 351, 355, 356
Mersenne, Marin, 38
Messe des morts
  (Gilles), 263
Metamorphoses
  (Ovid), 175
Micheau, Janine, 18
Milan, 26, 72
Miller, Leta E., 107
Minkowski, Marc, 18, 19, 132, 239
Molière, 28, 63, 64, 145, 225, 244, 336
Mondonville, Jean-Joseph de, 134, 136, 203, 209, 272, 276, 277
Montalvo, José, 20, 310, 311
Montargis, 230, 335
Montdorge, Antoine Gautier de, 119, 120, 121, 298, 343
Montéclair, Michel Pignolet de, 50, 53, 88, 177, 274, 275, 281
Montesquieu, 41, 68, 174, 270, 273, 277, 278, 336
Montpellier, 26, 50, 334
Moreau-Desproux, Pierre-Louis, 264
Mouret, Jean-Joseph, 117
Mozart, Wolfgang Amadeus, 113, 181, 210, 247, 250, 261, 279, 280

Muses galantes, Les
  (Rousseau), 139, 163, 219
Musette, 44, 85, 124, 160, 171, 181, 246
Music for the Royal Fireworks
  (Handel), 182
Naïs
  (Rameau), 180, 181, 200, 277, 288, 290, 306, 347
Naissance d'Osiris, La
  (Rameau), 239, 240, 278, 288, 290, 309, 310, 347
Nelée et Myrthis
  (Rameau), 240
Nemeitz, Joachim Christoph, 28, 85
Neveu de Rameau, Le
  (Diderot), 40, 41, 225, 279, 331, 337, 347, 355
Newton, Isaac, 40, 60, 104, 108, 139, 197, 223, 271, 274, 276
Niquet, Hervé, 19
Nivernais, Louis-Jules Mancini-Mazarini, duc de, 201, 202, 351
Noailles, Adrien Maurice de, 135
Nocturne
  (Britten), 130
Nouveau système de musique théorique
  (Rameau), 49, 104, 106, 217, 335
Nouvelles littéraires, 186, 192, 343, 348, 350
Nouvelles suites de pièces de clavecin
  (Rameau), 46, 98, 281, 335
Noverre, Jean-Charles, 76
Noverre, Jean-Georges, 99
Observations sur les écrits modernes
  (Desfontaines), 100, 107, 341, 342
Observations sur notre instinct pour la musique, et sur son principe
  (Rousseau), 218, 342, 344, 353
Octave rule, 26, 50
Œdipe
  (Voltaire), 60
Ólafsson, Víkingur, 17
Omphale
  (Destouches), 48, 177, 215, 278, 349
Opera buffa, 21, 208, 246, 261
Opéra de Lyon, 30
Opéra-ballet, 48, 57, 74, 92, 93, 94,

95, 121, 168, 175, 179, 242, 275
Opéra-Comique, 44
Orchestra of the Age of
   Enlightenment, 20, 295, 305, 310, 311
Origine des sciences, suivie d'une Controverse sur le même sujet
   (Rameau), 223
Orlando furioso
   (Ariosto), 244
Orléans, Philippe, duc d', 42, 59, 61, 68, 94, 191, 259, 272, 273
Orphée
   (Rameau), 17, 34
Orphée et Eurydice
   (Gluck), 264
Ovid, 112, 175
Page, Anthony, 20
Paladins, Les
   (Rameau), 20, 58, 244, 246, 247, 258, 279, 289, 290, 310, 337
Palais des Tuileries, 250
Palais-Royal, Paris, 42, 46, 55, 59, 62, 64, 67, 68, 69, 86, 94, 191, 219, 225, 250, 256, 259, 264, 280, 334, 335, 336, 345
Pamela
   (Richardson), 174
Pandore
   (Voltaire), 110, 133, 148
Parallèle des Italiens et des Français en ce que regarde la musique et les opéras
   (Raguenet), 207
Paris, 13, 15, 20, 21, 27, 29, 36, 37, 42, 43, 48, 55, 58, 59, 60, 61, 62, 63, 69, 74, 77, 86, 91, 92, 104, 107, 111, 112, 118, 126, 135, 137, 141, 143, 144, 145, 150, 162, 163, 166, 168, 173, 174, 176, 177, 179, 182, 187, 190, 191, 193, 206, 207, 210, 212, 227, 230, 232, 233, 238, 242, 250, 256, 258, 259, 260, 263, 270, 271, 272, 273, 274, 275, 276, 277, 278, 279, 280, 281, 282, 283, 284, 293, 294, 295, 296, 297, 298, 299, 300, 301, 302, 303, 304, 305, 306, 307, 308, 309, 310, 311, 331, 333, 334, 335, 336, 337, 338, 340, 341, 342, 343, 344, 345, 346, 347, 348, 349, 350, 351, 352, 354, 356
Passepied, 116
pastor fido, Il
   (Guarini), 49, 275
Pausanias, 151
Pélissier, Marie, 85, 99, 117, 125, 271, 277, 294, 296, 297, 299, 300, 335, 339
Pélleas et Mélisande
   (Debussy), 114, 246
Pellegrin, Simon-Joseph, 53, 55, 77, 78, 82, 87, 88, 119, 120, 177, 294, 335
Pelly, Laurent, 20
Pergolesi, Giovanni Battista, 207, 208, 211, 271, 275, 278
Petit chien qui secoue de l'argent et des pierreries, Le
   (La Fontaine), 244
Petitpas, Mlle, 45, 99, 294, 296, 297
Pharamond
   (Cahusac), 166
Philidor, François-André Danican, 163, 164, 263, 347
Pièces de clavecin
   (Rameau), 44
Pièces de clavecin en concert
   (Rameau), 134
Pièces de clavecin en sonates avec accompagnement de violon
   (Mondonville), 134
Piron, Alexis, 42, 44, 45, 51, 52, 53, 90, 135, 228, 293, 295, 334, 354
Pitt, William, 58
Platée
   (Rameau), 17, 20, 61, 145, 150, 151, 152, 153, 154, 155, 156, 175, 183, 211, 215, 223, 238, 239, 244, 246, 263, 264, 276, 288, 290, 301, 302, 303, 337, 346, 347
Poème de Fontenoy, Le
   (Voltaire), 157
Pomone
   (Cambert), 64

Pompadour, Jeanne-Antoinette
   Poisson, marquise de, 57, 58, 112,
   145, 149, 175, 179, 200, 201,
   202, 213, 242, 256, 262, 280, 306
Pour et contre, Le, 108, 109, 194, 342
Premier livre de pièces de clavecin
   (Rameau), 28, 29, 271, 272
Prévost, Antoine François, 108
Prideaux, Humphrey, 184
Prince de Noisy
   (Rebel and Francœur), 201
Princesse de Navarre, La
   (Rameau), 144, 146, 147, 148,
     150, 165, 258, 276, 280, 288,
     289, 290, 301, 304, 346
Principes généraux d'accoustique
   (Diderot), 194, 206
Pucelage, Le
   (Rameau), 45
Purcell, Henry, 97, 270, 332
Pygmalion
   (Rameau), 175, 176, 177, 178,
     200, 210, 239, 243, 264, 277,
     288, 290, 305, 306
Pyrame et Thisbé
   (Rebel and Francoeur), 183
Pythagoras, 195
Quam dilecta
   (Rameau), 31, 272, 286, 292
Querelle des bouffons, 165, 207, 210,
   211, 214, 223, 228, 232, 233,
   236, 239, 247, 248
Quinault, Philippe, 64, 77, 183
Racine, Jean, 77, 78, 82, 84, 132,
   225, 271, 294
Raguenet, François, 207
Rameau Project
   (University of Oxford), 20, 298,
     299, 300, 305, 310
Rameau, Claude Bernard, 24, 25, 30,
   34, 117, 227, 252
Rameau, Claude-François, 229, 265
Rameau, Claudine, 26
Rameau, Élisabeth, 24, 27, 33
Rameau, Jean, 23, 25, 26, 29, 30, 33
Rameau, Jean-François, 30, 225, 227,
   228, 333
Rameau, Marguerite, 24, 33
Rameau, Marie-Alexandrine, 139,
   202, 230, 259, 265, 335
Rameau, Marie-Claude, 24, 33, 252
Rameau, Marie-Louise, 229, 265
Rameau, Philippe-Eugène, 24
Raméide, La
   (J.-F. Rameau), 229, 333
Raynal, Guillaume Thomas François,
   119, 172, 192, 193, 194, 343,
   348, 350
Rebel, François, 183, 201, 203, 227,
   228, 263, 278
Recitative, 35, 49, 64, 74, 75, 82, 91,
   114, 116, 127, 128, 129, 131,
   176, 181, 188, 216, 243, 261
Réponse à la lettre de M. D'Alembert
   (Rameau), 221
*Réponse à une lettre imprimée de M.
   Rameau*
   (D'Alembert), 222
*Réponse de M. Rameau à MM. les
   éditeurs de l'Encyclopédie sur leur
   dernier avertissement*
   (Rameau), 220
Rétif de la Bretonne, 63, 334
Richardson, Samuel, 174
Richelieu, Louis François Armand de
   Vignerot du Plessis, duc de, 90,
   119, 139, 140, 144, 145, 146,
   147, 148, 149, 150, 156, 157,
   158, 164, 165, 179, 258, 259,
   260, 336, 339, 344, 345, 346,
   347, 356
Riquet, Pierre-Paul, 138
Rite of Spring
   (Stravinsky), 127
Robe de dissension, La
   (Rameau), 45, 274, 287, 290, 293
Robespierre, Maximilien, 28, 279
Rondelet, Marguerite, 30, 117
Rosbaud, Hans, 18
Rossbach (battle), 58
Rossi, Franco, 17
Rousseau, Jean-Jacques, 13, 21, 108,
   139, 156, 162, 163, 164, 165,
   177, 187, 191, 196, 207, 209,
   214, 215, 217, 218, 219, 221,
   223, 228, 230, 237, 272, 277,
   278, 279, 341, 342, 347, 352,
   353, 354

Rousset, Christophe, 19
Roy, Pierre-Charles, 102, 341
Royal College of Music
   (London), 20
Royal Opera, London, 19
Royal Society, London, 106, 108,
   191, 263, 342
Royer, Joseph-Nicolas-Pancrace, 21,
   28, 228, 236, 278
Sacchini, Antonio, 265
Sade, Donatien Alphonse François,
   Marquis de, 28, 259
Sadler, Graham, 53, 55, 243, 302,
   336, 341
Saint-Florentin, comte de, 167
Saint-Germain fair, 43, 44, 45, 93,
   293
Saint-Laurent fair, 45, 47, 77, 293,
   334
Saint-Mard, Toussaint Rémond de,
   101
Saint-Saëns, Camille, 17
Sallé, Marie, 76, 125, 131, 275, 301,
   344, 356
Samson
   (Handel), 148
   (Rameau), 88, 91, 92, 93, 98, 111,
      144, 146, 148, 275, 276, 287,
      289, 296, 340
Sauveur, Joseph, 38, 104, 109
Sawkins, Lionel, 258
Sculpture, La
   (Houdar de la Motte), 175
Seneca, 77
Sénéchal, Michel, 18
Serse
   (Handel), 210
Serva padrona, La
   (Pergolesi), 207, 208
Seven Years War, 58, 235, 240, 251,
   256, 279, 280
Shakespeare, William, 132, 152
Sheldonian Theatre
   (Oxford), 20
Simon Boccanegra
   (Verdi), 113
Sloane, Hans, 106
Song of Roland, 244
Stabat Mater
   (Pergolesi), 208
Stainville, Étienne François de
   Choiseul, comte de, 202, 351
Stamitz, Johann, 214
Stravinsky, Igor, 127
Stuart, Charles Edward, 178
Subdominant, 105, 113
Suite in D minor
   (Handel), 47
Surprises de l'Amour, Les
   (Rameau), 57, 112, 179, 200, 242,
      243, 288, 290
Swift, Jonathan, 107
Sybarites, Les
   (Rameau), 232, 234, 235, 242,
      278, 288, 290, 309
Tambourin, 96, 112, 122, 124, 127,
   128, 129, 181, 254, 258
Taylor, Brook, 106
Telemann, Georg Philipp, 47, 274,
   275, 332
Temple de la gloire, Le
   (Rameau), 157, 158, 159, 160,
      175, 276, 277, 303
Tencin, Claudine Guérin de, 147, 191
Téthis
   (Rameau), 34, 48, 272
Thaw, David, 18
Théâtre Italien, 111, 150, 166, 211,
   260, 274, 275
Thieriot, Nicolas-Claude, 91, 100,
   110, 118, 126, 133, 143, 339,
   341, 342, 343, 344, 353
Thuret, Eugène de, 73, 228, 236, 275,
   278, 337
Titon et l'Aurore
   (Mondonville), 209
Tonelli, Anna, 209
Toulouse, 26, 143, 166, 295, 297,
   302, 338
Tragédie lyrique, 21, 56, 64, 76, 88,
   93, 94, 95, 111, 127, 156, 183,
   186, 208, 236, 238, 255, 272, 349
Traité de l'harmonie
   (Rameau), 35, 36, 37, 38, 40, 41,
      49, 86, 104, 273
Treaty of Aix-la-Chapelle, 57, 178,
   277
Treaty of Paris, 256

Treaty of Utrecht, 31
Tribou, Denis-François, 85, 99, 117, 294, 297
Tuileries, 45, 62, 86, 94, 280, 339
University of Paris, 190, 192
Venice, 26, 72, 74, 143, 217, 261, 271, 272, 273
Verdi, Giuseppe, 113
Vérités également ignorées et intéressantes tirées du sein de la nature (Rameau), 257
Versailles, 31, 58, 63, 68, 93, 144, 145, 149, 157, 159, 165, 166, 169, 179, 181, 210, 232, 250, 256, 276, 277, 278, 280, 294, 296, 297, 298, 299, 300, 301, 302, 304, 305, 306, 307, 308, 309
Villenaud, Jean, 27
Villeroy, Mme de, 201
Vincennes, Château de, 193, 277
Viollier, Renée, 17
Vivaldi, Antonio, 142, 243, 272, 273, 276, 332, 354
Voisenon, Claude-Henri de Fusée de, 134
Voltaire, 13, 28, 53, 55, 58, 60, 61, 77, 86, 87, 88, 89, 90, 91, 92, 93, 100, 103, 107, 109, 111, 112, 118, 120, 125, 126, 129, 139, 144, 145, 146, 147, 148, 149, 157, 158, 159, 165, 184, 192, 220, 223, 225, 233, 234, 236, 237, 258, 259, 262, 263, 270, 274, 275, 276, 277, 279, 280, 296, 301, 303, 304, 336, 339, 340, 341, 342, 343, 344, 345, 346, 347, 349, 350, 353, 356

Wagner, Richard, 114
Walpole, Robert, 145, 273, 276
War of the Austrian Succession, 57, 144, 175, 178, 276, 277
War of the Spanish Succession, 31, 271, 272
Watteau, Jean-Antoine, 22, 94, 270, 272, 273
Williams, Jonathan, 20, 298, 299, 301, 305, 310
Written on Skin (Benjamin), 246
Zaïre (Voltaire), 88
Zaïs (Rameau), 172, 174, 200, 277, 288, 290, 305, 347
Zarlino, Gioseffo, 38, 110
Zéphyre (Rameau), 240
Zoroastre (Rameau), 16, 61, 175, 182, 183, 184, 185, 186, 187, 188, 200, 201, 241, 242, 247, 252, 264, 277, 279, 288, 289, 307, 337, 338, 347, 349, 355

THE AUTHOR

Simon Trowbridge was born in Oxford in 1961. He was educated at Wallingford School, King's College, London, and University College, London. He is the author of a history of the Comédie-Française. Before becoming a full-time writer, he worked at New College, Oxford, and the Taylor Institution, Oxford, and was a member of Congregation of the University of Oxford.

www.ingramcontent.com/pod-product-compliance
Lightning Source LLC
Chambersburg PA
CBHW020515080526
44583CB00013B/606